A Century of
New Testament Study

John Riches

Trinity Press International
Valley Forge, Pennsylvania

Trinity Press International
P.O. Box 851
Valley Forge, PA 19482-0851

Library of Congress Cataloging-in-Publication Data available.

Co-published with The Lutterworth Press, Cambridge, England

Printed in Great Britian

93 94 95 96 97 98   8 7 6 5 4 3 2 1

Acknowledgements

I am grateful to The Lutterworth Press for their invitation to contribute this volume on the New Testament to their series of retrospective accounts of different areas of theological studies. I have long thought that the history of interpretation of the New Testament was one of the best ways of introducing the subject to students and this invitation has been a spur to undertake a project that might otherwise (who knows what fate awaits British universities?) have waited indefinitely.

A number of people have assisted in the production of this book, including Colin Lester at Lutterworth with advice and comment, and Margie Balden, our Departmental secretary who over the years has learnt to decipher the (almost) indecipherable. To them many thanks.

I want also to record a debt of gratitude to those who, since the retirement of Ernest Best ten years ago, have come to Glasgow to teach and lecture, to inform and encourage debate: Kenneth Grayston, Kingsley Barrett, W. D. Davies, Jim Saunders and, for five glorious years, Christopher Evans. They have been with us as Alexander Robertson lecturers for generous periods that have allowed full discussion of many of the issues in this book. Other conversations, on briefer visits, have contributed to the writing of this book, not least with Ed Sanders, Gerd Theissen and Heikki Räisänen. Visits like these make an enormous contribution to the on-going debate within our Department.

It is, however, to my two New Testament colleagues, Ernest Best and John Barclay, that I owe the greatest debt. They have been ready to talk at all times, have informed me and criticised drafts. They are colleagues in the best sense. What more could one ask?

I am grateful to the following for permission to quote passages from the undermentioned works:

A. & C. Black for quotations from A. Schweitzer, *The Quest of the Historical Jesus*, London, 1910; A. Schweitzer, *The Mysticism of Paul the Apostle*, London, 1931.
T. & T. Clark for quotations from E. Best, *Mark: the Gospel as Story*, Edinburgh, 1983.
J. Louis Martyn for quotations from his *History and Theology in the Folurth Gospel*, New York, 1968.
The Edwin Mellon Press for quotations from M.J. Borg, *Conflict, Holiness and Politics in the Teachings of Jesus*, New York, 1984.
Oxford University Press for quotations from Karl Barth, *The Epistle to the Romans*, trs. Sir Edwyn Hoskyns, Bart, Oxford, 1933.
SCM Press for quotations from E. Käsemann, *Perspectives on Paul*, London, 1971; E. Käsemann, *The Testament of Jesus: A Study of the Gospel of John in the Light of Chapter 17*, London, 1968; E.P. Sanders, *Jesus and Judaism*, London, 1985; E.P. Sanders, *Paul and Palestinian Judaism*, London, 1977; R. Bultmann, *Theology of the New Testament*, Vol. 1, London, 1952, Vol 2, London, 1955; H. Räisänen, *Beyond New Testament Theology*, London, 1990.
SPCK for quotations from E. Schweizer, 'Mark's Theological Achievement', *Evangelische Theologie*, 24, 1964, in W. Telford, ed., *The Interpretation of Mark*, London, 1985, pp. 46-63; W.A. Meeks, 'The Man from Heaven in Johannine Sectarianism', *JBL* 91, 1972, 44-72 in J. Ashton, ed., *The Interpretation of John*, 141-73; C.K. Barrett, *New Testament Essays*, London, 1972.
Trinity Press International for quotations from H. Räisänen, *Beyond New Testament Theology*, Philadelphia, 1990.
Westminster/John Knox for quotations from E. Käsemann, *The Testament of Jesus: A Study of the Gospel of John in the Light of Chapter 17*, Louisville, 1968.
World Publishing Company for quotations from R. Bultmann, *Existence and Faith*, New York, 1960.
      for quotations from R. Bultmann, *Jesus and the Word*, London, 1934.
I am further grateful for permission to use material reprinted from:

Perspectives on Paul by E. Käsemann, copyright © 1971 Fortress Press, used by permission of Augsburg Press.
Jesus and Judaism by E.P. Sanders, copyright © 1985 Fortress Press, used by permission of Augsburg Fortress.
Paul and Palestinian Judaism by E.P. Sanders, copyright © 1977 Fortress Press, used by permission of Augsburg Fortress.

The Testament of Jesus: A Study of the Gospel of John in the Light of Chapter 17, copyright © 1968, used by permission of Augsburg Fortress.

Contents

This book is dedicated
with great affection
to my wife Nena

Introduction

Interest in the history of New Testament study has been growing of late. Within a relatively short span we have seen the new edition, revised by T. Wright, of Stephen Neill's *The Interpretation of the New Testament 1861-1986*, J. Rogerson, C. Rowland and B. Lindars' *The Study of the Bible*, R. Morgan with J. Barton's *Biblical Interpretation* and now E. J. Epp and G. W. Macrae's *The New Testament and its Modern Interpreters*. More detailed studies have appeared in the Issues in Religion and Theology series. Behind them stand three monumental works: W. G. Kümmel's *The New Testament: A History of the Investigation of its Problems*; and Albert Schweitzer's *The Quest of the Historical Jesus* (the 2nd enlarged edition is still [1993] not yet available in English) and his *Paul and his Interpreters*.

It is interesting to speculate on the reason for this renewal of interest. At one level, doubtless, it represents a proper recognition that the study of the New Testament is a corporate discipline, such that anyone who seeks to understand today's contributions is well advised to understand something of its history. What today's scholars write is part of a prolonged wrestling with a complex and interrelated set of questions — historical, literary, linguistic, methodological and theological. We need to be able to place a particular work in this complex and ongoing debate, if we are fully to understand what is being said.

At another level, such an interest in the history of the discipline may also indicate a shift of mood, even a measure of uncertainty and self-questioning. Scholars may feel that there is a need to take stock, to recover the major questions and strategies that have given the discipline its direction and dynamism over the years and which all too easily may be submerged in the welter of detailed arguments and debates that absorb scholars in the many specialised branches of the subject. It is invigorating to read again some of the great contributions to New Testament study, to appreciate the sharpness with which questions were put and solutions sought. It is important to gain an overview of the subject, if one is to plot the future direction of work. Such an approach to the subject is more a search for the — more or less — hidden springs of the discipline than simply an attempt to map out as comprehensively as time may allow its progress and development. At the same time, by highlighting certain debates and issues it also seeks to provide a basis for future work.

The present study makes no claims to comprehensiveness. Within the compass of this volume that would require too high a price in loss of detailed presentation and discussion of central works and figures. It is, if you like, less a map of the discipline, than a travel narrative, a record of my own wanderings in the history of a discipline that among all its many solid, workmanlike and (dare it be said) sometimes rather tedious offerings contains works of rare clarity, insight and acuity. Such works contribute not only to the understanding of our past, but also may thereby illuminate our present and our future. This volume will have succeeded in no small measure if it manages to recreate an audience for such figures by showing their place in the discipline, both in its past and its future.

One figure above all dominates the book, so much so that it might almost be called a journey around Rudolf Bultmann. This will not, I imagine, commend the book to all. Certainly those who accept the Stephen Neill view of New Testament studies — Cambridge balance and scholarship against German wilfulness and extravagance — will need convincing that giving such prominence to Bultmann is anything but a distortion. I must leave the book to make its case as best it can. What I have tried to show is first the way in which Bultmann dominated the discipline in this century by achieving a unique synthesis of theological and historical interpretation of the New Testament, and second the extent to which that synthesis has subsequently been undermined, in such a way that a complete reworking of it is now required. There will, of course, be those who will point to the demise of Bultmann's *Theology of the New Testament* as evidence of the folly of such an undertaking. They will feel that New Testament scholars should restrict themselves to historical explanations of ancient texts and the communities that produced them; attempts at 'actualising interpretation' will always be vulnerable to changes in the historical accounts which scholars have to offer. That is indeed one important issue and I shall return to it at the end of the book.

A word about the format of the book. It falls into three sections: the first (chapters 1-4) documents developments from 1892, which saw the publication of Johannes Weiss's *Jesus' Proclamation of the Kingdom of God* up to the publication of Bultmann's two great works, *The Gospel of John* and his *Theology of the New Testament*. Here I attempt to give some review of the main developments in the History of Religions School and to chart reactions to it, both in Germany and elsewhere. There then follows a chapter devoted to Bultmann's major works where I try to show how both the theological and historical aspects of Bultmann's interpretation of Paul and John complement and support each other. Much of the literature on Bultmann has tended to focus on either one side or the other. Any proper assessment of his achievement must do justice to their interrelatedness. Bultmann was a New Testament theologian; not simply a theologian who bent the New Testament to his will, nor a New Testament historian who made what use he could of theological ideas.

The manner of treatment changes again in the last five chapters. Here I look at what has happened in New Testament study since Bultmann, in five distinct areas: Jesus, Pauline, Markan and Johannine study, and New Testament Theology. Instead of attempting any comprehensive survey of these fields I have in each case picked out four or five major texts and allowed them to stand for much else. In a simple way I hope this will equip the student of the New Testament with a basic knowledge of the most important recent contributions in each of the chosen areas.

The advantage of this approach is twofold: it makes possible a much fuller account of each text and it allows one to draw out the discussion that has been engendered by the texts as they have interacted with the discipline and indeed with each other. The essence of a corporate discipline is that it should have its own internal dialogue and that this should be nurtured and clarified. It is the existence of such dialogue that provides the basis for hope and confidence in a discipline, which despite over two hundred years' vigorous and often heated activity, still retains the ability to produce new treasures out of old.

It is worth recalling that one of the founding acts of the discipline was the publication by Gotthold Ephrain Lessing of Reimarus's *Fragments*, notably the fragment *On the Purpose of Jesus and his Disciples*. Lessing had only recently abandoned his post as Director of the Hamburg Theatre. In describing his plans for publishing the *Fragments* he wrote to his brother: 'I would prefer to stage a little play with the theologians, if I had any need of the theatre. And in a sense that is what the material I have promised to send Herr Voss [his publisher] is about'. Lessing's 'play' has been running now for many seasons, and nothing could possibly recreate the shock with which he inaugurated the long-standing and varied dialogue. Perhaps, however, this book will help to sharpen and restate some of its major themes.

Of course, there is much that will be missed. The Synoptic Gospels are represented only by Mark, not Matthew and Luke. There is no sustained treatment of study of Christian origins, such as Chris Rowland's work of that title. The names of many who have contributed creatively and imaginatively to the discipline will not be found.

Moreover, I have paid what, to some, will be culpably little attention to new directions in biblical study, such as feminist readings and a wide range of literary approaches. My defence must be that what I am concerned with in this book is analysis of established patterns of work within the discipline. There is indeed a widening gulf between the growing number of 'new directions' which are pursued most energetically in North America and the historical approaches that have been normative in the discipline over the last hundred years. What I am trying to do in this book is to understand what has occasioned the crisis in the, till recently, dominant paradigms of New Testament study. It is diagnostic, not prescriptive. Without such a reading of the past, however, the discipline runs the risk of deep and destructive division. Those who remain committed to historical paradigms of study may simply end up going over old ground, tilling it finer and finer till it blows away in the wind; while those who reject the old paradigms may find themselves springing up quickly but withering away because they have no roots in the rich ground of historical study.

One last word by way of introduction. The three-fold pattern of the book corresponds to three distinct cultural moods that have informed the discipline. The earlier work of the History of Religions School still belongs to the period of cultural optimism of the Colonial age. Bultmann's work is a product of the interwar years in Germany, with its deep questioning of the past and its fateful search for the new. The post-war — and that also means post-Holocaust — studies that we are examining have their context in a world that at best (which is by no means always) is more conscious of cultural diversity, more conscious than before of the terrible effects of cultural imperialism, less willing to pass judgement on other cultures. I am not, of course, suggesting that there is direct causal relation between these different moods and the works of New Testament scholars. It is, however, important to be aware of these changes and in comparing the work of the three periods to see what correlations there are, not least with the underlying interpretative strategies that have directed work in New Testament study. This too may provide a valuable key to the future.

List of works cited

R. Bultmann, *Theology of the New Testament*, London, 1955

R. Bultmann, *The Gospel of John*, Oxford, 1971

S. Neill and T. Wright, *The Interpretation of the New Testament, 1861-1986*, Oxford, 1988

J. Rogerson, C. Rowland and B. Lindars, *The Study and Use of the Bible*, Basingstoke, 1988

R. Morgan with J. Barton, *Biblical Interpretation*, Oxford, 1988

E.J. Epp and G.W. Macrae, S.J., eds, *The New Testament and its Modern Interpreters*, Atlanta, Georgia, 1989

W.G. Kümmel, *The New Testament: A History of the Investigation of its Problems*, London, 1973

A. Schweitzer, *The Quest of the Historical Jesus*, London, 1910

A. Schweitzer, *Paul and his Interpreters*, London, 1912

J. Weiss, *Jesus' Proclamation of the Kingdom of God*, Philadelphia, 1971

Issues in Religion and Theology is published by the Society for Promoting Christian Knowledge [SPCK] and Fortress Press, London and Minneapolis

H.S. Reimarus, *Fragments*, ed. C.H. Talbert, London, 1971

1
New Testament Study at the End of the Nineteenth Century

New Testament study in the 1890s was, in more than one sense, nearing the end of an era. In the century or so since men like Semler (1725-91) had laid the foundations of the discipline, much had been done to fashion adequate historical tools for the study of the texts. In the first place, critical, scholarly editions of the New Testament writings themselves were now available. The work of Griesbach (1745-1812), Lachmann (1703-1851) and Tischendorf (1815-74) culminated in the critical edition of the New Testament by Westcott (1825-1901) and Hort (1828-92) in 1881. Much useful work had also been done on the language of the New Testament. Alongside the great dictionary of classical Greek by Liddell (1811-98) and Scott (1811-87) (first edition 1843), there had also appeared a number of important dictionaries specifically dedicated to the Greek of the New Testament. Of these the most important (1868) was probably that of Grimm (1807-91), which was in turn a revision of Wilke's (1786-1854) *Clavis Novi Testamenti* (second edition 1851).

At the same time scholars had been active in the enormous task of providing critical editions of other texts contemporary to the New Testament. Knowledge of the 'intertestamental' Jewish texts had been greatly enhanced by discoveries of apocalyptic texts in Ethiopia. Classical scholarship, which was in its heyday, was turning its attention to the world of popular Hellenism, its literature and religious beliefs. The year 1892 saw the beginning of a further revision of the great German Classical Encyclopaedia, subsequently known as Pauly-Wissowa. Harnack (1851-1930), Lightfoot (1828-89) and others produced major critical editions of early Christian texts outside the New Testament.

As well as these basic tools, a number of critical historical questions had also been discussed and, as far as it is possible with such matters, decided. Enormous amounts of scholarly energy in Germany had been poured into the question of the literary relationships among the first three Gospels. This had led to a consensus among critical scholars that came to be known as the two-document hypothesis: Mark was the earliest Gospel to be written; Matthew and Luke were compilations of Mark and another document, no longer extant, known as 'Q'.

Something like a critical consensus was also emerging over questions of the authorship of the books of the New Testament. There was broad agreement that not all the letters traditionally ascribed to Paul had actually been written by him. 1 Thessalonians, Galatians, 1 and 2 Corinthians, Romans, Philippians and Philemon were generally acknowledged as authentic. There was doubt about 2 Thessalonians and Colossians and even more about Ephesians; and the Pastorals were widely disputed. The apostolic authorship of the Gospels and of the Petrine and Johannine correspondence was under attack.

In all this a great deal had been done to introduce and make possible a more thorough-going historical approach to the New Testament. This was a solid foundation on which much could be built. From the start, however, there had been those who had raised wider, more searching questions about the nature of the religious beliefs that are to be found expressed in the New Testament writings. Such questions were of many kinds. Some asked about the origins of such beliefs in the cultures and religious traditions of the ancient world. Others raised questions about the development and diversity of beliefs within the emerging Christian communities. It was these questions that were now to give the discipline its real dynamic — not that all would by any means have agreed with that proposition.

Of course there are here a cluster of questions that, as we shall see, require careful definition. As early as the 1770s Lessing (1729-81) had been pressing the New Testament scholars of his day to take up the task of relating Jesus's particular beliefs about the Kingdom of God to contemporary Jewish beliefs on the one hand and to the beliefs of the early Christian community on the other. Semler responded not by dealing systematically and directly with Lessing's questions but by using his very considerable erudition to answer him point by point. It was what Albert Schweitzer (1875-1965) referred to as the beginnings of 'Yes-but' theology. It was a defensive, apologetic theology, unable to deny the force of the underlying questions that were raised by historical enquiry, but willing to use historical techniques to give a good defence of preferred theological positions.

Lessing's questions were taken up, developed and given provocative answers by the great Tübingen scholar F.C. Baur (1792-1860). Baur's magisterial studies of the growth and development of the earliest forms of Christianity were rooted in the Hegelian argument that there is an underlying order or 'logic' to major developments in human thought and culture, of which religion is the culmination. Such developments are 'dialectical'; they stem from the cut and thrust of debate and controversy among different groups who are the proper bearers of human culture. It is, moreover, through this process of intellectual struggle, rather than through the divine unveiling of eternal and infallible truths, that the world spirit comes to expression.

Baur's Hegelian beliefs liberated him from the need to find in the writings of the New Testament a uniform (non-self-contradictory) testimony to the timeless revelation of God. On the contrary, they inspired him to search out that diversity of belief which is the necessary form of any great development in human culture and religion and to uncover the particular groupings within earliest Christianity who had participated in the first theological controversies. In his *Church History* (1853) Baur drew a picture of Christianity divided between two main parties, the Petrine and the Pauline, the first committed to the Law, the second law-free. Out of the struggle between these two groups, so vividly recorded in the authentic Pauline epistles, came the synthesis of early Catholicism of which the Pastorals were, to him, clear evidence.

Baur's work was certainly not without its difficulties. On the one hand it might be felt that the picture he had given of the diversity and divisions within early Christianity was too schematic. His positing of a struggle between two parties with its resolution in early Catholicism read too much like an imposition of some Hegelian schema of thesis, antithesis and synthesis on the New Testament history, which in all probability was far more complex. More conservative scholars might have other grounds for objection. Any suggestion that the New Testament contained divergent views would of course be seen as an attack on the Bible's inerrancy. But here, at least for the Lutherans, there was more than a crumb of comfort. Paul still emerged as a dominant figure, boldly defending a law-free Gospel against the Petrine church. Baur's schema paid its debt to his own Lutheran heritage and subsequent New Testament study in Germany did little to disturb the theological pre-eminence of Paul —as seen through Martin Luther's (1483-1546) eyes. Baur's great pupil, Albrecht Ritschl (1822-89), attacked his master's portrayal of the earliest developments in the church in his *Origin of the Early Catholic Church* (1857), but he went on from there to give a sustained account of the Biblical doctrine of justification and reconciliation as a prelude to his own major work of systematic theology. In this, for all his debt to Immanuel Kant (1724-1804), he drew deeply on the Pauline-Lutheran tradition.

So we can say, simplifying shamelessly, that by the 1890s New Testament study was well advanced in equipping itself with the technical tools for a thorough historical investigation of the New Testament; that it already contained within its literature major works that had pressed hard on questions of the development of earliest Christianity; but that such works were still hotly contested by both liberals and conservatives.

It will not have gone unnoticed that in this very brief outline most of the figures I have referred to were German. This doubtless reflects something of a personal debt that I have to acknowledge. It is from the German *Neutestamentler* that I derived my own interest and enthusiasm for New Testament study, though this was not purely accidental. They were the scholars who raised the major philosophical and theological questions about the subject matter of the New Testament. For nearly two centuries they pursued them with an extraordinary rigour and intellectual energy, as anyone who has read Schweitzer's *The Quest of the Historical Jesus* (first German edition

1906) and *Paul and his Interpreters* (first German edition 1911) will see.

Why this should be is more difficult to say. In part it has something to do with the way the Lutheran tradition is rooted in Luther's own scholarly wrestling with the New Testament texts. In part, too, it has much to do with the way in which German theology, from the time of Schleiermacher (1768-1834), struggled to maintain its place within the general cultural developments of the nineteenth century. If the theological faculties were to retain a place within the universities, then they had fully to embrace historical and philosophical enquiry. Of course that, in a sense, is true of other countries. Maybe it was the Hegelian inheritance that encouraged German New Testament scholars to believe that an historical account of Christianity could be given which did justice both to the diversity and vagaries of the earliest Christian movements and to the truth that nevertheless was being realised in and through such diversity. In seeking to understand the 'logic' that underlay such diversity, scholars were attempting to give an account of one of the major developments in the history of human culture and religion. This commitment to historical modes of study and interpretation was to remain strong throughout most of our period. Only since the mid-1970s has it been challenged with determination.

Furthermore the scholars who devoted themselves to the study of early Christianity believed it to be a cultural and religious development of continuing significance for the world of nineteenth-century Europe. The enormous amount of intellectual energy expended on research into the Bible in nineteenth-century Germany would be unintelligible without this belief. Biblical scholars saw themselves as contributing to the creation of a new era of social and political life. After the Absolutism of eighteenth-century Germany, in which authoritarian rule was closely allied to authoritarian forms of confessional orthodoxy, liberal German Biblical scholars sought to recover the emancipatory and socially creative force of the Gospel. Thus developments in Biblical scholarship went hand in hand with the emergence of an independent and educated middle class with much greater political freedom. The name given to this new alliance was 'cultural Protestantism'.

It is no great exaggeration to say that Biblical study in England, by contrast, has until recently been to a large extent reactive, responding, often rather defensively, to developments in Germany, rather than exploring of its own accord the more fundamental, searching, historical questions. It has, as Stephen Neill (1900-84) enthusiastically documented in his *The Interpretation of the New Testament 1861-1961*, pursued its own agenda of historical and textual study, while largely holding back from the wider task of theological exposition. It has, too, been largely conservative, attempting to uphold its religious traditions against attack from historical criticism, and at most attempting to strengthen and revivify such traditions by providing a more contemporary interpretation as well as an historical justification for them. This is not to decry the great works of Westcott, Lightfoot and Hort, nor to suggest that they were illiberal in their scholarly or, indeed, political and social attitudes. Westcott, as Bishop of Durham, was remarkable in his day for his sympathies for the local miners. Nevertheless all these men, two of whom were bishops, were members of an established church that was still fundamentally conservative in orientation. It also has to be remembered that they were members of what was at the time the most powerful colonial power in the world. Perhaps it is not altogether accidental that some of the most creative English scholars came from outside the established church: C.H. Dodd, W.D. Davies, and C.K. Barrett.

It is worth looking a little more closely at this wider theological context in which New Testament study developed in England. In 1889 a group of Oxford scholars had just published a volume of essays, entitled *Lux Mundi*. In it they attempted 'to put the Catholic faith into its right relation to modern intellectual and moral problems' (vii).[1] They did so however, 'not as "guessers at truth", but as servants of the Catholic Creed and Church, aiming only at interpreting the faith we have received' (viii). Yet while they thus clearly pinned their colours to the mast of (Anglo-) Catholic orthodoxy, they equally clearly acknowledged the need to take due cognisance of developments in the natural and historical sciences as they impinged on theology.

The book aroused considerable criticism, principally because of its treatment of the doctrine of inspiration. This came in a chapter which its editor, Charles Gore (1853-1932), had himself written. There Gore attempted to outline a doctrine of inspiration that would do justice to some at least of the more recent views of the genesis and literary character of the Old Testament writings. He rejected impersonal metaphors which spoke of the Holy Spirit acting upon a man ' "like a plectrum striking a lyre" ', insisting that

> human activity was none the less free, conscious, rational, because the Spirit inspires it. The poet is a poet, the philosopher a philosopher, the historian an historian, each with his own idiosyncracies, ways and methods, to be interpreted each by the laws of his own literature (251).

The more we know about literature, the more we shall know about the literature of the Jews that the Holy Spirit inspired. Most significantly, what Gore emphasised was the gradual, historical development of theological understanding that occurred in Jewish literature. And this was clearly connected with his belief that every race has its own particular spiritual insight, its 'vocation, and we recognise in the great writers of each race the interpreters of that vocation. . . . Now every believer in God must see in these special missions of races a Divine inspiration' (250).

The views that Gore adopts here are close indeed to the Hegelian understanding of some progressive unfolding of the truth that occurs in different (racially defined) cultures throughout history. In England such views aroused considerable hostility and criticism against which Gore attempted to defend himself in the Preface to the tenth edition of *Lux Mundi* (September 1890).

What is interesting here is the way in which Gore attempts to blunt the force of radical, historical criticism. Having quoted the Bishop of Oxford's recent endorsement of historical criticism of the Old Testament, he goes on to sound a note that was to be heard again and again in English discussions of these matters:[2] 'the critical movement has been accompanied by all the arbitrariness and tendency to push things to extremes that appear to be an almost inseparable attendant upon living and vigorous movements, ecclesiastical and secular' (xvi). He goes on to suggest that it is the view of scholars like Graf Wellhausen (1844-1918) who represent such extremes that will in due course be rejected, as a more balanced, conservative scholarship wins the day.[3]

Such a tendency to pick and choose the critical scholarship with which he wished to engage in debate is perhaps an inevitable consequence of Gore's stated commitment to Christian orthodoxy. It is most apparent in his treatment of the New Testament where he apparently believed that there were no major questions raised by criticism that would seriously challenge the kind of Catholicism which he defended. He believed he could sufficiently justify the authoritative and inspired nature of the New Testament writings by appealing to their apostolic authorship and the careful instruction of the apostles by Jesus. It is true that to make this case he has to class Luke as sub-apostolic, but for the rest he is content to uphold the apostolic authorship not only of the other three Gospels, but also of the disputed Pauline epistles, of James, Jude and the Petrine and Johannine epistles.

This lack of even-handedness between his treatment of Old Testament as opposed to New Testament criticism can, it would seem, be explained only in terms of Gore's prior commitments to certain dogmatic positions. Certainly he offers no discussion of his disregard of important critical positions that do substantially challenge his views. What he does allow, however, which had significant consequences for his own christological views, is that Jesus held, or at least expressed, different views about the authorship of the Psalms and the Pentateuch from those of modern critical scholarship which Gore himself had come to accept: 'He shows no sign of transcending the history of His age' (1st edn, p.360 — a phrase which has been suitably mangled in the fourth edition).

One other contribution deserves mention here, that of E. S. Talbot (1844-1934), a former Warden of Keble College: 'The Preparation in History for Christ'. This raises the question of the kinds of historical accounts that can be given of the events which preceded Jesus's ministry. Talbot distinguishes two possible ways of approaching the question of Christ's appearing in the flesh: one that considers its 'own inherent truth and meaning'; the other that treats it 'as clothed in historical event, to be understood in its relations with what went before and followed after and stood around' (93). In considering the second approach Talbot takes as his starting point the Johannine declaration: 'The Word was made flesh'. This is not meant to fetter free enquiry; rather it means that a proper enquiry must be such as:

works in us the conviction that He both does, and does not, occur 'naturally' at the time and place when He appeared; that history leads up to Him and prepares His way, and yet that no force of natural antecedents can account for Him or His work (94).

Whatever the merits or otherwise of such a position, it is clear that it falls short of a thorough-going commitment to keep on searching for historical explanations, even where they are not immediately forthcoming. It encourages the enquirer to draw back and to leave an area of mystery and incomprehension around the figure of Jesus, rather than pressing on to find further clarification.

Talbot's remarks contrast sharply with the declared intentions of a group of scholars in Germany out of which there emerged at the turn of the century the so-called History of Religions School.[4] In 1868 Adolf Hausrath (1837-1909) had declared his intention to 'strive to fit New Testament history back again into the contemporary context in which it stood . . . to see it as . . . part of a general historical process.'[5] The same point was made more fully and forcefully by Otto Pfleiderer (1839-1908) in the introduction to his popular Berlin lectures of 1904, *Die Enstehung des Christentums*. Here Pfleiderer, following and referring to F.C. Baur (whose pupil he was), states unconditionally that a truly historical conception of the origins of Christianity cannot be reconciled with the 'presuppositions of Church faith'.

If Christianity has its origins in the descent of the second person of the Trinity from heaven to earth, in his becoming man in the womb of a Jewish virgin, in his bodily resurrection after his death on the cross and ascension into heaven: then the origin of Christianity is a complete miracle that escapes all historical explanation. For understanding a phenomenon historically means understanding its causal connections with the circumstances obtaining at a particular time and place in human life (1).

The entry of a suprahuman being into this world would be an event without any analogy in our experience and therefore one that we could not in any way comprehend historically.

Pfleiderer's introductory remarks contrast interestingly too with Gore's essay. Pfleiderer traces the rise of a truly historical understanding of the New Testament, as he sees it, from the eighteenth-century Deists, through the work of David Friedrich Strauss (1809-74) to F.C. Baur. Baur it was, he says, who introduced into New Testament study the notion of development and who saw that Christianity had to be explained in terms of the complex constellation of social and individual 'factors . . . whose combination and internal reconciliation with one another could not be achieved without internal contradictions and conflicts' (12). Baur's picture of the development of Christianity may have been modified by the work of later scholars, but his major achievement — that of offering an historical account — remains, because it was based not on speculation, but on careful investigation of the texts. He sought, that is, to set these texts in their cultural and religious context and so to make possible a differentiated picture of the history of the early Christian communities and their literature. In this respect his great achievement was to have identified the Fourth Gospel as a work, not of an apostolic eye-witness but of a later theologian of the church, writing a treatise on the incarnation of the Word.

Pfleiderer was, rather unusually for German theologians, well-read in English theology, and he concluded his brief survey with words which might almost have been addressed to Gore and his followers. While others before him had questioned the authenticity of this or that author, Baur was the first who had the courage:

> to free himself completely from that traditional fiction and, untroubled by the dogmatic fabrications of the Fathers, to scrutinise the New Testament writing with his own eyes, in order to determine in which particular time and place their own particular content, their religious character, their contemporary references placed them. Thus these writings became for him, not oracles of apostolic inspiration, which is what they are for the faith of the church, but witnesses of the natural process of development of the Christian religion and church (16).

Moreover, he dismisses as reactionary romanticism all calls 'to return to the tradition', which would be to allow dogma to dominate history. Rather he affirms his intention to investigate this history 'according to the same principles and methods as any other'. In this he will allow himself no other presuppositions than the following: 'the analogy of human experience, the likeness of human nature in past and present, the causal connection of all external events and all internal spiritual experience, in brief the regular order of the world, which has determined all human experience for all time' (*ibid.*).

Comparing figures like Gore and Pfleiderer in this way might suggest too sharp a contrast between the world of German New Testament scholarship and that of England. Certainly there were other major figures in Germany, not least Adolf Schlatter (1852-1938), who would hold very different views of the nature of the authorship and development of the New Testament writings. Nevertheless there were few in England who would have taken up a position more critical than that of Gore, and many who already regarded the position of *Lux Mundi* as dangerously liberal. In this regard the comparison is important and may usefully serve to set the scene for a more detailed consideration of developments in New Testament study.

It is important to be as clear as possible about the nature of the contrast. In the first place there is a fundamental difference of approach to the question of revelation. For Gore the revealed truth is something that has been delivered to the Church, whose task is then to preserve and administer it. This does not, evidently, mean that there is no need to restate or to continue to explore the richness of its meaning and in this exploration historical and indeed scientific enquiry may have important contributions to make. Nevertheless the Church stands or falls on its commitment to this truth and is not therefore in any significant sense in search of truth. On the contrary, it has received and is commissioned to spread abroad the 'light of the world'. Hence Gore's strictures about 'guessers after the truth'. On Gore's view, that is to say, the Bible is the prime witness to the revealed truth entrusted to the Church; it is therefore the task of the church theologian to guard the truth entrusted to him and in this task he may make judicious use of the tools of historical enquiry. They will serve him in the task of guarding against later distortion, of expounding and exploring the deeper meaning of the deposit of faith.

Such a position contrasts sharply with one of the foundation texts of the Enlightenment, Lessing's *Duplik*, in which he scourges the orthodox of his day for their reliance on received truth. It is not the truth that someone supposes he possesses but the striving after truth that constitutes true human worth. 'Possession makes people idle and arrogant'. Indeed were God to offer him in the one hand all truth and in the other 'the eternally active impulse to search after the truth, though with the condition that he would always err', he would fall on the latter and say ' "Father give! The pure truth is for you alone"' (from Lessing's *Duplik*, *LW*, 23, 58f).

Lessing's dictum comes in the course of a battle he is waging on two fronts. On the one hand he is attacking the orthodox who believe they have the untrammelled — because revealed — truth and that therefore human reason — because corrupt — cannot in any way presume to judge such revelation. On the other hand, more relevantly from our point of view, he is attacking those who, like Semler, believe that reason does have a role to play both in checking the credentials of supposed revelation and in presenting the arguments for its truth. Lessing agrees with the orthodox, against Semler, that divine revelation, if there be such, must simply overrule human reason. Not that he has any wish to support the orthodox claim to possess such knowledge: such possession would undermine human dignity and worth. But the orthodox are still not Lessing's main target. His principal opponent is Semler, who sought to press human reason into the service of revealed knowledge. Lessing's goal is to emancipate human reason from both religious and political authorities and he fears that Semler's attempt to wed the two will only emasculate human reason. Human reason must stand on its own; it must free itself from all inherited beliefs and prejudices, and in exercising its judgement listen only to its own voice, not the voice of church or state.

Central issues are raised here about the nature of our acquisition of the truth and the development of human virtue and morality. First there is the question about the 'possession' of truth, the manner of our knowing it. To what extent can we ever say that we lay hold of the truth? Is human life always, as Lessing seems to suggest, esentially a *search* for the truth? Is our knowledge, such as it is, always subject to revision and refutation? Baur and his followers affirm some such version of the nature of human knowledge and apply it to the account that they give of the history of the church. Gore characterises those who do not possess the full revealed truth as simply 'guessers after the truth'.

Second there is a question about the nature of human reason. How far are we are justified in speaking of human reason as if it were some sort of universal instrument, accessible to all without prior conditions or special beliefs, by which all men and women may arrive at objectively verifiable knowledge? Or must we admit that there are certain sorts of prior conditions of knowledge, particular kinds of religious or indeed moral experience that put those who enjoy them into a privileged position over against those who do not? Specifically, are those who have committed themselves to the teaching of the church in such a position?

This was a question which Newman (1801-90) had significantly addressed in his *Oxford University Sermons* (1843), a work that had deeply influenced the tradition to which Gore owed allegiance. In those sermons, and in his later *Essay in Aid of a Grammar of Assent* (1870), Newman had attempted to show how, in the judgements which people make about the truth of religion, a whole range of antecedent considerations play their significant, if not always acknowledged, part. Simple faith itself may be characterised as an acceptance of things as real, or as the simple acceptance of testimony. But the ratification of such assents which the reflective believer gives, depends upon a complex chain of reflection and judgement in which his own experience, moral, religious and aesthetic, may have its role to play. In this sense it may well be proper to speak of faith, the apprehension of and assent to the reality of the Gospel of God, as a necessary condition of the kind of complex assents which those who have engaged not only with the theological tradition but also with the historical and natural sciences, may come to make. At the same time this is not to say that it is in any way a sufficient condition of such assents being properly given. Newman's achievement was to have shown the interrelation of such 'antecedent considerations' and the historical and scientific judgements which also are part of the complex process by which believers may come to reaffirm their 'simple' faith.

Moreover we also have to ask whether those who are so committed do not enjoy a privileged position concerning the Biblical texts themselves. May it not be that it is only those with the 'eyes of faith' who can read the texts aright, who are in a position to grasp their central, living sense?

Newman also questions sharply Lessing's claim that resting in the possession of a truth encouraged both indolence and arrogance. In an age of autocracy, such as Lessing's, where secular and spiritual authorities claimed a monopoly of the truth and exercised a fierce censorship on aberrant views, one can understand why such a claim should be made. But it overlooked the point that, again, Newman makes in his *Grammar*: that there is an important sense in which those who truly and fully grasp certain truths or ideas are moulded by them, and have a moral authority and strength not shared by those whose very lack of such anchoring makes them lightweight, easily swayed and inconsequential. Alongside the ideal of the 'heilig Suchende' (she who is engaged in a holy God-given search), we need to place that of the one who in being mastered by the truth is freed and empowered to join in its service and exploration. Thus, at least on this issue, there is room for creative debate and disagreement.

Such reflections may help to show up the relative merits of Pfleiderer's and Gore's positions. Pfleiderer's insistence on a purely historical treatment of the Biblical documents — reading them, that is, as sources for a thorough-going history of Christian origins — attempts to situate such study within a universal, rational enquiry into human history and culture. It insists that the criteria by which such a history is to be written must be those which cover all such historiography: the priority of causal explanations and the primacy of analogical judgements based on common human experience.

Such stipulations cannot be lightly set aside. The search for historical explanation, the identification of antecedent events or congeries of events that provide, in the light of our experience, explanations for what otherwise seems strange and possibly inexplicable, is a necessary part of the discipline. Yet precisely because of historians' concern not to impose themselves on the subject but to allow the subject to speak for itself they must also be alert to the possibilities of great varieties of human experiences and motivations that may explain particular acts and courses of events. This is only to say that in seeking analogies for events in the past we need to be as open to the varieties of human experience as we can; and to realise that much of it may indeed be very strange to us. In the religious, as in the moral realm perhaps, only those who have seen deeply into such areas of human experience can be true guides. This is not to say, of course, that those who are false or superficial guides may not be gloriously exposed by those with a sharp sense of human dignity and worth!

At the same time we need specifically to recognise in the varieties of religious belief and activity a rich field of human experience that may lead to actions and patterns of behaviour of baffling unexpectedness to those outside the group. We need also to recognise the fundamentally problematic nature of such belief and activity, which lies in the essentially controversial nature of the claimed source and goal of such belief and behaviour: God.

Thus any programme such as that enunciated by Otto Pfleiderer needs both to be open to the specificity of the phenomenon of religion, and to attempt to portray it in a way that does not unnecessarily prejudge the final questions of the reality of its source and goal.

Such remarks might have seemed painfully obvious to men like Pfleiderer and the members of the History of Religions School, rooted as they were in a liberal, religious piety. They seem less obvious and more necessary today. We also still need to take seriously the position of those like Gore who, while prepared to engage in dialogue with such thorough-going historical enquiry, insist from the outset on their commitment to a particular view of the truth: who claim not only that the reality of God that they acknowledge has been mediated to them through the Biblical writings but also that their faith provides a vital key to the meaning of those scriptures.

There is a respectable and considerable line of those who have taken such a path and we shall take note of some at least of their achievements. We shall see how some indeed try to combine both a thorough-going history of religions approach with such theological commitment. Our task here will be to consider, so far as this can be judged, how far in practice such prior commitment has led to the advancement or otherwise of New Testament study; how far Biblical interpretations of this kind have informed thorough-going historical attempts; and how far the last have criticised and, indeed, totally undermined the positions of Biblical theologians.

The danger of a position like Gore's lies, we have already seen, in his reluctance to give the same attention to criticism of the New as he did to that of the Old Testament. But its virtues, too, should not be overlooked. It was sufficiently open to Biblical criticism to attend to the testing of traditional christology that arose from an awareness of Jesus's cultural limitations, 'his failure to transcend the history of His age'. Moreover, if one allows that theological beliefs may be valid, and acknowledges also that they cannot be established by means of historical enquiry (a point which Lessing stressed), then one has to offer some account of the interrelation of prior theological commitments and historical and rational enquiry into religious traditions. Gore's account may require further discussion but it provides the basis for such a discussion.

So far our discussion has concentrated on the theological and intellectual context of New Testament study in the 1890s. It may be unusual in a history of such study to advert to the wider political context, but it is not I think without point. For England and Germany the 1890s were a period of expansion and aggrandisement. The European conquest and exploitation of Africa was at its height: Britain was engaged in the subjugation of the Zulus at massive cost to human life on both sides — something against which Bishop Colenso (1814-83), himself a considerable historical critic of the Bible, protested at the cost of his position. Germany was shortly to destroy the Herero people in what was then German Southwest Africa, in an act of callous and arrogant genocide. Not that such acts of barbarity were the only features of colonial rule: it was, of course, a much more complex phenomenon, with commercial exploitation and missionary activity and education all playing significant roles. But what marks out and unites English and German theologians writing at this time is their cultural confidence that their religious beliefs are the ultimate or the highest form of all such beliefs, the essence of religion that lay at the heart of all true culture and society. This can be seen clearly in the *Kulturprotestantismus* of A. Ritschl, W. Hermann (1846-1922) and A. von Harnack (1851-1930).

Harnack, despite his awareness of forces in German culture deeply antipathetic to Christianity still believed that nineteenth-century Christian Europe came closer to the realisation of an ideal society than others before it. Such scholars may have been guided in part by Lessing's dictum about the continuing search for truth; but they had also been taught by Hegel (1770-1831) to see in German culture a significant stage in the coming to expression of the absolute Spirit. A similar belief in the cultural supremacy of Christianity can also be seen in the missionary confidence of the Anglo-Catholic movement of which Gore was a central figure. Societies like the Community of the Resurrection or the Society of St John the Evangelist went out to Africa and India to bring the light of the Christian Gospel to those who lacked its true fullness; the Church of England was to grow to become an Anglican Communion with provinces around the world. Yet, ironically, all this was occurring as the first signs of the breakdown of Western imperial hegemony were appearing and the first rumblings of European conflict began to be heard. We shall have occasion to observe how the political histories of England and Germany, which were subsequently very different, bore on their ways of doing theology and studying the New Testament.

Notes

1. Numbers in brackets directly following quotations refer to the page or pages where the quotation will be found in the work last cited.
2. It is a painfully recurring leitmotif of Bishop Stephen Neill's *The Interpretation of the New Testament 1861-1961*. Here Gore's theme of the racially distinctive contributions of different groups is developed into an obsession: English sense and balance contrast with German immoderation and extremism. It has been music to many English ears, but has hardly contributed to self-criticism and the development of the discipline.
3. Wellhausen was a leading Old Testament scholar whose theories about Pentateuchal sources (known as J, E, P and D) have lasted better than most scholarly hypotheses. He also wrote some excellent commentaries on the Synoptic Gospels.
4. The term 'History of Religions School' applies strictly to a group of scholars in Göttingen who reacted against Ritschl's biblical theology. Prominent figures included A. Eichhorn, W. Wrede, H. Gunkel, W. Bousset, and W. Heitmüller. J. Weiss was also associated with the group.
5. *Neutestamentliche Zeitgeschichte*, 1, ix, quoted in Kümmel, 206.

List of works cited

F.C. Baur, *The Church History of the First Three Centuries*, Tübingen, 1853-63 (German); London, 1878-9 (English)

C. Gore, ed, *Lux Mundi*, London, 1889, 5th edn, rev., May 1890, 10th edn, September 1890 [Quotations are from 15th, popular, later edition.]

G.E. Lessing, *Duplik*, in volume 23 of *Lessings Werke*, ed J Petersen and V. Olshausen, Berlin, 1926-35

S. Neill, *The Interpretation of the New Testament 1861-1961*, Oxford, 1966

J.H. Newman, *Oxford University Sermons*, Oxford, 1843

J.H. Newman, *Essay in Aid of a Grammar of Assent*, London, 1870

O. Pfleiderer, *Primitive Christianity: Its Writings and Teachings in their Historical Connection*, Munich, 1905 (German); London, 1906-11 (English)

A. Ritschl, *The Origin of the Early Catholic Church*, Bonn, 1850, 1857 (German)

A. Schweitzer, *The Quest of the Historical Jesus*, London, 1910

A. Schweitzer, *Paul and his Interpreters*, London, 1912

2

The History of Religions
and the Life of Jesus

In 1892 Johannes Weiss (1863-1914) published a small volume entitled
Jesus' Proclamation of the Kingdom of God. What distinguished it most
clearly from the hundreds of books about Jesus that had been published in
the course of the nineteenth century, was its determination to interpret
Jesus's preaching of the Kingdom in terms of beliefs and ideas that were
current in his day. The question he raised was 'whether and to what extent
the particular form of the idea which occurs in Jesus's proclamation had
models in the Old Testament or Judaism' (2nd edn, 2). Weiss recognised
that ideas have to be expressed in terms that are intelligible to their audience.
It was, therefore, essential, if one was to understand what Jesus was saying
about the Kingdom, to know what was the range of usage that such an
expression would have had among Jesus's contemporaries. If Jesus was to
be understood at all, we might say, he would have to pay his dues to such
usage.

In this task Weiss was greatly helped by recent studies of Jewish literature
of the time. When he asked what range of meanings the expression 'the
Kingdom of God' would have carried to Jesus's contemporaries, he could
refer not only to senses which might be garnered from a study of the Old
Testament, but also to texts more nearly contemporary with Jesus: the Aramaic
translations of the Old Testament which were done for synagogue readings
(the Targums); the collections of Rabbinic material, the Mishnah and the
Talmud; and the apocalyptic writings of the turn of the era. Weiss recognised
that there was in fact a range of senses current for the expression at the time
of Jesus. It might refer, as in many Old Testament texts, to the eternal rule of
God over the world. Connected with this sense, in the Rabbis and the Targums,
was the conviction that believers needed to acknowledge that rule in their
lives: 'taking the yoke of the Kingdom upon you'. Such a sense, according
to Weiss, was far removed from Jesus's proclamation:

> On the one hand (viz. in Jesus' preaching) the unleashing of an
> overwhelming divine storm, which blows freely, destroying and renew-
> ing, and which men and women can neither call up or influence; on

the other a permanently instituted order of things, which one can deny, from which one can withdraw but which one should submit to (5).

This former sense came closer to that of other texts, notably in apocalyptic literature, where what was said about the Kingdom referred to some expected state of affairs that would be brought about when God acted to put an end to the present evil age. Weiss traced a considerable body of tradition in the Old Testament and apocalyptic literature and found one text particularly significant, *The Assumption of Moses*. This text contrasted the coming Kingdom of God with the present Kingdom of Satan. Satan's rule would be done away with in a series of cosmic disasters and upheavals; the wicked would be destroyed and the righteous would enjoy eternal bliss (26f).

Weiss saw that there were phrases in the Gospels that were comparable to both the Rabbinic and the apocalyptic usage. 'Whoever does not receive the Kingdom of God like a child shall not enter it'(Mk.10:15) was like the Rabbinic usage (Weiss 7); but the portrayal of Jesus's temptation by Satan suggested that Satan was, indeed, temporarily the ruler of the world. It was this latter apocalyptic sense which Weiss believed found expression in Jesus's sayings about the coming of the Kingdom: 'If I by the finger of God cast out demons then the Kingdom of God has come upon you'(Lk.11:20; Weiss 88-95). In brief, Weiss believed that Jesus expected some cataclysmic end to the present order of things, an end that would be brought about by the direct intervention of God but which was, equally, associated with his own ministry and teaching. Thus those who heard him should repent and believe the Gospel and wait for the coming of the Kingdom. Mark 13 gives a vivid picture, both of what was expected and of what the proper response of Jesus's disciples was to be. Even if much of this chapter was taken over from contemporary Jewish expectations, Jesus's own expectations would not have been very different. Certainly, according to Weiss, he renounced any knowledge of the timing of the end (Mk. 13:32); but that does not mean to say that he did not expect such an end to occur (see Weiss *Das Markus-Evangelium*, 199).

All this stood in sharp contrast to the accepted views of Albrecht Ritschl and his followers. Weiss had delayed publication of his book until Ritschl's death, perhaps in view of his marriage to Ritschl's daughter. Ritschl had offered a view of Jesus's teaching of the Kingdom that we can now see owes at least as much to the philosopher Immanuel Kant as it did to Jesus. The Kingdom of God for Jesus was a 'Kingdom of Ends', a society in which all would be treated never merely as means but always as ends. It was a task given to people by Jesus of creating a new society here on earth that would be fulfilled in an eternal kingdom beyond death. Here on earth the kingdom was to be realised by 'man's self-activity' in response to the preaching of the kingdom. Interpreting the parable of the seed growing secretly (Mk .4:26-9), Ritschl argued that it referred to the seed of Jesus's teaching that was sown in history and which would come to fulfilment as a result of men's and women's response and faithfulness to the task that they were thereby set

(*Instruction in the Christian Religion* I.A, para. 5c,d). All of this was challenged by Weiss. The point about the parable was not the gradualness of the progress of God's will, as men and women responded to Jesus's charge, but the need for patience and quiet confidence and hope in the final fulfilment. It was not about 'men's self-activity' but about God's action. Jesus regarded the coming fulfilment of God's rule:

> in no way as the work of men and women, not even as his work, but as the work of God; his proclamation is the message that 'God will reign'. Men and women can do nothing other than prepare themselves for and make themselves worthy of this state of affairs (*Das Markus-Evangelium*, 115).

Weiss's work represented a major advance in the search for an historical understanding of the New Testament. It was not itself the result of great and original research, but it did make striking use of the historical studies of ancient Jewish texts that had been undertaken during the nineteenth century. Its real originality lay in pressing on the question of how we are to understand and to explain Jesus's utterances. The model of explanation which Weiss followed was essentially an historical, linguistic one. We have to explain Jesus's sayings in terms of the linguistic usage of the time; by so doing we shall be able to relate what he is saying to ideas about God's rule that were current at the time. One way of expressing such an approach was to say that historians have to explain their texts 'out of' the ideas of their time. This might be referred to as a 'genetic' mode of explanation. If we are to understand an idea, we have to know its family tree, where it comes from. We have, that is to say, to give a causal explanation in which Jesus's ideas are presented as the effects of certain antecedent ideas that were prevalent in his culture. Weiss's approach is less mechanical: he attempts to locate Jesus's usage in a range of contemporary options and thereby to discern its characteristic sense.

The genetic mode of explanation was attractive to those, like Pfleiderer, who sought to offer an account of the historical development of Christianity as one among a number of significant religious movements of its time. It was one that obviously exercised considerable fascination in an age where mechanistic understandings of causality were prevalent. Yet it is questionable whether such models do justice either to linguistic phenomena or, indeed, to the way in which people develop their own ideas in a particular culture. The point is this: it is true that we can communicate to our fellows only by using language in a way that they can recognise. We have to respect the conventions that obtain within a given natural language group or we simply would not be understood. But that does not mean that we are not free, within certain bounds, to use language creatively, wittily or metaphorically. Language is a living thing which is constantly being stretched, abused and developed. We need to grasp the innovations in linguistic usage as well as the debts to convention and established use in a given utterance, if we are to understand what is being said. The same is true about the development of ideas. Anyone who wants to communicate ideas about God to his fellows must at the very least relate what he or she has to say to current ideas about God. To enter into any intelligible discussion at all there must be at least some common base of beliefs that can be assumed, even if it may subsequently be challenged. This does not mean to say that original and sharp minds may not advance striking and unexpected thoughts which could not easily have been anticipated. Simply to reduce the beliefs of historical figures to products of the ideas current at their time is to miss the spark of wit and the creative moment when a new idea is born.

In this respect Weiss's work is instructive. It shows the necessity of a careful study of contemporary usage and beliefs if scholars are to avoid a crude modernising of Jesus's teaching. It demonstrates clearly that Ritschl's account of Jesus's teaching was in important respects too much of a reading into the texts of theological and philosophical notions of more recent date. Yet even here we must be careful. In the first place, Kant's notion of a 'Kingdom of Ends' owes much to the Protestant tradition with its own roots in Jesus and Paul. It is not a purely alien notion. Thus Ritschl's account of the Kingdom was not a straightforward imposition of alien ideas, but rather an attempt to render Jesus's thought into appropriate contemporary categories, undertaken with the specific intention of making proper use of historical scholarship. What Weiss showed was not the overall illegitimacy of Ritschl's Biblical theological project, but the inadequacies of its historical base. The point is not that Ritschl was deliberately modernising: how else can one interpret texts from the past, if not in categories that are presently intelligible? The point is rather that any attempt to do theology by expounding the Biblical texts will always be subject to revision in the light of developments in the historical study of the texts.

While Weiss was right to point out discrepancies between Ritschl's Biblical theology and his attempts to reconstruct the meaning of Jesus's sayings, his own method of working was also not without its risks. His search for historical antecedents for Jesus's teaching on the Kingdom meant that there was a danger of forcing Jesus's teaching into a strait-jacket. Too close an identification of Jesus's ideas with those of his contemporaries might conceal the creative and innovative elements in Jesus's thought, his — historical — particularity. It is important, not least in the light of subsequent debates about the distinctiveness of Jesus's teaching, to stress that this is an historical point. The historian is precisely concerned with particularity, with trying to grasp and recover the quite specific character of people, movements and events. In this the historian is therefore both trying to see how his or her subject fits into its contemporary setting and also trying to show how that subject stands out from its context: how it is significant, why it is interesting to recall, what is its 'contribution' to the historical developments of those times. The understanding of historical causality in the History of Religions School and its forerunners made this last task difficult and the results sometimes suspect.

There is another point of considerable political and practical significance. Theologians like Ritschl, Wilhelm Herrmann (1846-1922) and Adolf von Harnack tended to identify the religious and ethical community which Jesus charged his followers to realise with Western European Protestantism. The Reformation, they thought, had done much to restore Christianity to its original form, after its corruption by its intermingling with Greek philosophy. The Enlightenment, too, had removed much that was superstitious or unacceptable in the light of modern scientific knowledge. Now the scene was set for the realisation of a truly ethical and communal form of Christianity that could be the basis of a true human society and culture. The fact that such claims for Western European Christendom had to be made despite the conditions of the working classes in Western industrial society and the exploitation of the colonies, both of which were providing the basis for the development of radical forms of socialism, clearly did not trouble such theologians in any serious way. Marx (1818-1883) and Engels (1820-1895) were not thinkers that they engaged with. Disillusionment with this form of cultural Protestantism was to come in Germany after the disaster of the First World War. In England such disillusionment would in large measure have to wait for the dissolution of Empire after the costly 'victory' of the Second World War.

Weiss's work, which was picked up and developed by Albert Schweitzer, was, however, to provide powerful means with which to attack such a position. For him the Kingdom was not to be brought in by men's and women's moral activity, but by the sudden inbreaking of God's power. Human activity would be judged; what was required was patient waiting for the End. Clearly he was aware of the damage his work would do to Ritschl's theological position. Yet he never fully addressed himself to the radical questions that his study raised, either for drawing a picture of earliest Christianity, or indeed for Biblical theology in general. His own study of Christian origins, *Earliest Christianity: A History of the Period AD 30-150* (1914-17), remains a torso, incomplete when he died in 1914 at the age of 57. It is significant that he elected to start work on his projected second volume first, namely on the Gentile Mission and Paul. The proposed first volume, on Jesus and Early Christianity, was not completed.

Others were, however, ready to respond to the challenge which Weiss's view of Jesus presented both for the history of earliest Christianity and for Biblical theology.

Adolf von Harnack was principally a church historian, the author of histories of the dogma (*History of Dogma*, 1886-9) and mission of the church (*The Mission and Expansion of Christianity*, 1902), as well as of countless scholarly editions of early Christian texts. Nevertheless he also turned his hand to New Testament studies, wrote a book on St Luke, and produced a set of popular lectures on *What is Christianity?* (1900), in which he tried to answer the question historically. He pointed to its origins in the life and faith of Jesus of Nazareth and then attempted to demonstrate how the spirit of Jesus's religion had been distorted and overlaid by the subsequent history of the church. His work could be seen in one sense as little more than a restatement of Ritschlian Christianity: Harnack retained his commitment to liberal Christianity, even after the debacle of the First World War had led many German theologians, following Barth, to reject it. But it is also interesting to see in this work an historian's response to the work of Weiss.

Harnack starts by considering the sources for the life of Jesus, which for him are primarily the first three Gospels (19). He accepts Mark as being not only the earliest but as also providing an essentially reliable account of Jesus's life and work. That is to say, he saw no reason to try to get behind Mark's Gospel to the tradition that it recorded. In this he was merely following the standard critical view, which, however, was to be sharply challenged in the next two decades. For Harnack, the Gospels 'offer us a plain picture of Jesus' teaching, in regard both to its main features and to its individual application'; they show him leading his life and accepting death in faithfulness to his calling; and 'they describe the impression he made upon his disciples, and which they transmitted' (31).

Jesus' teaching is not a systematic treatise, dealing with different subjects *seriatim*. Thus, while his various sayings can be organised under different headings, they all point to the same reality, the gracious relationship between God and the believer. All his teaching represents different attempts to spell out and express the same central reality which he himself lived out: trust in God. His was a fresh vision, sharply contrasted by Harnack with the distorted understanding of God of contemporary Jewish leaders:

They thought of God as of a despot guarding the ceremonial observances in His household; he [sc. Jesus] breathed in the presence of God. They saw Him only in His law, which they had converted into a labyrinth of dark defiles, blind alleys and secret passages; he saw and felt Him everywhere'(50).

This character-assassination of first-century Judaism in order to portray the distinctiveness of Jesus is, as E. P. Sanders (b.1927) has more recently shown, a disturbing feature of many 'liberal' lives of Jesus.

When Jesus spoke of the coming of the Kingdom he was not, as Weiss suggested, simply taking over apocalyptic usage of the term and speaking of some future cataclysmic event in history. He shared such beliefs with his contemporaries; he did not initiate such beliefs but simply grew up with them and retained them (54). But that was not the heart of Jesus's teaching, that which was truly his own. The specific sense in which Jesus used such evocative language could be seen from his saying in Lk.17:20f: 'The Kingdom of God is not coming with signs to be observed; nor will they say, "Lo, here it is!" or "There!" for behold the Kingdom of God is in the midst of you'. Such sayings refer to the 'still and mighty power of God in the hearts of men' and women. Like Augustine, Harnack took 'in the midst of you' to mean 'in vestris cordibus', that is 'in your hearts'. Faith, the gracious relation between God and the believer, is not something that can be established by the believer himself. It has first to be established by God's:

coming to the individual, by entering into his soul and laying hold of it. True, the kingdom of God is the rule of God; but it is the rule of the holy God in the hearts of individuals; *it is God himself in his power*' (56).

The emphasis on the individual is undeniable in Harnack's treatment but needs to be carefully understood. Jesus taught the fatherhood of God and the infinite value of the human soul. In the Lord's Prayer he stressed the universal care and providence of God as Father: he also taught, in a series of Wisdom sayings, that as a child of God each person was of inestimable value to God. This is not a callous individualism that discourages the formation of strong social bonds, or disputes the duties of the wider family to care for the weaker members; it is an assertion of the worth of the individual that is rooted in his or her common relationship to the Father; 'a real reverence for humanity follows from the practical recognition of God as the Father of us all'. By his teaching, 'the value of the human race is enhanced' (70).

All of this comes out clearly enough in Jesus's ethical teaching. Jesus, says Harnack, rejected the legalism of the Pharisees, their concern with public worship and cultic observance, and preached a higher righteousness. Instead of insisting on detailed observation of the ceremonial law, he preached an ethic of intention (71). It was the purity of people's motives, their love for God and each other, and their humility, which properly expressed their true relationship to God. Humility 'is not a virtue by itself; but it is pure receptivity, the expression of inner need, the prayer for God's grace and forgiveness, in a word, the opening up of the heart to God'. It is a proper recognition of one's relationship to God and to one's fellows: it is 'the source and origin of the love of one's neighbour' (73).

Harnack's lectures have a perennial fascination. Their spirit lives on, popularly, in the works of W. Barclay (1907-78), who willingly acknowledged his debt to Harnack. For all that Harnack's views were about to be overtaken by a critical movement of great vigour, they gave expression to an enlightened, humane form of Christianity that continues to attract. Harnack saw the urgency of the recovery of such a view. He believed, indeed, that such a fresh 'naive', childlike view of life was essential if culture was to retain its health and its vigour. Nor was he overconfident: he realised that liberalism and Christianity had their detractors and enemies in Europe and he was to feel the force of that opposition in his own struggles to uphold them during the Weimar Republic.

Moreover Harnack's position is not without its historical strengths. He is not easily swayed by Weiss's adducing of apocalyptic parallels to Jesus's sayings. It is still important for Harnack to ask what specific use Jesus made of such language. Any answer to that question would require giving attention to the whole complex of Jesus's sayings. If Jesus, he might have argued, is to be considered as a fundamentally world-renouncing figure, announcing the end of this age and the judgement of all human deeds in the present, what point was there in Jesus's ethical teaching? Does not such teaching require to be lived out and realised in the creation of societies and cultures here on earth? And how does the reflective element in Jesus's teaching about the Fatherhood of God and the infinite worth of the soul accord with a view that sees this whole world as under judgement, ready to be rolled up?

Justified though such questions might be, they are questions raised precisely because of the striking similarities between Jesus's language about the Kingdom and the Son of Man, and texts like the *Assumptio Mosis* to which Weiss had so effectively drawn attention. As long as, however, the Synoptic Gospels were held to give a broadly accurate picture of Jesus's life and teaching, a strong case could be made for interpreting Jesus's Kingdom-sayings in the light of his Wisdom sayings and of his ethical teaching. Once that confidence in the Synoptics was shaken, other solutions would become more attractive. That would not alter the intrinsic worth of Harnack's study, which was to have sought the particular character of Jesus's teaching about the Kingdom by considering it in relation to the other contemporary uses of the term, and to the other beliefs that we may reasonably attribute to Jesus.

Before going on to consider the way in which confidence in the reliability of the Gospels as records of Jesus's life and teaching was shaken, we need to look briefly at one other attempt to discern the distinctiveness of Jesus's teaching.

Wilhelm Bousset (1865-1920) was another member of the Göttingen Faculty who belonged to the History of Religions School. His major work, *Kyrios Christos* (1913), will be discussed briefly in the next chapter. He also wrote a smaller work in reply to Weiss, *Jesus im Gegensatz zum Judentum* (1892; Jesus contrasted with Judaism). In this, Bousset disputes the connections between Jesus and the apocalyptic writings, arguing like Harnack later, that Jesus's piety was related to the piety of contemporary Judaism only in its external form. The whole figure of Jesus 'was not held under the spell of Judaism'. Rather 'the Gospel develops hidden elements in the Old Testament, but it protests against the ruling direction of Judaism'(see Kümmel, (b.1905) *Investigation*, 230-2). Jesus draws on the pure springs of Old Testament prophecy. He transcends the religious thought of his day and in a movement of the spirit recovers the deeply moral and religious vision of the prophets.

It is hard to know what sort of an historical explanation this is. On the one hand, it sets Jesus in his contemporary context; but on the other, it appeals to a movement of the spirit that both transcends that context and forges a link with the past. The problem is this: it is right to want to emphasise the distinctiveness of a particular historical figure, not to reduce him to the sum of the various cultural causes which are to be found in his environment; but in emphasising the distinctiveness of a particular figure, we still need to know how his or her particular vision of things relates to the specific situation, how it represents, as it were, a specific response to that situation. Simply to compare Jesus to the eighth- and seventh-century prophets does not explain why he should have adopted such a stance in his day. We would need to know, for example, more about the similarities between his situation and theirs before such comparisons could become illuminating and not simply a flight from historical explanation into appeals to the creativity of the human spirit. The question of the distinctiveness of Jesus's teaching is one that was to continue to fascinate scholars throughout our period; but we need to be aware of the quite distinct ways in which it may be raised. It might be raised in a search for the specific historical character of Jesus; or it might also be approached apologetically, in an attempt to set Jesus apart from his fellow Jews, as the bringer of a new, purer form of religion. The problem is that such very different enterprises cannot in practice always easily be distinguished.

We must return, however, to consideration of Weiss's impact on study of the life and teaching of Jesus. What Harnack's lectures showed, *inter alia*, was that so long as scholars continued to see the Gospels as broadly reliable accounts of Jesus's life and teaching, so long could the force of the parallels which Weiss adduced between Jesus's language of the Kingdom and Jewish apocalyptic be blunted by drawing attention to texts in the Gospels of an apparently very different kind, namely, the Wisdom sayings. Blunted, but not altogether removed. For the parallels to apocalyptic literature were striking, and they suggested ways of reading the texts that questioned liberal views of Jesus. Thus two routes lead from here. One was the further development of the apocalyptic view of Jesus which Weiss had sketched out in his book. The other was to attempt to open up the world of tradition which lay behind the Gospels themselves, and so to question the historical reliability of Mark.

One of the first works to challenge the widespread acceptance of Mark's trustworthiness was William Wrede's (1859-1906) *The Messianic Secret* (1901). Much has been written about this book and it is today seen mainly as the forerunner of redaction criticism, the sustained attempt to identify the theological stance of the Gospel writers themselves. But it is in many ways a much more complex book than that view might suggest. This is because Wrede had two principal aims in mind, both of which related to a basic intuition that Mark's Gospel was a product of the earliest Christian *community*. The first aim was to attack existing views of the historical Jesus, by showing the extent to which they were based on subsequent theological speculation by the early church; the second was to attempt a reconstruction of early Christian theological beliefs and apologetic.

As is well known, Wrede noticed that there were certain motifs in the Gospel that were not easily explained as straight, historical observations:

the command to silence to demons and to the disciples; similar commands to those healed; secret, private teaching to the disciples; a parable theory; and the disciples' lack of understanding. His own view was that these motifs gave expression to a unitary, theological conception that was the product of the early church and which represented a transitional form of christology:

We can find in Mark two ideas:

(1) Jesus keeps his Messiahship a secret as long as he is on earth;

(2) He does, of course, reveal himself to the disciples in contrast to the people, but to them too he remains in his revelations incomprehensible for the time being.

Both ideas, which frequently overlap, have behind them the common view that real knowledge of what Jesus is only begins with his resurrection (113f).

Thus such motifs could not be taken as evidence for the beliefs of Jesus himself; rather, they explained how the church could move from an early christological view, namely that Jesus was declared messiah at his resurrection, to later, more developed christologies that saw his whole life in messianic terms. The 'messianic secret' was a transitional form of christology, produced at a time when Jesus's life was already beginning to be seen in such messianic terms. By proclaiming (Mk. 9:9) that Jesus's messiahship was only to become public knowledge at his resurrection, it attempted to prevent too violent a clash with the earlier, still current, view that he became Messiah only at his resurrection (228f).

In short, Wrede drew attention to the diversity of the material in the Gospels and to the possibility that the accounts we have reflect the theological and practical interests of the communities or writers who handed them on. After Wrede it would no longer be quite possible for scholars to regard the Gospels as objective reports of the life and teaching of Jesus. Their theological bias had been revealed, and with that revelation came a growing awareness that between the Gospels and Jesus stood a perhaps quite complex process of tradition. The task of plotting the details of that process was to be taken up during and after the war years by the form-critics, foremost among whom were Martin Dibelius (1903-47), Rudolf Bultmann (1884-1976) and Karl Ludwig Schmidt (1891-1956).

What Wrede had suggested was that scholars could no longer take for granted that all the material attributed to Jesus in the Synoptics was, in fact, authentic to him. Thus if there was felt to be a tension between Jesus's apocalyptic sayings and the Wisdom sayings in the Gospels, the question would have to be raised: which of these sets of sayings did he actually utter? The same was true of tensions that might be found within certain groups of sayings. This at once left the way open for a much greater variety of interpretations of Jesus. It also led to a greater scepticism about the possibility of success and hence to the theological value of such an enterprise in historical interpretation. These options were to be variously taken up in the great tide of theological reaction to the debacle of the First World War.

Before turning to those developments, we need to retrace our steps. Weiss's book, we saw, raised serious questions about a particular interpretation of Jesus that had enjoyed considerable popularity and support because of its strong advocacy by Ritschl. This view was theologically attractive because of its strong ethical emphasis and its eschewal of metaphysics. It placed Jesus's ethical and social teaching at the heart of Christianity and played down the importance of traditional forms of doctrine, not least christology, which were becoming increasingly problematic. It was also, as we have noted, culturally attractive. It could be used to give credence to the view that Western European Protestantism was at least approaching the ideal of the Kingdom which Jesus had come to inaugurate. This was for two reasons: first because of the synthesis it achieved between Jesus's teaching and a Lutheran reading of Paul; and second because of its doctrine of history which saw the Gospel as a seed whose fruits would be slowly realised through men's and women's actions in history.

The complex theological and cultural implications of the Ritschlian view might account for the very diverse responses which Weiss's apocalyptic interpretation of Jesus brought forth. So far we have noticed the reactions of those like Harnack and Bousset who emphasised other elements in the Gospels, the prophetic or the Wisdom material, which is also attributed to Jesus and consequently felt free to minimise the significance of the parallels to apocalyptic literature which Weiss had adduced. The man who, of course, most fiercely challenged all such attempts to minimise the connections between Jesus and Jewish apocalyptic was Albert Schweitzer, notably in *The Mystery of the Kingdom of God* (1901).

Schweitzer's views, published in the same year as Wrede's *Messianic Secret*, were based on a reading of Mark's Gospel as a largely reliable historical account of Jesus's life and teaching. Thus certain incidents in Mark's Gospel, like the sending out of the disciples in Mark 6, and the incident at Caesarea Philippi and the journey to Jerusalem, provide a framework for his reconstruction of Jesus's ministry. While Jesus had a consistent view of the Kingdom, in one important respect, Schweitzer believed, he changed his mind.

Jesus believed in an imminent restoration of the Kingdom to Israel by an act of divine intervention. This Kingdom, as was taught in 'late Jewish Messianic expectation' (Enoch, Psalms of Solomon, Apocalypses of Baruch and Ezra), will be set up on earth by the Messianic Son of Man at the end of time. Jesus takes such teaching literally: he does not spiritualise it, as was suggested by liberal theologians like Holtzmann (1832-1910) and Harnack. But while he takes it literally, he fills it with his own ethical spirit, demanding 'a moral renewal in prospect of the accomplishment of the universal perfection in the future' (94). Thus his teaching is both eschatological and ethical:

In sovereign style Jesus effects the synthesis of the apocalyptic of Daniel with the ethics of the Prophets. With him it is not a question of eschatological ethics, rather is his world view an ethical eschatology. As such it is modern (256).

Jesus himself proclaimed publicly only the imminent coming of the Kingdom. Privately he believed that he would be revealed as the Messiah at the coming of the Kingdom. This was the secret that had been revealed to him at his baptism by John. Thus for Schweitzer the secret in Mark is not a theological motif explaining problems in early christology, but part of the historical consciousness of Jesus himself.

The coming of the Kingdom would be preceded by suffering, 'pre-messianic Affliction' on the part of the faithful. 'The believers must be prepared to pass with him through that time of trial, in which they are to prove themselves the Elect of the Kingdom by steadfast resistance to the last attack of the power of the world' (257). This suffering will have atoning power 'because God requires of the adherents of the Kingdom a satisfaction for the transgressions of this aeon' (258).

He sent out his disciples in the belief that this would bring about the Kingdom. When the disciples returned and told of their power over the evil spirits he believed that everything was ready. The fact that the Kingdom did not, however, come caused him to rethink his understanding of his role within its coming. Now he sees that God will bring about the Kingdom without the general affliction (266). He becomes convinced that he must take upon himself the messianic woes and so spare the elect the suffering that would otherwise have been theirs. At Caesarea Philippi he announces this to his disciples, together with his intention to go up to Jerusalem in order to bring in the Kingdom. He goes up to Jerusalem where he celebrates the Last Supper with his disciples in the expectation that they will celebrate it anew in the Kingdom. He is betrayed by Judas and condemned to death. The Kingdom he had expected does not come. Nevertheless Jesus's call to follow him, to seek out a new world, is still heard. The spirit of Christ that we know from his words and his teaching lives on in the hearts of those who hear and follow him out of this world into the new.

Schweitzer's work stands in a paradoxical relationship to the great quest for the historical Jesus which he chronicled so fully. It is continuous with that quest in so far as it continues to press on the historical questions that inaugurated it, and to believe that answers to them are possible. In this respect it is quite misleading to portray Schweitzer's work as a farewell to historical studies of Jesus. On the contrary, it is impossible today to read *The Mystery of the Kingdom of God* without being shocked by the extraordinary confidence with which Schweitzer reconstructs from the Gospels the fine detail of Jesus's last months. What he attacks is not the attempt to discover the Jesus of history but rather the attempt to construct a Jesus in the image of nineteenth-century society — what H. J. Cadbury (1883-1974) was to refer to as the 'peril of modernising Jesus'. So much of the later work on the historical Jesus 'forced

Jesus into conformity with our human standards and human psychology'. It weakened Jesus's 'imperative world-condemning demands upon individuals, that He might not come into conflict with our ethical ideals, and might tune His denial of the world to our acceptance of it'(*The Quest of the Historical Jesus*, 398). It was precisely the discovery of apocalyptic that undermined the modernising tendency of the Lives of Jesus:

> [T]heology was forced by genuine history to begin to doubt the artificial history with which it had thought to give new life to our Christianity, and to yield to the facts which, as Wrede strikingly said, are sometimes the most radical critics of all (399).

Such an appeal to genuine history also defines its role. It is there principally as a critic of all our attempts to modernise Jesus, to cast him in our own ethical mould. 'History will force it (theology) to find a way to transcend history, and to fight for the lordship and rule of Jesus over this world with weapons tempered in a different forge' (*ibid.*).

Thus history is to be transcended as yet another work by which men and women try to resist the demands of God. The Lutheran-Pauline connection is made:

> We are experiencing what Paul experienced. In the very moment when we were coming nearer to the historical Jesus than men had ever come before, and were already stretching out our hands to draw Him into our own time, we have been obliged to give up the attempt and acknowledge our failure in that paradoxical saying: 'If we have known Christ after the flesh yet henceforth we know him no more'. And further we must be prepared to find that the historical knowledge of the personality and life of Jesus will not be a help, but perhaps even an offence to religion (*ibid.*).

It is then in the individual's response to the words of Christ that she may discover who she is. History cannot:

> disengage that which is abiding and eternal in the being of Jesus from the historical forms in which it worked itself out. . . . The abiding and eternal in Jesus is absolutely independent of historical knowledge and can only be understood by contact with His spirit which is still at work in the world. In proportion as we have the Spirit of Jesus we have the true knowledge of Jesus (*ibid.*).

In the end, then, historical knowledge merely serves to show us that Jesus is a stranger to us. Certainly it undermines the liberal attempt to identify Christianity with the fruits of the Gospel. Rather it calls the individual out to fulfil the tasks which the living Christ sets, as Schweitzer himself responded to the call to go and care for the poor man at Europe's door.

Schweitzer's work has been enormously fruitful, though few in Germany wanted to follow the details of his historical reconstructions. In the main this was because the subsequent work of William Wrede, and K. L. Schmidt and the form-critics undermined scholars' confidence in Mark's Gospel as a trustworthy historical source. In England, rather strangely, he was better received: apparently the unorthodoxy of his account of Jesus's life and thought could be forgiven — even, with suitable modification, be taken up — as long as one could enlist his support for the reliability of Mark.

This can be seen clearly enough in W. Sanday's (1843-1920) *The Life of Christ in Recent Research* (1907). Sanday dismisses Wrede's *Messianic Secret* with uncharacteristic intellectual scorn — not with detailed argument: 'I cannot easily conceive anything more utterly artificial and impossible' (74). Wrede, according to Sanday, had argued that the view that Jesus was the Messiah had been developed by the early Church out of the belief in the Resurrection. For there was in the tradition a 'complete dearth of facts showing that He had made any such claim' (73f). According to Wrede, the early Church attempted to cope with this by introducing 'all these prohibitions and hints of esoteric teaching and imputations of dullness and the like'. But is that, asks Sanday, how 'an ancient' would have behaved? Would he not rather 'boldly go in and fill up the blank with the facts required?'(74) With this argument he is able to dispense himself from the need to give further detailed consideration to Wrede's book.

He is however much more sympathetic to Schweitzer, and remarkably seems ready to accept in large measure the latter's account of Jesus's ministry, his expectation of the Kingdom, his disappointment when it does not occur after the sending out of the 12 (Mk.10:23) and his subsequent realisation that he must take the Messianic suffering upon himself. Yet Sanday can do this only because he spiritualises the sense of Kingdom of God: 'Is it not the asserted and realised sovereignty of God, Divine influence and Divine power felt as energising in the souls of men?'(115). He quickly identifies this with the apostolic doctrine of the Holy Spirit, pointing to Pentecost as the moment at which a new access of such Divine power entered the world (*ibid.*).

Such an interpretation paid tribute to the connections between Jesus's language of the Kingdom and contemporary Jewish apocalyptic texts, but it spiritualised their meaning, offering what Sanday called a 'symbolic' inter-pretation of them. This meant, consequently, that a similar interpretation could be found for those terms in which Jesus, in Schweitzer's view, had spoken of himself: Son of Man, Son of God, Messiah. Here the strange attraction of Schweitzer's treatment becomes clear. Schweitzer asserted that Jesus thought of himself as Messiah; he believed that Jesus expected the inauguration of a new age with his death and that he was in this sense deluded. Sanday spiritualised Jesus's expectations, arguing that they were indeed ful-filled in the coming of the Spirit, and was then able to show how such a concept-ion of Jesus's teaching and self-understanding illuminated traditional christology.

Again the procedure is to broaden and spiritualise the terms employed. 'Son of Man' may have had a strictly transcendental sense in I Enoch, linked with a coming crisis in Israel's history, but in Jesus's usage it was reworked: 'I believe that our Lord rarely took up a Jewish idea without putting into it more than He found there. And this enrichment constantly came from His profound intimacy with the Old Testament' (127). Thus through Jesus's meditation on Psalm 8 he introduces into the notion of 'Son of Man' a representative element, showing that he stands for all humanity in the work that he undertakes.

Sanday's work thus opens the way for an acceptance of much of the findings of German New Testament scholars. But it is, as it were, a negotiated settlement: Sanday has his sticking points. The basic historicity of Mark's Gospel is not negotiable; nor is Jesus's Messianic self-consciousness. Nor will he entertain the possibility that Jesus may have been fundamentally mistaken in his expectations. What he does attempt is to construct an historical apologetic out of the work of the apocalyptic school, by dint of spiritualising the sense of the apocalyptic terminology used by Jesus, claiming, of course, that this was indeed its intended sense. Thus in a surprising transformation Schweitzer's work is used to buttress the very orthodoxy that he had sought to confound. This is certainly one way of trying to remain faithful to Gore's programme which we discussed in chapter one.

Two other responses by English scholars of the time may be considered. F. C. Burkitt (1864-1935) in *The Earliest Sources for the Life of Jesus* (new and rev. edn 1922), written after the publication of K. L. Schmidt's work on the framework of the Gospels, is still concerned to defend the fundamental historical trustworthiness of Mark. He is cautious about accepting Papias's account of how Mark's Gospel was written, namely that it was based on Peter's reminiscences:

> The impression I get on reading the Gospel according to Mark is that many of the tales may be traditional, told perhaps again and again, and that some are already on the point of becoming conventionalised and epic, but that the sequence of them, the general scheme of the Ministry as a whole, is being constructed for the first time (82f).

This statement effectively concedes Schmidt's main thesis: that Mark was responsible for the narrative framework of the Gospel and that therefore the Gospel could not provide adequate evidence for a life of Jesus. Burkitt nevertheless returns to a modified version of Papias's claim. Mark had received a good deal of his material from Peter. 'From the time of Caesarea Philippi we get a real sequence of events, conditioned by the nexus of the journey south to Jerusalem at the Passover' (93). Mark is still a reliable source for the life of Jesus. Elsewhere (*Jesus Christ: An Historical Outline*, 1932) he offers an argument of a rather different form: 'It appears to the present writer that the ultimate reason for regarding a narrative as historical is its consistency with the circumstances of the events which it narrates' (66). This strange sentence appears to mean that if you can make a coherent story out of it then the probabilities are that it is true. Subsequent scholarship was in fact to show how difficult it is to construct such a coherent picture out of Mark's Gospel. Even if it could be done, would that prove anything more than that Mark was a good story-teller?

One last figure may be referred to here: A. C. Headlam (1862-1947) who, with Sanday, wrote the ICC Commentary on Romans. In his *The Life and Teaching of Jesus the Christ* (1923), Headlam is as dismissive of Wrede as was Sanday before him. 'I am afraid that all criticism of this sort seems to me so baseless that I do not feel able to deal with it with that patience which no doubt I ought to display' (287ff, though Wrede is not mentioned by name). Headlam's general approach is also remarkably similar to Sanday's. He accepts the Markan account and offers a broadly spiritualising account of what Jesus meant by 'the Kingdom': but here there are striking resemblances to the old liberal interpretations of which Sanday had been scornful. The Kingdom of God:

> means a principle of life and conduct in men's hearts. . . . It is a process
> which is now working, not a new revelation to come from heaven, so
> it might be described as Christianity or the Christian dispensation, the
> new state of things inaugurated by the preaching of Jesus (255).

To interpret it as the Church would be to elicit too narrow a meaning. It would be better to say that it is Christianity looked on as a great power or process working in the world, of which process the Christian church is the definitely visible aspect. Beyond that, Headlam contended that 'The Kingdom ultimately will be the final consummation of all things'. Here the spiritualising of Jesus's teaching has been carried to such lengths that the whole force of the apocalyptic school's interpretation has been blunted. Equally, as we shall shortly see, the kind of reaction to liberalism that the disasters of the First World War occasioned in Germany, is nowhere in evidence. Indeed, as the remarkable preface makes clear, Headlam takes quite the opposite view. He draws parallels between the British Army's advances from Egypt to Palestine and ancient battles of the Biblical times and the crusades: 'English and Australian cavalry fought where Coeur de Lion had fought'; and he rejoices in the hope that Jesus's land 'may never again be brought under the blighting influence of Turkish and Mohammedan rule' (vii). He even, later, refers to the Treaty of Versailles (one assumes), in a passage of blinding self-delusion. In the section on love of one's enemies, he writes: 'Now towards masses of men we can hardly have the emotions which we call love, but we can (and we have attempted to) treat our enemies justly' (225). It is hardly a view which squares with the reparations that the victorious Allies exacted from Germany. Nor was it the view of those, like Jan Smuts, who pleaded in vain for greater magnanimity in victory.

Again such observations may seem out of place in a book such as this. Yet it is important to consider the wider context of works of scholarship. Sanday and Headlam were both Establishment figures who identified with the Church of England as the church of the nation. Sanday felt himself inhibited in his scholarship by what 'the nation at large' might be ready for (38). Headlam, more assertively, identified himself and the church with the nation's military triumph and seems to see in these the working out of a wider power or process in the world, of which process the (English?) Christian church is the definitely visible aspect. This cultural confidence, which had been so strikingly challenged by Weiss and Schweitzer, lives on by courtesy of a spiritualising interpretation of the Kingdom.

One last point now needs to be made. We noticed in the first chapter the contrast between Gore's stance, of one committed to the truth of the apostolic faith contrasting with those whom he described as 'guessers after truth'. Certainly Schweitzer, with his sustained attack on Alexandrian christology, made no secret of his rejection of traditional Christian doctrinal formulations; and he specifically invoked historical criticism to free himself from subsequent attempts to modernise Jesus, by conforming his teaching to the cultural norms of his day. For Schweitzer, though, this was precisely the point. Those who sought only to defend the inherited beliefs and values of their society could never hear the call of Jesus: the truth was greater than any of its cultural expressions and to restrict oneself to such forms would ultimately cut one off from new insight — even, indeed, from recovering old truths that had been subsequently overlaid.

List of Works

Wilhelm Bousset, *Kyrios Christos*, Göttingen, 1913 (German); Nashville, 1970 (English)
Wilhelm Bousset, *Jesus im Gegensatz zum Judentum*, Göttingen, 1892
F.C. Burkitt, *The Earliest Sources for the Life of Jesus*, new and rev. edn, London, 1922
F.C. Burkitt, *Jesus Christ: An Historical Outline*, London, 1932
A. von Harnack, *History of Dogma*, Leipzig, 1885-9 (German); London, 1894-9 (English)
A. von Harnack, *What is Christianity?*, Berlin, 1900 (German); London, 1901 (English), Philadelphia, 1986 (English)
A. von Harnack, *The Mission and Expansion of Christianity*, Leipzig, 1902 (German); London, 1904-5 (English)
A.C. Headlam, *The Life and Teaching of Jesus the Christ*, London, 1923
W.G. Kummel, *The New Testament: A History of the Investigation of its Problems*, London, 1973
A. Ritschl, *Instruction in the Christian Religion*, Bonn, 1875; in P. Heffner, ed, *Three Essays*, Philadelphia, 1972 (English)
W. Sanday, *The Life of Christ in Recent Research*, Oxford, 1907
A. Schweitzer, *The Mystery of the Kingdom of God*, Tübingen and Leipzig, 1901 (German); London, 1914 (English)
A. Schweitzer, *The Quest of the Historical Jesus*, Tübingen, 1906 (German); London, 1910 (English)
Johannes Weiss, *Jesus's Proclamation of the Kingdom of God*, Göttingen, 1892 (German); 2nd edn completely rev., 1900; English translation of first edition, Philadelphia, 1972
Johannes Weiss, 'Das Markus-Evangelium', in J. Weiss, ed, *Die Schriften des Neuen Testamentes, neu übersetzt und für die Gegenwart erklärt*, Göttingen, 1907
Johannes Weiss, *Earliest Christianity: A History of the Period AD 30-150*, Göttingen, 1914-17 (German); Gloucester, Mass., 1937, 1959 (English)
W. Wrede, *The Messianic Secret*, Göttingen, 1901 (German); Cambridge, 1971 (English)

3

The History of Religions School and Pauline Studies

The life of Jesus was not the only area of study in which the growing awareness of the first-century cultural context raised important new questions. In Pauline studies the wish to explain Paul's thought in terms of the wider context of Judaism and Hellenism raised issues of great complexity.

It will be recalled that Baur had already suggested that Pauline Christianity represented one pole of a sharp tension within early Christianity: law-free Christianity as opposed to Petrine Christianity with its commitment to the Law. But if it were once accepted that Paul had in this way parted company with his Jewish roots, a cluster of questions then arose: how far was Paul's thought to be seen as a development of Jesus's own messianic faith; how far should it be seen as a development of his inherited Jewish beliefs; and how far was it the result of some kind of interaction with the Hellenistic world in which he conducted his mission? Put simply, to cut Paul free from his own Jewish matrix raised the question of where to locate Paul's thought in the ancient world. This in turn raised questions about the relationship of Jesus and Paul which were to be vigorously canvassed.

Baur's own attempts to characterise Paul's thought were, however, not motivated simply by an historical interest in plotting the development of early Christianity. His real achievement was to have offered an interpretation of Paul's thought that was itself a significant work of theology. One way of putting this is to say that Baur read Paul in terms of Hegelian categories of spirit/mind. For Hegel (1770-1831), the human search for truth is an historical search. In the course of the history of the world, the universal world spirit first negates itself by entering into the sphere of the finite and transitory, of subjective spirit, that is of human minds and self-consciousness. This is, however, a necessary step in the manifestation of the spirit, a self-limitation by means of which finite minds may grasp the eternal truth. Thus the revelation of the truth occurs in the 'negation of the negation', as the limitations of finitude are overcome. If the human spirit thus thinks in opposites, 'dialectically', it nonetheless approaches the truth as it transcends those oppositions. The history of human culture, which finds its culmination in religion, is the history of the overcoming of these oppositions in human thought.

For Baur, it was christology that constituted the centre of Paul's theology. Christ, for Paul, is the one who unites all opposites in himself. In Christ, those subjective spirits that have the mind of Christ are united to the objective spirit. Pneuma, 'spirit' as opposed to 'flesh', denotes the sphere of the eternal, the absolute as opposed to the finite. Such spirit is not simply an understanding that acquires knowledge of the world of appearances around it, but is a knowledge of itself as caught up in the eternal spirit. Christian self-knowledge, in so far, that is, as Christians have the mind of Christ in them (1 Cor. 2:16), is 'identical' with the spirit of God itself:

> It is a truly spiritual consciousness, a relation of the spirit to itself, in which the spirit that exists in itself, reveals itself to the human spirit as it becomes the principle of human consciousness. As a spiritual consciousness in this sense, Christian consciousness is also absolutely free, unfettered by any finite limitations, open to the possibility of achieving complete clarity of absolute self-consciousness (*Paulus*, 2nd edn, 1886, II, 139, quoted in Bultmann, 'Geschichte der Paulus-Forschung', 308).

Such freedom expresses itself in action that is also free, no longer restricted 'by all that was limited, concealed and finite in the old covenant' (Baur, *Paulus,* 142). The Christian is able to see all things in terms of the idea that informs them, and can thus recognise the negativity of all that is relative and finite. It is in this sense that the Christian is free. Thus faith is the appropriation of the divine spirit by the human spirit: it is a recognition that one does, indeed, have the mind of Christ, and is thereby 'identical' with the spirit of God. For it is in Christ that such identification occurs supremely. Belief in Christ, then, is not simply knowledge about Christ; it is a recognition of Christ as determinative of one's own self-consciousness. It is such a recognition that constitutes our 'righteousness' in Pauline terms, for Baur our 'justified *being*'. However much as individuals we are limited and sinful, as united with Christ we are justified: *simul justus et peccator*.

This account of Paul's thought can all too easily be dismissed as merely an imposition of Hegelian categories on the apostle. Such dismissals (not unlike dismissals of Bultmann's thought as being merely an imposition of Heideggerean categories on Christian theology) are all too often simply an excuse for not attending to the real gains in understanding that accrue to those who attempt to interpret ancient theological texts in contemporary philosophical and metaphysical categories. Of course, in the end there may be a mismatch between Paul's theological beliefs and Hegel's. Yet the attempt to render one in terms of the other may still illuminate; it may be an important (even necessary) stage in the development of one's understanding of Paul. What Baur's account suggests most strongly to Bultmann, himself one of the major theological interpreters of Paul in this century, is this:

this interpretation is sustained by the recognition that, behind Paul's theological terms . . . there lies a particular understanding of human being. Baur's interpretation, in posing this question and in its determination to understand everything in its light, is quite simply exemplary (*GPF*, 32).

However much it was subsequently criticised in its detail, it could not be dismissed until such time as 'the radical question of Paul's underlying understanding of human being has been raised. And that is a question that can be raised only at the same time as one poses the question of one's own self-understanding' (*ibid.*). Thus any serious criticism of Baur should, in Bultmann's view, have taken as its starting-point his treatment of Paul's use of pneuma. Such criticism, however, was long delayed.

A first significant attempt was made by H. Lüdemann (1842-1910) in his *Die Anthropologie des Apostels Paulus* (1872). In this book Lüdemann argued that a key to the understanding of Paul's anthropology was to be found in the different senses in which he used the term 'flesh'. This could be found in a general, Jewish sense, referring to humanity in general, the finite as opposed to the infinite, as in the Hebrew *kol basar,* 'all flesh'. But there was another sense to be seen, which spoke of flesh as inherently sinful and corrupt, at war with the spirit, that from which men and women needed to be redeemed. What this indicated was: 'where the religious categories of Jewish consciousness appear alongside the speculative categories of Hellenism, there can no longer be any question of a uniform pattern of thought' (29).

Lüdemann believed that it was possible to discern in such usage evidence of a transition in Paul's thought from a Jewish to a more Hellenistic understanding of human nature, from one that saw the human will as still effectively intact, to one that saw it as no longer able to achieve the goals that it set itself. Coupled with this went a different appreciation of the nature of Christ's work. If the human will was seen as no longer able to respond to the demands of the Law then clearly some more radical solution was required to the human predicament. Nothing less than a recasting of that nature, a 'new creation', would do. Thus Lüdemann argued that it was possible to discern two concepts of salvation, one a juridical one where there is no real, objective change in the essential person, but an act of acquittal which at most establishes a new relationship between God and the believer; the other one where through baptism the body of sin of the one baptised is done away with, he or she is created anew, set free from the obligation to serve sin and receives the gift of the Holy Spirit. These two concepts do not simply stand alongside each other. There is a transition in Paul from one to the other which is never quite completed. Nevertheless, Lüdemann can say, the doctrine of substitutionary satisfaction is the 'portals through which the Christian who comes from Judaism must find access to salvation' that is revealed as 'the new creation and ultimate glorification of men and women mediated by Christ' (216). 'The consequence is that in the four major Pauline epistles we do not find a consistently maintained, uniform doctrine, but rather the witnesses to the apostle's most vigorous intellectual struggle with Judaism' (217).

Lüdemann's work clearly raises important questions for an understanding of both anthropology and theology in Paul. It also raises a number of more detailed historical questions. In the first place there are questions about the cultural milieu in which it was set. Was it Jewish or Hellenistic-dualist? How, more precisely, were those matrices to be defined? And then what about the unity of Paul's thought? Was there development? Was there inconsistency? Was there a centre to be perceived, or was Paul not the theologian that the Lutheran tradition had believed him to be but more a man of practical commitment and deep religious experience? How does Paul fit into the development of early Christianity? What might all this say about the Lutheran understanding of Paul as the proponent of justification by faith?

Thus in the debates that followed there was by no means a simple front between those who pursued these difficult and exciting historical questions, and more conservative and orthodox Lutherans. First there were substantial disagreements among the historians about the nature of Paul's debt to Judaism and Hellenism; second it would not only be the orthodox who would attempt to rescue Lutheran interpretations of Paul from the critical fire.

Obviously the attempt to place Paul in his cultural setting depends on the state of studies of that milieu at any particular time. The later decades of the nineteenth century and the early decades of the twentieth were a time of intense activity in the study of the ancient world. Not only, as we have seen, were Jewish apocalyptic texts of the turn of the era being recovered and published, but also there was a growing interest among Classicists in the religion and literature of the Hellenistic period. Scholars like Cumont (1868-1947), Reitzenstein (1861-1931) and Dieterich (1866-1933) were producing editions of texts from the Mystery Religions that had penetrated the Graeco-Roman world from the East. There was a renewed interest in Gnosticism and its historical origins. During the First World War Reitzenstein and Lidzbarski (1868-1918) would start to publish their studies of Mandaeanism, an early Syrian sect with links to Christianity and Gnosticism.

This meant that there was, in effect, a constantly changing picture of the world in which the New Testament was conceived and written, something that has continued with the major discoveries of ancient texts in the twentieth century. It also meant that certain texts, simply by virtue of their novelty, were likely to command more than their due attention. It is no more coincidental that New Testament studies since the early 1970s have been heavily dominated by the discoveries at Qumran, than it was that in the period around the turn of the century scholars explored possible links between the New Testament and the Mystery Religions to the full and, very arguably, to the detriment of other links with Jewish thought of the time.

As we have seen this debate was opened by Lüdemann. If Paul's anthropology had undergone development, or simply contained inconsistencies, where did the various components come from? An early answer to this question was given by Otto Pfleiderer his book on the origins of Christianity, *Primitive Christianity: Its Writings and Teachings in their Historical Connections* (Berlin, 1887). There Pfleiderer, in a manner close to Lüdemann, characterises Paul's theology as both 'Christianised Pharisaism' and as 'Christianised Hellenism' (G. 175).[1] On the one hand, he takes over from Pharisaism the belief in the sleep of the dead and their resurrection, coupled as it is with the belief that after judgement there will be a transformation of this world 'freeing it from enslavement to transitoriness' (G. 299). On the other, there is also to be found in Paul the idea taken from Platonic idealism that the 'earthly body is a prison house of the soul, which has its true home in the heavenly world into which the pious Christian will enter immediately upon the laying aside of his earthly body'; here the soul will receive a new body that 'has nothing to do with conditions as we know them on earth' (*ibid.*).

But Pfleiderer did not see any clear relationship between these two conceptions. It was 'simply impossible to get a unified picture of Pauline eschatology' (G. 301; cf I, 458). Rather the two currents of thought flowed alongside each other like two currents within one channel, 'yet without being really united' (G. 304 = I, 463). This may cause difficulties for those who feel the need to construct some system of doctrine out of Paul's theology, but it is of great significance for those who are attempting to construct a history of early Christianity. For it enables them to see the theology of the church as having come into being, not:

> as is erroneously assumed, by Jewish Christianity having prevailed over Paulinism, but quite the contrary, by the expurgation of the specifically Jewish (Pharisaic) elements from Paulinism and the free further development of his universally intelligible Hellenistic side (G. 305; cf I. 464).

Pfleiderer's work was developed and written in the period before research into the Mystery Religions had begun to make its impact on New Testament study. The next generation of scholars were, however, to take a lively interest in such work as they strove to understand religious beliefs not solely in relation to the prevailing theological doctrines but to a much broader range of popular religious belief and activity. In this they followed scholars working in the field of the history of religions who sought to demonstrate the relation of high-level theological and philosophical beliefs to lower-level popular beliefs and attitudes. This awareness marks the second generation of the History of Religions School whose work was particularly associated with the University of Göttingen. That is to say, where earlier proponents had sought to understand the writings and theology of the New Testament against the background of different theologies, the Göttingen school attempted to see how Christianity developed as a religious community that had to find its way in the world of popular first-century religious belief and practice.

Some of the early work in this field was carried out on the book of Revelation. H. Gunkel (1862-1932, see his *Creation and Chaos at the Beginning and the End of Time*, 1895) and W. Bousset attempted to show how widespread popular myths about some primal-creation struggle with the forces of darkness, can resurface in different forms as in the anti-Christ mythology of the book of Revelation. The goal of such enquiries was to trace the traditional forms of belief underlying a given text. Only so could the specific character of the beliefs in literary texts be ascertained.

Bousset's commentary on Revelation was published in 1896. Two years later A. Eichhorn (1856-1926) published a lecture on the Lord's Supper in the New Testament in which he tried to show how far the accounts of the Lord's Supper in the New Testament were influenced by 'the dogma and cultures of the church'. Again for him it was essential to attempt to map out the development of the tradition and to trace as far as possible the ways in which the beliefs of the church had moulded that development. Not that he believed that tracing the traditions back to their earliest form would take one back to an account of the original event. Rather, such a mapping of the tradition would show how it had developed in answer to the needs of the church. Eichhorn did not believe that the cultic meal had its real source in Jesus's last meal with his disciples. It was something that had been developed to answer the religious needs of the early Christian community. The task was to discern what other contemporary models there might have been for such a meal, for Judaism provided nothing adequate to explain its occurrence.

Such work laid the ground for a new approach to Paul and for a review of the idealist understanding of his doctrine of the Spirit that had dominated New Testament studies since Baur. Gunkel himself was the first to apply such a mode of study to Paul. In his *The Influences of the Holy Spirit in the Popular Views of the Apostolic Age and the Teaching of the Apostle Paul* (1888), he argued that 'pneuma' in Paul is not spirituality, the sphere of human self-consciousness, but supernatural power, evidenced by extraordinary psychic manifestations. Pneuma in itself can as easily be demonic as divine. It is holy only in so far as it is received in a particular community. Paul takes this popular understanding of the spirit and develops it by considering not only its outward manifestations but also its purpose, seeing the whole of Christian life as standing under its influence.

Eichhorn's study on the eucharist was followed shortly afterwards by W. Heitmüller's (1869-1926) work on the name of Jesus, and on baptism and the eucharist. In these works Heitmüller attempted to show how the invocation of the name of Jesus and the early Christian rites alike appealed to the popular, enthusiastic side of religious experience. In *In the Name of Jesus* (1903) he attempted to relate the invocation of the name of Jesus to similar views of the worth of the name, especially of the worth of holy names, held by Jews, Babylonians, Egyptians and Hellenists. In *Baptism and the Lord's Supper in Paul* (1903) he argued that the understanding of the sacraments in Paul was far removed from the Lutheran understanding of them as symbolic actions --means, that is, of awakening and strengthening faith in their recipients, an institutional form of the divine promise. For, in Romans 6, baptism is essentially 'incorporation into Christ' (9). It is a 'mystical, a physical-hyperphysical uniting with Christ, his death and his resurrection: in any case an altogether real process' (10). Nor is this the only way in which Paul explains the meaning of the rite. He also sees it as putting on Christ, as being freed from the powers of darkness, and as a washing away of the filth of sin. What is common to all these various accounts of baptism is, apart from the fact that baptism is only very marginally connected with ideas of justification and forgiveness of sins, that they all focus on experiences 'of a mystical, enthusiastic nature, on the reception of the spirit and, more, on union with Christ' (14). What makes someone a Christian is the possession of the spirit or 'being in Christ'.

What then, in the light of his understanding of baptism, does Paul mean by possession of the spirit? Something evidently very different, not only from Luther, but also from Baur. Indeed this latter contrast is much more to the fore when Heitmüller comes to discuss the meaning of spirit possession. Spirit is 'quite simply a supranatural, transcendent entity, in sharp contrast with the essence and being of humanity'. While it is true that in some sense this 'pneuma' forms a unity with the 'I' of the Christian, this union does not come into being by some process of psychological development, but by means of a revolution, a catastrophe, an event of a transcendental nature. However much for Paul the fruits of the spirit are to be found in ethical virtues, the spirit itself is, first and foremost, divine power. Paul, thanks to his 'animistically based psychology', thought of spirit in a far more material way than we do. The guarantee of the resurrection is that the spirit takes up residence in the Christian's body. The sanctification of believers is given by the holy spirit. By virtue of the close physical union between husband and wife, such sanctity can even be transferred from one to the other (1 Cor. 7:14). All of this is only one step removed from popular Christian beliefs in the transmission of the spirit through breathing on people or through the laying on of hands (18ff). In a trice, Paul is snatched away from the Lutherans and lodged dangerously close to the camp of popular Roman Catholicism. It is hard to imagine how such a message was received by the Associations of Scientific Preachers in Hanover and Brunswick to whom Heitmüller first delivered this material. His preface does not satisfy our curiosity; it merely records his pleasure in discovering agreements between his work and that recently published by Dieterich.

Similarly there are deep roots to the early Christian cultic meal in the primitive concept of the devouring of the godhead. Such ideas may have been found in the Mystery Religions but Heitmüller is cautious about drawing any too close connections. 'In light of our scanty sources, however, it is too precarious to wish to affirm a direct dependence on such specific phenomena'(52). It is enough to point to general tendencies in the time: 'Nascent Christianity lived in an atmosphere that, if you will permit the expression, was impregnated with the bacilli of the mysteries' (52).

Heitmüller's work was of course deeply disturbing. It attempted to explore the roots of Pauline Christianity in the popular religiosity of his day. In this it presented a view of Paul that must have seemed deeply alien to Lutherans in the early twentieth century. One can of course criticise him for pressing too hard the analogies between Paul's beliefs and those of Hellenistic religions; for failing, indeed, sometimes to regard them as analogies at all, but seeing them as largely determinative of what Paul and his communities believed and practised. Is he sufficiently sensitive to the way Paul distances himself from ecstatic and charismatic phenomena, to the emphasis on rationality as opposed to ecstasy (2 Cor. 5:13)? Does he do justice to the profoundly theological (as opposed to simply religious) character of Paul's letters? True, it was important to have explored the links between Paul and such mystical and charismatic experience in order, not least, to break with Baur's understanding of Paul's conception of spirit. But if the effect of Heitmüller's work was to dismantle Baur's understanding of Paul's thought, it was also to re-open the question of the relation of his theology to the religious life and practice of the early Christian community.

This question was taken up in two works that have been greatly influential and set the framework for much subsequent discussion both of Paul and of early Christianity: Wrede's *Paul* and Bousset's *Kyrios Christos*. Elsewhere Wrede argued that attempts to write theologies of the New Testament should be replaced with attempts to understand the religion of the New Testament communities. When he came to Paul, however, he had to concede that 'The religion of the apostle [Paul] is theological through and through; his theology is his religion' (76). Paul's doctrine is not a 'cold doctrine' that soars beyond the reach of mere piety; nor can his piety be described without 'mention of those *thoughts* in which he had apprehended Christ, his death and his resurrection. In the very moment of his conversion it was a clear, formulable thought that stamped the new impress upon his life' (76). That central thought is that 'Jesus is Messiah'; it is explicated in terms of Paul's beliefs about humanity's redemption from the radical misery of the state in which it is caught.

Wrede then attempts to show how Paul's theology controls all that he does and thinks. Central to his thought is his conviction that in Christ believers have been 'released from the misery of this whole present world'. It is not just release from sin, but from a state of the world that is radically in need of redemption, where humanity is held in thrall by dark powers that enslave it (see Gal. 1:4; 4:3, 9; 1 Cor. 2:6, 8). Release from this world of bondage and misery is effected by Christ's death and resurrection. In becoming man he takes upon himself the bondage of the world, becomes subject to the powers; but in dying he escapes from their power and in rising he enters on a new life of glory. As representative of humanity he thereby frees them, so that Paul can say: One died for all; therefore all died (2 Cor. 5:14). 'From the moment of his death all men are redeemed, as fully as himself, from the hostile powers, and together with his resurrection all are transferred into indestructible life' (100).

The benefits of such redemption are described by Paul when he says that believers have died to sin. This is not to be understood, as so frequently, in an ethical, figurative sense to refer to the successful struggle of the believer over sin. Rather, in so far as believers have died to the world *actually and literally*' (103), they are liberated from sin. Something has occurred objectively such that the powers that held them enthralled have lost their power over them.

Yet, on the other hand, 'every one of his exhortations presupposes that their power is not broken' (*ibid.*). Here Wrede points to a problem that was to continue to exercise scholars for the rest of the century. How does one reconcile the indicative, that believers are justified, freed from the power of sin, with the imperative —the injunctions not to give way to sin and to fall back into old ways? 'The whole Pauline conception of salvation is characterised by suspense; a suspense that strains forwards towards the final release, the actual death'. Yet for Paul, the redemption 'is already a perfect truth, because Christ *has already* died and risen again' (105, 104). Was then the realisation of salvation deferred? Not so. In the possession of the spirit, something of that realisation is already present. A supernatural force enters the believer, ' "dwells," works, and acts within him, "drives" him' (107). Through possession of the spirit, each believer becomes a 'son of God'. It is a manifestation of the last time that is shown in the power to heal, to speak prophetically and in tongues and also in the fruits of a moral life. Yet if here Paul comes close to modern conceptions of the holy spirit as a moral force, 'he does not think of the spirit as penetrating the inmost personality, and becoming one with it' (109). The spirit remains a supernatural entity, a pointer to the full realisation that is still to come.

Wrede's work is elegant and impressive in its coherence. Like Heitmüller he distances himself sharply from idealist interpretations of the spirit. Unlike him, he relates Paul's understanding of the spirit to a schema of redemption that is both cosmic and historical. It involves the breaking of powers that hold sway over the world and it still looks forward to some final act in this cosmic drama. Here patterns of thought can be discerned which may find their parallels in much Jewish apocalyptic material. Wrede in his (German) bibliography points to the work of scholars like R. Kabisch (1868-1914) and O. Everling (1864-1945), who had explored such material and its possible echoes in Paul's thought. He does not, however, discuss their work in detail, nor does he give any account of how Paul's view of cosmic history relates to Jewish apocalyptic views. Paul's view of Jesus as the Christ is formed by his experience at his conversion and by the demands of his mission to the Gentiles. Thus Wrede's account leaves questions about Paul's debt to Jewish beliefs unresolved. This was to have its legacy. A full discussion of Paul's debt to Jewish apocalyptic had to wait in the German academic establishment till the publication of Ernst Käsemann's (b.1906) commentary on Romans. Albert Schweitzer's work, which, as we shall shortly see, certainly attended to such questions, failed to command support within Germany.

The other work that was indeed powerfully influential in German academic circles (though much less so elsewhere) was W. Bousset's *Kyrios Christos*. In that work Bousset attempted to give a comprehensive account of the development of early Christian belief and practice. It was comprehensive in the sense that it attempted to trace the development of different forms of Christian belief and to show how they were influenced by contemporary religious belief and religiosity. Early forms of Christian belief developed as Jesus's teaching of the forgiveness of sins was combined with Jewish apocalyptic beliefs in the Son of Man. Jesus was identified with the glorious figure who would come to judge all at the end of time. The faith of the earliest — Palestinian — communities was characterised above all by expectation of the coming Son of Man. However, when Christianity moved outside the Palestinian context it entered a world where quite different forms of religiosity held sway. Here it was the worship of pagan deities present in cultic meals that constituted the centre of popular religiosity. Interestingly in such religions it is the title 'lord' (*kyrios*) which is characteristically used of the cultic God. Thus when Christianity moved into this world 'infant Christianity . . . *had* to assume this form of the *kyrios* faith and the *kyrios* worship; it could not at all turn out otherwise' (151). This is an astonishingly deterministic account of religious origins, which is representative of Bousset's approach. In his view religious communities, at least, have no alternative but to adopt the character of their environment.

It is such a cultically orientated Hellenistic Christianity that then provides the starting point for Paul's theology. Here it is that Paul encounters Christian belief in the spirit and in the Lord, beliefs, however, which he significantly remoulds. If communities are bound by laws of religious development, the human spirit, at least in the person of one as outstanding as Paul, is able to transcend those bounds and develop new forms of life and thought. If in the popular Christianity of the Hellenistic church spirit is related to the worship of the community and to individual manifestations, such as speaking in tongues, Paul 'makes the Pneuma into the element of the entire new Christian life, not only on its specially miraculous side but in its total ethical and religious attitude. As its fruits he enumerates all the virtues of the Christian life (Gal. 5:22-23). The great gracious gift of Christian liberty is the work or the life-expression of the Spirit (2 Cor. 3:17). This is a complete *metabasis eis allo genos'* (163). Paul creates a new religious psychology out of a communal, enthusiastic form of worship and in this way achieves one of the great moves forward in the history of the religion. In this way the whole of Christian existence — and not just certain extraordinary phenomena — is seen as miraculous. In a similar way, the 'Lord who governs the entire personal life of the Christian has developed out of the cultically present Kyrios' (160).

Thus Bousset sees Paul as a formative force within early Christianity. He is the figure that develops a new mode of human spirituality, which can then inform subsequent generations of Christianity. True, that spirituality will itself undergo numerous transformations; but, for all that, he has set Christianity off on this path. For Bousset such developments do not occur in a vacuum: they develop in a particular cultural and social environment and for Paul it is decisive that he lived in a Hellenistic environment. Paul's break with Judaism is taken to have been complete: his piety was formed by the worship of the early Hellenistic Christian communities. Yet his own mysticism and theology was the result of an imaginative, creative leap on his own part. Contrasted with the sacramental piety of the community and its belief in baptism, Paul's universalising of this belief in union with the death of Christ: 'knowing this that our old man was crucified, that the body of sin might be destroyed, that we might no longer serve sin', is innovative.

> These are new, unprecedented imaginations that now emerge out of the soul of the apostle. It is as if here a mysticism of a more personal note struggles free and flies upwards with freer strokes of the wings. But it takes its point of departure from the community's cult and sacrament (158).

Bousset's influence in Germany has been enormous. His thesis that there was an early form of Hellenistic Christianity that moulded Paul's thought gained widespread acceptance and was given almost canonical form in Bultmann's *Theology of the New Testament*. His sharp distinction between a Palestinian Jewish world and a Hellenistic world outside, was successfully challenged only in the late 1960s by Martin Hengel. The acceptance of this idea meant that two generations of scholars in Germany were to continue to seek to interpret Pauline Christianity almost entirely in terms of its links with various forms of Hellenism, not of Judaism. His more detailed interpretation of Paul was to receive a sharp challenge in Karl Barth's (1886-1968) onslaught on the whole of the History of Religions School. Even so, his contention that Paul was the founder of a particular Christian psychology was to have interesting echoes in Bultmann's existential interpretation of Paul.

There is, of course, much to challenge in Bousset's work. His derivation of Paul's thought from Hellenism is surprisingly one-sided and, at least on the face of it, implausible. Did Paul retain nothing of his Jewish heritage? What, at the simplest level, of Paul's use of the Old Testament and of the many other Jewish motifs in his thought? The construction of a pre-Pauline

Hellenistic form of Christianity is in one sense a much more interesting undertaking. There must, indeed, have been something there before Paul and the evidence of Paul's interaction with it in Acts is at the very least ambiguous. But is the sheer determinism of Bousset's account of its dependence on popular Hellenistic piety persuasive? Again, why exclude from this early stage of Christianity's development Jewish motifs and influences? This wholesale suppression of Jewish motifs in Paul's thought is a disturbing feature in one who was both a rigorous historian and well-read in Jewish literature of the time.

Part, at least, of the blame for this must be laid at the door of Bousset's own views of history, which were much influenced by Thomas Carlyle (1795-1881). History was created by the great heroes who were able to transcend their time and to lead men and women to God. 'For, as I take it, Universal History, the history of what man has accomplished in this world, is at bottom the History of the Great Men who have worked here' (*On Heroes and Hero-Worship*, 1). As Jesus rises above the Judaism of his day, so Paul rises above the Hellenism of the rest of the first-century Mediterranean world. It is the 'Thoughts that dwelt in the Great Men sent into the world' that are responsible for 'all things that we see standing accomplished in the world'. Part of the blame, again, one suspects, lies deeper in a conviction in the inherent superiority of 'cultural Protestantism' (to which Bousset gave expression in his *The Essence of Religion*). Neither of these views makes for good history or for a balanced estimate of the worth and relationships of different religious traditions.

There were others who did not share Bousset's view of the dominant influence of Hellenism on Paul's thought. In his study of Pauline scholarship, *Paul and his Interpreters* (1911), Albert Schweitzer attempted to rehabilitate those who, like Otto Everling and Richard Kabisch, had explored the links between Paul's beliefs and popular Jewish beliefs about angelology, demonology and eschatology. What Schweitzer argued against Bousset and the dominant History of Religions School of his time was that it was not possible to escape the underlying apocalyptic form of Paul's thought. Paul thought of himself as living in the overlapping of the ages. The old age still endured but the new age through the resurrection of Christ was already here, though its fulfilment was still awaited. To suppose that Paul's thought could be transposed into a form of Hellenism, with its essentially dualistic contrast between the earthly transitory world and the eternal heavenly world, was like trying to play 'a piece in two-four time and a piece in three-four time together, and to imagine that one hears an identical rhythm in both' (223).

This is not to say that Schweitzer believed that it was possible to demonstrate the consistency of Paul's thought. He, too, accepted that there was an important distinction to be made between the juridical doctrine of justification by faith and the mystical language of participation in Christ, such as that to which Lüdemann had drawn attention. Schweitzer however believed that both these sides of Paul's thought were conceived within an essentially Jewish matrix and that the doctrine of righteousness by faith was derived from his mystical doctrine of incorporation into Christ. In Galatians, that connection is clearly to be seen, while in Romans, Paul has attempted to set it on a more independent footing.

Schweitzer's own views on Paul were set out more fully in his *The Mysticism of Paul the Apostle* that he completed only in 1929. The specific key to Paul's 'mysticism' lay not in the Hellenistic Mystery Religions but in Jewish apocalyptic, specifically in Jewish beliefs about the coming of the Messianic Kingdom and the end of the world. For Paul, those who believe in Jesus as the coming Messiah will live with him in the coming Messianic Kingdom in a supra-earthly form of existence; those who do not will sleep in the grave until the end of the messianic age, when the general resurrection and the final judgement will occur. This difference between believers and non-believers is to be explained in terms of the particular mode of corporeality that the believers have in common with Christ. Because of this the powers of death and resurrection that brought about Jesus's raising from the dead, are also at work on the believers. In this sense they are no longer natural men and women like others; they have become beings who are being transformed from their natural to their supernatural state, who only have the appearance of natural human beings, which they will discard at the dawning of the messianic age.

Paul's mysticism is thus intimately tied to his imminent expectation of a dramatic, cosmic event. It is also indissolubly connected to his sense of community with Christ. It is from this that he derives his ethics. The Law is for those who belong to the passing age, not for those who are already participating in the age to come. Knowledge of what is truly good is derived for the believer immediately from the spirit of Christ. This spirit is the heavenly power of life that is preparing the believers for their existence in the resurrection state. It compels them to behave differently from those who are still in the world and finds its clearest manifestation in love. Paul's mysticism is thus, at bottom, an ethical one. Paul lays down the supremacy of the ethical in religion with the words 'But now remain these three: faith, hope and love: but the greatest of these is love' (see *My Life and Thought*, 248-51).

Schweitzer's work is much concerned with the details of Paul's eschatological schema. He takes what might seem some of the most speculative, and indeed unsystematic, parts of Paul and creates from them a detailed account of the end, which then functions to explain the rest of Paul's theology. This mode of procedure is baffling. Apocalyptic visions of the end are rarely consistent in themselves; to construct a system out of scattered utterances by someone for whom they scarcely constitute the centre of his thought is courting disaster. On the other hand, however speculative his construction of Paul's theology, Schweitzer does show how great are the connections with Jewish thought of the time, and proposes at least a solution to the relation of Paul's statements about the state of being of Christians to the ethical demands that he makes upon them.

It is interesting, too, to note what Schweitzer and the History of Religions School have in common. It is, partly, the interest in explaining the beliefs of Christianity 'out of' existing beliefs of the time. This they shared, though of course they differed as to which contemporary beliefs and practices they considered particularly influential in Paul's case. They both attempted to give some account of the development of early Christianity from its origins in Judaism to its development as a form of Hellenistic religion. This, too, they shared, though they differed about the point at which the boundary between Judaism and Hellenism had been crossed.

This was not all. They both also attempted to make sense of Paul's piety by relating it to basic forms of human religiosity, such as the human desire to be united to the godhead in some kind of sacramental meal. It is in this context that Schweitzer uses the term 'mysticism' that was subsequently to attract such unfavourable attention in German theological circles, but which probably endeared him to English theologians raised on Platonism and Dean Inge (1860-1954). Mysticism is to be found 'when we find a human being looking upon the division between earthly and super-earthly, temporal and eternal, as transcended, and feeling himself, while still externally amid the earthly and temporal, to belong to the super-earthly and eternal' (*Mysticism*, 1). Such phenomena are, then, by definition widespread and diverse. They embrace the primitive and the developed forms of mysticism. Primitive forms of mysticism are to be found in sacrificial feasts, whereby 'the partaker becomes in some way one with the divinity' (*ibid.*). A more developed form of such magical mysticism is to be found in the Greek Mystery Religions whereby the believer achieves union with the divinity and becomes a partaker in the immortality for which he yearns. 'Through these sacraments he ceases to be a natural man and is born again into a higher state of being' (*ibid.*).

There is a further stage in the development of mysticism which Schweitzer refers to as intellectual mysticism. It is reached at that point where 'man reflects upon his relation to the totality of being and to Being in itself'. Union with the eternal is achieved by an act of reflection whereby the thinker:

> raises himself above that illusion of the senses which makes him regard himself as in bondage in the present life to the earthly and temporal.
> . . . Recognising the unity of all things in God, in Being as such, it passes beyond the unquiet flux of becoming and disintegration into the peace of timeless being, and is conscious of itself as being in God, and in every moment eternal (*ibid.*).

This is a form of religion to be found in Hinduism and Buddhism, in

Platonism, Stoicism, in Spinoza (1632-1677), Schopenhauer (1788-1860) and in Hegel.

Paul, interestingly, stands somewhere between primitive magical mysticism and the more developed forms of intellectual mysticism. His 'religious conceptions . . . stand high above those of primitive mysticism'. On the other hand, he does not speak of being one with God. Rather, for Paul, union with the eternal is mediated through union with Christ:

> Thus, higher and lower mysticism here interpenetrate. In Paul there is no God-mysticism; only a Christ-mysticism by means of which man comes into relation to God. The fundamental thought of Pauline mysticism runs thus: I am in Christ; in Him I know myself as a being who is raised above this sensuous, sinful, and transient world and already belongs to the transcendent; in Him I am assured of resurrection; in Him I am a child of God.

> Another distinctive characteristic of this mysticism is that being in Christ is conceived as a having died and risen again with Him, in consequence of which the participant has been freed from sin and from the Law, possesses the Spirit of Christ, and is assured of resurrection. This 'being-in-Christ' is the prime enigma of the Pauline teaching: once it is grasped it gives the clue to the whole (3).

Thus Schweitzer rejected the suggestion of scholars like Heitmüller that Paul's view of the sacraments was to be explained in terms of some form of magical mysticism, which was the necessary form that his religiosity had to take if he was to communicate effectively to people in the Hellenistic world. Instead he argued that the sacraments in Paul were part of an eschatological mysticism that was focused specifically on the notion of union with Christ. In such union the believer transcended the limitation of her earthly existence and already enjoyed the future state of the resurrected life which Christ had entered at his crucifixion and resurrection.

To call this an eschatological mysticism is to draw attention to the way in which, for Schweitzer, Paul's conception of the relation of the temporal to the eternal is conceived in linear, chronological terms, rather than spatial ones. The old age of corruption and decay will give way to a new age of fulfilment in which the righteous will enjoy the fruits of everlasting life and come into the presence of God. But with the resurrection of the one man Jesus, the simple schema of a present evil age to be followed by a future age of fulfilment ushered in by the general resurrection of — at least — the righteous, is changed. Because the age to come had already been anticipated by Jesus's resurrection, Paul believed that he was living now 'between the ages'. Those who believed in Christ were already participating in the age to come, although its full revelation was still awaited. Baptism was an 'eschatological sacrament' whereby Christians were united with Christ in his death and resurrection and sealed against the coming judgement.

Schweitzer's views, which had of course already been propounded with some vigour in *Paul and his Interpreters*, commanded little support in Germany in the period up to the end of the First World War. Scholars like Bousset were not easily persuaded by Schweitzer's view that the sacraments of the early Christian church were, in fact, derived from Jewish ideas of some kind of sacramental sealing of the elect in the face of the coming judgement and fulfilment. They preferred, as we have just seen, to explain the development of the Christian sacraments as the consequence of the early Christian movement from a Jewish to a Hellenistic environment. For them the essential difference was between Jewish Christian expectation of the coming Son of Man and Hellenistic Christianity's worship of the Lord present in the cult. Schweitzer's point was that the distinctive character of Pauline thought was to be found in a subtle combination of both these elements of expectation and shared presence.

Thus Bousset and others gave a very different picture of the development of early Christianity from Schweitzer. Schweitzer attempted to show how the Messianic faith of Jesus was modified by the community and Paul in the light of their belief in his resurrection. Paul could then be seen as constituting an important bridge between Jesus's Messianism and the later Hellenistic mysticism of the Gospel of John and Ignatius. For Bousset, the break between Jesus and Paul was much sharper: Paul, himself, is the product of a Christianity that is already imbued with the spirit of Hellenism, even though he effectively transcends it. The faith of the early Christian community is thus closely related to that of other forms of popular Hellenistic religion and equally clearly distinguished from that of Jesus, and, on his better days, at least, Paul.

The questions raised by these debates at the beginning of the century remain as a permanent contribution to the discipline. The debates themselves were cut off by the sharp reaction after the war, in Germany at least, to the whole liberal theological enterprise, of which the History of Religions School was a part. In Britain there was far less reaction to the work on Paul than there had been to that on Jesus. Schweitzer's work was translated and he was a frequent visitor. F. C. Burkitt's brief preface to *The Mysticism of Paul the Apostle* betrays sympathy and a sharp sense of where the major theological import of the work lies. He notes that Paul has gone out of favour in Britain and that there is little understanding in Britain for the difficult adaptations which Christianity had to make in order to become intelligible and attractive to Christians living in the Empire. Nevertheless if:

> Christianity is to renew its youth in this our changing age it can only do so through Christians learning to understand the inner developments of Christianity in former ages, even though these developments do not directly satisfy our present religious needs (vi).

A fuller reaction to the work of the History of Religions School on Paul is to be discerned in C. H. Dodd's (1884-1973) *The Meaning of Paul for*

Today (1920). Here Dodd presents a view of Paul that is still clearly indebted to Idealist interpretations, while carefully distancing itself from Heitmüller's and Bousset's attacks on that tradition.

What, according to Dodd, is central to Paul's thought is a doctrine of history that saw the church as the instrument whereby God would redeem a humanity that had disintegrated, and establish a new Divine Commonwealth. God's purposes had been prepared before the coming of Christ by the selection of a small remnant; the turning-point came with Christ, who lived out the new life which was to be the heart of the new redeemed humanity; from Christ's coming flowed 'the reintegration of the race, the inclusion, step by step, of the "rejected," and the attainment of final unity for all that is, in the perfected Sovereignty or Kingdom of God' (41).

Such a view was expressed, in part at least, in terms drawn from 'Oriental' views of the decay of the world. However at the heart of Paul's views lay the belief that what was essentially wrong with the world was what was 'wrong with men':

The problem of reality is at bottom a problem of personal relations. No purely physical speculations will ever solve for us the problem of this tangled universe. Personality holds the clue; and the solution is personal and practical. The spiritual aspirations of man, faithfully followed, let us into the secret of evolution and give the only hint we get of its purposes (33).

Hence when Dodd comes to discuss Paul's doctrine of emancipation it is no surprise to find that he sees it, in a way not so very far different from that of F. C.Baur, as lying centrally in the appropriation of the mind and spirit of Christ. Faith is an acceptance of God's working in us:

The immense energy of the religious life is rooted in a moment of passivity in which God acts. . . . The righteousness of Christ is a real achievement of God's own Spirit in man. It is a permanent and growing possession of humanity. It is historic and integral to our world (112f).

Paul's language of the spirit finds its analogies in the world of the Mystery Religions, and his converts may have understood baptism in such a way. These, however, are merely the analogies that Paul's converts would have perceived. They are not, as they were for Heitmüller, the very source of the church's religious experience. Rather, Paul points to the deeper reality that underlies the Christian life in the spirit:

The initiation into the Christian life . . . is 'baptism in the Spirit,' the steeping of the whole being in the Spirit of Christ. This is the true baptism, of which the immersion in water is only the effectual sign. It means the implanting within our human nature of a divine element, present indeed in germ and in potentiality before, but woefully obscured and frustrated by our participation in the wrongness that infects all human society as it is (130f).

Dodd's book in a sense is no more than an elegant republication of Idealist views of Paul. By presenting the similarities between the Mysteries cults and the Christian sacraments simply as analogies perceived by Paul's converts, rather than as keys to the understanding of the nature of early Christian religion, Dodd attempts to neutralise the force of Heitmüller's criticisms of Baur. What he leaves unanswered is the question of how such a purely symbolic baptism came into being in a world in which such actions were *conventionally* understood very differently. If this was the way Paul's converts understood them, and Paul did not single-handedly introduce the Christian sacraments, what does this tell us about the way they were understood in the churches before Paul's theological analysis of baptism?

Nor does Dodd choose the way out of this reading of the sacraments of the early church favoured by Albert Schweitzer as early as his *Paul and his Interpreters*, namely a reading of them in terms of Jewish apocalyptic. Dodd's treatment of the apocalyptic roots of Paul's thought is uneasy. He acknowledges that Paul's view of the world as a slave to decay is 'Oriental'; he recognises, too, that in Paul's view of the world, principalities and powers have a role to play in humanity's enslavement; but he prefers to see all this as centrally focussed in a dualistic view of reality where there are 'two planes of being, the one eternal, the other temporal; the one visible, the other invisible' (55). He recognises that Paul's views of the end of things owed a good deal initially to Jewish apocalyptic views of the End, but argues that Paul underwent a change of mind which led to the more mature view in Romans (and, importantly, in Colossians and Ephesians).

There is here a serious ideological clash. Apocalyptic interpretations of Paul, such as Schweitzer's, suggest that there is a major rupture between this world and the new age which Paul announces. Apocalyptic views of reality are world-renouncing, not simply world-reforming. In the end, Dodd sees Paul as advocating a view of history that is evolutionary; which, for all that it sees disintegration in the world, nevertheless also sees continuity. Moreover Dodd, not least in his treatment of Romans, can point to powerful elements in Paul's thought that do indeed stress the continuity between God's actions in the past and his present action in Christ. The debate which such a contrast of readings of Paul might have opened up is one about the precise nature of Paul's understanding of the renewal of the world.

Certainly the questions raised by Schweitzer and others about the ways in which Christianity adapted to a changing environment are of perennial interest and significance. They bring home to the student the way in which any vigorous religion must constantly be adapting and searching for new ways of expressing its fundamental beliefs if it is to remain true to its fundamental intuitions. Equally importantly, we need to be aware of the way in which any religion is always indebted to, and in dialogue with, the inherited beliefs of its own culture and that too represents an important challenge to more traditional understandings of revelation.

The History of Religions School raised another question, which is also of continuing interest, relating to the nature of the religious experience of the early Christian community. Can we place the beliefs of Paul and his community on some map of human religious experience? Does early Christian practice of the sacraments and invocation of the name of Jesus belong to some form of enthusiastic, magical kind of religion? Is it a manifestation of some more developed form of mysticism, which yet needs to be distinguished from the religion of Spinoza? What categories, indeed, do we have for describing and comparing different sorts of religious phenomena? These are major questions of an interpretative kind that were, however, soon to be dismissed from the scene in the aftermath of the terrible events of the First World War. Perhaps such questions can only easily be handled in an age either of complete confidence in one's own culture, or (is it too much to hope?) in an age where people may catch a vision of the positive value of the rich diversity of cultures that the world contains.

Notes

1. References of the form 'G.175' are to the German edition, which differs substantially from the English translation which is referred to by volume and page num ber, e.g. 'I, 463'.

List of works cited

F.C. Baur, *Paulus, der Apostel Jesu*, Leipzig, 1845; 2nd edn, Leipzig, 1866-7

W. Bousset, *Kyrios Christos*, Göttingen, 1913 (German); Nashville, 1970 (English)

W. Bousset, *Das Wesen der Religion dargestellt an ihrer Geschichte*, Halle, 1903

R. Bultmann, 'Geschichte der Paulus-Forschung', *Theologische Rundschau*, NF 1, 1929, 26-59

T. Carlyle, *On Heroes, Hero-Worship and the Heroic in History*, London, 1840, popular edn, London, 1872

C.H. Dodd, *The Meaning of Paul for Today*, London, 1920

A. Eichhorn, 'Das Abendmahl im Neuen Testament', Supplement to *Die Christliche Welt*, 36, 1898

O. Everling, *Die paulinische Angelologie und Dämonologie*, Göttingen, 1888

H. Gunkel, *Die Wirkungen des heiligen Geistes nach der populären Anschauungen der apostolischen Zeit und nach der Lehre des Apostels Paulus*, Göttingen, 1888

H. Gunkel, *Schöpfung und Chaos in Urzeit und Endzeit*, Göttingen, 1895

W. Heitmüller, *'Im Namen Jesu'. Eine sprach- und religionsgeschichtliche Untersuchung zum neuen Testament, speziell zur altchristlichen Taufe*, Göttingen, 1903

W. Heitmüller, *Taufe und Abendmahl bei Paulus*, Göttingen, 1903

R. Kabisch, *Die Eschatologie des Apostels Paulus in ihren Zusammenhängen mit dem Gesamtbegriff des Paulinismus*, Göttingen, 1893

H. Lüdemann, *Die Anthropologie des Apostels Paulus*, Kiel, 1872

O. Pfleiderer, *Primitive Christianity: Its Writings and Teachings in their Historical Connections*, 1, Berlin, 1887 (German); London, 1906 (English)

A. Schweitzer, *Paul and his Interpreters*, Tübingen, 1911 (German); London, 1912 (English)

A. Schweitzer, *The Mysticism of Paul the Apostle*, Tübingen, 1930 (German); London, 1931 (English)

A. Schweitzer, *My Life and Thought*, Leipzig, 1931 (German); London, 1933 (English)

W. Wrede, *Paul*, Göttingen, 1904 (German); London, 1907 (English)

4

From Barth to Bultmann: New Testament Study in the Aftermath of the First World War

The First World War interrupted and disturbed New Testament study in different ways. In a strange sense it was a time of great productivity. Bultmann, it is said, wrote his *History of the Synoptic Tradition* on the kitchen table. Straitened circumstances and a dearth of students perhaps concentrated the mind and made possible the intense work on the New Testament documents that the form-critics achieved during the War years. Such studies raised radical new questions for the study of the Gospels. Just as importantly, the terrible carnage of the war posed deep question marks against the cultural optimism which had affected Europe. In Germany, Liberalism came increasingly under attack: the new Weimar Republic was unable to withstand the political pressures of socialism, nationalism and fascism. Theology under the leadership of Karl Barth underwent a major change. New Testament study, in Germany at least, discarded the historical apologetic that was characteristic of scholars like Harnack and Bousset and sought new strategies for interpreting the central texts.

Three major works of form-criticism appeared within short succession after the First World War: in 1919 Martin Dibelius (1883-1947) published his *Formgeschichte des Evangeliums (From Tradition to Gospel*, 1934) and Karl Ludwig Schmidt (1891-1956) his *Der Rahmen der Geschichte Jesu* ('the framework of the history of Jesus'; not available [1993] in English); in 1921 Rudolf Bultmann published his *Die Geschichte der synoptischen Tradition (The History of the Synoptic Tradition*, 1963).

What these works had in common was a desire to trace out the history of the tradition that lay behind the Gospels. The key to such an undertaking was, they held, the study of the *forms* of the individual units of material that were contained in the Gospels. In '*Kleinliteratur*' (works not written for a self-consciously literary public), Dibelius maintained, the individual had an insignificant role in the composition of a work: its form was a supra-individual entity, the product of particular needs and situations within his community.

The material in the Gospels was of this kind: stories and sayings whose actual form was much more the product of the particular cultural and social context in which they were retailed than it was of any particular individual inspiration. The evangelists were principally collectors of their material, not its creators (*From Tradition to Gospel*, 1-3). Furthermore, the form-critics believed that it was possible to discern certain regularities in the modifications which stories and sayings underwent in the course of their transmission. What all this meant was that it was in principle possible to determine the setting in life (*Sitz im Leben*) of the individual Gospel units (*pericopae*) and to trace out the subsequent history of the tradition of such units before they were finally written down. If this could be done then a clearer picture could emerge not only of the earliest forms of the traditional material in the Gospels, but also of the history of the communities that had produced and transmitted them. The three works contributed in various ways to this task.

Schmidt's book (to be followed later by a magisterial study of the Gospel form, 'Die Stellung der Evangelien in der allgemeinen Literaturgeschichte') was restricted to a consideration of the framework which the evangelists had created for the stories and discourse material which they collected. What he showed convincingly was that this framework was a loosely constructed expedient by which the evangelist was able to draw together a mass of traditional material into a coherent narrative. It was, that is to say, an editorial device by means of which collectors of the tradition could arrange their material, not a reliable historical account of the outline of Jesus's life and death. Source criticism, by identifying Mark as the oldest Gospel, had led many to suppose that it was, therefore, a reliable source of information about the course of Jesus's life. Schmidt's work simply undermined such a view. The evangelists were collectors of folk-tales, not reporters of historical events. The overarching story they created was just that: a creation. One consequence of this was that attempts to trace the development of Jesus's self-understanding had simply to be abandoned for lack of any kind of reliable chronology in which to place stories and sayings. More significantly, perhaps, Schmidt's work established the view that, as Dibelius put it, the evangelists are 'only to the smallest extent authors. They are principally collectors, vehicles of tradition, editors. Before all else their labour consists in handing down, grouping, and working over the material which has come to them' (*From Tradition to Gospel*, 3).

Dibelius and Bultmann, in their different ways, undertook the major task of giving an account of the *history* of the Synoptic tradition. They wanted to show, that is, how particular types of stories and sayings emerged within a particular setting and then were handed on until they reached the stage in which, variously, we find them in the Gospels. As Bultmann states, such a task, like all historical tasks, is circular. The setting in life of the sayings can illuminate our understanding of the sayings; but equally, it is our understanding of the sayings that may enable us to posit what was their original setting in life. It is possible, therefore, to take either a 'constructive' approach (as does Dibelius), seeking to determine first the different setting in which the stories and sayings of the tradition emerged, and then showing how they developed and related to such settings; or it is possible to proceed 'analytically' (as does Bultmann), classifying the sayings and moving from there to an account of the community and its needs. The two procedures are complementary. What Bultmann insists upon, however, is that in neither case can one neglect judgements about the authenticity of the material in the tradition. The task is not simply one of aesthetic analysis; it is, rather, an historical one that seeks to place the stories and sayings within the development of the early Christian community's faith (*HST*, 5). In simple terms this meant distinguishing between those sayings whose earliest form went back to Jesus himself and those which were the creation of the community. It also, importantly, meant attempting to identify those tendencies that had shaped the material as it was handed on in the community. Sayings that were original to Jesus might still have been substantially recast by the community in the course of transmission.

We shall see shortly how Bultmann developed his account. Here we need to note the extent to which this work dealt damaging blows to the increasingly uneasy alliance between historical studies of the New Testament and liberal theology. In Germany this alliance had been, for the most part, struck up between liberal theologians and source critics. Mark's Gospel, as the earliest and most reliable source for the life of Jesus, could be read in a way that presented Jesus as embodying in his own faith and teaching the highest form of religion, a truly ethical and spiritual faith. Of course, Schweitzer had proposed very different ways of reading Mark's Gospel, but they were intriguing and possible, rather than compelling. Form-critical studies of the Synoptic tradition now showed how difficult it was to trace the line back from even the earliest written Gospel to the events and sayings which it retailed. This, in time, was to prove to be far more corrosive of liberal views of Jesus than were Schweitzer's alternative readings of Mark's Gospel.

There were, however, quite different reasons for the growing disaffection with the older, liberal forms of theology in Germany. Germany's defeat in the First World War destroyed (if not forever) the belief that Western European Protestantism was the finest flowering of the seeds of the Kingdom sown in the words and teaching of Jesus. Western Europe had committed an appalling act of mutual genocide. Theologians and church leaders had done little, if anything, to check the fiercely militant nationalism of their imperialistic states. The ruthlessness with which Britain, France and Germany had pursued their imperial ambitions in Africa and India was now visited on their own youth with terrifying thoroughness, and among the vanquished some, at least, had time to repent of their political and cultural imperialism. For the British, who had now effectively removed some of the immediate obstacles to their colonial ambitions, such a process of repentance was to be far less acceptable.

The main attack on liberal theology, as is well known, came from Karl Barth in his *The Epistle to the Romans* (1919; 2nd edn 1921). This is a work of extraordinary rhetorical force, which derives its power from Barth's majestic vision of the transcendence and otherness of the Word of God. In its sight all human history stands judged; all attempts to identify human goals and achievements with the will and activity of God are condemned outright as religion (as opposed to faith), as the most dangerous and deluding expressions of human sinfulness. Faith, by contrast, is not, as the liberals had (at least in some forms) suggested, a particular form of human attitude, piety or self-consciousness that can be communicated from one person to another: it is the total openness to the living, transcendent Word of God that is created by the sovereign Word as it judges and liberates the heart, which is turned in on itself.

What, then, is this Word of God which, as it were, provides the link between the wholly other God and sinful men and women in their isolation? 'It is as though we had been transfixed by an arrow launched at us from beyond an impassable river' (238). It speaks to us, judging and calling. But the God who speaks through it cannot be grasped; cannot be made known except as he who is wholly other. 'Woe be to us . . . if we do not speak of that of which the unobservability alone is observable' (*ibid.*). Nor do his judgement and call themselves take human historical form. They cannot be embodied in laws, in human codes, in human culture. God's Word is free; it has to be heard again and again, always new. Like the manna in the wilderness, it must be gathered anew every morning. If people attempt to hold on to it, to tame it, to make it their own, it will only turn mouldy.

Barth's *Romans* is, of course, itself a work of New Testament interpretation, but one that it is almost impossible to classify. Like Calvin, Barth sought to battle away at the centuries-old barrier between himself and Paul until he heard him speak as if such a time gap no longer existed. 'Dialectical theology' is essentially a dialogue with the texts and their subject matter which, Barth assumes, is the transcendent, wholly other God. 'The conversation between the original record and the reader moves round the subject-matter, until a distinction between yesterday and to-day becomes impossible' (7). Such an emphasis on a theological interpretation of the Bible was, of course, intended as a corrective to much of what passed for exegesis in New Testament study, but it is important to see where Barth's criticisms are directed. He was not at all dismissive of New Testament scholarship, in so far as it could help him to pull down the historical barrier that divided him from his text. He recognised fully the need for an historical interpretation of the words of the text. But he was deeply critical of such study in so far as it failed to distinguish, as he saw it, between cultural and religious-historical studies of the texts on the one hand, and theological interpretation on the other (6-10).

What Barth is attacking here is the kind of explanation that is offered by the History of Religions School, and others. Such scholars are content to offer an explanation of a difficult passage in Paul in terms of the 'religious thought, feeling, experience, conscience or conviction, — of Paul!' or by attributing it to 'later Judaism, to Hellenism, or, in fact, to any exegetical semi-divinity of the ancient world!' (7f). Barth overshoots the mark by suggesting that this is no explanation at all. He is correct, none the less, to point out that this is not a theological explanation, that is one that attempts to see how what Paul is saying illuminates the — assumed — central subject matter of his texts, namely the revelation of the transcendent God in Jesus Christ. It is not that he, Barth, rejects criticism; it is rather that the critical historian requires to be more critical:

> The commentator must be possessed of a wider intelligence than that which moves within the boundaries of his own natural appreciation. True apprehension can be achieved only by a strict determination to face, as far as is possible without rigidity of mind, the tension displayed more or less clearly in the ideas written in the text. Criticism (*krinein*) applied to historical documents means for me the measuring of words and phrases by the standard of that about which the documents are speaking — unless indeed the whole be nonsense. . . . The Word ought to be exposed in the words. Intelligent comment means that I am driven on till I stand with nothing before me but the enigma of the matter; till the document seems hardly to exist as a document; till I have almost forgotten that I am not its author; till I know the author so well that I allow him to speak in my name and am even able to speak in his name myself (8).

It is important to understand the argument at this point, for it is central to the understanding of subsequent attempts to do New Testament theology. The question here is what might count as a theological explanation of a particular text. In a sense there are two issues here: first what kind of explanation would do justice to a particular kind of text, namely a text that purports to talk *about God*; and second what kind of theological account would actually serve to *explain* the meaning of such texts? Barth is surely right to point out that there is a *prima facie* requirement on interpreters of religious texts that they should deal with the stated subject matter of such texts. The fact is that not all theological interpretations of texts actually explain them. There are two quite distinct reasons for this. In the first place, as Barth recognises, there are theological accounts of, for example, Pauline texts, which have not wrestled with the meaning of the text, but simply made arbitrary decisions to identify it with theological beliefs which the interpreter himself holds. These fail because they are not interpretations of the text itself. In the second place, there are theological explanations that fail to explain — at least to some — because they offer an explanation in terms of something to which the hearer can attach no sense. Barth's explanation in terms of the transcendent wholly other God speaking to the believer would not count as an explanation at all to non-believers who can attach no sense to such a notion. One attempt to extricate New Testament theologians from this dilemma (of failing to offer acceptable theological explanations to one's non-believing students and academic colleagues) is to suggest that explanations should be offered in terms of some neutral concept of religion (acceptable, that is, to believers and non-believers alike), which would allow non-believers to make sense of what was being said and believers the freedom to go on and identify what was being talked about with their experience of the encounter with the living God. This is argued, for instance, in R. Morgan's (b.1940) *Biblical Interpretation.*

Barth's great *Nein* to religion, to all attempts to identify human hopes and aspirations, goals and desires with the self-revelation of the transcendent God, clearly bears on such programmes of Biblical interpretation, but its bearing is not simple. In the first place, he is, clearly enough, wanting to make a radical disjunction between religious phenomena, that which can be perceived and observed, and the encounter with the living God which is mediated through the Word. Of course there is, at the very least, a temporal connection between the two. If Barth heard the Word of God address him as he studied Paul in Safenwil, then that encounter occurred as he was engaged in an activity that falls quite properly within the scope of, say, sociologists and psychologists of religion. The question which Barth's negation raises, but which Barth himself left open, is whether, in fact, a distanced study of such phenomena can in any way assist in the understanding of that encounter with the living God, which for him was wholly different from the human aspirations and activities that he dismissed as sinful and religious. He might have allowed that there was a temporal connection between his efforts in his study and God's act of self-revelation; but he would have argued that such a connection was, in human terms, accidental — not causally explicable — even though it lay within the providence of God.

Barth's concern was, of course, principally to cut the knot between knowledge of God and human religious activity and experience. It was, as he subsequently maintained, a prophetic word, intended to call into question any identification of human experience and activity with the activity and will of God. Such a protest has its place in the aftermath of the First World War; just as it continues to raise questions as to how far a general definition of religion that can do justice to the believer's claims about his experience is at all possible. To that we shall return.

There were other questions which Barth's contemporaries, even those who were strongly sympathetic to his cause, wanted to raise. In his review of the second edition of *The Epistle to the Romans*, Bultmann welcomes Barth's emphasis on the transcendence of the Word. It is the spirit of the Reformers and of Soren Kierkegaard (1813-1855) and the prophets that breathes in this remarkable work. But the question for Bultmann, in the end, is this: if we stress the transcendence of God, the sense in which God cannot be grasped in human words, then how can we understand him at all? If we do not allow that God in some sense takes human, historical form, that the encounter with the living God leaves at least its marks in the human self-understanding, how do we know that such an encounter has occurred at all? If the conjunction, that is, of human thought and action and willing with the self-revelation of God is purely external and accidental, in what sense does it touch men and women at all? Are we not in danger of simple unintelligibility in attempting to speak of such a thing? Is faith, when it is beyond consciousness, anything at all real? What sense can we attach to talk of God? In what sense can we speak of or about God at all? Faith, for Paul, 'is the conscious acceptance of the message of salvation, the conscious obedience under God's new saving ordinance' (57).

Such questions are pivotal for Bultmann's work on the New Testament. There has been in his work a fusion between philosophical and theological interests on the one hand and historical and sociological ones on the other, which is without parallel in the twentieth century. If our discussion of New Testament study between the wars is largely dominated by his work, it is because of this fusion and because of his remarkable ability in both areas.

Like Barth, Bultmann was taught by the great German liberal theologians and Biblical scholars of the outgoing nineteenth century: Harnack, Hermann, Jülicher (1857-1938) and Weiss. For Bultmann, also like Barth, the First World War marked an important turning point in his intellectual development. Bultmann's development, however, should not be too closely related to Barth's. As significant as his reaction to Barth's *Epistle to the Romans* is his co-operation in Marburg with the German philosopher Martin Heidegger (1889-1976). What characterised the latter's work in *Being and Time* (1927) was, on the one hand, his rejection of conventional, received attitudes and norms and, on the other, his search for meaning, for 'authenticity', that is human existence in the sphere of human 'inwardness'. With the collapse of pre-war Germany and the monarchy, German intellectuals who were sensitive to the major cultural changes that had occurred turned again to such fundamental questions of the basis of true human fulfilment and life. Heidegger sought to offer an analysis of what it was to be human, an analysis of *Da-sein* (being-there) which would bring out the specific aspects of human existence in time that distinguished it from that of things. Such an analysis would need to be significantly different from that of traditional analyses of substance that, following Aristotle, had analysed them in terms of fixed qualities or attributes; for human existence is precisely not predetermined in the way that the existence of inanimate objects is. On the contrary, it is part of what it is to be human, Heidegger maintained, that we should choose what we are to be. We are what we are, not in the acceptance of the everyday conventional mores of our mass culture, but in the exercise of our will as we choose those possibilities of existence that are most truly our own.

Heidegger's analysis of the modes of human existence, which is a remarkable and complex piece of work, was written during a period of close co-operation with Bultmann in Marburg. The subject of Bultmann's debt to Heidegger has been often enough discussed, but it is, perhaps, helpful to distinguish two areas where their interests were close. In the first place, as we shall see, Bultmann needed a conceptual framework that would enable him to give an account of human self-consciousness that was intelligible and acceptable to Christianity's 'cultured despisers'. In Heidegger he could find such an account of human inwardness that, for Bultmann, was the place of encounter with the transcendent Word. Here their positions are quite close: though one must remember that what is borrowed is itself the fruit of Bultmann and Heidegger's common study of the tradition of Augustine, Luther and Kierkegaard. Yet though they shared certain intuitions, they developed them in very different ways. Both, indeed, shared a sense that inherited values or codes could not of themselves provide an adequate basis for true human existence, that true 'meaning' — truth, indeed — was to be found in the sphere of human inwardness. For Bultmann such meaning can be found only when the individual encounters the transcendent Word of God and in obedience to it finds release from his preoccupation with the cares of this world and freedom to serve the living God.

It is here, significantly, that Bultmann both learns from and parts company with Barth. Both see in the transcendent Word the source of Christian faith; but for Barth faith is not to be identified with the transformed self-consciousness of those who are encountered by the Word. It is a *Hohlraum*, 'an empty space', which is filled — again and again — by the free Word of God. Does it therefore follow that we are not conscious in any way of such an encounter? Is faith, if it is beyond consciousness, any kind of reality at all? 'Certainly, our justification is . . . present with God, even without our knowing about it. And of it we can only say that we believe it' (*RBInt*, 57). But can we say of faith itself that we can only believe it: that while it does, indeed, have its observable side, *true faith* as the eternal step into that which is wholly unobservable is itself unobservable?

Such a faith beyond consciousness would not be Paul's, for whom faith is 'conscious obedience under God's new saving ordinance'(*ibid.*). Faith beyond consciousness would not be the 'impossible possibility' but would be, in every sense, an absurdity. For while faith is not identical with the 'psychic' processes that occur in the believer, it is an event that occurs in the conscious life of the believer perhaps without great reflection but not without some acknowledgement, some *confession*, whether in thought or words or deeds.

Bultmann's work in a sense never ceases to grapple with the doubts that he raised so sharply over Barth's *Epistle to the Romans*. Despite that work's polemics against attempts to base faith on the historical Jesus, Bultmann's first contribution to this continuing debate was his book *Jesus and the Word* (1926).

This book, which was published, rather oddly, in a series entitled 'Spiritual Heroes of Humanity', has often been overlooked and rarely fully understood. Precisely because Bultmann himself later set his face against attempts to base faith on historical knowledge of Jesus, scholars have often discussed his oeuvre as if the book had never been written. It is a problematic book, which is capable of being read in two quite diverse ways. In one way, it is a continuation of historical, critical studies of the life and teaching of Jesus, that we have already documented and which had been greatly furthered by Bultmann's own studies of the history of the Synoptic tradition. It is a work, as we shall see, that proposes its own solutions to the questions raised by Weiss and Wrede, but which certainly does attempt a reconstruction and explanation of Jesus's teaching. It says little, it is true, about the details of Jesus's life: but it is at least as specific as, say, Harnack; indeed it says rather more.

In another sense it is a response to the problems of biblical interpretation which Barth had raised. Barth, as we saw, had not rejected historical, critical studies as such; he had, rather criticised the lack of any sustained attempt to *interpret* the texts. Critics merely attempted to explain, linguistically and historically, 'what was there' - 'what is in the text'. Barth wanted more, to attempt to think through what was being said, to discover the subject that is being spoken of, which can only be the same for us as for the author. Bultmann's Jesus is, more rigorously than Barth's *The Epistle to the Romans*, an attempt to put this kind of programme into action. He invites his readers to hear Jesus addressing those questions of human existence, of its transitoriness, of its questionableness and fragility, in short, its hopes and its fears, which concern both them and Jesus's original hearers. This represents a position substantially different from Bultmann's later rejection of all attempts to derive such a message from study of the Jesus tradition: but it is only a step to his finding in the text of John and Paul a firmer base for his existential interpretation of the church's *kerygma*. We need to read the book both ways if we are to have a fuller appreciation of it.

I suggested in the second chapter that the problems raised by Weiss, namely of the close analogies between parts of the Synoptic tradition and contemporary Jewish apocalyptic, could be seriously tackled only when confidence in the historical reliability of Mark's Gospel and of document Q had been shaken: until such time it would always be possible to interpret the apocalyptic material in the light of the very substantial body of Wisdom and legal material which could be found elsewhere. What Wrede and now form-criticism had shown was that such confidence was misplaced: that, in fact, by no means all the material in the Synoptic tradition could with certainty be seen as original to Jesus, and that even what was original might well have in part undergone considerable transformation.

This meant, of course, that scholars would have to approach the task of writing a study of Jesus with the presumption that not all the sayings attributed to him were in fact authentic. In consequence, they needed to devise strategies for establishing at least a core of material that they judged to be authentic and which would provide the basis for their interpretation of Jesus's message.

The task of identifying the authentic sayings of Jesus had been, in a sense, re-defined by the form-critics themselves. In his *History of the Synoptic Tradition*, Bultmann had classified the sayings material into two main headings: apophthegms and dominical sayings. The former are sayings that are formally related to narratives; the latter are independent sayings, though they may be gathered into larger collections. The dominical sayings are then further classified into logia (Wisdom sayings), prophetic and apocalyptic sayings, Legal sayings and community rules, I-sayings and, lastly, parables. One advantage of this classification is the way in which it clearly spells out the diversity of material attributed to Jesus. Is it likely that one man would have uttered all the different types of sayings to be found in the Synoptics? How are we to decide which of the sayings is authentic?

Bultmann's approach to such a task has often, I think, been misrepresented. He has been presented by some as having devised certain tests or criteria for solving questions of the authenticity of the Gospel sayings. In fact, his treatment is far less rigid than this might suggest. He first classifies sayings and narratives formally. In most instances this does not, in Bultmann's view, shed much light on the authenticity of the sayings: the forms derived from the legal, Wisdom and prophetic-apocalyptic traditions are, for the most part, at home in the first-century Palestinian milieu which Jesus inhabited. But in a few cases, say community rules such as some of the material in Matthew 18:15-17, 21-22 (*HST*, 141), there are clearly grounds for supposing that these owe their present form to the early church. More light is shed on the authenticity of certain sayings and collections of sayings by a consideration of their history. Consider, for example, Mark 7:1-23 (*HST*, 17f). Here we have a collection of material about purity that appears *as a collection* to have undergone a considerable process of development and correction. It falls into two sections probably originally independent of each other, vv. 1-13 and 14-23. In the second section v.15, which is a doublet of v.18, appears originally to have been an independent saying which has been given an initial interpretation: vv.18,19 (together with an editorial comment v.19b) and then a further commentary vv.20-23 which makes use of a list of vices similar to those found, for example, in Galatians 5, Colossians 3 and Romans 1, which are almost certainly Hellenistic in origin and in this context almost without question later additions. What all this suggests is that this section has been built up over some length of time and that, therefore, the original saying v.15, around which the rest of the material has accrued, is, substantially, early. It does not prove that it is authentic, merely that it is early. Proof of authenticity cannot come purely from considerations either of the form of the material or of the history of particular units of material or collections. Indeed, proof of authenticity in the strict sense is not possible. Nevertheless a consideration of what is most characteristic in the sayings, which may be thought to be early on traditio-historical grounds, may help.

Here we are faced with the basic dilemma. Even when we have pared down the Synoptic tradition to include only material that is early and which is innocent of any later theological tendencies, we are left with a substantial body of material derived from the legal, Wisdom and prophetic-apocalyptic material. Here a judgement has to be made; Bultmann's is unequivocal. The Wisdom sayings, for the most part at least, breathe a spirit of 'childlike belief in providence and a naive optimism in his view of nature and the world' (*Jesus*, 115). Such sayings are in marked contrast to the radical urgency and seriousness of much, if not all, the prophetic-apocalyptic material attributed to Jesus. Bultmann weighs the matter carefully. On the one hand, he does not think that Jesus would have specifically repudiated such beliefs 'since they are consistent with the typically Jewish belief in God' (116). On the other hand, such sayings do not for the most part represent what is most characteristic in Jesus's thought and may well have been brought into the tradition for practical reasons. For the most part, Bultmann rejects the Wisdom sayings in favour of Jesus's apocalyptic and prophetic sayings. This still leaves a corpus of legal sayings that may be attributable to Jesus. A good part of the dynamic of the book derives from Bultmann's attempt to offer an interpretation of the legal and the prophetic-apocalyptic sayings that makes sense of both.

Even here there are fine judgements to be made about the authenticity of the remaining material. Bultmann does not by any means accept the authenticity of all the prophetic-apocalyptic sayings. Certain predictions, like that of the destruction of Jerusalem, he regards as prophecies after the event (*vaticinia ex eventu*). Nor does he believe, in the light of Jesus's recorded refusal to give signs, that the detailed predictions of the events of the End, such as are found in Mark 13, are original to Jesus. 'Jesus rejects the whole content of apocalyptic speculation' (36). Bultmann believed, indeed, that most of Mark 13 was based on a Jewish apocalyptic source that had been taken over by the early church and given a Christian reference (*HST*, 122f).

Even allowing for such qualifications, how does he proceed to interpret the legal and prophetic-apocalyptic material? The answer lies in his attempts at understanding apocalyptic. Here a somewhat later work may help to interpret his own *Jesus*. In *Jesus Christ and Mythology* (see esp. ch. 2). Bultmann makes a comparison between Greek views of human transitoriness and futility and Biblical views. In Greek drama and philosophy, human finitude is expressed in terms of contingency: the coming in to being and passing away of men and women, their insignificance in the cosmos. Their task is to recognise this reality, to obey, to live a life in accordance with the nature of things; not to delude themselves into believing that they can escape the eternal law of providence. Such a sense of the transitoriness of life is widespread: it can be found in Shakespeare as it can in Sophocles and Pindar. It is, however, given a particular form in the Biblical writers, where human existence is not simply contrasted with the eternal, unchanging reality of Being, but with the holiness and otherness of God. 'For the prophets and for Jesus God is the Holy One, who demands right and righteousness, who therefore is the judge of all human thoughts and actions' (*JCM*, 26). Here men and women are perceived, not merely as finite, contingent beings who must 'obey' the law of providence and nature, but as sinners who must bow before the holiness and law of God. Moreover this contrast between creatures and a holy God is heightened in mythological eschatology where God is experienced as a distant God who will come to judge his world for its disobedience and to establish his rule over it. On such a view eschatology and law are indeed intimately connected: law is both a measure of the present generation's disobedience, and also the expression of God's will that all will acknowledge who survive the wrath to come.

Bultmann's discussion attempts to show how such eschatology relates to a basic human apprehension of the questionableness of existence. Such apprehension may be expressed in Greek writers in terms of cosmic laws of nature and providence, in eschatological mythology in terms of cosmic events in the future. One may use spatial metaphors to express the transcendence of infinite Being over the finite, the other chronological terms to speak of the coming judgement which God will exercise over his creatures. Both, however, express a sense that in and of itself human life is incomplete, questionable, futile; that it is only when it is related to the source of all light and life - to the law of life - that it makes sense and is fulfilled. Bultmann's *Jesus* attempts to interpret Jesus's teaching by showing how Jesus's language and sayings address themselves to such questions, and, more significantly, how by helping others to read them in such a way, they may themselves be addressed by such sayings, may be questioned and enlightened in their own search for meaning, 'integrity' and 'authenticity'.

It is easiest to start with Bultmann's exposition of Jesus's teaching about the Law. His central thesis is here that Jesus does not come to teach a set of ethical values, nor to establish some kind of political or social programme (81); what he does is to confront people with the Will of God *for them* and to call them to obedience. The rich, young man asks Jesus what he should do to inherit eternal life. Jesus, having reminded him of the commandments, challenges him to sell all that he has. In this, says Bultmann, Jesus is not preaching an ideal of poverty or asceticism. He is making two points: first that 'the will of God claims the man completely'; and second that it is not formal goodness which is required but true obedience. 'Truly when a man asks after the way of life, there is nothing in particular to say to him. He is to do what is right, what everyone knows. But if then a special demand confronts the whole man, it becomes plain whether the *whole* man was involved in that right conduct, whether that doing of what is right really rests on the decision for the good' (74). Will he subordinate his own inclinations to the Will of God, will he obey with his whole heart; not in blind, mindless obedience, but willingly and knowingly sacrificing his own interests to the call and Will of God? Again, in treating the question of love of enemies Bultmann argues that what is significant about Jesus's command here is not its content. In that respect, he thinks there is not anything specifically new. In Bultmann's view, what is important is the way in which such a command challenges precisely our own deepest instincts and interests and so calls us most clearly to total obedience (70). Such obedience is given not to a code but to the living Word of God as it speaks concretely to each person.

How then does such a sense of obedience, as each person's obedience *here and now* to the present call of God's Word, relate to eschatological language about the future coming of God's judgement and Kingdom? What sense can Jesus's sayings about the coming of the Kingdom have for us if we are already challenged to obey God's Word in the present moment?

Bultmann's strategy here (28-47) is sophisticated. He starts with a summary statement of Jesus's 'proclamation of deliverance and call to repentance'. Jesus preached the coming of the Kingdom of God as a present reality. 'Happy are the eyes that see what you see!' (Lk. 10:23). In his exorcisms and healings the power of God's rule is evidenced and the promise of the prophets fulfilled (Mt. 11:5). In this last hour, 'the hour of decision', Jesus is sent to confront men and women with the ultimate decision, 'the Either-Or. To decide for the Kingdom is to sacrifice for it all things else' (30). Such a call is a call to repentance which calls men and women to reject the world and 'to put the Kingdom of God above all other things. It makes its claim not on man's frivolous desire for pleasure but on his will' (32).

If then the core of Jesus's preaching is a call to decision, if that is to say his message is essentially a message addressed to men and women's wills, what sense attaches to the phrase 'Kingdom of God'? In the simplest sense it is 'deliverance for men . . . which confronts man as an Either-Or' (33). Thus it is not some highest good, continuous with other human values and goals. The parable of the seed growing secretly (Mk 4:26-9), with its stress on the miraculous ripening of the grain, points to the miraculous character of the coming of the Kingdom. It is not achieved by human agency but by the action of God. It is not to 'be realised in any organisation of world fellowship' (35). In all this, of course, Bultmann repeats Weiss's criticism of Ritschl. But he also importantly echoes Barth's insistence on the super-historical character of the Word of God.

What can be said more positively of the Kingdom? What sort of events were associated with its coming? Here Bultmann carefully distinguishes Jesus's use of eschatological language from that of his contemporaries. Jesus was not untouched by such beliefs. 'There can be no doubt that Jesus like his contemporaries expected a tremendous eschatological drama' (35). Yet, at the same time, he rejected Jewish apocalyptic speculation about the signs of the End itself, which for Bultmann represented a dimming of the prophetic perception of human existence in the face of the holiness of God. While there are such speculative elements in the Synoptic tradition these stand in sharp contrast with Jesus's rejection elsewhere of the demand for signs, and are therefore of doubtful originality (36f). Jesus does use the language of God's coming, but he uses it not to speculate, but to stress the sense in which human existence must always be open to the future, the call of God. Whereas his Jewish contemporaries prayed for the deliverance of Israel and the gathering in of the dispersed tribes, Jesus's language in prayer is shorn of all such detail: 'Thy kingdom come, thy will be done'. The notion of the coming of the Kingdom expresses, that is to say, a fundamental either/or of human existence. Those who are obedient to God's Word as it encounters them, will find themselves, that is they will discover what it is truly to be human; those who reject it will lose themselves.

Jesus, that is to say, is taking the language of contemporary mythology and drawing out its full existential sense. He does not see the Kingdom principally as some event in the future about which one can speculate, but as a 'power *which, although it is entirely future, wholly determines the present. . . .* If men are standing in the crisis of decision, and if precisely this crisis is the essential characteristic of their humanity, then every hour is the last hour, and we can understand that for Jesus the whole contemporary mythology is pressed into the service of this conception of human existence. Thus he understood and proclaimed his hour as the last hour.'(44f.) In that last hour, men and women are confronted precisely with the Will of God as that which can determine their existence for good; it is in *obedience* to the call which Jesus brings that the new existence comes to fruition.

In this way Bultmann is able to offer a consistent interpretation both of Jesus's eschatological preaching and of his teaching about the Law. He is also able to relate Jesus's preaching and teaching to fundamental questions of human existence which press on his own readers an awareness which Bultmann sees as a necessary condition for approaching the subject. Thus the focus of Bultmann's interpretation is on the sphere of human inwardness. His dialogue with the text - or at least with his reconstructed text of Jesus's sayings - is an existential dialogue that seeks to allow Jesus's words to address his readers' questions about human finitude, transitoriness and the quest for meaning and wholeness.

In all this there is, of course, a sharp break with the earlier, liberal traditions that had stressed the historical continuity between Jesus and the church, his theological and ethical legacy (the seed sown in history) which was given in Christian culture and society. For Bultmann, history is at most the site in which an individual may encounter the - transcendent - Word of God that addresses him and calls him to a mode of existence which is the contrary of his present ways. Like Barth's, Bultmann's 'Conversion' from liberal theology is clearly related to the massive loss of confidence in Western culture after the First World War. Thus he is drawn to those elements in Jesus's sayings that stress God's transcendence over his world: sayings about judgement, about forgiveness and the possibility of new life, the radical commands to obedience that cut across all human desires and interests. At the same time he has, as it were, to strip such sayings of their 'objectifying' content. Sayings about the End are not — or not centrally — sayings about future historical (supra-historical) events, they are sayings about events in the highly personal sphere of human inwardness. Commands to sell one's goods or to love one's enemies are not statements of universal, ethical principles, but quite concrete, specific commands to individuals. The realm of faith is no longer the public, historical world of the existential moment that can transform and renew the individual and provide him with a firm ground in the shifting sands of history and culture.

It is fascinating at this point to compare Bultmann's *Jesus* with Dodd's *The Parables of the Kingdom*, published in the very different world of England in 1935. Dodd does not refer to Bultmann's *Jesus* and is more influenced by the earlier work of Jülicher on the parables (1892) and the original work by R. Otto (1869-1937), *Kingdom of God and Son of Man* (1934). Dodd's aim is to offer an interpretation of the parables, as these, he believes, have a freshness and originality that authenticate them as few other parts of the material ascribed to Jesus can be authenticated. Nevertheless while he thus pleads for the substantial originality of the Synoptic parables, he recognises that the parables have been subject to distortion and development and makes some limited use of the work of the form-critics in his search for their original form and meaning.

Dodd's strategy is two-fold: one stage is formal, the next traditio-historical. Parables, asserts Dodd — and here he follows Jülicher — are similes (16). If we look at the broad spectrum of material that can be classed as such, we find, following Bultmann, at the one end simple *Bildworte* (figurative sayings) and, at the other, extended narratives. But in each case the sayings and the stories serve to make a comparison that is properly concerned to make only one point (18). A scene, character or event from life is compared with (some aspect of) God's Kingdom in respect of some shared characteristic (*tertium comparationis*). What we need to do is to discover what was the original setting, the context of the utterance of the parable, in order that we may discover with what the parable is being compared (26).

All this was, of course, as Jülicher had argued extensively, very different from traditional, allegorical forms of parable interpretation that we find in the Gospels in the interpretation of the Parable of the Sower (Mk. 4:14-20), and which became standard in the subsequent history of the church. Where Dodd differed from Jülicher was in the account he offered of the subject of the parabolic comparison. The latter believed that the parables were intended to illustrate and illuminate general theological principles. As Dodd succinctly remarks, 'this method of interpretation makes the parables to be forcible illustrations of eminently sound moral and religious principles, but undeniably its general effect is rather flattening' (25). Dodd believed they cast light on the nature of Jesus's ministry and of the proper response to it (26).

Dodd's formal analysis of parables as single-point comparisons provides him with a key to the tradition-history, or at least a broad principle by which to reconstruct the original. Allegorical details may be excised, conclusions that appear to draw further lessons from the parable than that suggested by the main ductus of the story may be removed, as may details that appear to disturb the realism of the parable. Thus in broad principle, rather than by detailed analysis, Dodd establishes his basic text.

Before he can begin to determine what the parables meant, however, he has to face a major problem. If, as he argued, parables are comparisons, we have to know what is being compared with the story or saying. For Dodd, the connection was concrete: the parables related to situations in the life of Jesus. The heart of the problem lay, however, in determining what were the specific situations. Dodd's analysis of the material showed him that there had been, at least in some cases, a clear reworking of the parables to apply them to later situations in the life of the church. How could one any longer know what their reference was in the life of Jesus?

Dodd's answer is characteristically subtle. We can, he believed, find some parables or parabolic sayings where the connection between the parable and the situation seems to have been clearly preserved: the Children Playing in the Market Place (Mt. 11:16-19), with its reference to Jesus and John the Baptist, is one such case (28). But in most cases we cannot be so sure of the original connection, and here we have to be guided by the other clue that we have: the frequent reference to the Kingdom of God in the introductions to the parables. Thus before he comes to discuss the sense of the parables at all, Dodd turns to a consideration of the meaning of Jesus's sayings about the Kingdom and the Son of Man (chs. 2 & 3).

Dodd's views on Jesus's eschatology are well known. Jesus proclaimed that in his ministry the Kingdom of God had drawn near: the eternal had entered history in his life, judging and offering promise to those who would hear. In him Jewish hopes were fulfilled, God's Kingdom was 'realised'. His argument was based partly on a linguistic treatment of the Greek *eggiken* in the phrase, 'the Kingdom has drawn near' (Mk. 1:15) (44f); and partly on a reading of the predictive material (notably in Mk .13) as genuine predictions of the disasters that would befall Jerusalem because of its rejection of the Son of Man (56-66). In this Jesus followed in the steps of the prophets.

The rest of Dodd's book is something of an anti-climax. Once we know what it is that the parables refer to and elucidate there are few great surprises in what follows. The parable of the Sower refers not, as in its Synoptic version, to the different types of converts (an allegorical interpretation that relates more obviously to the missionary situation of the early church), but, as originally uttered by Jesus, to the opportunities for missionary work that were there for the disciples as a result of Jesus's ministry: 'pray ye therefore the Lord of the harvest'(180-3). Parables like the Lost Coin (119f) or the Pearl of Great Price (112f) bring home to people the urgency of the call of the Kingdom. Here is something for which one must be prepared to give everything, for it is beyond price.

Dodd's book has been enormously influential, more than its slimness, and, it has to be said, the thinness of its exegesis might suggest. It is, of course, elegantly and persuasively written. It responded to issues in New Testament scholarship quite freely, and it appeared to offer a way of identifying the heart of Jesus's message by concentrating on the distinctive parabolic material. But the sureness of Dodd's method is deceptive. His reading of the parables is ultimately determined by his reading of the much more problematic apocalyptic material attributed to Jesus. Here he pays little attention to the work of the form-critics, accepts Mark 13 as largely authentic, and bases his reading on a prophetic interpretation of its predictions together with an exegesis of the Greek of Mk. 1:15, which is probably a Markan summary rather than a saying of Jesus. He does, of course, attempt to get back to the Aramaic behind the Greek, but this extra step only weakens his argument.

Where Dodd has left his mark on the discipline has been, above all, in his concentration on the question of the timing of the Kingdom. What was distinctive about Jesus's teaching of the Kingdom was that he taught that it was already here (which Dodd dubbed 'realised eschatology'). Jewish apocalyptic, by contrast, taught that it was still to come in the future. Dodd, under pressure from the exegetically much more detailed and powerful work of Jeremias (1900-1979), *The Parables of Jesus*, was eventually to concede that Jesus did indeed still envisage some future stage of fulfilment: but even this debate was still couched largely in terms of the timing of the Kingdom. It says little, if anything, about the nature of that rule which arrives or is inaugurated with Jesus's ministry, though interestingly Dodd is alive to the question and refers, almost incidentally, to the fact that Jesus's teaching does indeed presuppose a very different view of the character of God's rule from much of contemporary Judaism.[1]

What, then, was the reason for the great popularity and influence of Dodd's book? Questions of this kind cannot easily be answered, as inevitably one must speculate about the connection between elements in the book and what one takes to be predispositions or cultural attitudes on the part of Dodd's readers. In one sense there is little doubt that Dodd provided an account of Jesus's teaching which appeared to deal with form-critical/traditio-historical problems in studies of Jesus's teaching in such a way as to leave a core of Jesus's teaching which could be interpreted in a positive sense. This was doubtless reassuring to English scholars and indeed to a wider public. Form-criticism had received only limited attention in England. Only Dibelius's work was translated before the Second World War and by and large reaction to the form-critics was hostile. Yet this alone would not have explained the work's attraction to an English readership which, while largely conservative in its religious opinions, was none the less aware of the problems of interpretation of Jesus's sayings that had been raised by Schweitzer and others.

Probably what was most attractive in Dodd's work was its republication of the liberal views of Christian history that had previously been advocated by Ritschl, Harnack and others and which, as we have seen, had been so radically rejected by the new generation of German-speaking scholars after the First World War. We saw in chapter two, notably in the work of Headlam, how English scholars' confidence in — English — Christianity was enhanced by the outcome of the Great War. England's age of post-imperial self-doubt was still to come. Meanwhile it was only the more perceptive theologians who subjected the English Christian tradition to radical self-criticism, and figures such as Studdert-Kennedy (1883-1929) appear to have had few exemplars among New Testament scholars.

We need to be careful in assessing that doctrine of history which Dodd uses to interpret Jesus's parables and, in the first instance, his sayings about the Kingdom. The first thing to note is, however, that it is, precisely, in terms of a doctrine of history that Dodd interprets Jesus's sayings. This is, of course, in stark contrast to the interpretation offered by Bultmann in his *Jesus* with its emphasis on the Word as it impinges on the human self-consciousness. For Dodd, the eternal has entered the sphere of human history with Jesus and his ministry and this, once and for all, radically changes the course of that history. Not that such a coming has automatic or inevitable consequences. On the contrary, such coming requires a response from those who encounter Jesus, and that response is expressed not only in the sphere of human inwardness, but also on the plane of human history. 'But Jesus declares that this ultimate, the Kingdom of God, has come into history, and He takes upon Himself the "eschatological" role of "Son of Man". The absolute, the "wholly other", has entered into time and space'. The eternal is not subsumed in the movement of history ('The historical order, however, cannot contain the whole meaning of the absolute'), but it may be perceived as an active principle within history, bringing God's purposes to fulfilment ('judgement and blessedness have come into human experience', 107f). Thus in the end (and this, perhaps, comes out most clearly in his much later *The Founder of Christianity*), Dodd does see Christian culture as the outworking, albeit through many vicissitudes, of the Christian Gospel which has its roots in the life and ministry of Jesus.

This resurgence of liberal Christian views of history in England after the First World War reflects the markedly different political climate in England in the last decades of its colonial supremacy. It is also clearly, if more subtly, expressed in Dodd's earlier *The Meaning of Paul for To-day* (1920). As we noticed in our discussion in chapter three, Dodd's reading of Paul is essentially evolutionary. Christ's coming represents the major step forward in the quest for the divine Commonwealth, which God will bring about through his chosen instrument, the church. Dodd is ready enough to acknowledge the historical failings of the church but also sees clearly the missionary implications of such a view. Christianity is superior to Judaism (Dodd's portrayal of which is surprisingly shrill). When Christianity is faithful to its missionary task 'it is an indication of the true method of building the brotherhood of man in which the Kingdom of God may find expression'. Where it enters 'into an unnatural alliance with national ascendancies and all the superstitions of Empire, it stultifies itself' (48). For all its moderation, such a view still asserts the cultural superiority of Christianity and the need for the transformation, at least, of other forms of religion. What it does not do is to tackle the radical critique of all religion that was offered by Barth, or to engage seriously with a prophetic view of religion that sees all forms of human religiosity as constantly in need of criticism from a transcendental source.

Thus there is in this period a parting of the ways between English and German New Testament study that was to be further aggravated by the forced separation of the coming War years. Of course, such separation was not total. Hoskyns (1884-1937), in Cambridge, translated Barth's *Epistle to the Romans* and encouraged his students to visit Germany. In his *Cambridge Sermons* he showed himself more sympathetic to the rediscovery of eschatology than his other Cambridge colleagues.[2] But the roots of the division were deep and ran down into very different perceptions of reality, shaped by very different political and cultural experiences.

Perhaps this last observation provides confirmation, at least, of Barth's contention that theological interpretation should be a dialogue with the text about its central subject matter. On such a view it is clear that the dialogue will be conducted in very different terms by those who have widely divergent perspectives on that subject matter.

Notes

1. 'While formally the new and original element in the teaching of Jesus is that the Kingdom of God, long expected, has come, there is an even more profound originality in the new content given to the idea through His revelation of God Himself' *Parables*, (79). Dodd refers in a note to R. Otto (*Kingdom of God*): 'All his works and words . . . are directly or indirectly inspired by the idea of a divine power breaking in, to *save*. This has its immediate correlate in the 'new' God whom He brings, the God who does not consume sinners, but *seeks* sinners; the Father-God, who has now once again *drawn near* out of His transcendence, who asks for the child-mind and childlike trust'(83).
2. See his remark: 'The Lady Margaret Professor of Divinity (Bethune-Baker) recently defined the immediate task of Christian theology to be the re-expression of Christian faith in terms of evolution. I would venture to suggest that the task of the Christian theologian is rather to preserve the Christian doctrine of God from the corrupting influence of the dogma of evolution, at least as that doctrine is popularly understood' (34f).

List of works cited

K. Barth, *The Epistle to the Romans*, Bern, 1919, 1921 German); Oxford, 1933 (English)

R. Bultmann, *The History of the Synoptic Tradition*, Göttingen, 1921 (German); Oxford, 1963 (English)

R. Bultmann, Review of Barth's *The Epistle to the Romans*, in *Anfänge der dialektischen Theologie*, ed. J. Moltmann, Munich, 1966, 119-42 (English in ed. R. Johnson, *Rudolf Bultmann. Interpreting the Faith for the Modern Era*, London, 1987, 54-65)

R. Bultmann, *Jesus and the Word*, Berlin, 1926 (German); London, 1934 (English)

R. Bultmann, *Jesus Christ and Mythology*, London, 1960

M. Dibelius, *From Tradition to Gospel*, Tübingen, 1919, 2nd ed, Tübingen, 1933 (German); London, 1934 (English)

C.H. Dodd, *The Parables of the Kingdom*, London, 1935

C.H. Dodd, *The Founder of Christianity*, London, 1970

M. Heidegger, *Being and Time*, Tübingen, 1927 (German); London, 1962 (English)

R. Morgan with J. Barton, *Biblical Interpretation*, Oxford, 1988

R. Otto, *The Kingdom of God and the Son of Man*, Munich, 1934 (German); London, 1938 (German)

K.L. Schmidt, *Der Rahmen der Geschichte Jesu*, Berlin, 1919.

K.L. Schmidt, 'Die Stellung der Evangelien in der allgemeinen Literaturgeschichte', *Eucharisterion*, Göttingen, 1923

5

The Development of an Existential Interpretation of the Bible: Paul and John

We saw in the last chapter how Barth directed a fierce attack against all attempts to ground Christian faith in the sphere of the observable, the historical, the outward world of sense and appearance. The object of faith was essentially transcendent, wholly other; God's Word was something that could only be believed and not known. Even faith itself was not to be equated with anything that occurred within the sphere of human self-consciousness, but was the unobservable act by which the believer appropriated the transcendent gift of divine justice/justification, an act that itself could only be believed.

Bultmann was clearly deeply influenced by Barth's *Romans*, but from the start he raised questions about the intelligibility of such a faith. If we could neither observe nor register the consequences of faith in our human self-consciousness, then in what sense could we be said to believe at all? His *Jesus* was an attempt to give an account of the way the free, transcendent Word of God does, indeed, impinge on the individual, as it — again and again, in a quite specific personal sense — challenges and calls them out. This challenge and call can be spoken of only indirectly, almost, as it were, improperly. To generalise about it is in itself to stand back, to distance oneself from the specific, particular encounter which alone is the point at which we may in the act of faith apprehend the reality of God as it overpowers us and reorientates our lives.

Such a call can occur only in the words and sentences of a given time. It speaks directly to a person, offering her the possibility of a new existence that is there to be accepted in faith. Those who respond can speak of their new self-understanding again only in the language of their time, and such attempts at reflection on their new 'believing self-understanding' are the only evidence that we have of its existence.

This three-fold distinction between the *challenge and call* (the kerygma), as opening up to the individual possibilities of self-understanding not otherwise available, *belief* as the concrete act of realising such possibilities, and *theological thoughts* as the development of 'faith's understanding of

God, the world, and man' (II, 237) provides the basic conceptual structure for Bultmann's major work of New Testament interpretation, his *Theology of the New Testament* (1952-55). What marks out this undertaking from his book on Jesus is, foremost, the conviction that the kerygma is mediated to us, not by our reconstructions of the preaching of the historical Jesus, but by the expressions of it that we encounter in the central documents of the New Testament: the Pauline and the Johannine literature.

In his *Theology* Bultmann gives an account of the 'theological thoughts of the New Testament', tracing them in their variety as they are presented in the different books. He does not, that is, attempt to systematise them, but rather to show the variety of expressions of the 'believing self-understanding' of its writers and communities. In giving such an account, his aim is not to present the theological doctrines of the New Testament as propositions that are the object of faith, but to show them as different ways, more or less adequate, of giving expression to the self-understanding of the early Church. Indeed, the task of giving expression to that understanding of God is a perennial one which 'permits only ever-repeated solutions, or attempts at solution, each in its particular historical situation' (*ibid.*).

It is, therefore, an exercise that is both historical and theological, and in Bultmann's hands the historical stands in the service of the theological interpretation. It is historical in that the reading of such culturally specific texts requires the interpreter to locate them in their particular linguistic and cultural context; that is to see them in their relation to the history of the emerging Christian church with its different attempts at explication of its 'believing self-understanding'. It is theological in so far as it seeks to show their meaning for the present. This, for Bultmann, is a two-fold task. It involves a critical assessment of what is being said by the authors, seeking to understand them better than they understand themselves (what Bultmann calls *Sachkritik*, 'content-criticism', II, 238). It also involves an attempt to translate the substance of what is being expressed into an idiom that can be appropriated by modern readers. Hence the importance for Bultmann of showing such expressions as explications of a 'believing self-understanding' which is also a possibility of self-understanding for people today.

Bultmann's reading of Paul has been enormously influential. It was developed through a series of highly original articles and then set out systematically in his *Theology of the New Testament*. His central concern is to shift attention away from the christological and, indeed, soteriological doctrines that can at least be inferred from certain passages in Paul, and to concentrate attention on the understanding of human existence which breathes through Paul's pages. This can be seen clearly in his treatment in the *Theology of the New Testament* where the overall structure of his treatment is given by the two main headings, 'Man Prior to the Revelation of Faith' and 'Man under Faith'.

It is important to understand what it is that is being proposed here. It might seem, as indeed it did to some of Bultmann's own followers, that he was abandoning any attempt to produce a New Testament theology and instead attempting to read the New Testament as a document of our common humanity, as an expression of humanity's search for fulfilment and authenticity. This is to misunderstand both what Bultmann is opposing and what he is proposing.

Bultmann denies that Paul is the kind of theologian who views God and Christ, the world and humanity, from a distance and attempts to fit them all into a coherent system of knowledge. In this respect his views are significantly at variance with those of Oscar Cullmann (b.1902) and Krister Stendahl (b.1921), which we shall discuss in chapter ten. This is not to deny that Paul is a theologian in any sense. The fact that many of Paul's utterances are occasional and fragmentary does not mean that he was merely a devout and pious man, but without theological grounding. His response to the pressing questions with which he has to deal is grounded in a fundamentally theological position that is made explicit in a fairly complete manner in the Epistle to the Romans.

But what kind of theology? In Bultmann's view, what Paul does is solely to lift 'the knowledge inherent in faith itself into the clarity of conscious knowing' (I, 190). The act of believing is always at the same time an act of apprehending; but what kind of apprehending? What is grasped is not some kind of speculative knowledge about God in his nature as such, but rather God is known only as he is significant for people, for their life and salvation. In the same way, Paul talks about the world and humanity only in their relation to God. 'Every assertion about God is simultaneously an assertion about man and *vice-versa*. For this reason and *in this sense* [my emphasis] Paul's theology is, at the same time, anthropology' (I, 191). It follows from this that when Paul speaks about God's relation with humanity and the world he does so historically, out of the experience of God's dealings with his people; as it follows that his christology is concerned not with theoretical questions of the relationship of Christ's natures, but with the Christ 'through whom God is working for the salvation of the world and man'. In this sense then 'Paul's christology is simultaneously soteriology' (*ibid.*); not, of course, soteriology in an abstract sense, but always as the explication of that fundamental apprehension of human existence under God that is given in faith.

The sheer achievement of Bultmann's account of Paul's theology in his *Theology of the New Testament* can hardly be overstated. His first task is to show how Paul has forged a language in which to express an understanding of human existence that is open to its restlessness and creativity, its possibilities and failure. To be human is not to possess some predetermined essence; it is rather to be faced with responsibility and choice, with the possibility of finding oneself and losing oneself. In the flow of existence, people may come to themselves, may find freedom and authentic, owned existence; they may also lose themselves. We may speak about the nature of human existence in two ways: formally, 'ontologically', referring to the structures of human being which as it were sustain the flow of human existence; and specifically, 'ontically', as individuals confess their own particular experience of existence, their own 'self-understanding'.

Thus Bultmann introduces his account of Paul's theology with a discussion of Paul's anthropological terms which argues that Paul does, indeed, have an understanding of human existence in which a person is seen as striving for fulfilment, for life, but as doing so in a way which demands that she must come to terms with herself. The human person, that is to say, is conceived of by Paul as fundamentally in relation to herself; but this relationship may lead either to bondage or to freedom and life.

Bultmann's work here deserves and, it has to be said, requires close reading. The task is formidable. It means following Paul's use of particular terms -- *soma* (body), *psyche* (soul), *pneuma* (spirit), *zoe* (life), *nous* (mind), *syneidesis* (conscience) and *kardia* (heart) -- through his letters, and attempting to detect a dominant anthropological sense. A closer look at what Bultmann says about *soma* (I, 192ff) may shed light on the difficulties and the remarkable nature of his achievement.

It is clear, says Bultmann, that for Paul the term *soma* refers to something constitutive of human being; Paul cannot conceive of human existence, even after death, without a body of some kind — unlike some of his opponents in Corinth (1 Cor. 15:35ff). Precisely at this point a problem arises, for here Paul talks about the body and its various manifestations as if it were a form that could be imprinted on different kinds of matter — fleshly and spiritual. That such use is not typical of Paul can be seen from other passages, such as Romans 6:12: 'Do not let sin reign in your mortal bodies' or Romans 12:1: 'Present your bodies therefore a living, holy sacrifice, acceptable to the Lord'. For here *soma* refers to the whole person, though admittedly in a particular respect. Thus from the start it is clear that any interpretation of Paul's usage will have to be a discriminating one (*Sachkritik*), discerning those senses that are, as it were, most characteristic of him, relegating usages that were, perhaps, prompted by the context and polemical situation in which he found himself.

There is, further, need to set Paul's usage of *soma* against the wider contemporary use of the term, which was by no means uniform. Clearly the most common usage of the term in Hellenistic Greek is to refer to the physical body, and this is frequently contrasted with the soul or the spirit. Such use can be found in 1 Thessalonians 5:23; 1 Corinthians 5:3 and 7:34; and is widespread in Paul. But there are a number of occurrences where it is clear that the body is not something that, as it were, adheres to the human 'I'. Rather it belongs essentially to it, in such a way that 'we can say man does not *have a soma*; he is *soma*' (194). This is clear enough from Romans 12:1 and is well illustrated by Romans 6:12ff, where not presenting one's members (used as equivalent to 'body' in the immediately preceding verse) is paralleled to presenting 'yourselves' to God.

The question therefore arises, if *soma* can refer to the whole person, in what respect? Bultmann's answer is as follows: '[A person] *is called soma in respect to his being able to make himself the object of his own action or to experience himself as the subject to whom something happens.* He can be called *soma*, that is, as having a relationship to himself' (195f; Bultmann's italics).

This is a crucial notion for Bultmann, for it refers to the inner dialogue within a person that is one of the proper characteristics of what it is to be human. As human beings we can, as it were, stand back from ourselves, act upon ourselves, but also experience ourselves as being acted upon by forces beyond our control. There is, in other words, an existential dialectic, which makes it possible for people both to be at one with themselves, and also to be at odds, to be alienated from themselves. There is the possibility of being in control of oneself and there is the possibility of losing control and experiencing oneself as being under some alien power. Moreover such an alien power may be experienced as malevolent, alienating a person from herself; or as beneficent, bringing the person who is alienated from herself back to herself (196). Even this account, which is no more than a paraphrase of what Bultmann writes in this section, is obviously metaphorical, and it makes use of the language of cosmic myth and dualism, as it draws, again metaphorically, on the language of materialist social analysis — alienation. One of the central questions for any such account of human existence is, precisely, what are or is the referent or referents of such metaphorical terms, as they are employed to characterise the human condition. Are the powers that possess men and women in their alienated state the powers of economic and social interest groups, which oppress and divide people from the fruits of their labours; are they spiritual forces that possess their minds and bodies; or is the alienation an ultimately self-determined alienation, resultant on the failure to seize the opportunity of life when it presented itself? These are questions as much for Bultmann as for Paul; but precisely because he so closely identifies himself with Paul's self-understanding it is often, in what follows, difficult to disentangle what is Bultmann and what is Paul. In this respect, as in many others, Bultmann has drunk deep at Karl Barth's well.

Nevertheless it is important to attempt to distinguish Bultmann's and Paul's positions and the different role that the language of cosmic dualism plays in their writing. Where Bultmann is concerned, there is little question but that he is wishing to use the language of such dualism metaphorically. For him the alien powers that possess people are indeed the function of their refusal to submit to the Word of God, or alternatively of their never having encountered such a challenge that could have released them from their divided state. Whether such an account can do justice even to his existentially interpreted Pauline understanding of the self is then the question. In his following of Paul, is he not committed to a view of the universality of sin which it is hard to reconcile with the emphasis which he himself wishes to place on human choice and responsibility?[1]

For Paul, by contrast, the matter is quite different. He is, even in Bultmann's view, perfectly capable of a quite literal use of the language of cosmic dualism, of dark powers that possess the creation and human beings (Rom. 8:18ff, 38f; 1 Cor. 10:20; 11:30). On the other hand, as we have seen, there is also a strong case to be made for seeing his language as expressive of a dialectical understanding of human existence. Is Bultmann then justified in seeing Paul's use of cosmological language (at least in significant passages) as substantially modified from its literal contemporary sense (which would be to say that Paul himself is already engaged in the process of demythologising such language)? Or is Bultmann's interpretation itself a creative reworking of the Pauline Epistles?

Such questions are most properly addressed to what Bultmann refers to as Paul's 'ontic' statements about humanity, that is statements about the actual state of human existence. Here the main centre of attention lies in Paul's statements about sin. Even the terms which Paul uses, as it were neutrally, to describe the formal structures of being, often shade over into a more specific sense. *Soma* can be spoken of as a body of sin (Rom. 6:6). *Nous* can refer to the, albeit, vain search for the good (Rom. 7:23). Desiring, *epithymein*, can take the negative sense of evil desires. In all this, according to Bultmann, we can see that for Paul, '*Man has always already missed the existence that at heart he seeks (sein eigentliches Sein)*'(I, 227).

The key term around which turn the questions of men and women's 'fallenness', their sense of alienation from themselves, is *sarx* ('flesh'). Again, as with *soma*, this can have a fairly straightforward, neutral sense, referring to transitory existence in the body (Rom. 3:20). It is the sphere that we can observe, which comes into and goes out of existence, but which is not, of itself, necessarily perverted. But in Paul's usage, when 'flesh' qualifies certain verbs — such as walking 'according to the flesh' — then it takes on, as a rule, an altogether more negative sense (237). For here a person's whole orientation has been distorted, he no longer sets his heart on God, but attempts to find life in the sphere of that which is 'merely human, the earthly-transitory' (238) over which he believes he can exercise control.

Consideration of what Bultmann says about Romans 7[2] may help to clarify his interpretation here. In Romans 7:15 Paul states, 'I do not understand my own actions. For I do not do what I want, but I do the very thing that I hate'. This has often been taken to mean that I am prevented from doing what I want to do by lower, baser instincts, 'the flesh'. But this suggests that for Paul the will operates on a conscious level (E&F, 177), whereas:

> according to Paul's view, human existence transcends the sphere of consciousness. This is clearly expressed when he holds that man wills and acts under the domination either of 'flesh' or of 'Spirit'. . . . From the standpoint of a subjectivistic anthropology, these 'powers' under which a man stands can only be understood as mythological entities or else interpreted in the sense of a naturalistic dualism. I hope that the

interpretation of Romans 7 will show that these *'powers' in truth designate the possibilities of historical existence (ibid.*; my italics).

The problem for Paul is not that those who set out to obey the Law actually fail to do so. The term 'parabasis' (transgression) does not occur. The point is rather the fundamental dividedness of those under the Law: that what people will is indeed life, but that what they achieve (*katergazesthai*, v. 15) is death. 'Everything that is done is from the beginning directed against its own real intention.' (E&F, 183). The fundamental desire of the *nous* to do the good, to achieve life (v.23) is frustrated, is not achieved because man himself is fundamentally misdirected, as man seeks to control his own existence:

> to raise claims for himself, to be like God. Inasmuch then, as this 'sin' brings 'death', it becomes evident (1) that the man who wants to be himself loses himself; instead of the 'I', 'sin', becomes the subject (vs. 9); and (2) that being a self nevertheless belongs to man, for in losing himself he dies (vss. 9f.); but also that his self is not realised when he himself tries to lay hold of it by disposing of his own existence, but only when he surrenders himself to the claim of God and exists for him. This would be 'life' for him; then he would exist in his *authenticity*. (*E&F*, 184).

Instead of submitting themselves in obedience to God, men and women — and here Paul refers generally to their situation before or outside faith — falsely imagine that they can achieve life of their own efforts, and in this lies their guilt and sin.

All this, of course, has to be understood against the background of Paul's understanding of God and creation. As we have seen, Paul does not speak of God abstractly, but, rather, always in relation to men and women as his creatures. God is the creator, who is the source of light and truth for his creatures. The root of sin is the 'turning away from the Creator, the giver of life, and a turning toward the creation — and to do that is to trust in one's self as being able to procure life by the use of the earthly and through one's own strength and accomplishment' (see Rom. 8:7; *TNT*,I, 239). Conversely, it is only in relation to God, in obedience and service to him, that men and women can truly find themselves and can therefore live undivided lives and find true freedom.

Yet the fact is, for Paul, that it is because men and women *always* fall short of such obedience, that they have not found such freedom. The claim here is a universal one: 'For as in Adam all die, so also in Christ shall all be made alive'(1 Cor. 15:22); 'For as by one man's disobedience many were made sinners, so by one man's obedience many will be made righteous' (Rom. 5:19). Here Bultmann recognises clearly enough the mightily mythological character of Paul's language: 'through Adam, sin and death came into the world as dominant powers' (TNT, I, 227). In what sense, for Paul, do all sin in Adam? Is it some inherited condition, something passed on from one generation to another? Bultmann proposes (TNT, I, 252) that we need to grasp Paul's meaning from consideration of the second halves of the verses. What is certain for Paul is that the righteousness which Christ brings is not automatic, not something that is independent of men and women's choice or decision. It has to be appropriated in an act of faith. In the same way each and every person has to make their own choice, choose to 'fall' like Adam, to deny themselves by seeking to be like gods, to deny their being as creatures of God who find their life in obedience to him.

> Because man is a self who is concerned with his authenticity and can find it (as that of a creature) only when he surrenders himself to the claim of God, there is the possibility of sin. Because from the beginning the claim of God has to do with man's authentic existence, there is the possibility of misunderstanding: the man who is called to authenticity falsely wills to be himself (*E&F*, 185).

There is, as subsequent commentators have pointed out, an apparent tension between Bultmann's claim that Paul always speaks historically of God and the way that Paul's statements here are apparently dehistoricized, taken to refer to a universal human dilemma that is repeated in each and every person. Yet the tension, for Bultmann at least, is apparent rather than real. The drama that repeats itself is indeed '*geschichtlich*' ('historic'), in the sense that it determines the manner of existence of all people, determines their relationship to their God and to themselves. What Paul has done, according to Bultmann, is to give a concrete, 'existential' interpretation of the myth. It now no longer refers to some event whose effects on men and women are wholly beyond their control but to a universal condition that, nevertheless, is conditional upon the existential decision of each one.

What then can rescue people from this 'body of death'? Men and women are divided from themselves: that with which they should be united is itself a source of death and guilt. Their willing is perverted and brings death, even though it is imagined to be itself pleasing to God. Certainly salvation cannot come from traditions and culture, which can all too easily become the sphere over which we imagine we have control and responsibility. Only a word that cuts across the historical continuum, which both judges and redeems, can bring respite. It alone can restore men and women to their proper relationship to their creator. Such a word reveals both the *orge* (wrath) and the *dikaiosune* (righteousness/justification) of God. Where is such a word to be found? What is its ground and its content?

It is a word that is revealed, which is preached by the apostles, and whose authority and power lies in its ability to transform and free from the slavery of sin. In it the salvation-occurrence, which puts an end to the old aeon, is present. 'It is, by nature, personal address that accosts each individual, throwing the person himself into question by rendering his self-understanding problematic, and demanding a decision of him' (*TNT*, I, 307). It is a word of the Cross that means not a doctrine of atonement, nor some account of God's dealings with the world and its guilt, but rather a word that cuts across all human ideas of how salvation is to be achieved, judging even the highest ideals of Jew and Christian and proposing instead a strange righteousness which is a gift (*charis*).

Above all, then, the Word proclaims the gift of God's righteousness by which God brings men and women into relationship with himself, freeing them from their sins and their guilt. Bultmann insists that, for Paul, *dikaiosune* is essentially a forensic term. It refers to men and women's relation to God, their standing in his sight. What is grace and life to Paul is that such right standing before God is now revealed to men and women to be not something that they can achieve for themselves *ex ergon nomou* (on the basis of works of the Law) but which can only come *ek theou* ('from God'; Phil. 3:9):

> As 'their own' or 'my own' means the righteousness which man exerts himself to achieve by fulfilling the 'works of the Law,' so 'God's righteousness' means the righteousness from God that is conferred upon him as a gift by God's free grace alone' (*TNT*, I, 285).

Such righteousness, moreover, by contrast with Judaism, is proclaimed by Paul as a present gift, not something to be awaited in the future.

What this means is that men and women are now released from their bondage to the 'flesh', to their vain attempts to find life and fulfilment through their own efforts, and are instead freed to live a life of obedience in the Spirit. The fundamental act of faith — the acceptance of God's judgement and the gift, the *charis* of his righteousness — transforms men and women's life so that now they are freed to fulfil the law of Christ, to live out of the Spirit, producing fruits of love, patience and long suffering.

This brings out the particular character of Paul's ethics which Bultmann had pointed to in a famous essay of 1924, 'The Problem of Ethics in Paul'. In that essay Bultmann examines the apparent contradiction often pointed out by scholars contained in sentences of Paul that *both* speak of a person's sinlessness, (namely, his being justified), *and* exhort him to lead a life of righteousness (Rom. 6:1-7:6; 8:1-17; Gal. 5:13-25; 1 Cor. 6:9-11). Is this a contradiction, to be explained in terms of the historical and psychological circumstances in which Paul wrote, or is it a genuine antinomy pointing to an underlying reality that can perhaps only be so understood?

Bultmann is critical of historical and psychological explanations. On such views, the fundamental sense of *dikaiotheis* is that woman is indeed justified, that the eschatological time of salvation has already arrived and that she has been given the grace to share in it. In that sense she is taken out of this world, and injunctions not to sin, to lead a life in accordance with the law, stem more from the present circumstances of Paul's letters than from his theology proper.

What, according to Bultmann, is right about such accounts is the emphasis on the eschatological nature of justification, its total character, bringing the justified into contact with the transcendent God. What is overlooked is the sense in which for Paul both indicative and imperative are closely — not accidentally — associated: *ei zomen pneumati, pneumati kai stoichomen*

('If we live in the Spirit, let us also walk by the Spirit' Gal. 5:25). Moreover, such interpretations are based on an idealist understanding of righteousness or sinlessness: that it is a condition of the human will, the embracing of a principle of good. In contrast, in Bultmann's view, for Paul it is principally something negative: freedom from the power of sin. The justified person, for Paul, is a miracle, an eschatological phenomenon, not a person about to develop his highest moral abilities.

If Paul's statements do not rest on a contradiction, what gives the antinomy its underlying sense? Paul's language, says Bultmann, owes not a little to the world of Hellenistic mysticism. But whereas in Hellenistic mysticism there is a divorce between the sphere of the flesh and the transcendent, such that the 'real' person, the particle of light imprisoned in the tomb of the body, is taken up into the eternal sphere where it finds light, in Paul, justification is an event whereby God embraces the individual, particular sinner and declares him forgiven or just. It is a particular act that embraces the whole person, not simply some eternal particle of light or some reborn, undifferentiated part of the person that now represents the true reality.

Justification is an eternal transcendent act that is appropriated in and by faith and the acceptance of God's eschatological verdict, which declares a person just, not simply by setting aside past sins (so that he or she must now from hence-forward strive not to sin again), but by declaring the sinner justified. Only so does the sinner know his sin, as he experiences the grace of God; and in faith, which is the acceptance of such grace, he commits himself in obedience to God. Justification, then, is not something observable: it is transcendent, eternal; it is an act of a God who saves, of a gracious God who embraces the individual sinner. For Paul 'the notion of transcendence is determined by its relationship to the individual, concrete person' (*Das Problem*, 135). Such 'justification' is none the less transcendent: it is there before it is believed (see Bultmann's review of Barth's *The Epistle to the Romans*). Additionally it can only be believed: it is not some act of the person, some change in his ethical quality, some mystical experience. It can only be believed in an act of 'obedience to God's saving deed which renounces any claim to be able of oneself to establish a relationship to God' (*ibid.*).

In what sense then does such justification make a difference? Is the behaviour of the justified noticeably different; does he or she have a different understanding of the Law? Not, according to Bultmann, in principle. The one who accepts God's justification gives himself totally to God. As such he does indeed obey the Law, but nothing is demanded which would not be demanded of another: 'The moral demand has not gained *any new content* and his moral behaviour is distinguished from that of others only in that it bears the character of obedience' (*Das Problem*, 138). Such obedience and the imperative that expresses it are now not something imposed on the believer which she has to fulfil in order to remain within the sphere of grace; rather they are themselves part of the gift — the mode of being that is conferred on the sinner by God's eschatological act of justification.

Thus Bultmann's Pauline interpretation returns full circle to his discussion of Barth's *The Epistle to the Romans*. It presents Paul as a theologian reflecting on the apprehension of God contained in the central act of faith, which is the appropriation of God's act of justification. In his reflection, Paul relates this to his general understanding of human existence, of men and women's striving for fulfilment and life, of the tragedy of human alienation and self-division. Only in the acknowledgement of the grace of God in Christ, of that alien power that frees and which offers life to those who renounce all attempts to achieve their 'own' justification, can there be reconciliation, a recovery of self. Here the dark powers that hold men and women in bondage are forsaken precisely as the 'inner man', the *nous*, is freed from its preoccupation with self-justification and is thus able to live out of its God-given relationship to its creator. This 'indicative', this given, is not static: It is life, a life of obedience and freedom which issues in the presenting of oneself fully and wholly to the Lord: 'then walk in the Spirit'.

It is interesting to consider the relation of this interpretation to the interpretations we documented in chapter three. Bultmann clearly acknowledges his debt to Baur's interpretation of Paul (not least in his article on the history of Pauline research, 'Zur Geschichte der Paulus-Forschung'). For him, Baur is the theologian who saw above all that 'underlying Paul's theological concepts, which are to be interpreted, there is a particular view of human existence (*Sein des Menschen*, 32). Baur's interpretation is 'quite simply exemplary' in its continuing search for this underlying understanding and in its determination to see the details in Paul's thought in its light. Such a search, for Bultmann, can be undertaken only at the same time as one explores 'the question of one's own understanding of existence' (*ibid.*). Where Bultmann parts company with Baur is in the understanding of existence that he attributes to Paul. Baur saw human self-consciousness, at its highest ('insofar as it is spiritual', 30), as 'identical' with the Spirit of God itself. For Bultmann, men and women find themselves in obedience to the call of a transcendent God. Such obedience, in contrast to Barth's view, does, indeed, make a difference to a person's actual (ontic) self-understanding, but its essence lies in the sense of the qualitative difference between the believer and God. Yet, importantly, to stress the qualitative difference between the believer and the creator God is not to deny his grace or to erect insuperable barriers between the two. The difference is manifested precisely in the grace of God that is the source of life for the believer.

Such a reading of Paul's understanding of existence clearly sets a sharp divide between Bultmann and Baur, not only with regard to the question of identity, but also, consequentially, with regard to the understanding of universal history. Baur's stress on the unity of the human and the divine spirit is related to a doctrine of universal history according to which the cultural and religious history of the world is itself a manifestation of the divine Spirit. Bultmann, by contrast, sees the relationship between the believer and the divine Word almost as punctiliar, something that occurs 'again and again' as the divine Word speaks and challenges. Hence, whereas Baur can see the discussion of salvation history in Romans 9-11 as crucial to an understanding of the epistle, for Bultmann, the key to Paul's message in Romans is to be found in the understanding of human existence that is forged in Romans 5-8. Baur, like Dodd, is able to take up the cosmological and historical elements in Paul's writing; Bultmann seeks to excise such elements by giving them an 'existential interpretation'.

In this sense Bultmann is the prophet of a radical Lutheranism that locates faith in the realm of the 'pro me', God's gracious empowering of the individual sinner. Such an interpretation of course sets him at a distance from the work of scholars like Heitmüller who had emphasised Paul's closeness to the popular religiosity of the time. Bultmann's debt to the History of Religions School is, however, not inconsiderable. In the first place he accepts their criticisms of Baur. Paul's understanding of spirit cannot be adequately rendered in terms of idealist doctrines of the identification of the finite and infinite spirit. For Paul the spirit is the divine power that overwhelms and transforms the believers. But whereas Heitmüller and others saw such manifestations of divine power as having their prime seat in the cultic life of the community, for Bultmann Paul, by contrast, locates the operation of the Spirit within the relationship of Word and faith between God and the believer. In this, of course, he is following a lead given by Bousset when he contrasted Paul's creative spirituality with the cultic piety of the Hellenistic church. For Bultmann Paul is not simply a creative genius who attains greater spiritual insight through the excercise of the free spirit; Paul's theology is the faithful expression of the new 'self-understanding' that is brought by the gospel in its transcendent power. Paul's 'greatness', that is to say, lies not in his originality, but in his obedience, his faithful reflection of the gift of the gospel in his tireless struggle to find adequate theological forms of expression for it. Whether Bultmann's uneasy relation with the History of Religions School is something that can be sustained is something we shall discuss in chapter seven.

If Bultmann's treatment of Paul uncovers the complexities of Paul's understanding of existence in a quite remarkable way, then his reading of the Fourth Gospel is a *tour de force* of exegetical ingenuity in finding a reading of the text that is congenial to his own emphasis on Word and Faith. For it is not obvious that John's Gospel, with its clear emphasis on the contemplation of God's glory in the incarnate Christ can easily be read as supporting a view of faith as an obediential response to a non-objectifiable transcendent Word. In order to argue this case Bultmann has to use all his skills as literary critic and historian of religion. He has to distinguish different layers of meaning within the text, just as he has to develop a complex theory of its disruption and subsequent reconstruction by a later editor. In so doing, in straining every sinew of his exegetical force and perception, he set the agenda for subsequent Johannine studies, even though few have followed him in the main lines of his interpretation. *The Gospel of John* (1941) remains, for all that, the greatest single work of New Testament exegesis of the century.

Bultmann's primary weapon in turning the Fourth Gospel into a work of remarkably Pauline theology is the complex literary analysis to which he subjects it. The Gospel, as we know it, he argues, is no longer in its original form. Chapter 21 is clearly an appendix: there is already a perfectly good conclusion to the Gospel in 20:30, on which, indeed, the concluding verse of chapter 21 is modelled. But there is other evidence. The section in 3:31f, as it stands, refers to Jesus and John the Baptist, but the contrast between the one from above and the one from the earth, who speaks of the earth, applies unhappily to the Baptist, and the whole section would fit in better to the discourse with Nicodemus earlier in the chapter. The present order of chapters 5 and 6 causes unnecessary complications in Jesus's itinerary, and chapter 6 itself is jerky and disjointed. Moreover it contains one section (6:51b-58) whose eucharistic theology seems, to Bultmann at least, wholly out of keeping with the rest of the chapter, indeed of the work.

There are other problems: 8:12 seems to introduce an extended discourse on the light, and such a discourse can be reconstructed only with great ingenuity. The farewell discourses interrupt the narrative of the disciples' progress with Jesus from the Last Supper to the Garden. Other shorter passages have a marked sacramental or future eschatological emphasis that can easily be seen as insertions into the original text (3:5; 19:37; 5:28f; 6:39, 40, 44). On this basis — and the seriousness with which subsequent commentators have taken all these points is witness to the acuteness of his observations — Bultmann offers both a detailed reconstruction of the original text and an analysis of the redactor's own contributions. The latter, which therefore do not constitute part of the Evangelist's theology, consist mainly in the introduction of sacramental theology and a future eschatology by contrast with the essentially realised eschatology of the Evangelist.

Even when the original form of the Gospel is thus reconstructed, the question still has to be put: what was its literary history? What sources did the Fourth Evangelist use? How did he use and edit them? We can only list Bultmann's views at this point. He believed that the Fourth Gospel was not in any way dependent on the Synoptics; and in this he is still followed by a majority of scholars. Bultmann did, however, believe that the Fourth Evangelist had a narrative source for his miracle stories (the *semeia*-source), just as he had a Passion narrative source that was substantially different from the Synoptic account(s). Again this view, with variations, has enjoyed distinguished support. Where however Bultmann is most controversial is in his views of the discourse material. The problems caused by this material are substantial. It is extremely difficult to find close, formal parallels to it, as subsequent discussions continue to show. Bultmann believed that John had used a set of 'revelation discourses' which bore formal resemblance to the discourses in the Mandaean writings then recently published by a Göttingen scholar, Lidzbarski. Admittedly, the Ginza which he published could not be traced back earlier than the sixth century AD, though the Mandaeans, a Syrian Gnostic sect, had connections with the Baptist and may well have substantially predated the Ginza.

This was not all. Bultmann further proposed that John had used a revelation discourse source, which was Gnostic in content as well as form, and had then revised it and edited it to serve his own theological purposes. This proposal, as we shall see, is crucial to his general interpretative strategy.

Bultmann's approach consists in distinguishing between the sense of the source itself and the sense that it has when taken up and edited by the Evangelist. Thus where the narrative material is concerned, he argues that there is a substantial difference between the sense of the miracle stories in the source and the sense given to them by John. The miracle stories as they stand stress the miraculous element in the action, and see the miracles themselves as productive of belief. Thus in the healing of the official's son (a variant of the Synoptic healing of the centurion's servant), the healing is set at a distance and the story focuses on the miraculous display of power by Jesus, rather than on the centurion's prior faith. But in the story as it stands in the Fourth Gospel, Jesus specifically distances himself from such belief based on miracles. In a remark that is oddly addressed to the worried father, he complains: 'Except you see signs and wonders will you never believe' (4.48). Moreover, Bultmann argues, the stories are given a symbolic, rather then literal or historical, sense, as, for example, the stories of the marriage at Cana and the cleansing of the Temple, which form an opening diptych symbolising the fullness of revelation and the judgement which Jesus brings.

Significantly for Bultmann this means that the Evangelist does not in any way attempt to link faith to the observable occurrences that are the stuff of narrative. Such stories for him serve only to point beyond themselves to the transcendent reality of the incarnate Word, which certainly enters into the world of the historical and the observable, but in such a way that it becomes perfectly hidden: 'the Revealer is nothing but a man' (*GJ*, 62).

Bultmann's postulation of a Gnostic revelation-discourse source owes a lot to the work of the History of Religions School and their positing of a widespread Gnostic myth of a Redeemed redeemer. Such a myth could be seen in its fullest form in later works like the Ginza, but it was reflected in many other works of Hellenism and, in the views of such scholars, substantially pre-dated the schemes of Gnostic heretics of the second century like Valentinus and Basilides.

In substance the reconstructed myth told of a pre-cosmic fall where the sons of light fell from heaven and were imprisoned in the world that they created. This world was surrounded by spheres and powers that kept the sons of light entrapped. Salvation comes only when the Redeemer himself descends into the earthly sphere, reveals himself to the sons of light, who in turn recognise him, and he imparts to them the knowledge (gnosis) by which they can find their way out of their worldly prison. He himself precedes them and they follow to the heavenly home that he has prepared for them, escaping the powers of darkness and entering into the sphere of light where they enjoy eternal life.

It is not difficult to recognise elements of such a story in the Fourth Gospel. Jesus is the one who descends to this earth to bear witness to what he has seen in heaven (3:12); he knows his sheep and they recognise his voice (10:3f); he is the light (8:12), the way, the truth and the life (14.6) and he goes before them to prepare a heavenly place (14:2).

Yet there are other elements that are not present: there is no speculation about a pre-cosmic fall, only the confrontation of Nicodemus with the impossible possibility of being born anew (3:5-8). Jesus claims that he will bear witness to what he has seen and heard in heaven, but apart from the reference to the many mansions in chapter 14, there is nothing comparable to apocalyptic visions of heaven, or the speculations of the Hermetic literature. Indeed, in Bultmann's view, if one asks what it is that the revealer reveals, what he imparts, the answer is only that he is the revealer.

Why, if the myth is thus stripped of its cosmological and speculative elements, does the Evangelist make use of such 'a source'? What is the knowledge given, what the significance of the strongly dualist language of light and darkness that forms such a striking part of the Evangelist's vocabulary?

A closer look at the Nicodemus discourse in chapter 3 may help to elucidate Bultmann's views. Bultmann sees the chapter as a free composition of the Evangelist's, as it were, on the text of his source, using also a saying from the tradition such as Matthew 18:3. In the source (as opposed to the Evangelist's version as we now have it) the discourse referred to the fact that only those who were born from above (*anothen*) could have eternal life; for only they possessed the metaphysical qualifications to make the ascent out of this world to the heavenly habitation to which the revealer had come to bear witness. However in the Evangelist's version, as Nicodemus's question, with its clear misunderstanding (a favourite device of the Evangelist) makes clear, the point is made differently: those who want to enter the Kingdom must be born anew (taking another, equally possible, sense of anothen), must receive a new origin; must move from being 'of the flesh' to being 'of the Spirit'. Nicodemus's misunderstanding ('how can one enter again his mother's womb') makes the point dramatically: the man 'of the flesh' can only conceive of renewal in fleshly terms, cannot even grasp the meaning of new life when it is made. Only a radically new birth 'in the Spirit' can release him from his bondage.

In the human sphere it is impossible for there to be anything like rebirth. For rebirth means — and this is precisely the point made by Nicodemus's misunderstanding — something more than an improvement in man; it means that man receives a new origin, and this is manifestly something that he cannot give himself (136f).

What is retained here of the myth is then not its cosmological explanation of the human predicament, but its sense of human bondage, of the need for salvation which lies beyond its own potentialities, of the need to pass into a new mode of existence in order to find true life. It is, in brief, the theological anthropological sense that attracts the Evangelist, not its speculative explication.

Again, the myth points to the coming of a divine, heavenly figure who will bring knowledge and bear witness to that which is above, revealing both 'earthly' and 'heavenly' mysteries (v.12), truths about the origins of the cosmos in a pre-existent fall and about the nature of the heavens and the way of salvation. But, as we have seen, such revelation is not given. Instead, the notion of witness is focused on the revealer's claim to be the 'one whom the Father has sent': 'for the word of God which he speaks is nothing more nor less than the witness *that* he is the Revealer, *that* he speaks God's word!' (160f). John points to the transcendence of the Word which Jesus brings, but does not attempt in any way to 'objectify it' or at least to develop the speculative aspects of the myth. He uses the myth solely

> to bring out the nature of the word of revelation as a word which 1) comes from outside man's sphere to confront man, which cannot be checked and which cannot be arrived at on the basis of man's observation and reasoning, and 2) which is an authoritative word binding its hearer to obedience (145).

What is essential about the revealer is that he calls those he encounters to come to him, to believe, and it is on this decision that life and death, light and darkness depend. That is to say, the dualism of the Fourth Gospel is not a cosmological dualism where the world is divided into darkness and light on the basis of its relationship to some cosmic power of good or evil: the ultimate divide depends on the *decision* made by each individual as he or she is encountered by the Word of God in the Son inviting them to enter into the reality of the divine life, to 'dwell in him'. It is a dualism of decision.

What, then, finally is it for the Fourth Evangelist to declare that 'the Word became flesh and we beheld his glory'; what kind of divine reality and what kind of vision is it?

For Bultmann, verse 14 of the Prologue introduces a new and solemn note into the hymn. The entry of the Word into the sphere of flesh, of the transitory, means that it becomes hidden, incognito. The Word cannot appear, cannot manifest itself in the sphere of the transitory, and the assertion that it becomes flesh means effectively that 'the Revealer is nothing but a man' (62). Yet those who encounter and believe the Word confess that they have seen the glory of the Word. Again, this is not some contemplation of the divine glory manifest in the flesh. Such vision which, in Bultmann's view, is in no way aesthetic, is an apprehension of the revealer as he really is for us. For the revealer is what he is in virtue of what he is *for us*. 'The *doxa* (glory) (of the Revealer) consists in what he is as *Revealer* for men, and he possesses the *doxa really* . . . when that which he himself is has been *actualised* in the believer' (68f). It is as we know him, as the one who gives us a new understanding of our existence, that he is the revealer for us and that we know him as he is. The vision of the glory results 'in the upturning of all man's natural aims in life' (*ibid.*). Such a vision can only be experienced in the immediacy of the encounter with the Word; it cannot be given objectifiable content.

Bultmann's *John*, viewed as a work of exegesis, is both wilful and illuminating. It offers a view of the Gospel that plays down striking (not to be denied?) narrative and mythological elements in the work and brings out the emphasis, which is also clearly present, on belief in the words of Jesus as being critical for life and death. Those who accept have already passed through judgement; those who refuse remain in their sins. The references to the dead rising from the graves at the last day are by the redactor; the eschatology of the Fourth Evangelist is wholly realised.

It is in this emphasis on the realised eschatology of the Fourth Gospel that Bultmann's own understanding of religion, of faith and history is most deeply seen. In a strange way it is here in his interpretation of John, for all its — real or apparent — wilfulness, that there is the clearest consonance between his own theological stance and his reading of his text. The believer's encounter with the transcendent Word is that which transforms his existence. The Johannine Christian understanding of God is of a God who is free and transcendent, not to be caught or embraced in the realm of the transitory — and yet one who enters this realm and transforms the existence of those who have turned in on themselves and have sought life in the sphere of the transitory, of that over which they believe they can have control. But, according to Bultmann, for John it is only in radical openness to the transcendence of God — in acceptance of the revealer's claim to reveal the fullness of life — that men and women can break out of their entrapment in the sphere of the transitory and become themselves free, friends of the son.

This transformation of the believer's self-understanding is truly historical; an event not just in the sphere of the observable and transitory, but one that transforms the human self-understanding and is the source of meaning and life. Of course, such a use of the word 'historical' is puzzling to English-speaking readers. Bultmann distinguishes '*Historie*', the sphere of the observable ruled by an iron law of causality, from '*Geschichte*', the realm of human decision-making and creativity, self-understanding. Bultmann brings this distinction to bear against those, like Pfleiderer and Hausrath, who had seen the task of New Testament study as being to show the causal connections between the beliefs of the early Christian writers and communities and other contemporary religious movements and ideas. True belief is not simply a product of intellectual and cultural forces in a given environment. It is rather something that stems from an encounter with transcendent reality, which then enables the believer to take a critical stance against the cultural forces of his day. For Bultmann such an encounter occurred as believers were confronted with the Word of God in the preaching of the Gospel, in the kerygma. In obedience to the Gospel believers would find freedom from the constraints of inherited culture, as they found their own values and goals turned upside down. In this sense they were bearers of new meaning.

It is striking, of course, that in this account of human transformation Bultmann abandons the language of aesthetics that pervades the Fourth Gospel. It is, at least on a straightforward reading, in beholding the glory of the incarnate Logos that the believers receive life, grace and truth (John 1:14; 17:2). Bultmann attempts to show the Evangelist as ridding the Gnostic myth of all its cosmological elements — which is to say all those elements that might be contemplated by the believer — and simply taking over those elements that speak of the human predicament. For him the realm of the aesthetic is to be sharply contrasted with the sphere of human inwardness which is the true locus of our encounter with the transcendent. The road to proper self-understanding lies through an 'existential dialectic' that exposes the contradictions and paradoxes of our human striving for fulfilment. Read like this the Fourth Gospel is a work that dismantles myth. But is it not just as plausible, indeed in the light of the history of its subsequent readings, far more plausible, to see it as one of the great works of Christian mythopoiesis? Here the elements of a radically new myth are being forged which were to be the inspiration for Christian piety, art and literature for the next two millennia.

Bultmann's study the New Testament presents a remarkably rounded theological interpretation of the corpus. He reads it, that is, against an explicit understanding of what religion — belief in God — is. That understanding, as we have seen, is greatly indebted to Barth's emphasis on the transcendence and freedom of God, but equally importantly stems from the rejection of the philosophies of history and culture that had informed German theological liberalism. Instead, Bultmann seeks the source of human meaning not in the sphere of inherited culture, but in that of human inwardness, the particular individual meaning that only an individual can discover through the exercise of a particular and deliberate choice or decision. That such a view of religion distinguishes it from the realm of the corporate, of the social, should be clear; and that in this sense it represents a withdrawal from the sphere of the cultural and political should also be clear. Bultmann was, indeed, active in the struggles of the confessing church, but such engagement came from his own judgement about the situation, rather than from any specific theological implication of his religious belief. What his belief did was to free him to obey the will of God which, in turn, could be perceived clearly enough in the light of reason and the natural law.

Such a view of the relation between religion and politics owes doubtless not a little to important strains in the Enlightenment: the rejection of an improper religious interference in the sphere of politics and the fear of a religious ethic that overrides the clear dictates of natural reason. But it fails to do justice to or to take adequate account of the way in which religious belief, precisely because it involves the whole person with all her network of social relations, does have deep social and political implications, cannot be understood without reference to these, and is constantly on the way to various forms of social embodiment. The era through which Bultmann lived made such thoughts difficult to sustain, but in the period after the war they were to become increasingly pressing both in Europe and in the States.

Notes

1. This is, of course, not to disregard the way in which those in the tradition of Immanuel Kant, for all the emphasis that they wished to place on the human will and its role in human decision-making, nevertheless also saw the need to recognise 'radical evil' in human nature. See I. Kant, *Religion within the Limits of Reason Alone*, Book 1.

2. See, as well as his treatment in Theology of the New Testament 212, 259-69, 'Romans 7 and the Anthropology of Paul', in R. Bultmann, *Existence and Faith*, 1964, 173-185.

List of works cited

R. Bultmann, 'Das Problem der Ethik bei Paulus', *ZNW*, 23, 1923, 123-40

R. Bultmann, 'Zur Geschichte der Paulus-Forschung', *Theologische Rundschau*, NF 1, 1929, 26-59

R. Bultmann, *The Gospel of John*, Göttingen, 1941 (German); Oxford, 1971 (English)

R. Bultmann, *Theology of the New Testament*, Tübingen, 1948ff (German); London, 1952-5 (English)

R. Bultmann, 'Romans 7 and the Anthropology of Paul', in R. Bultmann, *Existence and Faith*, London, 1964, 173-85

I. Kant, *Religion within the Limits of Reason Alone*, New York, 1960

6

New Studies of Jesus

Bultmann's legacy to students of the life and teaching of Jesus was, as has been rather too infrequently noticed, more than a little ambiguous. On the one hand he insisted that historical knowledge of Jesus was of no value whatever for faith, which must stem from the encounter with the living word of the Gospel. On the other, as we have already seen, he had himself written a book on Jesus, which had shown him as a remarkably kerygmatic figure, addressing matters of existential concern as real to us as to his own hearers.

Bultmann's insistence that historical knowledge of Jesus is of no value for faith needs clarification if we are to understand the quite intense debates that were conducted among his pupils in the 1950s. Bultmann distinguished between two sorts of historical knowledge: objective ('objectifying') knowledge of the facts of history ('*Historie*') and the appropriation and interpretation of such facts in such a way that they inform the self-understanding of the historian ('*Geschichte*'). He also claimed, and it is important to see this as a separate claim, that saving knowledge of Jesus, the knowledge that liberates and opens up the possibility of a truly authentic existence, is derived from the church's proclamation of Jesus as Lord. That is to say, the church's proclamation is being given a privileged status. It is that mode of appropriation and interpretation of the 'facts' of Jesus's life and death that alone brings authentic self-understanding. This spiritual, life-giving understanding of Jesus as Lord is the only true understanding; all others are 'fleshly', natural understandings (2 Cor. 5:16). The justification for such a claim is that it is through such proclamation that God chooses to act, to address men and women and call them to that radical decision which can bring life. Only when God so acts, do men and women in fact have the possibility of gaining authentic existence. By their own efforts they can achieve nothing.

This position combines a broadly existentialist understanding of history with a Lutheran epistemology that asserts that true knowledge of God, through which we know him as judge and redeemer, comes not by our own efforts but by the grace of God himself. Such knowledge is not 'objective' knowledge of God as First Cause, or of his acts in history; it is personal, life-giving knowledge of God as the one who judges men and women's vain attempts to find security and life for themselves, and at the same time makes them the gracious gift of that life as he calls them to obedience and freedom.

We shall return to this discussion when we come to consider questions of New Testament theology. It also forms a necessary part of the background to the debates in the 1950s about the 'new quest for the historical Jesus'. Scholars like E. Käsemann, G. Bornkamm (b.1905), E. Fuchs (1903-83) and H. Conzelmann (b.1915) had no wish to relinquish the claim that it was only in the divine 'address' of the kerygma that we could come to authentic knowledge of God and so find true existence. They sought to establish a place within such saving knowledge of God for the kind of historical enquiry that New Testament study had been pursuing for some two hundred years into the life and teaching of Jesus.

One work must stand for all. In the opening chapter of his *Jesus of Nazareth* (1956), G. Bornkamm attempts to justify historical study of Jesus by reference to the New Testament witness to Jesus. The Gospels 'bring before our eyes, in very different fashion from what is customary in chronicles and presentations of history, the *historical person* of Jesus with the utmost vividness' (24; my italics). The Gospels are concerned with the historical reality of Jesus; even if the community has handled the tradition of stories and sayings freely, behind the tradition lies a sense of the power and authority of the one from whom they stem and whom the community confesses as Lord. Thus from the start Bornkamm's field of vision is specified by the horizon of the New Testament texts themselves. What he seeks to draw out from them is, as it were, the historical controls that guide and inform the tradition. Such historical controls are not purely objective facts: they spring from the community's apprehension of the meaning and significance for them of the man Jesus of Nazareth, that is to say of his authority and power over their lives. This authority — and here the New Testament witness is to be distinguished from the myth — is not grounded in some ahistorical story, but in the experienced reality of Jesus himself, something, indeed, which can only be confessed and proclaimed by those who have so experienced it.

Thus Bornkamm's task is to search for the roots of such experience of Jesus in the life and sayings of Jesus himself. It is at this point that there is obvious continuity with earlier work on the history of the Synoptic tradition and with the wider historical enquiries into the life of Jesus. Bornkamm has, indeed, to acknowledge the very real difficulties that exist in discerning those elements of the tradition that are original to Jesus or which provide essentially accurate reports of incidents in his life. What he appeals to is the distinctiveness of Jesus's deeds and utterances, which in turn, of course, is perceived by the community as that which is authoritative about Jesus himself. In his call to simple obedience, which is contrasted with the legalism of Pharisaic interpretations of the Law ('you have heard it said, but I say unto you'), Jesus enables people to perceive the Will of God and to respond freely to it. He:

points the disciples, with the greatest emphasis, to God — the God who will come and is already present and active. . . . Yet it is equally clear that Jesus is present in the sayings in no other way than in his words, completely one with his words (108).

In this sense Bornkamm can speak about the 'christology' of the Sermon on the Mount.

Käsemann's contribution to the new quest, which he can in many ways claim to have initiated, runs along similar lines to Bornkamm's. What Käsemann offered in a lecture 'The Problem of the Historical Jesus' (1953) was a more determined attempt to formulate procedures for distinguishing authentic sayings of Jesus, arguing that as a minimum one needed to search for those sayings that were significantly unlike sayings that one would otherwise have expected to hear from the lips of a first-century Jew; and also significantly unlike those which might have stemmed from the earliest Christian communities with their particular cultural milieux and interests. He pointed to the saying in Mark 7:15 as an example which would have been virtually unthinkable from a first-century Jew and which, indeed, proved difficult for many early Jewish Christians to accept. Such a saying, moreover, with its total rejection of the distinction between the sacred and the profane, was radically innovative in the first century and points to the distinctive authority of Jesus over his world.

Interestingly, while Bornkamm, like Bultmann, emphasises Jesus's call to obedience and connects this with a certain kind of authority that Jesus himself has, he is not specifically interested in the content of the teaching, or his role as a teacher. What is significant for Bornkamm is the radical call to obedience itself, not Jesus's specific interpretation of the Law. Jesus points men and women to the boundless mercy of God, rejecting human notions of divine rewards for works of the Law (143).

Significantly, Bornkamm and the other scholars in this group added very little that was new to the understanding of the Jewish world which Jesus inhabited; nor were they able to draw very much on innovative work in that field by other scholars. To a large extent they were indebted to views of Judaism that saw it through Lutheran-Pauline eyes. Judaism was — unduly — concerned with works-righteousness, with earning salvation in the sight of God through performance of works of the Law, many of which were concerned only with outward ceremonial and ritual observance. This lack of interest in exploring the nature of contemporary Judaism may have had its source in an existentialist lack of concern with ethical principles and values (there is, for instance, no serious discussion of the *content* of Jesus's command to love one's enemies, which might seem to relate interestingly to contemporary Jewish teaching on love of neighbour). It may also derive from the desire to set Jesus apart from his contemporaries and to see his most characteristic (and, to be fair, historically most ascertainable) features in that which was most untypically Jewish about him. Either way it is a sad comment on this period of intense theological activity that ultimately the picture of Jesus that is presented hangs in the air and has little historical reality, precisely because it is so divorced from its specific cultural and social context.

There were exceptions. Joachim Jeremias, notably in his work on the parables, *The Parables of Jesus* (1947), continued and developed the methods of interpretation that had been pioneered by Jülicher and Dodd. What distinguished Jeremias's work was his great knowledge of and love for contemporary Jewish sources, together with his assiduous attention to the detailed interpretation of the stories themselves. There is in Jeremias's work a strange mixture of historical and scholarly enquiry into first-century Judaism and Jesus's place within it, and a strong apologetic which derives from his own firmly held, Pietistic convictions. The result, as E.P. Sanders (b.1927) has recently argued, is often to distort; but there is still much to be derived from this remarkable scholar.

It was, however, with the publication of M. Hengel's (b.1924) *Judaism and Hellenism* (1968) and his *The Charismatic Leader and his Followers* (1968) that a more thorough-going historical approach to Jesus was achieved. Hengel's work on the interrelation of Judaism and Hellenism was, at least as far as New Testament scholars were concerned, a major breakthrough. It broke with the simplified notion that there was a straightforward geographical distinction between Judaism which was located in Palestine and Hellenism (and Hellenistic Judaism) which was located outside it. Palestine had for centuries been influenced and infiltrated by Hellenistic culture, and in a work of impressive scholarship Hengel set out to document this in relation to Jewish literature and culture. It may seem strange to include a work which in fact deals only with the period up to the turn of the era in a chapter about study of Jesus. But the work which Hengel undertook in this study, together with his study of *The Zealots* (1966), had the effect of providing a more sharply focused view of the Jewish context in which Jesus lived than had previously been available — a necessary condition of more serious study of Jesus himself.

Just how beneficial such preparatory studies could be was shown by Hengel's own inaugural lecture, *The Charismatic Leader*. Sanders has described this as 'a masterpiece, possibly the best single treatment of a synoptic pericope ever done' (*Jesus and Judaism*, 133). Like Bornkamm, Hengel sets out to explore the nature of Jesus's authority, his call to people to follow him and the nature of that relationship. He takes a single pericope of Matthew, 8:21f and subjects it to rigorous scrutiny with all the means available to the New Testament historian, 'redaction and form-criticism, plus Religionsgeschichte' (*CL* 3). By means of redaction and form-criticism he is able to establish with some confidence the original form of the pericope in Q: 'Another said: let me first go and bury my father; but he said to him: follow me and leave the dead to bury their dead' (4).

Hengel argues for the authenticity of the logion on the grounds of its dissimilarity from the tradition either of the Jewish or the later community. Such a deliberate flouting of the deepest ethical perceptions of the community is, indeed, remarkable. Burying one's parents was held to be the highest of the works of love incumbent upon Jews and to dispense even from the obligations of Torah. Jesus's saying is not entirely without parallels within Judaism or indeed Hellenism: the high priests might be dispensed from their obligations, the prophets might be commanded neither to rejoice nor to mourn as a sign of God's coming judgement. Charges were made against Socrates that he was educating his pupils to 'condemn their ancestors and relations' (12). The background to such a saying, however, can best be sought in the apocalyptic idea of the destruction of the family and its ties in the end-time. The question is why Jesus linked such a radical break with family ties with following him. Thus Hengel is led to:

> suppose that this relentless hardness on Jesus's part as to the unconditional nature of following him can no longer primarily be understood from the standpoint of Jesus's activity as a 'teacher', but is to be explained only on the basis of his unique authority as the proclaimer of the *imminent Kingdom of God*. In the light of its urgent proximity, there was no more time to be lost and so he had to be followed without procrastination and to the abandonment of all human considerations and ties. The phenomenon must therefore be investigated no longer only in relation to the teacher-pupil relationship on the lines of the rabbinical parallels but above all from an *eschatological* angle and - must we not say? - in the light of the *messianic authority of Jesus* (15).

Hengel's work exploring Jesus's contemporary cultural context did not stand alone. In England Geza Vermes (b.1924) was conducting important studies of contemporary Jewish language and thought which bore its first fruit in the reopening of the question of the meaning of the phrase 'son of man'. He also published a lively book *Jesus the Jew* (1973) exploring the parallels between Jesus and the Jewish 'men of deed': charismatic figures, men of healing and prayer, like the first-century Hanina ben Dosa. This has been followed by two further studies, *Jesus and the World of Judaism* (1983) and *The Religion of Jesus the Jew* (1993).

Vermes's work on the Son of Man is, of course, only an example of the way that developments in historical studies of first-century Judaism by both Jewish and Christian scholars have continued through the period of the 1960s, 1970s and 1980s to illuminate the life and teaching of Jesus, and of other areas of the New Testament as well. Vermes himself, together with M. Black (b.1908) and F. Millar (b.1935), has been responsible for the new edition of E. Schürer's (1844-1910) *The History of the Jewish People*, which is a mine of information about the history, settlement (a quite fascinating survey of the history of the cities of Palestine), beliefs and literature of the Judaism of the time. S. Safrai and M. Stern have been engaged since 1974 in bringing out the *Compendium Rerum Iudaicarum ad Novum Testamentum* which covers a wide range of historical, theological and literary topics, with particularly interesting material on the agriculture, economy and political and religious institutions of first-century Judaism. In the United States J. Neusner (b.1932) has published extensively on the Rabbinic traditions, attempting to devise satisfactory critical procedures for distinguishing the layers of tradition within the Rabbinic corpus. W.D. Davies (b.1914) has devoted a life-time of study to the setting of the New Testament within Judaism, and some of this has been forcefully driven home by his pupil E.P. Sanders. There has also been important archaeological work done by Israeli and American teams which is beginning to cast more light on the history of the time; and there has been the gradual publication of the Dead Sea Scrolls, which has provided scholars with a whole library of contemporary Jewish texts.

One other factor must be taken into account before we proceed to review more recent work on Jesus and the particular issues it raises. The dominant models of explanation underlying studies of Jesus in the earlier part of the twentieth century were theological and anthropological: that is to say, interpreters were concerned to discover what Jesus's theological beliefs were and how they related to his understanding of human existence. The work of scholars like Vermes, Millar, Black, Safrai and Stern now provided a wealth of information about the social, political and economic conditions of the time. What was needed was a model of explanation to enable scholars to relate this background to the religious beliefs and actions of figures like Jesus who were not obviously or overtly political, or at least not in any way that we would presently recognise as such.

In this respect the work of G. Theissen (b.1944) in Germany acted as a great catalyst. In a series of essays and in his book *The First Followers of Jesus* (1977) Theissen attempted to outline 'the aims and methods of a sociology of the Jesus movement' (1) This, of course, was not the same as trying to give an account of the particular teaching and practice of Jesus himself. Theissen's aim was to 'describe typical social attitudes and behaviour within the Jesus movement and to analyse its interaction with Jewish society in Palestine generally' (*ibid.*). Specifically he tried to analyse the various roles that were adopted by different people within the Jesus movement, for these are indicative of typical patterns of behaviour within the movement. Early Christianity, he believed, was propagated by wandering charismatics, in turn supported by more sedentary groups in towns and villages. The pattern of a rootless existence also has its analogies in the surrounding society, both in the mendicants and in the freedom fighters, Josephus's 'fourth philosophy'. Analysis of such roles and discussion of similar patterns of behaviour in the surrounding society enables one to understand more about how the behaviour of a particular group fits into its general social context. The more analogies, 'the more widespread a pattern of behaviour was in Palestinian Jewish society, the more we may assume that it was socially conditioned' (3).

Talk of social conditioning also raises the question of the relationship between social factors and particular patterns of behaviour. Theissen speaks of economic, ecological, political and cultural factors and regards them all as being able to influence typical patterns of behaviour within a particular society. He is at some pains to insist that he is not looking for a social 'first cause', one kind of social factor that outweighs all others and is the 'real' cause of all else (as in some kinds of materialist analysis); rather he aims to show a consonance between various constellations of social factors and certain patterns of behaviour within that group. This does not mean that all behaviour within a particular society is determined in a strict sense by such social factors; only, but importantly, that certain patterns of behaviour become more likely. Nor does this mean, evidently, that individual courses of action are simply the product of social forces. Nevertheless it is important to establish the existence of such general patterns of behaviour to see how 'individual elements stand out from what is universal and typical'. He quotes Burckhardt: 'On average, generalised facts, like those of cultural history, may prove more important that particular facts; happenings that recur may be more important than those which are unique' (4).

Nor should it be thought that the sole aim of a sociological description of patterns of behaviour within the Christian movement is to show the way in which various social factors have contributed to or constrained them. A sociology of the Jesus movement, for Theissen, seeks to understand the interaction between society and religion, and therefore has to consider the function of religious beliefs and practices within the society as a whole. Religious groups and movements may have many different functions in their society, contributing to the basic aims of a society to integrate its members and to resolve conflict. Thus they may contribute either repressively to social integration, by various forms of internalised social pressure; or more creatively, by contributing to the 'extension and enrichment of human possibilities' (2). In the same way, their contribution to dealing with conflict in society may vary: restrictively, by suggesting illusory forms of compensation to those who are the victims of such conflicts; or creatively, by suggesting new ways of resolving such conflicts.

Theissen's work in the sociology of the New Testament has properly been concerned with the description of patterns of behaviour within the communities whose literary remains it contains. We shall encounter it again when we come to consider recent work in Pauline studies. Its significance for studies of Jesus himself is therefore indirect, lying principally in the ways in which he attempts to construe the patterns of behaviour among Jewish groups of the time. What is most significant here is his thesis that Jewish society of the time showed signs of social anomie, that is of a breakdown in the prevailing social norms of the community. Evidence for this is found in the various forms of social rootlessness in first-century Palestine: emigration, resettlement, brigandage, mendicancy and vagabondage. All this in turn has its counterpart within the Jewish renewal movement: the inner emigration of Qumran, the armed resistance of the Zealots, the various prophetic groups who looked to some act of divine intervention to help resolve Israel's difficulties. What this suggests is: first, that we have to see first-century Palestinian society as undergoing a deep social crisis, stemming from the prolonged erosion of Jewish norms by foreign domination and occupation; and, second, that we need to see the Jewish renewal movement as part of a pattern of social responses to such a situation. This, of course, leaves the way clear for asking how Jesus himself with his own particular vision and activity relates to the Jewish renewal movement of which he was a part.

This is not to say that Theissen has solved all the problems that such a task implies. His work here is addressed principally to patterns of social behaviour and there is much which needs to be done in order to show how all this relates to the ways in which inherited beliefs are reworked or revised in order to reshape or make sense of the dissonance between a people's traditional expectations (arising from their inherited beliefs) and their actual experience. There is, that is to say, a need to provide an account of how high-level theological beliefs relate to ethical prescriptions, to social attitudes and expectations, such that we can discern how changes in theological beliefs occur and interact with changing patterns of behaviour within a particular group. Nevertheless it provided important resources for subsequent discussions of Jesus himself and, together with Hengel's work, contributed to a growing interest in social history which informed a new series of studies of Jesus that began to appear at the end of the 1970s, beginning with Ben Meyer's (b.1927) *The Aims of Jesus*. Some have wished to see this as a 'third quest'; but that suggests more homogeneity about the work than is the case.

Historical study of Jesus, in Meyer's view, has been too much controlled by the wrong sort of aims: either apologetic or polemical — and not enough by purely historical aims — trying to discover who Jesus was. The nature of historical enquiry has been seriously misconstrued, not least by the acceptance of the principle, enunciated by Ernst Troeltsch (1865-1923), that historical judgements are fundamentally analogical judgements.

The principle of analogical reasoning in historiography prescribes that the historian must base his judgements about the trustworthiness of his sources on his or her experience of analogous phenomena in the contemporary world. Too often, as construed by historians engaged in the quest for the historical Jesus, this has meant imposing on Jesus, not merely the idea that he was a man, but also that he was 'a mere man' (18).

Meyer is therefore sharply critical of much that has been offered by those engaged in the quest for the historical Jesus, not least by the great polemicist Reimarus (1694-1768). Nevertheless it was Reimarus who first enunciated the question that forms the title of his own book. The question was, indeed, a good, historical one, designed to set Jesus in relation to the general aims and aspirations of his contemporaries. Reimarus's treatment of it was, however, deeply marred by his own desire to 'strip the figure of Jesus of transcendental meaning' (19).

It is nevertheless with Reimarus's question that Meyer's book is principally concerned. What were Jesus's aims? How did they relate to the shared aims of his countrymen? He asks this question as one designed to subserve his principal aim, which is 'to understand the Jesus of ancient Palestine' (*ibid.*). Figures such as Strauss, Wrede and Bultmann were, he rightly remarks, not deeply interested in this aim. They were too much caught up in their own academic and theological agenda to be seriously interested in the world which Jesus inhabited, except as so 'much "background" as was necessary to make his idea of Jesus intelligible' (*ibid.*).

> But this is not history. Nor is a survey of the teaching of Jesus history
> in the proper sense. Nor is history merely the minute examination of
> gospel data with a view to passing judgments of historicity on them.
> History is reconstruction through hypothesis and verification. Its topic
> is 'aims and consequences', for history involves, first of all, the grasp
> of aims in relation to the dynamics of the time, i.e. the springs of actually
> advancing movements (*ibid.*).

Meyer's fundamental contention is that Jesus, like many of his contemporaries, was concerned with the restoration of Israel. It is this theme that informs and makes intelligible Jesus's preaching of the Kingdom of God. Jesus encountered such hopes principally in the person of John the Baptist and his preaching, and his own baptism by John is an indication of how fully he entered into those hopes: 'Like the Baptist, he understood this restoration not as a divine act exclusively reserved for post-historical realisation (located, that is, on the far side of a still future judgement) but as called for now and already begun!' (128).

Meyer then introduces a distinction between Jesus's public and private ministry and teaching. This distinction is to be found in the Gospels and, so Meyer believes, goes back to Jesus himself. In his proclamation of the Kingdom and in public acts of exorcism, healing and table fellowship, Jesus announced the hoped-for restoration of Israel. This was linked specifically to God's healing of the afflicted and forgiveness of the sinners and outcast. Such public acts symbolised the nature of the restoration, whereby all Israel would be reconciled to God and the nations brought into his reign (Mt. 8:11). In his parables Jesus attempted to persuade the righteous to accept this offer of forgiveness to the sinners, but it remained deeply offensive to Jewish leaders.

Privately Jesus taught his disciples that the hoped-for restoration could only come after a conflict between the people of Israel and God's prophet. He himself must suffer and die, but he would be vindicated on the day of the Son of Man: the smitten shepherd would return to lead the reassembled flock, the new temple would be built.

Meyer's thesis is striking and refreshing. It does indeed try to do serious history, to set Jesus back into the history of Palestine with its hopes and fears. It attempts to put the pieces of the Gospel data into an intelligible form, which makes sense in its contemporary context and which is coherent in itself. In all these ways it is a remarkably creative and helpfully innovative work.

There are, of course, problems. Meyer is critical of attempts like those of Norman Perrin's (1921-1976) to concentrate on isolated pericopae where he can be sure of their authenticity. On the other hand, he himself relies on the coherence of the picture which his hypothesis creates of Jesus's teaching and activity. That is to say, if the Gospel data can be fitted into a coherent picture of Jesus's work, they can be accepted as historical. Of course if such data were part of a coherent yet erroneous picture that the early church had developed of Jesus's life and ministry, they would also satisfy Meyer's test of a good hypothesis. His largely uncritical acceptance of Jesus's teaching given in private to his disciples is a mark of his insensitivity to the concerns of the traditio-historical critics.

At another point, too, Meyer's work needs extension and amplification. His treatment of Jesus's relation to contemporary Jewish aims and aspirations is largely concentrated on Jesus's relation to John. This is clearly a very significant part of that relationship, but it too needs to be seen in the context of a much fuller picture of contemporary Judaism which, at the time Meyer wrote, was only just becoming available through the works of Jewish and Christian scholars. These questions will recur in the discussion of the other works in this phase of the enquiry.

It is a somewhat delicate matter to write about one's own work in the context of a review of others' work. I can only hope that what I say will not be unduly partisan and will contain at least a measure of self-criticism. My *(b.1939) Jesus and the Transformation of Judaism* appeared in 1980. It is interesting, looking back, to see how much the approaches and indeed the questions of Meyer's book and mine overlap, and the same, as we shall see, is true with Anthony Harvey's (b.1930) book. Meyer concentrated firmly on the question of the aims of Jesus and traced that question back to Reimarus. In the same way, my own decision to write a book about Jesus, despite the very contrary conditioning I had received when a student in Germany, came from reading not only Reimarus himself, but the fiercely combative literature that was occasioned by Lessing's publication of sections of Reimarus's text.

In the end, I find Meyer's treatment of Reimarus somewhat unsympathetic and indeed a little unhistorical. It is true that there is a good deal of hatred of conventional religion in Reimarus's attack on traditional accounts of Jesus, but one has to remember that Reimarus was unwilling to publish at all during his lifetime for fear that he would be imprisoned and his family dishonoured. At the same time that hatred is strongly disciplined in much of the work: Reimarus's criticisms of the biblical bases of traditional christology and of eighteenth-century apologetics are founded on a detailed philological enquiry into the biblical texts, which has stood the test of time. While it is true that his own hypothetical reconstruction of the aims and purposes of Jesus and his disciples is inadequate, we need to understand the enormous psychological difficulties confronting someone like Reimarus in making sense of religious figures of the past when his own experience of religion was so negative. Despite all that, he is carried beyond his natural antipathy to ask genuinely historical questions about the details of the texts, for he has a natural curiosity about the strange and the odd which does not fit his or other people's preconceived ideas about the history and he follows it where he can. However, it required a person of broader spirit, the dramatist and critic G.E. Lessing, to glimpse the possibility of a treatment of Jesus that would be able to portray him as one whose deep religious beliefs and instincts were intimately related to, indeed the means of directing and expressing, his and his people's aspirations for peace and freedom, justice and truth. That is to say, Lessing wills to see Jesus as playing a role in the ongoing human quest for freedom, emancipation and enlightenment, which he himself so resourcefully attempted to advance, not least by his publication of Reimarus.

If reading Reimarus and Lessing raised questions about placing Jesus in relation to contemporary Jewish hopes and aspirations, a reading of Schweitzer and Weiss raised other questions about the nature of historical explanation.

The specific problem was this: what sort of explanation can one offer of the growth and development of religious ideas and beliefs? Historians of religion, as we saw, have tended to offer genealogies of beliefs, explaining one set of beliefs 'out of' other prior beliefs held in the world of a particular religious figure: Paul's beliefs were explained in terms of Pharisaic Judaism and Hellenism (Pfleiderer) and Jesus's in terms of contemporary Jewish apocalyptic (Weiss, Schweitzer). The dangers here of a kind of reductionism are great. Religious figures are seen as wholly constrained by the beliefs of their time, even though there is the possibility of some development in their intermingling. In practice, what this has more often than not meant is that in order to explain the meaning of a sentence, say, of Jesus, historians of religion have sought a similar saying in other contemporary literature and attributed to Jesus's sentence the meaning that they believed the other contemporary saying to have. Quite apart from the problems that there may be in accurately identifying the meaning of the 'parallel' saying, there is a further question about the extent to which anyone who wishes to communicate to his contemporaries is constrained by existing patterns of usage, to what extent he may be free to adapt and modify them in order to say new things.

That was one question which was central to my book; another was the question of the relation of high-level theological beliefs to lower-level beliefs about social and political matters, indeed to attitudes and expectations of a quite wide variety. If we are to understand Jesus's aims, we have to understand how the quite specifically religious beliefs that he held related to a broad range of human aspirations and expectations. This will help us to grasp the social and political implications of what he was saying. Moreover, this concern with teasing out the social implications turns out not simply to be a matter of *adding* to our understanding of high level theological statements; it might, indeed, more properly be said that, if we are to understand such statements at all, then we need to know what their social and political implications are. Otherwise they may remain rather vacuous.

In attempting to answer such broad theoretical questions I was extraordinarily fortunate to have the help of a philosopher of language who is also a philosopher of religion, Alan Millar (b.1947) of Stirling University. Millar's views are not easy to summarise and need to be read for themselves. Perhaps one could say in a simplifying way that he suggests that interpreting texts is a matter of discovering in as much detail as possible what is the network of beliefs and expectations which is expressed in the sentences in the text.

The distinction between sentences and the beliefs/propositions that they express is a crucial one: the same proposition may be expressed by two quite different sentences, as, indeed, the same sentence may express two quite different propositions. The interpreter's problem is most fundamentally to move from the sentences to the propositions which they express.

Further, the notion of a network of sentences and beliefs is vital for the understanding of how language works, how it 'carries' meaning. When I utter a particular sentence, others who understand the natural language I am using will immediately link that sentence up with a number of others and with a number of experiences they might expect to have if what I have said is true. If you ask one of my hearers what I meant by saying: 'It's drizzling' he might reply that I meant that it's raining lightly, that if you go outside you would get gently wet but not soaked, and so on. The network of sentences and expectations is the means through which we understand what is meant; and it relates to a similar network or system of beliefs which we understand to be expressed by that set of sentences and experiences. What holds the network of sentences together and makes linguistic communication possible, at least between members of the same natural language group, is the linguistic conventions that govern it. I know, and I know that you know, that if I say 'it's drizzling', then you and others will take it to be linked to a particular set of sentences and experiences.

This very simple account may at least help to explain the answers to the two puzzles that intrigued me in writing *Jesus and the Transformation of Judaism*.

First there is the question of innovation in religious belief. In what sense is it possible to say something new? How far are our beliefs determined by the beliefs we inherit? How far can we ever do more than reshuffle the pack and produce what is only seemingly new?

What I was arguing here was that within any given natural language community the standard conventional senses of sentences do, indeed, constrain our beliefs, do condition the way we make sense of our world. For Jesus to say: 'The Kingdom of God is come upon you' would have been to invoke certain standard beliefs and expectations in his hearers. Such constraints operate in the form of linguistic conventions that are essential if there is to be any communication at all; hence it is imperative that we discover what we can about such conventions as were in force at the time of Jesus. However while such conventions do indeed constrain the way people look at the world and the conceptual apparatus in terms of which only they can begin to make sense of it, their constraining power should not be misunderstood. It is possible to modify existing linguistic usage in such a way that quite new ideas may be expressed. Thus Jesus could modify the contemporary senses of the term 'Kingdom' by altering its conventional associations, deleting some, adding others. If he announced the coming of the Kingdom at the same time as celebrating meals with collaborators and those who flagrantly broke Jewish laws, then he was clearly saying something significantly new about the nature of God's rule, the way he would deal with his enemies and those who flouted his will (87-111).

The point is simply this: conceptual change occurs not by simply flouting the linguistic conventions of a particular society, but by modifying them in a way that has to be sufficiently clearly signalled to be understood. Thus such a view concurs with that of the History of Religions School that new religious ideas are importantly continuous with the inherited beliefs of a community; but it also allows for a greater degree of modification and change by showing how, within such constraints, it is possible for new ideas to be expressed.

The second point concerns the relation between theology and politics in its broadest sense. It is certainly true that in much that has been done in the name of New Testament study, theological beliefs have been treated in almost entire isolation from their social and political implications. Indeed it has perhaps often not been perceived that they have such implications at all. The suggestion that we communicate by evoking a network of sentences and expectations, however, makes the point strongly that such implications are an integral part of the meaning of high-level theological beliefs, and that understanding such implications is therefore also an integral part of understanding the high-level beliefs themselves. Fully to understand what Jesus is saying about the coming of the Kingdom is to understand not only what this means about the nature of the way God will exercise his rule, but also what it means about the way people will be expected to behave, who will exercise power in Israel's affairs, how one should treat enemies of the people, and so on.

What continue to interest me in the book are two things: the examination of the nature of the language of kingship and of the way in which Jesus modified it; and the discussion of the interrelation between the sayings about purity and his teaching about love of enemies.

Interestingly, Norman Perrin, in his book *Jesus and the Language of the Kingdom* (1976) had drawn attention to the richness of the term 'Kingdom of God' in Jewish religious usage. Following the American philosopher P. Wheelwright (b.1901), he had suggested that the term Kingdom of God was in fact a 'tensive symbol' which pointed to a reality so rich that it could only be evoked by a range of ideas and associations. My own attention had been drawn to discussions of religious symbols by Raymond Firth (b.1901) and Mary Douglas (b.1921). There is a rich literature in philosophy and social anthropology which deals with this matter. I was particularly interested in Mary Douglas's analysis of theological language and ritual in *Purity and Danger* (1966) which suggested that it functioned both at a conscious, literal level and on an unconscious, sociological level. Stories which in a literal sense were about gods and men and women, had another level of meaning that related to social attitudes and practices, group discipline and the maintenance of the internal and external boundaries of the group. Language about Kingdom, then, might speak on the one hand literally about God's guidance and rule over Israel, possibly through human kings who were his sons; it might also inculcate into Jews, in an underhand kind of way, a sense of group discipline and loyalty, and a strong sense of corporate identity against other nations and their rulers.

In an earlier version of my book I had, in fact, offered an analysis of Jesus's kingdom language in such terms. What Alan Millar proposed was that one could understand the interrelation of theological and sociological senses better, if one understood how the linguistic conventions prevailing in a particular natural language community worked to communicate a range of sense contents when a particular sentence was uttered, or a ritual enacted. In this way the richness of meaning of a particular term may be explained, in part at least, by the range of conventional associations that are linked with it. If you uttered the Aramaic equivalent of 'the Kingdom of God has come upon you' in first-century Palestine, you would be understood by other Aramaic-speaking Palestinians to accept a whole range of other sentences about the way God had acted, the appropriate responses on the part of his subjects and what one might expect to see and experience: the overthrow and subjection of his enemies, the restoration of Jewish sovereignty, peace and prosperity for his subjects. Thus terms like 'the Kingdom of God' are not so much of a quite different kind from others — 'symbols' as opposed to ones which express clearly defined concepts; they are rather ones which carry in the language a particularly wide range of associations and which therefore have the power to motivate people at a quite deep level.

This might again seem to suggest that Jesus was restricted in what he could say and communicate by such powerful linguistic conventions. Yet, in fact, it opens up the possibility, more so than does Mary Douglas's analysis, of showing how such terms may be modified, some of their key senses changed without their necessarily losing the power to move and inspire. Jesus, in using the term 'Kingdom', was certainly using a term that was strongly associated with Jewish hopes for independence and sovereignty. But it was also associated, at least in some Jewish groups, with notions of power that were defined in terms of military might, the destruction of those who resisted the ruler's will and the reward of those who were faithful. Jesus, I argued, was able to modify the meaning of the term by deleting some of these associations, adding new ones, while still retaining some of its traditional associations that made it such a powerful term for his contemporaries. To announce the Kingdom of God at the same time as sharing meals with tax-collectors and sinners was, I suggested, a striking means of modifying the way in which the term 'Kingdom' had, till then, been used to think about God's rule. God's rule was no longer to be exercised by the destruction of his enemies but by inviting them into the circle of his followers.

The suggestion that religious beliefs form part of a network or interconnected system was also fruitful for dealing with a problem that had not always been fully grasped by biblical exegetes, namely the relation between Jesus's ethical teaching about love of neighbour, love of enemies, and his rejection of the notion and practice of purity.

It was certainly the case that for many scholars, Jesus's ethic had been seen primarily as an ethic of intention, a *Gesinnungsethik*, while the Pharisaic interest in ceremonial and ritual legislation was, by contrast, seen as a rule-based ethic, concerned with 'outward' observance, casuistic and legalistic. In this sense Jesus's rejection of purity laws in Mark 7 was, of course, perfectly intelligible, merely the reverse of his own emphasis on sincerity or 'purity' of intention. But such a reading of Pharisaic purity laws quite fails to explain how it was that such laws became the basis of a Judaism that was able to survive the crisis of the destruction of the Temple in AD 70 and to spawn a whole family of Judaisms that sustained ethical traditions of great standing.

Thus some other explanation of purity rules was required; and that in turn would require a different account of the relation of Jesus's rejection of them to his own positive teaching. Here I can give only a brief account. Mary Douglas argued in *Purity and Danger* that purity rules constitute an important means of framing our lives, of marking out key distinctions in our society. Above all they are concerned with reinforcing the boundaries that we set up between our society or group and the outside world; and with the boundaries that we establish within our group, between one family and another, and among different classes and sorts of people. This is an enormously important insight, though one which Douglas expounds in a not altogether satisfactory way. She sees the relation between theological stories that underwrite purity regulations and the powerful sociological sense of such stories as being unconscious or hidden. The regulations themselves are, she believes, figurative. They prescribe ways of regulating ingress to and egress from the body's orifices. Bodily emissions must be kept in their proper place; the body must not ingest or come into contact with certain foods and substances which are thought to be 'unclean'. In this the body works as an image or figure of the body politic. Just as we need to guard our physical bodies from contact with what is 'impure', so we need to guard the entrances and exits of the body politic against the infiltration of what is alien and dangerous. Purity regulations are an unconscious reminder to the group to be on its guard against danger from without and disorder within.

In fact it seems to me that within the Old Testament tradition there is evidence that at least at certain stages this link between the specific sense of the regulations, for example not eating pork, and its sociological sense, that is not having dealings with that which was alien or anomalous to the group, is perfectly well understood. It is precisely to remind the Jews of the distinction between themselves as the chosen people and the Gentiles who disobey the law and are an abomination to God that such laws have been laid down and that God has distinguished clean from unclean beasts (Lev. 20:22-26; see the discussion in ch.6 of my book). The pursuit of holiness and purity is part of a complex strategy of maintaining the distinctiveness of the group and its mores over against other groups who threatened the Jews and their way of life, more or less. In fact it would be better to say that the pursuit of holiness in this sense spawned a whole host of strategies, from those of the early priestly holiness code, to those of the Pharisees and the Essenes. Part, at least, of what occasioned the variety in such strategies was the variation in the understandings of the nature of the chosen community.

No matter what the variety, the point that unites all such strategies is that they are designed to defend the group from alien influences by erecting strong boundaries around the group. If this is the case then, of course, it becomes relatively simple to see how Jesus's commands to love one's neighbour *and* one's enemy relates to his rejection of purity regulations in Mark 7. They are not rejected because they are legalistic, concerned only with outward observance. They are rejected because they are the basis of a far-reaching religious strategy that can maintain the central emphasis of Jewish tradition only at the cost of erecting tight barriers against all that is alien. What Jesus advocates is a strategy of embracing that which is alien, a missionary strategy which springs from a confidence that one's own moral and religious insights will withstand all the pressures of alien codes.

I have already dwelt too long on my own work; some of its themes will recur in discussion of other recent works. Let me offer, at least, a few words of self-criticism, an indication of what after ten years I would want to do differently. I think it is true to some extent that, like Meyer's work, it came a little early to take account of the work of Sanders and others on Palestinian Judaism. Indeed my own belief still is to some extent that our knowledge of Pharisaism before AD 70 is so shaky that we have to be careful about building too much on it. My own strategy was to look for what was good evidence of contemporary linguistic use, from whatever source, and to derive the meaning of Jesus's sayings from his use and reworking of such linguistic conventions as could be established. Linguistic conventions are probably less liable to change over a period within traditional cultures, than are the actual beliefs that are expressed by their means. So Old Testament texts and texts from Qumran, and reports about the Zealots from Josephus, serve to provide the clues to contemporary linguistic use, whereas what we can tell about Jesus's own specific use of such conventions must in the end be the guide to his own meanings. Some have seen this as concentrating too much on groups who were on the outskirts of Jewish society and ignoring those like the Pharisees and the sages who were more central. I agree that the Pharisees would eventually come to determine the mainstream of Jewish development after AD 70. It would certainly be proper after the wealth of work that has been done recently to take them more into account and to see how their approach to the problems of the time compares with Jesus's. But I would still want to insist that the prime aim of the book was not comparative but interpretive: trying to grasp the distinctive character of Jesus's use of contemporary idiom in order to hear his own specific historical voice, a voice that is distinctively Jewish, but which, like many of his contemporaries', has its own views on the burning issues of the day.

I would like to make one last point. It has sometimes been suggested that the book is rather idealist in its treatment of Jesus, that it does not deal sufficiently closely with the political and sociological aspects of Jesus's life, that it is still too much interested in the theological claims made by Jesus. I would agree that it is interested in theology, indeed, that most energy went into teasing out the sense of sayings that are quite explicitly theological, not least Jesus's Wisdom sayings that I attempted to rehabilitate after their dismissal by Bultmann. But I do not see that as in any sense inimical to the task of understanding the sociological import of Jesus's teaching. Jesus was, after all, an essentially religious figure. His preaching was an attempt to spell out the values for the new age that he anticipated, in some sense indeed to embody them in his whole life. For him, certainly, such values were rooted in the will of God, and were therefore deeply theological. But, also, they were concerned with laying down the basis for the new age that would be brought in, and in that sense they were clearly political, and would have been seen by Jesus, and, indeed, other more perceptive contemporaries, as such.

We must now turn to another work that appeared two years later, Anthony Harvey's *Jesus and the Constraints of History* (1982), which is certainly one of the most elegant and cogently argued of recent works on Jesus. It is also essentially a work of orthodox Christian apologetic. To say that is not in any way to detract from its historical rigour and scholarship. Here, as with Bultmann, there is a remarkable marriage of historical critical acumen and orthodox christological conviction, such that, however, each informs the other. Unlike with Bultmann, the leading christological question is not so much 'What does Christ mean for me?' but, more starkly, 'Who is Christ?'

For this reason, Harvey has to start by countering much of the historical scepticism about Jesus which Bultmann had been happy to encourage. For Bultmann, indeed, it was not ultimately knowledge of the historical Jesus, 'knowing Jesus after the flesh' (2 Cor. 5:16), that could transform people's lives, but rather the encounter with the living word of the Gospel. For Harvey, I conjecture, it is important to fill out the christological claims of the Christian creeds with as much knowledge as can reasonably be garnered from a study of the biblical texts. One may detect here some strains, at least, of *Lux Mundi*.

Harvey's argument starts by giving a rather different assessment of the overall reliability of the Gospel narratives than has often been assumed. Archaeological evidence has shown many of the details of the narrative to reflect closely the practices of the period. There is a verisimilitude about the details of the Gospel stories that should predispose us to trust them. Moreover the general coherence and consistency of the story about Jesus that they tell is itself a further ground for seeing the Gospels as valuable historical sources. Jesus, we may be sure, was a teacher, performed healings that were regarded as miraculous, engaged in controversy with his fellow Jews over the Law of Moses, and was crucified by the Roman authorities.

We need, however, to press on beyond this to some way of countering a more resistant form of scepticism, that about the details of Jesus's teaching and preaching. To this end Harvey proposes not only recourse to a rather flexible version of the dissimilarity test - 'odd is true' - but to a new way of describing Jesus and checking the Gospel records which provides the title of his book. In essence what he proposes is this: precisely because Jesus was a man of his time who lived according to the cultural, social and linguistic conventions of his people, and had to do so in order to communicate at all, he had only certain options open to him in the way he behaved, addressed himself to his people and, in general, attempted to achieve his purposes. Such options do not simply determine behaviour: they can be handled more or less creatively. But they do constrain it, and the fact that they do so is instructive. By considering the various options that a particular historical personage in a particular culture chooses of those available to him, we can begin to build up a profile of him. The general list of facts about Jesus can thus be given 'objective content' and 'we can begin to build up a profile which is independent of Christian sources and which offers some kind of test by which the reliability of these sources can be checked' (7f).

This is an interesting set of proposals, and it is characteristically subtle. It does not offer some guaranteed set of procedures that will assure us of the accuracy of the Gospel picture of Jesus. It suggests, rather, a way of building up a picture of Jesus which draws heavily on the new resources of knowledge of first-century Judaism which have come to us from the Dead Sea Scrolls and study of other contemporary or near-contemporary Jewish literature. These tell us more than we knew before about the ways in which Jews of the first century related to each other, and thus suggest alternative role models which Jesus had at his disposal, but it does not simply impose a set of options on Jesus. It is sufficiently flexible to allow us to perceive where Jesus may have differed from his contemporaries and where he may have modified the contemporary conventions to suit his special needs. As such it does not provide a wholly independent check on the Gospels. The profile which is built up will always have to be drawn up with reference to the Gospel records themselves, and it is here that recourse to the dissimilarity principle, 'odd is true', will have its use. Nevertheless, as we shall see, it is knowledge of the contemporary options which provided the outlines of Harvey's treatment, not the details of the Gospel text. Thus the process of corroboration of the accuracy of Jesus's sayings in the Gospels is complex, and always rather provisional. This is both a strength and a weakness of the approach, as I hope to indicate.

Harvey's first major chapter, 'Political Constraints: The Crucifixion', represents a rather oblique application of his procedure, for here he is concerned with Jesus's crucifixion, specifically with the ways, judicial or otherwise, which were open to his opponents for dealing with him. In a detailed and carefully balanced argument, Harvey suggests that Jesus was handed over to the Romans by the Jewish authorities, more for reasons of political expediency than because he had been worthy of death for any specific religious offence. There is certainly the suggestion that the Jews sought to find religious reasons for condemning Jesus, but the overwhelming impression given is that while Jesus's actions and preaching were such as to raise questions about their legality, those who comprised the Jewish court were also so far divided among themselves that they were not able to reach any verdict. In the end, it would seem (in Harvey's view, taking his lead from Luke), they handed him over to Pilate on the grounds that he had been 'giving himself out as an anointed king' (20:2). All this leaves us with a strong presumption that whatever sort of a figure Jesus was, he was not one that fitted easily into any easily identifiable Jewish category, and that he himself must have made some kind of claim to authority which could have aroused anxieties about him on the part of the authorities and have plausibly led to the charges of royal pretensions levelled against him.

The rest of the book attempts to sharpen this initial impression, and we quickly see how neatly and cumulatively Harvey builds up his case. Here, too, his procedure works more directly. In the chapter on the Law, Harvey considers what options were open to Jesus in relation to the Law. In one sense, precisely because the Law was, in respect of most aspects of Jewish life, simply the law of the land, there were not a lot of options open to people. You either obeyed or you chose to flout it and to take the consequences. Hence a prior question is whether Jesus deliberately broke the Law. Harvey argues that there is little evidence to support the view that he did. The two areas where the Gospels suggest that he might have broken the Law are in respect of the Sabbath and of the food laws. Sabbath laws, such as were later recorded in the Mishnah, were almost certainly in place at the time of Jesus. Charges against him occur principally in connection with healings on the Sabbath, but it is only the Fourth Gospel that records actions of Jesus — making paste and commanding a man to carry his bed — which would clearly infringe the Sabbath regulations. This may well reflect a later division between the church and the synagogue, while the Synoptics may give a more accurate picture, portraying Jesus as arousing hostility on the part of the Pharisees for breaking the spirit of the Sabbath by not healing only when it was strictly necessary. The saying of Jesus recorded at Mark 7:15 which Mark suggests 'declares all foods clean' would, if it were authentic and if Mark gave the correct interpretation, clearly constitute a rejection of substantial parts of the Levitical code and a breach of contemporary Jewish practice which had the force of a deeply entrenched taboo. Harvey's dismissal of this possibility is complete:

> That he should have done such a thing seems highly improbable; there is nothing else in the records about him that comes anywhere near such a forthright repudiation of a central feature of the culture in which he lived, nor is there any hint that when the church had to make a decision on the question whether these food taboos should apply to gentile converts they knew of any clear declaration on the subject by Jesus' (39).

What, then, can we say more positively about Jesus's behaviour in relation to the Law? If he did not deliberately flout it, but observed it, what part did it play in his religious view of things? Here we need to consider the significance of one of the established facts about Jesus, namely that he was a teacher. What kinds of teachers were there in Jesus's day? What options were open to him if he wished to offer instruction in matters of Law and generally of human behaviour? Apart from 'the people of the earth' — those who were satisfied with maintaining a fairly basic minimal observance of the Law — there were three main groups among the Jews of the time who were 'zealous' for the Law. There were sectarians like the Qumran community (which Harvey wishes to distinguish from the Essenes) who cut themselves off from the rest of society in order to develop a system of observance that was quite distinct from that of the rest of the population. There were, at the other extreme, those who sought to express their Jewish faith by involvement in the life of the nation, notably the Sadducees. And there were those, like the Pharisees, who sought to 'pursu[e] a more elaborate pattern of religious observance and piety amid the normal pursuits of daily life' (43).

Jesus fairly obviously does not fit either of the two more radical options, the sectarian or the nationalistic one. His teaching does, however, bear interesting similarities to that of the Pharisees, though fairly evidently he was not one of them. He was both like and unlike them. Like them, he sought to develop a 'way of life in which religion would seem relevant to every activity; like them, he based his teaching on the will of God as revealed in the law; like them, he addressed much of his teaching to a public far wider than his immediate followers' (51). Nevertheless there are significant differences, as is clearly indicated by the stories of controversies between Jesus and the Pharisees, even allowing for the fact that some of these (especially those in Matthew) may have been influenced by subsequent debates between the church and the synagogue. Jesus did not accept the oral tradition by which the Pharisees interpreted the written Law. Did he also reject the written Law? Here the crucial texts are the so-called 'antitheses' in Matthew where Jesus contrasts the traditional teaching with his own: 'You have heard it said . . . but I say unto you'. But here Harvey notes two things: first that this concerns oral not written teaching; and second that while there are indeed references to the written Law they are also, at least in some cases, associated with a further interpretation of those sayings ('and whoever kills shall be subject to judgement'; ' and hate your enemy'). Hence it is reasonable to see these sayings as directed not against the Law itself, but against particular interpretations of the Law (55). Moreover if we consider the actual content of the sayings themselves, there is little in them to suggest that they reject the Law: to urge someone to refrain not only from killing his brother, but from being angry against him is not flouting the Law but making an application of it (*ibid.*).

Nevertheless there are aspects of Jesus's teaching which do not simply fit into the pattern of legal interpretation and which are better seen by analogy with prophetic activity and utterance. When Jesus commands one of his followers to 'Leave the dead to bury their dead', there is a radicalness about the charge which finds its nearest analogy in the story of Elisha's request to Elijah to take leave of his parents (1 Kings 19:20). Jesus's command, which is shocking by any ancient standards of filial piety, is justified because of the urgency of the situation. That is to say, his teaching reflects the particular situation in which he finds himself, as it were on the edge of a new world. 'Jesus, as prophet, could set aside even fundamental duties in view of the urgency of the task' (61). Such prophetic urgency is also reflected in that side of his teaching, notably, for example, in the Sermon on the Mount, which has often been felt to be utopian. This is not simply an interim ethic, something possible to those who see this present age as about to pass wholly away (as Albert Schweitzer argued), but, rather, something that has a perennial ability to tempt us out beyond the 'limit of what is attainable by anyone caught up in the normal responsibilities and complexities of everyday life' (64). In this prophetic side of his teaching Jesus was effectively claiming that, because of the exceptional circumstances of the time, there could be no detailed, systematic interpretation of the Law. 'Thus the follower of Jesus will always be in a special situation; and only a fresh return to the basic commandments will enable him to discover the response that is demanded of him' (65).

I have spent a good deal of time on this section of Harvey's book because it demonstrates clearly the approach that he takes to his subject and raises a number of central questions. The rest of the book is no less compelling, examining Jesus's miracles, his entry into Jerusalem and action in the Temple, and his claims to authority and sonship. Throughout we are presented with an enquiry that presses, as it were, in two directions. On the one hand Harvey is constantly striving to set Jesus in his contemporary world; to see him as one who is bound by cultural, social and linguistic links to his fellows and who only has existence in terms of such conventions. If we are to know him, to know him better through the reading of the Gospels, then we shall have to see him as intimately a part of that web of relationships, a man of his time communicating to others of his time. But to see him in such a web is not to see him as imprisoned or tied. The very links that tie us to our fellows are those that enable us to develop our own personalities, to find our own voice, to say and do what we would do. The constraints enable us to find ourselves, and the task of the historian is therefore to see how the individual uses and, indeed, adapts them in order to attain his purposes. There is, that is to say, a very proper historical concern with the distinctive character of any figure. Of course such a concern with Jesus's distinctiveness may serve an apologetic purpose in directing attention to those aspects of his character which set him apart from all men and women. The question that has to be put to a work such as Harvey's (and, indeed, to my own book) is not whether his historical enquiry is *eo ipso* vitiated because it also subserves apologetic ends, but whether it is sufficiently rigorous historically. There may also be a further question as to whether the picture that emerges is sufficiently close to that which orthodoxy requires.

A number of questions may be raised about the adequacy of Harvey's enquiry. In the first place, the list of facts from which he starts is remarkably restricted and has a certain generality about it that serves, in a way, to isolate the enquiry from the stranger aspects of first-century Jewish life. As we shall shortly see, when we come to consider E.P. Sanders's study of Jesus, the list could have been drawn up very differently, in such a way, indeed, to set Jesus more closely in relation to more radical forms of Jewish eschatological thought. The fact of Jesus's baptism by John is something on which few scholars would wish to cast doubt; as is the fact that he gathered disciples and led an itinerant, mendicant existence. All of this may suggest that he was much closer to a strand of Judaism that saw the end of this world as imminent and was therefore much less concerned with the working out of an understanding of the Law for this present world. As we have seen, Harvey does indeed address himself to this question in the chapter on the Law, and he returns to it importantly in the next chapter on the constraint of an ending, where he suggests that Jesus's belief in some imminent (within, anyway, the next fifty years) end to the present order was, even if mistaken, nevertheless the only way available to him of suggesting the kind of urgency that he wished to convey. It is this element of utopianism in his teaching that is important to Harvey, the sense in which it is constantly teasing his followers to reach out beyond what they perceive as the limits of the possible. So much may well give an illuminating account of the way in which such beliefs do, in fact, function. What Harvey's account does not do is to look more closely at what Jesus may actually have expected: what role he expected himself or his disciples to play in the new age; what would be the place of the Temple and the Temple hierarchy; and what would be the fate of the Gentiles. Such questions may be, indeed, almost impossible to answer, although Harvey's method would at least help to spell out the options that were available to Jesus. But his treatment of Jewish apocalyptic is perhaps the least convincing aspect of his book, concentrating as it does on the literary speculations of works like 2 Esdras and identifying apocalyptic seers more or less exclusively with apocalyptic savants. Further discussion of this will have to wait till we come to discuss Sanders's *Jesus and Judaism*, but it is crucial to the assessment of Harvey's work.

A final point of a rather different kind, which has already been raised in discussion of B. Meyer's book and was also to be raised again by Sanders, is that Harvey's aim is avowedly to build up a profile or portrait of Jesus. As I suggested above, his underlying question is a christological one: who is Christ? But in so far as the attempt to build up a portrait of Jesus on the basis of our knowledge drawn from the Gospels and other contemporary Jewish evidence is an historical one, we might properly ask if this is a sufficient aim for an historian? Nobody can stop historians asking: what sort of a person was he? But if the questioning remains there, is there not a whole range of unanswered questions about his 'aims in relation to the dynamics of the time, i.e. the springs of actually advancing movements' (Meyer, *Aims of Jesus*, 19) clamouring for a hearing? Do we not, that is to say, need to set the pictures that we paint of historical personages back more fully into the history of their age? Do we not need to see the historical constraints that bear on them as themselves the product of an historical process, with its social, economic, political and cultural aspects? Such questions are muted in Harvey's book, and this has the effect of making Jesus strangely indifferent to his time. He may, as it were, have to accept the limitations of the options that are available to him for his purposes; his purposes themselves, however, are timeless, directed towards individuals wherever they may find themselves on the temporal continuum.

It is interesting to see how this carries over into Harvey's own very real concern with contemporary social and political issues. As one of the major architects of the Church of England's important report *Faith in the City*, he was responsible for the chapter on the theological principles behind the report's findings. There, Jesus's preaching and teaching is said to be directed principally to individuals, and it has therefore little specifically to contribute to the wider issues of social justice and ethics. Is this not the point at which the apologetic concern to see Jesus as transcending his time takes its toll?

Social, historical and phenomenological modes of explanation provide the basis for an original treatment of the subject by Marcus Borg (b.1942). His *Conflict, Holiness and Politics in the Teachings of Jesus* was published in 1984, but written without reference to either Harvey's book or mine. Taking his lead from G. Theissen, Borg sees the need to set Jesus's teachings in the context of first-century Judaism's attempts to deal with the conflict between itself and Rome. This is of particular interest in view of the questions raised about the various modes of interpreting Torah which were identified by Harvey. What was the thrust behind such attempts to sustain and renew observance of the Law?

Borg suggests that central to Jewish renewal movements of the first century was 'the quest for holiness'. This provided 'the dominant cultural dynamic of Israel's corporate life' (51), consisting principally in an attempt to imitate God's holiness which put great emphasis on the need for Israel to separate from all that was alien. Different groups interpreted this differently: Qumran withdrew and separated itself from all those who did not follow its path; the Pharisees 'intensified the quest for holiness so as to require a separation *within* society' (57). They:

> sought to counter directly the corrosive effects of Roman political control and Gentile influence. Purity laws required separation from all that was unclean, including Gentiles and many Gentile practices. Socially, the emphasis upon purity was intended to insulate and isolate Israel from the practices of the heathen, to protect her against assimilation and corruption; religiously, the emphasis flowed out of devotion to Yahweh as the holy one. Meticulous tithing of all agricultural products addressed the greatest source of non-observance, the double system of Jewish and Roman taxation. All tithes were to be paid and a person who would be holy could not eat untithed food (59).

Such a thesis is very close to some of the views that I put forward in my book, prompted initially by Mary Douglas's treatment of the notion of purity (which Borg appears not to know). Groups under pressure from external forces attempt to strengthen both their external and their internal boundaries by means of purity regulations which both reinforce the group's self-consciousness as distinct from those forces which they identify as polluting and help to bond the people to their acknowledged source of goodness and wholeness, in this case the God of Temple and Torah. Borg is, it is true, a good deal more confident about his ability to read back from the regulations of the Mishnah to the practices of the Pharisees in the first century than many scholars, but can find powerful support for his views from J. Neusner (b.1932). Sanders, as we shall shortly see, was to be more cautious about some of these judgements.

The question then is: how did Jesus react to such a strategy? In a word, Borg claims that he sought to replace the quest for holiness with his teaching of God's mercy; to replace, that is, a strategy that was exclusive with one that was inclusive. Evidence for this can be found in his meals with tax-collectors and sinners, in his healings on the sabbath and in his attitude to tithes. Of particular interest, not least in the light of subsequent discussions, are his views on Jesus's meals. Meals were of particular importance to the Pharisees. Not only did they express intimacy and fellowship, as they did throughout the ancient Near East, but also they were the point at which two concerns of the Pharisees converged: purity and tithing. 'No fewer than 229 of the 341 rabbinic pericopae attributed to the houses of Shammai and Hillel pertain to table-fellowship. The Pharisees were thus "a table-fellowship sect"' (80). Members of a Pharisaic *havurah* (not all Pharisees, but consisting exclusively of Pharisees) 'were committed to the tithing of all food and to eating every meal in that degree of purity observed by officiating priests in the Temple' (80f). Thus the *haver* could not be the guest of one who was untrustworthy; nor could he share a table with one 'whose presence might defile the meal' (81). Jesus's meals with sinners and tax-collectors offended, in Borg's view, on two counts. The term 'sinners' could, indeed, mean a number of things, but what was essentially offensive to the Pharisees was that sinners, however understood, 'did not accept in practice the Pharisaic programme of holiness for Israel and could not be trusted with regard to tithing and cleanness' (84). The fact that a public figure like Jesus shared meals with such people was therefore seen by his opponents as a serious challenge to their programme of reform which was intended to make Israel a holy community, a kingdom of priests. Further, Jesus's contact with tax-collectors posed a further threat for it 'implied an acceptance of quisling behaviour and thereby threatened to shatter "the closed ranks of the community against their enemy," to break down the cohesiveness necessary to the survival of a society immersed in conflict' (85f).

Jesus's meals, by contrast with Pharisaic policies of separation, pointed to the mercy of God, as a God who was 'forgiving, accepting, nourishing of righteous and sinner alike'. And for Israel this 'pointed toward greater inclusiveness, toward an overcoming of the "intra-cultural segregation" which increasingly marked her life' (137). There is much in the detail of Borg's discussion which is of interest. Clearly, too, the general thesis is one that comes close to positions for which I have argued. But a number of points need to be made, some of which will be discussed again in connection with Sanders's work. The first point concerns the development of the Pharisaic tradition. To what extent were the regulations concerning the *haverim* and meals with *non-haverim* in force at the time of Jesus? Clearly much of the legislation in the Mishnah was developed after the Fall of Jerusalem in AD 70; equally clearly much of this development would have concerned questions of purity and their detailed application. This observation might seem to undermine the thesis which Borg is advancing, but it is not fatal. The point is that there were resources in the Pharisaic tradition that could be drawn on and developed after AD 70. That these contributed to the development of a 'quest for holiness' and were themselves part of such a quest is also scarcely in doubt. We can see Jesus's meals, in so far as they represent a policy of drawing that which was faithless and therefore alien into the fold, as constituting a very different response to the conflict between Israel and the powerful occupying forces which threatened it, from that of the Pharisees or, indeed, their successors. What is more difficult is to determine to what extent Jesus actually offended against Pharisaic regulations then in force. How far indeed, even if they were in force, would they have applied to other Jews, even *non-haver* Pharisees? In short, was the offence of Jesus's eating with sinners one concerned with purity regulations as such, or with the correlate of such regulations: avoidance of those outside the group? The point can be made like this. Purity regulations reinforce the external and internal boundaries of a group by reminding people, consciously or unconsciously, of the dangers of association with what is alien to the group. It is difficult to know, given the state of our knowledge of the purity regulations actually in force at the time of Jesus, to what extent he was guilty of technical infringements of such regulations. What we can say with some confidence is that Jesus's meals with tax-collectors and sinners would have sent very different signals about the importance of maintaining tight group boundaries from those which were already being sent by Jews who were beginning to develop more carefully guarded communities, in which development purity regulations would come to play an increasingly important part.

The last point concerns Jesus's view of the future. To talk about Jesus's alternative strategy to that of the Pharisees tends at least to suggest that it was significantly like their strategy in so far as it was a plan of action that could be carried out by reforming and reshaping the life of the Jewish nation. If, on the other hand, it were thought that Jesus actually envisaged a radical transformation of Israel as a result of some future action of God, then clearly what he was advocating would be of a very different character. For here the prime initiative would lie with God. Borg's attempts to deal with this question, not unlike Harvey's, fail to convince because he does not attempt to spell out exactly what it is that Jesus did expect. He points to changing views of Jesus's expectations as arguments against the early views of scholars like Weiss and Schweitzer, but he does not deal satisfactorily with Jesus's relation to John the Baptist, or indeed with the question of the disciples' role in the coming Kingdom. In this sense, talk of Jesus's 'strategy' is less than concrete.

One further feature of Borg's work should be noticed. While he is mainly concerned with explaining Jesus's teachings in terms of their place within first-century Jewish responses to conflict, he also develops a further type of explanation which is certainly rare in New Testament study. He attempts, that is, to classify the type of religious experience that underlies Jesus's teaching, his particular sense of the numinous. Jesus, suggests Borg, was a holy man, one who was in touch with the divine power; he differed however from other holy men in that he founded a renewal movement. It is hard not to see here a running together of different categories. On the one hand Jesus is being compared to an ideal type in social anthropological studies, the shaman who is 'the delegate of the tribe to the other realm'. On the other he is being compared to the 'men of deed', figures in first-century Judaism who were remarkable for their prayer and miracles and whom Vermes has compared with Jesus. The fact that Jesus started a renewal movement does not make him any the less a holy man in the first sense; though it does certainly distinguish him from figures like Honi the Circle-drawer.

A more substantial difficulty with this approach is that of finding adequate evidence for Jesus's own religious experience. It is true that we are told that he was remarkable for going apart to pray; but in many ways we know less about him than we do about the prophets, certainly a good deal less than we do about Paul. Borg seeks to derive evidence for his religious type from the Wisdom material in the Gospels, which has often been thought to be spurious. He suggests that Jesus's mysticism was of a kind that did not lead to complete union with the Godhead but did entail a direct, intuitive knowledge of God. This is reflected both in Jesus's address of God as *abba* (something that he shares with some of the 'men of deed') and also in his confident description of God's nature which we find in passages like Matthew 6:26-30 and Luke 12:6-7. It is on the basis of such knowledge that Jesus assumes the role of prophet. Borg goes on to suggest that Jesus is to be seen as a sage, and draws again on the Wisdom material in the Gospels.

This is a less than satisfactory treatment: Jesus scarcely emerges as an integrated figure; the material is used uncritically and its relation to Jesus's inner life is not argued for; and Jesus's prophetic role is seen less as a matter of divine call than of his own initiative based on his mystical experience. But despite this the question itself should not be allowed to pass unnoticed. The question of the manner in which experience of the numinous is mediated in Christianity is potentially a fruitful one.

The issues raised by Marcus Borg's book were also vigorously discussed by E. P. Sanders in his *Jesus and Judaism*, published the following year (1985). Sanders had already made an important contribution to Pauline studies with his *Paul and Palestinian Judaism*(1977), in which he had attempted to free Pauline studies from its predominantly low estimate of Judaism, which Sanders attributed largely to the influence of Lutheran scholars. Judaism was not a narrow, legalistic creed: it believed in God's grace and election too. However, that grace took the form of a binding covenant with obligations on both sides that were enshrined in the Law. We shall discuss this more fully later, but here two comments are needed. The significance of Sanders's work is that it countered one-sided characterizations of Judaism, based on isolated texts that might indicate a legalistic side to Judaism, by referring them back to the central, basic tenets of Judaism, which he described as 'covenantal nomism'. But having isolated that central core of Jewish beliefs, he did not adequately explain how and why it was that that it could generate so many different systems of belief in the first and second centuries. Hence while rejecting 'legalistic' interpretations of, for example, Pharisaic interest in purity regulations, he offers no positive account of his own of why in the first century, and increasingly in the second, Jewish scholars gave so much attention to this subject. This has led one prominent Jewish scholar to dismiss the book as 'cosmically irrelevant' to the study of Judaism. It is certainly not that, but it does leave much unexplained.

The second point is of a rather different kind. Sanders's work can be seen as a reaction not only to confessional interpretations of Paul, specifically Lutheran ones. Perhaps more illuminatingly, it can be seen as a reaction to the cultural over-confidence of American Protestantism and an attempt to give a reading of the New Testament which reflects more nearly the multicultural environment in which religions are studied in American Liberal Arts Colleges and schools. What this means in practice is both that he is quick to discern and castigate value judgements about the merits of one religion over another; and also that he is reluctant to explore the nature of the relationships between Paul and Palestinian Judaism or indeed between Jesus and Judaism. This latter reluctance, however, does inhibit the very process of historical explanation that he is keen to advance.

Sanders is above all anxious to promote an historical approach to the New Testament, as he puts it, 'to free history and exegesis from the control of theology' (333). To do this one needs to have good historical questions, to take a critical view of the sources and to formulate 'good', intelligent and sensible hypotheses. The question that he formulates is one about Jesus's intention. What were Jesus's aims: how do they relate to the course of his life, his death, and the subsequent behaviour of his followers, leading to the emergence of the Christian church? (18-22; 166f). The difficulty Sanders perceives with such a question is that there is a great deal of smoke — sayings attributed to Jesus and his followers, stories about him and the early doings of the Christian church - but no easily discernible connection between all this smoke and the fire which produced it: Jesus and his intentional activity. But there is a further difficulty that he is less aware of, namely that the question itself does not ask how Jesus's intentionality relates to that of his contemporaries. We shall return to that point at the end of our discussion.

Sanders's awareness of the problem of identifying the fire behind the smoke leads him to propose a relatively novel route to discovering Jesus's intentions. It is usually thought that the most obvious way to discovering

Jesus's intentions lies via his utterances; Sanders, deeply sceptical of our ability to determine which of the sayings attributed to Jesus most accurately reflect his views, proposes to take as his starting-point certain assured facts and to use these as the basis of his explanatory hypothesis.

It is the overwhelming probability of facts like the fact that 'Jesus did something in the temple and said something about its destruction' (61), or that he was baptised by John the Baptist and called twelve disciples, which attracts Sanders, as opposed to the uncertainties of trying to ascribe sayings to Jesus and to uncover their senses. But here Sanders hardly does justice to what seems to me an important point: facts allow of different modes of description: 'thin' descriptions and 'thick' descriptions, to use a helpful distinction of Gilbert Ryle's (1900-1976). It is one thing to say someone moved his lower eyelid; another to say he gave a knowing, or warning wink. To say, for example, that 'Jesus did something in the temple', is to offer a thin description; to say that his overturning of the tables symbolized its destruction and restoration a quite thick one. Thin descriptions remain at the level of surface observations; thick ones may give an account of such phenomena as significant actions within a particular cultural matrix and it is this which we require if we are to illumine Jesus's intention and his relationship to his contemporaries in Judaism — as Sanders, by his own discussion, is fully aware. The difficulty is this: we can be pretty confident about certain facts about Jesus, thinly described, but this will not take us very far; we can be a good deal less confident about offering accounts of their meaning within his particular cultural context, and it is this which we require if we are to say much about Jesus's intentions. This is not to dismiss the value of Sanders's work; it is to question the confidence of some of its stronger claims.

It would nevertheless be foolish to disregard the fact that we can be pretty confident about certain facts about Jesus, as indeed Anthony Harvey argued. Moreover, and this is Harvey's point again, the more we know about the cultural matrix in which such events occurred, the better placed we shall be to interpret those facts. Our confidence will, that is to say, be directly proportionate to our confidence in our knowledge of Jesus's milieu; even so, there will still be needed a complex process of reading those facts before we can offer suitably thick descriptions of their meaning.

What, then, of Sanders's main thesis? His basic contention is that certain unassailable facts about Jesus's life and activity locate him firmly within Jewish restoration eschatology: the fact that he was baptized by John; that he called twelve disciples, was a Galilean who preached and healed; and that he confined his activity to Israel and engaged in controversy about the temple. All of these place him in the context of Jewish hopes for the restoration of Israel. Equally we know that Jesus was crucified and that the Jews had some part in the process, certainly that Jesus aroused substantial opposition among the Jewish people. Sanders's explanation for this is that

Jesus's meals with tax collectors and sinners were the cause of such fierce opposition. The reason for this is that Jesus 'may have offered them inclusion within the kingdom not only *while they were still sinners* but also *without* requiring repentance as normally understood [i.e. as involving restitution as prescribed by the Law], and therefore he could have been accused of being a friend of people who indefinitely *remained* sinners' (206). Thus Jesus by not requiring sinners to follow the prescriptions of the Law (possibly because he thought they had no time to create a new life for themselves) deeply offended some of his fellow religionists, and this was a contributory cause of his death. Jesus did not break with the Law as such. Indeed many of his followers remained faithful to the Law after his death. The early church remained faithful to Jesus's expectation of an imminent end as it did to the Law. It was 'pushed towards another stance on the law only by the pressures of the Gentile mission and the efforts of a few creative and remarkable apostles and other leaders'. For it was not simply a continuation of Jesus's own work:

> It lacked 'fellowship' with sinners. It appears that at least this one important nuance of Jesus's message, and a point at which he went beyond John the Baptist, was taken over only in a modified form: they should repent and adapt their lives to the requirements of the law. This provision, however, was seldom successfully enforced on Gentile converts, and it was one form of the Gentile mission which finally separated the Christian movement from the law' (323f).

Sanders's thesis thus offers an account of Jesus's relation to contemporary Judaism (like them he expected the restoration of Israel), of his differences from his fellow Jews (his offer of inclusion in the kingdom to sinners) and of the development of the church as a law-free community (it emerged from the exigencies of the — eschatologically — inspired mission to the Gentiles).

The thesis is attractive. It certainly sets Jesus firmly within first-century Judaism and it does so in such a way as to suggest how he could have aroused deep antagonism among his contemporaries without breaking the bonds of the Judaism of his day. It also offers a plausible account of subsequent developments, though this is only briefly sketched out. The problems with his thesis come, of course, in the accounts Sanders offers of the 'facts' on which he bases his argument.

I have discussed this more fully elsewhere ('Works and Words of Jesus the Jew') so here I shall content myself with some summary remarks. In his treatment of the temple incident Sanders, having discounted views that suggest that it was a direct attack on the temple trade (necessary for the conduct of the temple cult) argues that it was a symbolic act. What it signified was the destruction of the temple - and its restoration. The difficulties with this view are manifold. Does the overturning of some tables in the temple obviously symbolize its destruction (quite possibly, I think)? Why should it then also symbolize its restoration? Because, we are told, Jesus could only have undertaken to attack what 'was ordained by God' if such destruction in turn looked towards restoration (71). This involves Sanders in a fascinating discussion of contemporary Jewish expectations about the temple. Here the difficulties are legion. Many of the texts do not explicitly refer to the temple, but rather to Jerusalem. Few, if any, before AD 70 refer both to the destruction and restoration of the temple. The most promising is 1 Enoch 90:28, but this may well not refer to the restoration of the temple, so much as to the restoration of Jerusalem. Certainly there is nothing compelling in the evidence to suggest that Jesus looked for its restoration. But Sanders might well ask, 'Is it really likely that a first century Jew could have contemplated the destruction of the temple as part of the realisation of God's kingdom? Is it not precisely at such points that we have to guard against theology colouring and affecting our judgement?' It is, but that does not in itself answer the question. Certainly one New Testament writer with deep Jewish roots could contemplate a new Jerusalem without a temple (Rev. 21:22). Do we not need at least to ask what the attitude of people in the country districts was to the temple in Jerusalem? Of course there was a deep attachment to it evidenced by the attendance at the festivals. Yet is it unthinkable that a restoration prophet like Jesus should have conceived of a restoration of Israel that went back to the days before there was a temple at all? And may such a vision not have been fuelled by antipathy to the powerful rulers of the temple and the obvious links between the Hellenistic building and those who dominated the land politically and economically? In the end, Sanders's treatment here is hampered by his not having offered a sufficiently differentiated account of first-century Judaism.

To what extent did the very different ways in which first-century Jews developed their beliefs in the covenant, Law and election reflect the economic, political and social differences between them, reflect different strategies for confronting the forces, not least those of an alien occupying culture, which threatened Jewish norms and mores?

Again, what of Jesus's meals with sinners? Sanders argues that the cause of offence was that Jesus offered inclusion to sinners without 'conversion to the Law', without making due restitution. This is a bold and attractive thesis, in that it seems to do justice to what we know of the facts. But does he fully draw out its implications? Here it seems to me he may be hampered by his reluctance to present Jesus as passing judgement on Judaism in any way. For if it is true that Jesus's 'table-fellowship' was a sign 'that the wicked who heeded him would be included in the kingdom, even though they did not repent as it was universally understood' (207), what does that mean about the nature of God's rule? Surely that cannot leave standard conventional ideas of God's rule unchanged? It is not enough to present this as merely a temporary setting aside of the requirements of the law. A more fundamental change in understanding is signalled which, while it may not by any means represent a wholesale rejection of previous notions, may none the less pave the way for fundamental changes in the basic assumptions on which a new society is to be grounded. Sanders, for all that he wants to offer an account of Jesus's intentions which will explain the continuity and change between Judaism and early Christianity, seems to be unwilling to consider the way in which prophetic, liminal figures may indeed anticipate major shifts in consciousness and values. Maybe here his own ideological concerns (guarding against some form of theological anti-Semitism) interfere with his historical judgement.

The same point can be made perhaps less contentiously with regard to Sanders's treatment of the relation between Jesus and John the Baptist. Sanders is, quite rightly, troubled by the relative paucity of reference to repentance in the Synoptic sayings of Jesus. Did Jesus not believe in repentance (surely unthinkable for a first-century Jew), or was it perhaps that because John had laid such great stress on it Jesus felt 'he did not himself have to do it all'? (227). After John's call to Israel to repent, Jesus then set out to promise inclusion to the most obvious outsiders. This raises all sorts of neat problems. In the first place, while Sanders has stressed that the sense of 'sinners' (as in Jesus's meals with tax collectors and sinners) has to refer to those flagrantly in breach of the Law, John's call seems to have been addressed more widely to all those who felt that they had fallen short of the Law. This would suggest a different notion of repentance. Secondly, it suggests too continuous a relationship between Jesus and John. It is not that John was a forerunner of Jesus; Jesus was more probably his disciple. The point is that we should at least be on the alert for substantial variations in vision among different prophetic figures, even if they have at times been associated. Jesus's vision of a Kingdom that would include the sinners and tax collectors may have been a rather different one from John's with its terrifying symbols of the threshing-floor and winnowing fork, the axe laid to the root of the tree.

Thus in the end Sanders's hypothesis falls short of providing an adequate historical explanation, precisely because of its unwillingness to engage in sustained reflection on the relation of Jesus to the different forms of first-century Judaism. He seems more content to be able to locate him generally within a certain broad movement in Judaism and then to offer some account of the continuities and discontinuities between Jesus and the early church. What is lacking is a broader explanatory framework that could do justice to the major shifts in historical consciousness which are taking place at this juncture of history and which have their issue in the twin birth of Rabbinic Judaism and early Christianity.

At least the discussion of these recent contributions to the quest for the historical Jesus should make it clear that the quest itself is alive and well. Although there is by no means unanimity among the various scholars' findings, it is more than just a 'mood' that has overcome the discipline.

There is a growing confidence in the basic conditions of the possibility of such a quest. What is the basis of such confidence, which is still not shared by all?

In the first place it rests on a conviction that we do know that Jesus lived and died and that we know at least certain basic facts about his life with at least as much confidence as we could know similar facts about any other figure in ancient history. Compared with many ancient historians, New Testament scholars are in a relatively fortunate position.

The second factor is a greater confidence in our ability to understand Jesus's social world, the world of first-century Judaism and its various renewal movements. This is obviously significant. We could possess a great deal of authentic material about someone from the past and still be largely at a loss as to how to interpret it, if we were largely ignorant of its historical context. The most obvious case of this would be if it was in a wholly unknown language. But ignorance of social conventions, of political and cultural factors which might bear on such texts and remains would also make it difficult for us to give much of a reading. The discovery of the Qumran texts, and the growing contribution of Israeli, European and American Jewish scholars to the study of the first century have made possible a clearer understanding of Jesus's context, and this is a vital step forward in any attempt to make sense of the records we possess.

All of this may serve to overcome the crippling sense of historical scepticism that had been engendered, not least by the uncertainties of any attempt to reconstruct the history of the tradition behind the Synoptic Gospels. Significantly, few of the books we have been reviewing make great use of such attempts (my own being the principal exception and its use is quite severely constrained). This is not to say that there is any consensus, either about the way Jesus is to be situated within his Jewish context, or indeed about the most appropriate way of undertaking the task.

At this point it may be worth listing what appear to be the main points of agreement and disagreement:
1. It is agreed that there was a man called Jesus of Nazareth who was a prominent religious figure of his day.
2. He was baptized by and was an associate of John the Baptist.
3. He called disciples (probably 12), performed works of healing and exorcism, taught his disciples and a wider audience and engaged in controversy with Jewish teachers of the Law.
4. He associated with tax collectors and sinners and this caused offence to some of the Jewish devout.
5. He performed some kind of prophetic action in the Temple.
6. He was crucified by the Romans at the instigation of some of the Jewish leaders.

On the other hand there are fruitful areas of debate and disagreement about among other things:

1. The nature of Jesus's relation to the Baptist. Did he simply assume the Baptist's preaching about repentance? Or was his own view of the future a substantial reworking of the Baptist's?

2. The extent to which Jesus should be seen primarily as a teacher of the Law, or rather as a prophet of Jewish renewal; whether indeed either of these categories will suffice to describe him.

3. The extent to which Jesus did or did not advocate views that were essentially at odds with the Law, either in the sense that they proposed alternative courses of action which were acceptable or unacceptable to God, or indeed that they specifically challenged established interpretations of the Law.

There are also more detailed points of contention:

1. Did Jesus explicitly set aside the laws of purity?

2. Did his actions in the Temple symbolise its destruction *and* restoration?

3. What was the precise nature of the offence that was given by Jesus's meals with tax-collectors and sinners? Was it related to some Jews' beliefs and practices about purity? Was it related to Jewish beliefs about repentance and restitution?

4. Did Jesus expect an imminent end to the present age? To what extent would the new age be continuous with the old? How far would Jesus and his followers be responsible for 'bringing it in'?

Alongside these specific views about Jesus there are also agreements and disagreements about a number of broader interpretative issues. It is perhaps worth noting the rather obvious point that all the scholars whom we have discussed here are firmly committed to an historical mode of enquiry into Jesus's life and work. Whereas elsewhere New Testament study is in some measure divided over the question of whether to embrace literary or historical paradigms of study, here there are no texts as such that stem from Jesus and the subject matter himself can only be grasped through some process of historical reconstruction. There is however some scope for literary-critical studies of the sayings of Jesus and more notably his parables, and this is an area of study that may contribute more fully to our understanding of Jesus in the future.

There is, however, disagreement over the historical strategies that are to be employed.

1. There is still by no means a consensus about the appropriate means for determining which of the sayings attributed to Jesus in the Synoptic Gospels are, at least broadly, authentic. Confidence in the dissimilarity test, as we have seen, has somewhat ebbed. Harvey's 'Odd is true' is a formulation that certainly suggests a rather more flexible and less confident way of applying it. Coherence with what we elsewhere know of Jesus by our careful construal of the facts about which we are certain may be a more useful way of distinguishing the authentic voice of Jesus. Yet even such a path is not without its dangers, both of excluding sayings that might have enlarged our understanding of his teaching as of assuming

too readily that Jesus never changed his mind, or underwent any development in his thinking.

2. Again even where there is broad agreement about which facts we know about Jesus, there is perhaps more disagreement than might first meet the eye about how they are to be related to the cultural matrix in which they are set. Sanders approach is essentially to pigeon-hole Jesus into the category of Jewish restoration eschatology. Harvey portrays him as operating fairly firmly within the constraints imposed by first-century Jewish culture, while at the same time he allows Jesus, as it were, to choose between the various options that were open to him. Some of these choices single him out, if in no other way than that he refuses to conform to any single type — prophet or teacher. Yet neither Sanders nor Harvey offers very much by way of explanation of Jesus's interaction with contemporary Jewish beliefs and practice. Borg and I, however, do suggest that there is a greater freedom on Jesus's part to transcend or to modify, to transform, the beliefs of his contemporaries. That may to some seem like a thinly veiled form of apologetic; but it is, at least consciously, more part of an attempt to grasp the historical particularity of the man than to argue for the superiority or uniqueness of his beliefs. Both books try to show how Jesus proposed ways of dealing with the contemporary crisis rather different from those of groups like the Pharisees and the followers of Judas the Galilean which attempted to set tight boundaries around their people, the better to resist foreign infiltration. Yet even here there are differences: Borg is content to spell out the difference in approach: what I attempted was to show how linguistic conventions can themselves be modified in order to enunciate novel ideas.

3. Nevertheless even these two latter attempts do not offer any cohesive account of what motivated Jesus's radical shift away from contemporary modes of resisting external forces - if indeed this is what he was advocating. This is a significant point. Much of the debate turns on a particular scholar's judgement of what is possible by way of innovation within a given cultural matrix. To what extent could any first century-Jew have deliberately flouted the Law, if he in any way cherished religious goals? This is a question which it requires more than commonsense to answer. A satisfactory answer must, it seems to me, satisfy at least two demands. It must at least be consistent with what we can learn about religious change and innovation from other times and places: attention to the work of religious historians, anthropologists and sociologists of religion will be of considerable assistance. It must also fit into a broader hypothesis about the development of Christianity and Rabbinic Judaism in the first and second centuries. Clearly, during this period enormous changes occurred in the beliefs and practices of Judaism, which was in any case a fairly diverse phenomenon at the beginning of the era. Relating Jesus to this complex matrix and equally to subsequent developments in

Judaism and Christianity can hardly be done without some understanding of the nature of religious change in general and of the details of this process of change in particular.

A further, by no means insignificant, point arises. If it is true that in order to make judgements about Jesus's relation to his inherited Jewish culture we need to reflect more fully on questions about the nature of religious change, then it will also follow that where such reflection is lacking scholars may be most likely to allow their own preferred options to dictate their reading of the situation. Those who see religion as essentially subversive, may be more willing to see the innovative elements in Jesus's teaching and praxis as dominant; while those who see religion as giving cohesion and permanence to societies may prefer a reading that explores the ways in which Jesus may have attempted to reform and strengthen contemporary Judaism. But we need to be aware of the many diverse ways in which religion may function in order to make informed judgements about the process of change that occurred in the first and second centuries, and such awareness may — to a degree at least — free us from the force of our own preferences.

List of works cited

M.J. Borg, Conflict, *Holiness and Politics in the Teachings of Jesus*, New York, 1984

G. Bornkamm, *Jesus of Nazareth*, Stuttgart, 1956 (German); London, 1960 (English)

Compendium Rerum Judaicarum ad Novum Testamentum, ed S. Safrai and M. Stern, Assen, 1974ff

M. Douglas, *Purity and Danger*, London, 1966

A.E. Harvey, *Jesus and the Constraints of History*, London, 1982

A.E. Harvey, *Faith in the City: A Call for Action by Church and Nation*, Report of the Archbishop of Canterbury's Commission of Urban Priority Areas, London, 1985

M. Hengel, *Judaism and Hellenism*, Tübingen, 1968 (German); London, 1974 (English)

M. Hengel, *The Charismatic Leader and his Followers*, Berlin, 1968 (German); Edinburgh, 1981 (English)

M. Hengel, *The Zealots*, Leiden, 1966 (German); Edinburgh, 1988 (English)

E. Käsemann, 'The Problem of the Historical Jesus', *ZThK*, 51 (1954), 125-53 (German); *Essays on New Testament Themes*, London, 1964, 15-47 (English)

J. Jeremias, *The Parables of Jesus*, Göttingen, 1947 (German); London, 1963 (English)

B. Meyer, *The Aims of Jesus*, London, 1979

N. Perrin, *Jesus and the Language of the Kingdom*, London, 1976

J. Riches, *Jesus and the Transformation of Judaism*, London, 1980

J. Riches, 'Works and Words of Jesus the Jew', in *Heythrop Journal*, 17, 1986, 53-62

E.P. Sanders, *Jesus and Judaism*, London, 1985

E.P. Sanders, *Paul and Palestinian Judaism*, London, 1977

E. Schürer, *The History of the Jewish People*, ed G. Vermes, F. Millar, M. Black, Edinburgh, 1973, 1979ff

G. Theissen, *The First Followers of Jesus*, Munich, 1977 (German); London, 1978 (English)

G. Theissen, *The Shadow of the Galilean: The Quest of the Historical Jesus in Narrative Form*, London, 1987

G. Vermes, *Jesus the Jew*, London, 1973

G. Vermes, *Jesus and the World of Judaism*, London, 1983

G. Vermes, *The Religion of Jesus the Jew*, London, 1993

7

Recent Study of Paul

If, as I suggested, Bultmann's *Gospel of John* is the greatest single work of New Testament exegesis of the century, then it is probably also true to say that his work on Paul, in his essays and in the *Theology of the New Testament*, was the most influential single body of work in New Testament studies. Bultmann's view of Paul dominated the discipline in the 1950s and 1960s. Its powerful attraction stemmed from his combination of detailed philological studies of Paul's language and thought with a searching theological analysis. While his interpretation was indeed deeply Lutheran in inspiration (albeit a Luther understood as a prophet of radical human freedom), it was also worked out in dialogue with significant contemporary attempts to make sense of human existence. Paul emerges not as the purveyor of arcane, pre-scientific myths, but as the father of a rich tradition of spirituality, including among its representatives Augustine (353-430), Luther, Pascal (1623-1662) and Kierkegaard, which charts and illumines the inwardness of men's and women's existence under God.

Reactions to his reading of Paul came from within and without, the more important of which we shall survey. First in the 1960s and early 1970s, Käsemann challenged the emphasis which Bultmann had placed on Paul's anthropology, insisting on the cosmological aspects of Paul's preaching of justification. At the same time Krister Stendahl questioned more radically whether the tradition of Christian inwardness was right to lay claim to Paul as its founder at all. Was it not more the product of the introspective conscience of the West? Paul's concern was with the place of Jews and Gentiles in God's dispensation. Further attacks on the Lutheran nature of Bultmann's reading of Paul came from E.P. Sanders, based on his re-reading of first century Judaism and of Paul's place within it. Subsequently, Theissen, Meeks (b.1932) and others have attempted to provide a reading of Paul which was more alert to the social setting of his missionary preaching.

Ernst Käsemann was probably the most influential, certainly the most creative, of Bultmann's pupils, who dominated the field in German New Testament studies in the 1950s and 1950s. His early work was published in the thirties, during which time he worked as a pastor in the Ruhr. Subsequently he saw service in the war. During this period he was deeply involved in the German Church struggle. He was a member of the Confessing Church, was arrested by the Gestapo in 1937 and wrote the first draft of his study of Hebrews in prison. Eventually he resigned from the Confessing Church in Westfalia because of its cooperation with the German Christians. After the war he held chairs in Mainz, Göttingen and Tübingen. He was in all his work concerned with maintaining the dialogue between church life and theological science, which 'is, like all true companionship, only fruitful if it remains in a state of tension. The dialogue has to lead the parties involved away from traditional horizons into paths till then untrodden; and the unavoidable conflicts must not be shunned' (*Perspectives*, 33). Certainly, Käsemann's career was marked by its own share of conflict with the religiously orthodox. Sadly, in the 1970s it was overshadowed by the murder of his daughter by the Argentinian regime. Käsemann's commitment to the recovery of a Gospel which addresses itself to the pressing questions of the world has never faltered.

For Käsemann the centre of the New Testament is to be found in the theology of Paul. Unlike Bultmann, who tried to give a Pauline reading of John, Käsemann attempted to displace the Johannine writings from the centre of the New Testament by arguing for their docetic character. Not that this left Paul in a position of undisputed superiority: too many questions had been raised about the nature and unity of Paul's theology for that. Moreover, Käsemann's task was not simply to argue for the unity of Paul's thought; nor even to argue for the centrality to it of the notion of justification. It was to recover the meaning of the central Pauline concepts of justification and the righteousness of God from interpretations that diminished and privatised them.

Much of Käsemann's work on Paul is to be found in articles, many of which are published in his *Perspectives on Paul* (1969). The fullest statement is given in his *Commentary on Romans* which was published in 1973. It is not an easy book: it eschews introductions and summaries of Paul's theology. True to Bultmann's views of exegesis, Käsemann believes that the meaning of the text should emerge in the course of sustained examination of the text itself, using all the means at the exegete's disposal: religio-historical, philological, and theological. In consequence the answers he gives to detailed historical questions, as well as his account of Paul's theology, have to be garnered from across the volume. In unpicking these threads, there is a considerable danger of destroying the quite subtle interrelationships among the various arguments. Nevertheless for the sake of simplicity some such listing of Käsemann's views must be undertaken.

One of the questions that had engaged New Testament scholars since the time of the History of Religions School was that of the particular cultural milieu against which Paul writes. Scholars like Heitmüller and Reitzenstein, as we have seen, attempted to read Paul against a background of popular Hellenistic religion. Gunkel stressed the materialistic conception of spirit which was to be found in such religion; others (Reitzenstein) suggested parallels between the Mystery Religions with their initiation rites and Pauline sacramentalism. 'In Christ' believers undergo a fundamental transformation of their nature, they become a 'new creation'.

Such considerations of the cultural milieu of Paul's Epistles also prompted questions about the unity of Paul's thought. For alongside this mystical or sacramental language and thought, there was also present in Paul's writings a way of thinking more juridical in character. The language of justification by faith, of forgiveness of sins, of law and obedience, suggested a way of thought more Jewish in character, ethical rather than mystical. Men and women were not so sinful that only a transformation of their nature would help; rather what was required was forgiveness, repentance, faith and obedience. Scholars were divided as to which of these two sides of Paul's thought was to be seen as dominant: some stressed justification by faith, while others saw it as merely a subsidiary theme in contrast to the central Pauline notion of participation in Christ.

In attempting to address these complex questions Käsemann starts from two broad assumptions: that the Reformers had gained important insights into the nature of Pauline theology; and that the text has one 'central concern and a remarkable inner logic that may no longer be entirely comprehensible to us' (viii). That concern crystallizes around the notion of the righteousness of God. Moreover, when this term is seen against the background of certain forms of contemporary Judaism, ways are opened up of reading the Epistle as a unity which other derivations of Paul's language had made impossible.

Käsemann's own attempt to understand the notion of the righteousness of God starts from an examination of its roots in the Old Testament and Judaism (24f). A hundred years of debate had discredited the notion that it was to be derived from Greek notions of a norm or ethical attribute. Rather, the biblical usage was recognized to be forensic in character, referring to a *relationship* in which one is placed, namely, the standing that ensues from the recognition of one's innocence. In Jewish apocalyptic this usage is further extended to apply to the judgement of justification at the last judgement. What previously was a condition of salvation now becomes the very thing to be given in salvation (cf Phil 3:9, where the righteousness of God seems to be specifically defined as the righteousness from God). Thus Bultmann argued that what was distinctive about the Pauline use was that such justification was now seen to be presently given to believers, whereas previously it had been at most hoped for. The apocalyptic dimension was as it were swallowed up in the present moment.

According to Käsemann, however, since the discovery of the Qumran literature (and he laid particular emphasis on the Thanksgiving Hymns, [25]) one can no longer see the emphasis on righteousness as a present gift as a distinctively Pauline view. Rather than such an emphasis removing Paul from a strictly apocalyptic view of things, it sets him more firmly into such a context. The gift of righteousness, presently received, is concerned precisely with God's judgement of this world; with, that is, his establishment of his right over his world, a right that will finally be established only at the end. Equally importantly, the Qumran texts give evidence of a use where the phrase 'the righteousness of God' can refer both to the *gift* from God to believers of being brought back into his presence and ways, and to the *power* of God which works such righteousness in his people and strives towards the final setting of his world to rights. The difference between Paul and Qumran, in Käsemann's view, lies in their attitude to the Law, not in their views on present eschatology. For Qumran, the gift of righteousness could lead only to an intensification of one's observance of the Law. For Paul, righteousness is *sine lege*, it is the righteousness of faith, the acceptance of the gospel of Jesus which removes men and women from bondage to the Law and frees them for the service of the Lord Jesus Christ. Thus to remain on the level of a purely historical explanation of Paul's usage, it is one that stands closest to certain strands of Jewish apocalyptic as found in Qumran, but which is modified importantly in the light of his christology. So Käsemann can assert that justification by faith 'is the specifically Pauline interpretation of christology just as the latter is the basis of the former' (24).

The move away from Bultmann's interpretation of Paul is clear. For Bultmann, justification by faith referred to a gift from God whereby the individual was able to enter into his or her own authentic mode of existence. In the Word of the Gospel she was confronted by a demand that had to be responded to; it was in that demand or address of the Word (*Anrede*) that its 'power for salvation' (Rom. 1:16) lay, namely in its power to release people, to free them for a new existence. For Käsemann its power was not to be identified with the transformation of the individual. The work of the Gospel would be completed only when the whole creation was set to rights under the Lordship of Christ and so acknowledged the rule of God. The transformation of the individual was part of this process but the process should not be identified with that individual transformation.

So far we have seen how Käsemann provided a significantly different reading of the language of justification from that which had been previously offered by those who stressed the ethical or anthropological side of Paul's thought. What of those elements, the language of Adam/Christ, the sacramental language of chapter 6 and the flesh/spirit language of chapter 7 which had seemed to lie close to Hellenistic religious belief and practice? Is a reading of these passages in terms of contemporary Jewish modes of thought possible? Will such a reading offer a means of showing the consistency of Paul's thought in these passages with his understanding of justification?

Paul's Adam/Christ language, so Käsemann argues (144ff), takes its rise in Jewish speculation about the heavenly Sophia as the mediator of creation. Whereas this Sophia was widely identified with Torah, in Hellenistic Judaism it was identified with the Logos, or in Philo (*de conf. ling.* 146) with the mythical figure of the Primal man. While in Judaism this figure is understood as a mediator of creation, it is not difficult to see how such Sophia speculation could be associated in early Christianity with Christ as not only the mediator of creation but also as the saviour figure in whom Wisdom came to expression (1 Cor. 10:4; 8:6; Col. 1:15f). Paul's Adam/Christ typology emerges when this is read against a background of the apocalyptic notion of the two ages. Then the first and last Adam can be contrasted and brought together in a framework of a primal and a final age. This also offers the possibility of seeing the mediator of creation as the beginning and the inaugurator of the general resurrection of the dead, and of seeing the event of baptism as an anticipation of the work of the last Adam. 'In dualistic contrast Christ and Adam are now the bearers of destiny [*Schicksalsträger*] for the world determined by them' (146).

If Paul's thought in chapter 5 bears the marks of apocalyptic thought, Käsemann concedes that the Hellenistic Mystery Religions have influenced the language of being buried with Christ in chapter 6 (160ff). But, he argues, Paul's views are here being expressed polemically. Against those who believe that they are already transformed into the new creation in Christ, he insists that the reign of Christ, while already inaugurated, is still to be completed. Thus while we are indeed to be conformed to Christ's death and resurrection, for the present it is the crucifixion which is the mark of Christian existence under the Lordship of Christ. Paul, that is to say, uses the notion of 'with Christ' to sharpen the understanding of Christ as the bearer of our fate. Baptism is a placing under the rule of Christ, an initiation into that rule which must be worked out in a period of testing in the realm in which the divine spirit shines out.

Similarly the dualistic language of spirit and flesh in chapters 7 and 8 can be explained in terms of the fundamental change in the allegiance of the Christian who now lives in the power of the spirit of the risen Christ, free from the Law and the desires of the flesh that are the mark of men's and women's slavery to the dark powers. Precisely because such dualism is a dualism of lords rather than an ethical or metaphysical dualism, Paul can do justice both to the element of givenness of salvation and to the continuing testing of the Christian in the new obedience of the life of the spirit. It is, moreover, an advantage of such an understanding of chapter 7 that it can take account of the historic differences between Jews and Gentiles before Christ. Again, it is in terms of a christologically interpreted apocalypticism that Käsemann sees Paul's usage here.

If Käsemann in this way has succeeded in offering a uniform account of the religio-historical background of Paul's language, what of the problem of the theological unity of the epistle? For Käsemann the question to be answered is of the relation between justification and saving-history (see his essay of that title in *Perspectives on Paul*). It is only too easy to see an irreconcilable tension between the individualism (expiation of personal sin and guilt, the gift of a new self-understanding, and so on) of Paul's doctrine of justification and the cosmic view of God's action in history to be found in chapters 4 and

5, and 9 to 11. Again, it is in the notion of *dikaiosune theou* (the righteousness of God) that Käsemann finds the central axis of Paul's theology, but understood in a way that does justice to the cosmic perspectives of 1:18 to 3:20, and chapters 4, 5, 9 to 11.

As we saw above, both Qumran and Paul use the phrase 'the righteousness of God' to mean on the one hand God's gift of salvation, realized now in the believer but to be consummated in the future, and on the other hand God's active power bringing the world back into the realm of his justice and right. It is such an emphasis on both the power and the gift that, according to Käsemann, accounts for the various aspects of Paul's thought that can so easily be contrasted and seen as disparate and irreconcilable. But it is not enough simply to give a religio-historical explanation of the term; what is required is a theological account of Paul's use of the term, an account which shows what Paul's central concern is when he writes in this way.

It is, in short, christology that underlies Paul's particular use of the 'righteousness of God' as both gift and power. The central theme of Paul's christology is that Christ is God's supreme gift to us and no less our Lord who rules over us. *Charis* (gift, grace) for Paul means mainly the power of grace and yet takes concrete form in the individual charisma. Similarly, he speaks of the God 'who brings back the fallen world into the sphere of his legitimate claim . . . whether in promise or demand, in new creation or forgiveness, or in the making possible of service, and — what must be no less considered according to Gal 5.5 — who sets us in the state of confident hope and, according to Phil 3.12 constant earthly change' (29). The Qumran texts which speak of present justification have the same gift-power structure, but because they are not christologically determined they can speak only of the renewal of the old covenant in an intensified observation of the Law. It is, Käsemann believes, his christology which causes Paul to identify the righteousness of God with the righteousness of faith and so to put the stress on the gift of salvation.

What does it mean to say that it is Paul's christology which determines his treatment of the notion of justification over against Qumran, to say indeed that justification is Paul's specific interpretation of christology? The key lies in Paul's conviction that Christ died for the ungodly, that salvation in Christ is not salvation of the righteous Jew but of those who accept the gospel of God's judgement and grace. It is this which is the specific content of Paul's doctrine of justification; the righteousness of God is a power that brings freedom and sonship to those who are weak, to those who are enemies, just as Jesus saw his mission as being to the sick (Mk. 2:17). The apostle in his theology has reflected as fundamentally, as no one else, on that which according to Mk.2:17 determined Jesus's word and deed (317). Again it is, as we have already suggested, Paul's christology which underlies the gift-power structure of the righteousness of God. Christ is both the inaugurator and representative of the new humanity that stands opposed to the old

Adamitic man. Christ by his obedience inaugurates a new age, just as his obedience is the mark of those who are created anew and who submit in freedom to his rule. Thus Paul's doctrine of the righteousness of God is not simply a doctrine about the assuaging of individual guilt. Rather it is the specific shape that Paul gives to his belief in the 'attack of grace on the world' in Christ. It is cosmic and apocalyptic in the sense that it speaks of the creator God re-establishing his rule over the world in a process that awaits its completion at the final judgement, but that is already now inaugurated in the event of Christ. It is deeply christological in that it speaks of the God who comes to heal those who have need of a physician, who raises the dead, who creates *ex nihilo* and who establishes a new covenant with those who in faith are obedient and free.

It is now possible to see how Paul's doctrine of justification related to those passages in which he speaks of God's action in *history*, notably 1:18-3:20, chapters 4-5 and 9-11. Clearly Paul's view of justification as bringing the world back into the sphere of God's right is itself a doctrine about saving-history. Anyone who divides world history into epochs characterized by Adam, Abraham, Moses and Christ, has a view of saving-history; but is it one where God's plan is revealed clearly to his chosen people and executed through them? For that would be precisely counter to Paul's view of the justification of the godless. Or is it one where the history of salvation is seen as Augustine saw it as the battlefield of the *civitas dei* and the *civitas terrena*? Christians are not, like the Corinthian enthusiasts, to live simply in enthusiastic anticipation of the final victory. Rather their place is under the cross; the final victory belongs 'to the dying, the tempted, the mocked, the weak -- in short, believers' (*Perspectives*, 67f). Thus God's plan of salvation is deeply hidden in this world of darkness, even though Paul can speak of continuity in salvation history (4:12ff; 9:6ff). God does, indeed, act in history, at particular times and places, and his promises and actions will be vindicated. Yet men and women should not be too anxious to discover the particular shape of that vindication:

> Abraham does not know the country to which his exodus is to take him. He hears the promise of heirs without understanding how that promise can be fulfilled. . . . Sarah's laughter is faith's constant companion. . . . For Paul, salvation history is therefore exodus under the sign of the Word and in the face of Sarah's justifiable laughter. Its continuity is paradoxical because it can only endure when God's Word, contrary to the earthly realities, creates for itself children and communities of the pure in spirit (*ibid.*, [124]).

Thus the tensions between saving-history and justification which rested on an individualistic interpretation of the latter are done away with by Käsemann's apocalyptic and cosmic interpretation of justification, which yet insists on the present reality of the individual's righteousness. So, too, the tension often felt between sacraments and ethics in Paul is dissipated when baptism is seen as the placing of the believer, visibly and publicly, under the rule of Christ, in the *nova oboedientia* which is a continuation, a continual *reditus ad baptismum*. Again, the tension between justification and sanctification where often the one is seen as a second stage in the life of the Christian subsequent on justification, is resolved when it is seen as 'justification maintained in the field of action and suffering' (174). Sanctification is the 'anthropological obverse of his christology' (176).

Ultimately, then, what holds Käsemann's view of Paul's theology together is his insistence on the centrality to it of Paul's christology. The real mark of that christology is the way in which it opens up on to a deeper understanding of both God and of man. In it, God is revealed as the God who creates *ex nihilo*, who justifies the godless and who raises the dead; men and women are revealed as those who are most deeply at odds with themselves in their disobedience to God and who find freedom and hope in obedience to their lord Jesus Christ.

Käsemann's interpretation of Paul's theology in his Romans' Commentary is a major work of both historical and theological interpretation. Its main thrust was anticipated in a letter to Bultmann in 1949,[1] where he announced to Bultmann that he had been attacking him recently in lectures:

That God establishes his right over this earth is indeed something different from what you call our new understanding of being, and is, as it seems to me, the subject which strangely unites the New Testament writings in all their diversity. You doubtless would only be able to call this message mythological. But the message stands and falls precisely with this mythological message, at least in my view!

This raises very neatly the central interpretative question that Käsemann's work poses. Against Bultmann he insists on bringing out precisely those mythological elements of which Bultmann had offered an anthropological interpretation, that is, in terms of some common and presently intelligible understanding of human existence. It is the cosmological claims that are being made in the Gospel that, for Käsemann, cannot be abandoned without at the same time forfeiting the Gospel as a whole. The charge against Bultmann is not that his programme of existential interpretation is reductive because it translates myths that are cosmological into statements about human existence, but rather that Bultmann is misled by his programme of existential interpretation into overlooking or playing down the cosmological elements in Paul in favour of those which are concerned with human inwardness.

This is interestingly reminiscent of a passage in Bonhoeffer's (1906-1945) *Letters and Papers* (not, however, published until two years after Käsemann had written his letter) where he complains that Bultmann has stripped the mythological elements away from the Gospel in a 'liberal' attempt to reduce it to its essence. We need, writes Bonhoeffer, to 'maintain the full content, including the mythological concepts'. However 'the concepts must be interpreted in such a way as not to make religion a pre-condition of faith' (110). It is at this point that one feels the lack in Käsemann of a conscious interpretative strategy. He is in a sense more a polemicist, more, perhaps, even a preacher, than a theologian. The problem, that is to say, is not that he has sought to offer a theological interpretation of Paul, but that he has chosen to do this by modifying the details of Bultmann's account rather than rethinking its fundamental approach, his programme of existential interpretation. If Bultmann's strategy cannot do justice to the cosmological elements in the Christian myth, then we need one that can.

I propose now taking a step back from Käsemann's 1973 commentary to an essay published in 1963 by Krister Stendahl and vigorously responded to by Käsemann in his lecture 'Justification and Saving History' which he delivered in various parts of the States in 1965-6. Stendahl's essay 'The Apostle Paul and the Introspective Conscience of the West' argues that the tradition of interpretation that runs from Augustine through to the Reformation and on into modern Western interpretations of Paul owes more to the particular questions concerning human inwardness and self-understanding which intrigued Augustine and Luther than to Paul himself. What Paul was concerned with were the questions: '1) What happens to the Law (the Torah, the actual Law of Moses, not the principle of legalism) when the Messiah has come? 2) What are the ramifications of the Messiah's arrival for the relation between Jews and Gentiles?' (84). Western interpretations of Paul have, by contrast, supposed that the central question which intrigued and, indeed, tormented Paul was 'How do I get a just God?' This is achieved by erecting the question of the status of the Law into a universal human problem by rereading it as a question about men's and women's ability to satisfy their consciences. However, when in Phil. 3 Paul talks about his life as a Jew, he gives no evidence for his having been troubled by his conscience (80). It means that questions which are secondary for Paul are made primary, and that the questions which intrigued him are seen as peripheral or, indeed, problematical. Romans 9-11, which deals with the place of Israel within God's plan of salvation, is the climax of Paul's discussion of the questions which Stendahl believes were of central importance to Paul. For much Lutheran interpretation it has represented a major difficulty.

Thus Stendahl sees justification by faith as not the central aspect of Paul's theology but, with Schweitzer and others, as a 'secondary crater'. But how does he understand it? He sees it as a doctrine advanced in order to justify or defend the way of life of Gentile Christians against the attacks of Jewish Christians who wished them to comply with all the demands of the Law, including, of course, circumcision. If Jews had thought that justification was by works of the Law, then, for Paul, Gentiles were 'justified' by faith. It was not his central doctrine; rather an apologetic, as opposed to polemical argument, in order to protect his churches from being thrown off course by Judaising Christians.

Käsemann responds to Stendahl's attack on central theological positions of the Reformation with characteristic vigour. It is hard not to be reminded of some great giant dealing out heavy blows to a more agile and elegant opponent. In the end the conflict is inconclusive, because little contact is actually made. In its course each performs feats of great strength and skill.

Käsemann chooses not to deal in detail with the particular readings of Pauline texts offered by Stendahl. Instead he discusses the broad subject of justification by faith and saving-history in the Epistle to the Romans. At the same time he chooses to lump Stendahl together with scholars like Munck (b.1904) and Cullmann and to characterize them all equally as conspirators against the Reformation heritage. Further, he simply misunderstands Stendahl when he (Käsemann) credits him with the view that the doctrine of justification by faith is a 'fighting doctrine, directed against Judaism'. As Stendahl was under pains to point out subsequently, his view is that its 'place and function, especially in Romans, are not primarily polemic, but apologetic as he defends the right of Gentile converts to be full members of the people of God' (130).

Thus there are two separate principal questions being pursued here: whether Paul propounds a view of saving-history and, if so, what kind of saving-history it is; and whether Paul, in his doctrine of justification by faith, was engaged in an attack on Judaism and its way of life based on Torah. There is also a secondary question of whether Paul's polemic, if such it was, has any continuing significance for the church.

As far as the first topic is concerned, the two men are more united than their debates might lead one to suppose. Käsemann, as we have seen, was at great pains to distance himself from the anthropological reductionism of his teacher, Bultmann, and to assert that Paul's doctrine of faith was about God's — historical — action in setting his world to rights. Where he takes issue with Stendahl is over the precise nature of God's action in establishing his justice. The strength of Käsemann's position is in his insistence on the paradoxicality of Paul's belief in the power of the Gospel. It is in God's justifying of the ungodly that his rule is established, in a way that merits the laughter of Sarah and that brings victory out of defeat. To this side of Käsemann's lecture Stendahl subsequently gave no attention.

Equally, Käsemann pays little attention to what is one of the main thrusts of Stendahl's paper, namely that Lutheran interpretations of Paul have often seen far too great an opposition between Paul's doctrine of justification by faith and Jewish piety of his day (works-righteousness). The primary aim of Stendahl's paper is to portray Paul's teaching of justification as a way of defending the new way of life of Gentile Christians as a proper response to the new way of salvation which has been opened up by the coming of the Messiah, rather than an attack on the old way that is now superseded. The question that this debate might have opened up (but didn't) is this: To what extent did Paul, if he saw the life of Gentile Christians as having superseded that of Jews, also see it as contrasted or indeed opposed? Stendahl is very persuasive when he shows up the strategies by which subsequent interpreters have increasingly universalised the Law, taking it to mean not just the Mosaic laws but any demands of the human conscience. He is also right to point out that Paul in Romans 7 argues primarily that the Law is holy and good. Yet that still leaves open the question of how far the way of life under the Law could bring salvation, why indeed obedience to the Law is now seen by Paul as inimical to the way of life adopted by Christian converts.

One of Stendahl's continuing themes, which we shall consider in chapter 10, is that we should not allow our desire to find a contemporary meaning for texts to blind us to the particular meaning which they had in their original setting. This leads him to point up the very substantial differences that there are between Paul's attempts to locate the Law within God's overall purposes and subsequent Lutheran accounts of 'justification by faith'. Käsemann argues that however much the particular point of Paul's polemic against justification by works may be seen as a particular debate between Jewish and Gentile Christians, it is still a debate that has continuing significance for us. For what the Jewish nomism that Paul attacks represents, according to Käsemann, is the 'community of 'good' people which turns God's promises into their own privileges and God's commandments into the instruments of self-sanctification' (72). Thus Käsemann agrees with Stendahl that it is a misreading of Paul's doctrine to see it as principally concerned with the Law as an ethical matter and so to read it in principally psychological terms. For Paul the Law was an entity, comprising both the ethical and the cultic which had its place in saving-history and indeed in the cosmos. It was an entity which had its own power that 'leads man astray into the ways of demonstrable piety. It creates the sphere within which man tries to sunder himself from immorality and godlessness, views the history of his fathers' redemption as the guarantee of his own election and claims God's grace as his personal privilege.' Such an attitude Paul calls sin because it is an 'attempt to bring God into dependence on us' (72). The problem that the Gospel lays bare is indeed not men's and women's subjective feelings of guilt but 'the objective fallenness of man . . . which displays itself in its most sinister form in his reliance on his own goodness'. What Paul sets against this is a doctrine of God's justification of the ungodly which is an interpretation of his underlying christology. For 'the true God joins himself to the ungodly and brings them salvation, as he did through Jesus — the ungodly, but not the Pharisees, the Zealots or the men of Qumran' (73).

Käsemann's rejoinder to Stendahl is clearly powerful: it opens up the christological dimensions of Paul's texts and it ties his doctrine of justification into a swingeing attack on Jewish nomism. It is, it has to be said too, argued without too great attention to the text. How can the view that the Law 'leads man astray' be equated with Paul's claims that the Law is holy and good? To see Paul's theology as 'anti-judaistic' in this way is actually to miss a great deal of the pathos of his work, the dilemma into which he is forced by on the one hand his belief in the goodness of the Law and the purposes of God in and through Israel, and on the other his belief in the radically new life that is made possible in Christ and which makes all other forms of life look like bondage. Simply to portray Pauline theology as a polemic against Judaism is to flatten the dialectic -- and to produce a severely distorted picture of contemporary Judaism. This does not, however, mean that what Käsemann says positively about the justification of the ungodly is wrong. Here his reading of Paul comes to life, and he uncovers meanings within the text that will ensure his writing a place in history of New Testament study.

Käsemann's view of 'Jewish nomism' was, of course, by no means original to him. It was widespread within a long-standing tradition of German scholarship which was attacked with fire by the Texan scholar E.P. Sanders. In his *Paul and Palestinian Judaism* (1977) he attacked a whole line of scholarship which had presented the Judaism contemporary to Paul in terms all too reminiscent of the Lutheran portrayal of late-medieval Catholicism. The key term in any such discussion is 'works-righteousness'. Luther had argued that late-mediaeval piety, with its penitential disciplines, sale of indulgences and masses for the dead made salvation depend on the individual's performance of good works rather than on God's grace. So, too, scholars like Ferdinand Weber (1836-1879), Schürer, Bousset, Billerbeck (1853-1932), and Bultmann suggested that salvation for Jews in the first century depended on the performance of 'works of the Law'. Men and women, as it were, run up an account with God where their good and bad deeds are weighed, and it is on the final reckoning that their salvation depends. Billerbeck concluded: 'the old Jewish religion is thus a religion of the most complete self-redemption; it has no room for a redeemer-saviour who dies for the sins of the world' (quoted in *PPJ*, 43). This view, with modifications, pervaded German scholarship until the 1970s and was, as can be readily seen, still influential in the work of Käsemann. It sat all too comfortably with a Lutheran interpretation of Paul as the apostle of justification by faith, for it was the latter doctrine which provided much of the inspiration for such a reading of Judaism.

Sanders's *Paul and Palestinian Judaism* is largely devoted to a close scrutiny of contemporary Jewish texts, attacking such a view of Judaism and establishing instead an alternative view which he entitles 'covenantal nomism'. The alternative view he offers is part of an attempt to discern the 'pattern of Jewish religion', to see, that is, how it functions as a whole, rather than simply to extract some essential characteristics (works as opposed to faith, law as opposed to liberty) or simply to examine certain themes or motifs. We need, he argues, to see how such motifs function within a whole system of beliefs and practices before we can really make sense of them. Equally, before we can compare, for example, Paul and Judaism, we need to see each of them whole and entire, only then going on to compare and contrast.

The notion of 'pattern of religion' is important for Sanders. He is attempting not to offer an account of the whole development of a particular religious community, but rather to discern and describe certain basic patterns of belief and practice which are present in and hold together a perhaps quite considerable degree of diversity of religious communities, such as Lutherans. 'The term "pattern" points toward the question of how one moves from the logical starting point to the logical conclusion of the religion'. It is the 'description of how a religion is perceived by its adherents to function. "Perceived to function" has the sense not of what an adherent does on a day-to-day basis, but of *how getting in and staying in are understood* ' (17).

So the object of the book is to offer an account of two patterns of religion — first-century Judaism and Paul — and to compare them. In the end it is the descriptive rather than the comparative exercise that intrigues Sanders most; he does, however, assert very clearly the distinctiveness of the two patterns.

After some 400 pages of detailed discussion of Jewish texts, Sanders offers the following summary of the pattern of religion which is common to the various Jewish communities and writers whom he has examined:

The 'pattern' or 'structure' of covenantal nomism is this: (1) God has chosen Israel and (2) given the law. The law implies both (3) God's promise to maintain the election and (4) the requirement to obey. (5) God rewards obedience and punishes transgression. (6) The law provides for means of atonement, and atonement results in (7) maintenance or re-establishment of the covenantal relationship. (8) All those who are maintained in the covenant by obedience, atonement and God's mercy belong to the group which will be saved. An important interpretation of the first and last points is that election and ultimately salvation are considered to be by God's mercy rather than human achievement (422).

It is clear that such a description of Judaism is fundamentally opposed to the standard German Protestant view which we outlined above. Here salvation is not solely dependent on men's and women's efforts to build up a sufficient tally of good works but principally on the gracious election of Israel by God; principally, but not exclusively. Ultimately, a Jew's salvation depends not only on his election but also on his obedience. For, as Sanders says, *'obedience maintains one's position in the covenant, but it does not earn God's grace as such.* It simply keeps an individual in the group which is the recipient of God's grace' (420). It is, that is to say, God's grace which alone is responsible for someone's getting into the group; obedience (along with atonement and God's mercy) is what keeps someone in. Of course, salvation depends not merely on getting in but on staying in.

So on Sanders's own admission, works do count in Judaism. Moreover, it seems to me, there is nothing so very surprising in that. It is part of the moral seriousness of Judaism that it is passionately interested in God's will for the world, for the way it should be ordered and that therefore men and women should behave. Those who reject his will, who are disobedient and reject even his offers of forgiveness and restitution, are excluded. Yet there seems to be a strange reluctance on Sanders's part to give full recognition to Jewish delight in *doing* the Law. It is almost as if Sanders, in order to correct Lutheran portrayals of Judaism as pelagian (that is, as making salvation dependent solely on men and women's efforts) has striven to portray it in terms that are as Augustinian (salvation dependent solely on the divine grace) as possible. In fact on such a scale Judaism seems largely (though 4 Ezra might be thought to be an exception) to be semi-pelagian, representing salvation as dependent on a conjunction of God's mercy and men's and women's obedient response. Of course, as Sanders could well point out, this does not mean that Jews and semi-pelagians share the same pattern of religion. How God's mercy is mediated, what the precise nature of God's will is, who the covenant people are, these and many other questions would distinguish their different patterns of religion. But on the question of 'grace and works' they might be said to share similar views.

None of this is to deny the enormous service which Sanders has rendered to the guild of New Testament scholars. His fierce polemic and detailed re-examination of the Jewish texts have made scholars deeply aware of the dangers of misrepresenting Judaism when seeing it through Christian dogmatic eyes. Yet it would have to be said that Sanders's own difficulties in giving full weight to the importance of Law in the Jewish pattern of religion themselves demonstrate what a massive task it is for people to think themselves out of their own inherited traditions.

When Sanders turns to Paul, his polemic is, not surprisingly, directed against Lutheran interpretations which see Paul's doctrine of justification by faith as the centre of his theology. Referring to Schweitzer, Sanders's argues that justification by faith cannot be central because: (1) where it first occurs in Galatians it is worked out with the help of other, better established notions related to the notion of 'in-Christ'; (2) it only occurs where the question of the Law has to be dealt with; and (3) Paul does not draw on the notion when seeking a 'basis for ethics, nor in the doctrines of baptism and Lord's Supper' (Schweitzer, *Mysticism*, quoted in *PPJ* [439]). It is rather two other notions which centrally determine Paul's life and thought: '(1) that Jesus Christ is Lord, that in him God has provided for the salvation of all who believe (in the general sense of "be converted"), and that he will soon return to bring all things to an end; (2) that he, Paul, was called to be the apostle to the Gentiles' (441f).

Paul, that is to say, did not start with a deep human problem to which he sought an answer, as Luther did with his question: 'how do I find a just God?'. He started with a solution, namely the conviction that in Jesus Christ life and salvation had been given to the world and that he, Paul, was commissioned to bring the news of this to the Gentiles. His subsequent reflections about the nature of the Law and of its place in God's purposes were just that: subsequent. They were an attempt, with diverse expressions, to think through his basic conviction that in Christ there was life. The problem with Judaism, for Paul, was not that it had produced a deep division within him (Phil. 3 gives no evidence of that); it was that it was not Christianity (552). For it was in Christ, rather than in Judaism, that he had discovered life.

How, then, did Paul spell out his central conviction that Jesus was Lord and that he, Paul, was his apostle, called to announce the Gospel to the Gentiles before the end of the ages? What kind of pattern of religion did Paul develop? In simple terms for Paul '[o]ne enters by becoming one with Christ Jesus and one stays in by remaining "pure and blameless" and by not engaging in unions which are destructive of the union with Christ'. From this a sequence of thought is developed which Sanders summarizes as follows:

God has sent Christ to be the saviour of all, both Jew and Gentile (and has called Paul to be the apostle to the Gentiles); one participates in salvation by becoming one person with Christ, dying with him to sin and sharing the promise of his resurrection; the transformation, however, will not be completed until the Lord returns; meanwhile one who is in Christ has been freed from the power of sin and the uncleanness of transgression, and his behaviour should be determined by his new situation; since Christ died to save all, all men must have been under the dominion of sin, 'in the flesh' as opposed to being in the Spirit. It seems reasonable to call this way of thinking 'participationist eschatology' (549).

It may be helpful here to ask two questions: what place does the notion of justification by faith have within this — Pauline — 'pattern of religion'; and, what is the relation of this pattern to the Jewish pattern of covenantal nomism? These are both matters that Sanders rightly discusses fully.

In the first instance, it is Sanders's view that 'justification by faith' is for Paul a transfer term. It refers, that is, to 'getting in' rather than 'staying in'. To say that Christian believers are justified by faith is to say that it is in some sense by virtue of their faith that they have become one with Christ. But in what sense? 'Faith' or 'believing' is, for Paul, the principal word for participation in the saving action of God in Jesus Christ (447). It is, that is to say, a central term which is clearly associated within the Pauline corpus with other key terms such as 'in Christ', which refer to the reality of the union between believers and Christ which is at the heart of Paul's perception of the new life he enjoys. The phrase 'justification by faith', however, is by no means such a central term. It occurs only in specific contexts, principally in Galatians and Romans, and there predominantly in an antithetical use. 'Justification by faith' is contrasted with 'justification by (works of) the Law' in order to make the point that life in Christ cannot be the end result of works of the Law. Paul's point here is not that observance of the Law in itself is responsible for the human predicament (as in Käsemann's view, above) but that it does not, as a matter of fact, lead to life in Christ.

Why does Paul choose to use the language of justification here, which in current Jewish use referred principally to the right standing of men and women before God? In the face of debates with Jewish Christians about the observation of the Law Paul, so Sanders argues, is led to reflect further on the human predicament (to which participation in Christ is a solution) and to describe it in terms of transgression, as opposed to the language of slavery and bondage which he uses elsewhere. In so far, that is to say, as the human plight is to be seen as exclusion from God because of past transgressions, Paul denies that it can be resolved by works of the Law. All of this is, however, not the central thrust of Paul's theology, which asserts rather that life is to be had as a result of accepting the Lordship of Christ. Moreover, when Paul reflects on the life and freedom in the Spirit that such participation in Christ brings he is more inclined to see his former condition as one of bondage than of transgression.

This is a useful clarification of Paul's language which facilitates comparison of the two patterns of Pauline and Jewish religion. One of the intellectual excitements of Sanders's work is the way in which he is able to pull the results of detailed exegetical work together and is not afraid to synthesize and compare. Taken in the round, he asserts, Pauline and Jewish religion constitute two very different patterns of religion. If Judaism affirms that entrance to the covenant-people of Israel is by God's election, Paul asserts that entrance into the people of God is by faith in Christ. For Jews, staying in is dependant on obedience to the Law, repentance for transgressions and God's forgiveness of such failures. For Paul staying in, too, depends on obedience; but for him this is spelt out in terms of remaining 'pure and blameless', of not engaging in unions which are alien to the Christian believers' life in Christ. The difference between the two patterns of religion can, moreover, be brought out by a consideration of the different way the same word groups are used. In Jewish literature *dik*-words (words with a common stem which lie behind translations like 'justify'. righteousness', etc.) are predominantly used substantively to refer to those within the covenant-people who are obedient; it is a status term. In Paul as we have seen it is used more often verbally as a transfer term referring to the believers' entering into union with Christ (here there are some parallels in Qumran). For Jews, 'repentance' is a central term relating to the overcoming of transgressions of those within the covenant. In Paul, the term has virtually disappeared. Again, 'sin' in Judaism refers 'uniformly' to transgressions. While such uses are to be found in Paul (notably in Rom. 1-3) the dominant concept is of sin as a power from which one must be freed in order to be saved. 'One must transfer from the lordship of sin to the lordship of Christ' (547).

The language used for describing what it is to 'stay in' is also different. *'Both Judaism and Paul take full account of the individual and the group'* (547). In Judaism God's covenant-relation is with Israel; the individual within the covenant must remain pious, right with God. 'In Paul one comes to be among the saved by the act of faith which results in participating *in Christ*. One shares the inheritance by becoming a "joint heir" and *participates* in Christ's resurrection' (547). But the notion of participation in Christ, difficult as it is to define, is not like that of membership of the covenant people, one of simple group membership. There are no parallel expressions in Judaism to Paul's notion of becoming one person in Christ (Gal. 3:28).

Finally with the possible exception of Qumran there is no parallel in Judaism to Paul's notion that all must transfer into the new community.

This is the extent of Sanders's comparison and contrast of Judaism with Paul. What he does not do is to suggest that either of these patterns of religion is superior to the other. 'In saying that participationist eschatology is different from covenantal nomism, I mean only to say that it is different, not that the difference is instructive for seeing the error of Judaism's way' (552). In this sense Sanders parts company with earlier *Religionsgeschichtler* who had often been all too ready to set out their evaluations of different types of religion. At the same time, unlike them he offers no explanation of the genesis of Paul's pattern of religion—hazarding only that behind them there may lie differences of experience which are however 'much more opaque for research than is thought' (549).

Equally, Sanders makes no attempt to explain, other than in negative terms, what Paul meant by participation in Christ. 'We seem to lack a category of "reality" — real participation in Christ, real possession of the Spirit — which lies between naive cosmological speculation and belief in magical transference on the one hand and a revised self-understanding on the other' (522). Like Käsemann, that is, he sees the inadequacy of Bultmann's anthropological reading of Paul; unlike Käsemann he recognizes that merely to restate Paul's doctrine in mythological terms is not the same as interpreting it. Much, indeed, of what Paul thought was falsified by events. While others (like Bultmann) may pick up the themes which have proved more durable and construct a theology out of them, such a course does not offer a 'real and exhaustive interpretation of what Paul meant. What he really thought was just what he said: that Christ was appointed Lord by God for the salvation of all who believe, that those who believe belong to the Lord and become one with him, and that in virtue of their incorporation in the Lord they will be saved on the Day of the Lord' (523).

It is hard not to see a powerful theological (or anti-theological) agenda at work here. Sanders laudably wishes to destroy Christian misrepresentations of Judaism which have too close connections with anti-Semitism. He wishes further to set Pauline Christianity and Judaism alongside each other as indifferently valuable religions, and finally he wants to cut the ground away from at least Lutheran forms of Christianity by denying them their prime witness, Paul. Such an agenda may, indeed, have powerful attractions for those who teach in Departments of Religion; it may importantly reflect the needs and perceptions of a multicultural society like the United States or indeed the United Kingdom. One might well reflect on the sharp contrast in view that there is between Sanders's presentation of Paul and that of dominant views in the Southern States. Nevertheless one may ask whether in this grand design, in his purging of anti-Semitism, of conservative denominationalism (and much else), some grain of truth has not been lost, whether indeed in a strange and paradoxical way, the search for the truth itself has not been prematurely suspended. Bultmann's attempt to interpret Paul's message existentially may, in practice, have amounted to a reduction of that message; but that does not mean that the enterprise was, in principle, misconceived. Sanders's concluding remark that what Paul thought was what he said (523) is systematically misleading: is Sanders equating Paul's beliefs with his linguistic expressions of them, such that no other expressions of them would do? Or is he simply affirming that, in his linguistic utterances, he did indeed give expression to what he believed? The first reading would make any attempt at interpreting anything vain — for only the original words would do; the second simply opens up all the old questions about how we are to interpret Paul, that is to find contemporary linguistic expressions which do adequately express his thoughts.

Such a task may be beyond us. Perhaps it is true that we do not have such terms, that at most we can attempt to define negatively (as in fact Sanders does) what Paul means by 'in Christ'. But before abandoning such a task we should perhaps explore the language of religious experience more thoroughly.

Again, while there may be important matters in which Paul was wrong (such as his expectation of an imminent end to the present world), we do not, as a consequence, have the right to consign all that he said to the past. It is refreshing to have such questions vigorously raised; one might have wished that they had been raised in a less polemical, more explorative way. The danger is that such wholesale dismissals may lead us to neglect important insights into the nature of reality.

While Sanders's work thus runs out into a declaration of failure, as he is confronted with the task of attempting to make sense of Paul's 'participationist eschatology', others have sought to find new ways of tackling the task.

As we have seen, Schweitzer, who had pioneered such a view of Paul's theology, had sought an understanding of it by attempting to set it within a broad classification of types of mysticism. Sanders declares, not without some justification, that types of religious experience are hard to track down by the methods of research available to us. Few presently would be disposed to challenge this view, though G. Theissen's *Psychological Perpectives* (1983) is a lone exception to this view which still awaits a receptive readership. There are major tasks here as yet largely unaddressed.

Theissen's work in another field has, however, proved extremely fruitful. In a series of essays, *The Social Setting of Pauline Christianity* (1982) published originally in 1974-5 in German, he opened the way for a sociological approach to the study of Paul that has inspired a rich debate and led indirectly at least to the production of works like W. A. Meeks's *The First Urban Christians* (1983) reviewed later in this chapter.

Theissen's study of the Corinthian community attempts at one level to describe the 'social setting' of Pauline Christianity. Here there are clearly problems, for the texts do not themselves offer descriptions of a such setting;

or only indirectly. When Paul writes that there are not many of noble birth in the community (1 Cor. 1:26-9), this is certainly not part of an objective social description of the community, rather it is part of an attempt to create unity within his congregation. Thus, the kind of descriptive task which Theissen sets himself requires some sophistication. How can we move from the particular historical situation which Paul addresses to judgments about the social status of the addressees, and beyond that to judgments about the broader social context in which they were set? Theissen sees in this question one of the central points of tension between historical studies and sociological studies (typical and generalized). What he attempts here is a form of social history: the attempt to read texts is such as to illuminate the particular situations to which they refer, while setting them within a wider nexus which pays particular attention to those forces/factors within it which shape and will shape patterns of human interaction.

It is, as he has himself made clear, part of a wider quest for a critical understanding of religious belief and practice which attempts to extend the debate which Sanders was later to abandon (see esp. Theissen's *On Having a Critical Faith*, 1978).

Let us consider an example of Theissen's workings here. In his essay on 'Social Stratification in the Corinthian Community' (69-119), he argues that Paul's claim that among the Corinthian Christians there are not many wise, not many powerful, not many of noble birth (1 Cor. 1:26-9) should not be read simply as a direct statement that the Corinthian Church was predominantly a church of the poor and the powerless. At the very least it suggests that there were some who were powerful, and Paul's letters refer specifically to some — Stephanas, Gaius, Crispus, Sosthenes — who clearly fell into this class. Much of the essay which follows is taken up with a fascinating analysis of the various hints which Paul and Acts provide about the status and activities of at least some members of Paul's churches. Of course, merely identifying the social status of the various members would do little of itself to explain social interrelationships within the Corinthian congregation which create the problems to which Paul addresses himself , nor to explain the interaction, either individual or social, between Corinthian Christians and the world of the city-states which they inhabited. Here the situations of conflict within the congregations serve to provide illumination. For in such situations we may perceive more than just a clash of personalities, more simply than a clash of theological views, but the point at which complex networks of social forces interact and create problems. 'Conflicts are also atypical events, but in most cases they expose to view the structures which transcend individuals' (181). Actions, attitudes and beliefs which are unproblematic in one social setting may be read as deeply threatening and deviant in another. In newly emerging communities such conflicts may reveal much about the contrasting worlds·from which new members come.

In this respect the conflict over eating meat offered to idols is instructive

(121-43). Not everyone in the ancient world would have eaten meat with any regularity. For the poorer members of society the occasions on which they ate meat would have principally been restricted to particular public occasions such as the celebration of victory or to public sacrificial meals and religious festivals. That is to say, eating meat was not part of their regular way of life; when they did eat it, it was usually in connection with some pagan religious rite (125-9). By contrast, for the wealthier, meat eating would have been more frequent. As well as in the public occasions mentioned they would also have participated in private meals at temples, and this would have been an integral part of the pattern of social life and commerce that sustained and constituted their social standing. Non-participation in such events would have caused difficulties, raised doubts about their standing in society and created obstacles to their exercise of their rights and duties. The city treasurer Erastus (Rom. 16:23) may have had designs on office as overseer of public places and buildings where consecrated meat was sold. To have publicly dissociated himself from such meats would clearly have undermined his position (130).

Against this background we can begin to discern something about the nature of the conflict over eating meats sacrificed to idols which Paul addresses in 1 Cor. 8 and 10. At its simplest, the problem is that while for the poorer members their new life in Christ can be lived out by making a clean break with their pagan past (at least as far as attendance at public festivals is concerned), for those of higher social status such a break is more complicated and threatening. It would mean a rupture with their existing patterns of social life which underpinned their status. The 'weak', by contrast, in breaking with former patterns of life, would be fully compensated for what they gave up by 'access in the congregation to the upper classes who could use their wealth to serve the congregation and thus to serve the socially weaker' (132).

The success of this analysis of the conflict is striking, and is what has attracted most attention and imitation. But Theissen's analysis of Paul's response to the problems should not be overlooked. Paul's position has often been criticized as inconsistent. On the one hand he argues that idols are nothing (1 Cor. 8:4ff) and that to those who possess such knowledge there is therefore no danger or problem with eating meats which have been sacrificed. On the other he asserts that Christians cannot both participate in Christ and in demons (1 Cor. 10:20). Such arguments may have been directed respectively to the 'strong' and the 'weak'. Theissen suggests that an appeal to 'knowledge' may be typically characteristic of higher social-status groups, and that in 1 Cor. 8f. Paul is addressing himself principally to the strong. Paul's approach is clear. It is to plead with the 'strong' to show consideration to the weak. Paul does not, that is to say, prohibit attendance at all meals, rather at those which will easily come to the attention of the wider congregation. Private dinner parties form a convenient exception (1 Cor. 10:23ff). This discriminates against the weak, whose sole opportunities for meat eating, namely at public festivals, are hereby cut off. But Paul's stance in 1 Cor. 11 will reinforce the weak's resolve to break with their former pattern of life and integrate into the new community. Thus Paul's vacillating theological stance subserves a broad policy of 'love-patriarchalism', whereby existing social inequities are taken up and integrated into a more coherent whole by transfusing them 'with a spirit of concern, of respect, and of personal solicitude' (139).

Two things may be noticed here. What Theissen writes about Paul's attempts to integrate the conflicting parties in Corinth into a more cohesive society is in its way an attempt to understand Paul's 'participationist eschatology'. It does so, not by identifying it with any particular type of religious experience, nor by simply reducing it to the expression of a particular set of needs in a particular group, but rather by attending to its social function. On such a view the function of religious language has to be distinguished from the particular intention of its author. Religious utterances may have social effects which are real and recurrent and which form no part of their author's intention. Such functions may be variously classified, as designed to produce order or to control conflict, as creative or conservative. In identifying the integrative role of Paul's arguments about food offered to idols, Theissen offers one explanation of the way in which Paul's doctrines of participation in Christ function: serve, that is, to integrate people into a new society and group (see J.H. Schütz's, b.1933, excellent introduction, p. 16).

It is interesting to note how, for Theissen, this, in broad outline at least, forms part of a wider explanatory exercise. The notion that Paul is here developing a form of 'love-patriarchalism' which enables the effective integration of socially distinct groups is taken up into a wider thesis about the reasons for Christianity's emergence as the dominant religion in the Roman world. Because attempts to extend social and economic power to the lower levels of society often failed (for lack of resources), a form of love-patriarchalism could emerge as a more successful way of dealing with social conflicts and division. What Paul is working out in the microcosm of the church in Corinth will become part of a much wider strategy for dealing with conflict in the Mediterranean world (107-10). This is both to show how the significance of Paul's letters extends well beyond their immediate sense and purpose, and, however, to tie them in firmly to a world of the Roman Mediterranean which will in due course be superseded by other forms of political economy. The functionalist account also serves to explain the wider significance of the Pauline synthesis. The explanation, however, also ties the texts back into their world: love-patriarchalism may have served the particular needs of the early centuries of our era. It is not a continuing recipe for social integration and self-realisation.

Another form of functionalist analysis, freely acknowledging its debt to Theissen, was offered by W. A. Meeks in *The First Urban Christians* (1983).

Meeks describes himself as a 'moderate functionalist' (7); the questions to be asked about the early Christian movement are those about how it worked.

> Society is viewed as a process, in which personal identity and social forms are mutually and continuously created by interactions that occur by means of symbols. Culture, as Geertz puts it, consists of 'webs of significance'. Moreover, there is some real but complex relation between social structure and symbolic structure, and religion is an integral part of the cultural web (6).

Such a functionalism, that is to say, is interested in the interactions between the personal beliefs, norms and self-understanding that make up a person's identity, and the social forms which regulate patterns of association within particular societies. Such interaction, so it is claimed, is mediated through networks of symbols, part of which is provided by religious belief, ritual and practice. Such a view is not reductionist; it does not, that is to say, reduce the significance of religious belief and ritual to its capacity to effect social change. Indeed, it is open to the way in which there may be interaction through the medium of such networks of communication between individuals and the social forms and structures which they inhabit. Nor is it committed to a particular view of the function of religious belief. Meeks distances himself from the views of Geertz which he sees as linking religion too closely to an integrative function. 'In fact, it may be disruptive or, paradoxically, integrative for a disruptive movement' (6).

In all this Meeks is in broad agreement with Theissen. Neither is reductionist; neither is committed to a particular functionalist explanation of religious beliefs. Nevertheless there are interesting variations in the way the broad perspective is developed in their work. Theissen's work, as we have seen, is principally concerned with the way in which religious belief served to overcome the conflicts occasioned within the Corinthian church by the differing social status of its members; Meeks attempts a broader task, a description of the social structures and forms of the Pauline churches on the one hand: social level, formation of the *ekklesia*, governance, ritual; and an account of patterns of belief and life on the other. In a brief but fascinating last section he attempts a sketch of possible correlations between social structures and symbolic systems: 'the ways in which sacred symbols affect reality and social experience affects symbolization' (190). The difference is more one of descriptive style than of overall strategy. Meeks is more comprehensive and also offers a 'thicker' description (this is, of course, explained in no small measure by the difference between an extended monograph and a series of essays).

Again, it is interesting to consider what account Meeks offers of Paul's 'participationist eschatology'. In a sense, of course, the whole book is an attempt to answer the question: how did the beliefs and rituals of the Pauline Churches bind its members together? Here we can only select part of the discussion.

Meeks opens his account with an extended treatment of Paul's urban environment. The social structures of the Pauline churches are located, of course, within a particular existing society with its own forms of association. The fact that the church did not simply adopt an existing pattern of association must have led to tensions for its members, as is evidenced by the issue of food offered to idols. Meeks treats this as a particular case of boundary definition for the church. Whereas the synagogue was able to draw more or less tight boundaries around itself by the development of purity regulations, dietary rules, sabbath observance, avoidance of pagan ritual, etc. — rules which deliberately separated them from the Gentiles (92, 97, 103) — the introduction of such rules was fiercely rejected by Paul for the obvious reason that he was attempting to create a community out of both Jews and Gentiles. Within Paul's community the introduction of such rules would have created a sharply differentiated and stratified community, one that differed from the familial one that developed. This is not to say that the group had no divisions, internal or external; nor that in the course of its development it did not develop, precisely through its use of familial language, more hierarchical forms (76f); but such divisions are of a different order.

The dispute about food offered to idols (97-100) raises such questions in a particularly difficult form. On the one hand it raises questions about the external boundaries. Prohibitions on.participation would have made continued participation in other forms of urban life very difficult for some; nevertheless its continued practice offers difficulties for the life of the *ekklesia* because of the different cultural significance such actions had for the strong and the weak. So Paul cautions discretion.

Such a compromise can hardly have been very stable. The love-patriarchalism which Theissen identifies needs buttressing in other ways and Meeks goes on to detail some of these, such as injunctions to holiness in sexual relations and the rejection, for the most part, of divorce. There is also the more subtle impact of specifically Christian beliefs: that they had received a peculiar revelation, that their lives were conformed to the pattern of a suffering and glorified Messiah. Here expectations are being created that the community and its members will meet with opposition and suffering, and these will be reinforced by actual experience of opposition. Certainly Paul, by emphasizing his own experience of suffering and encouraging his churches to imitate him, is assisting this process with some vigour.

Equally, in its rituals the community possesses powerful means for reinforcing a sense of the group's identity. Meeks discusses this in two sections (88ff and 157ff), as he considers the use of language and ritual in the formation of the community. What he shows very powerfully is the way in which the baptismal rite, with its symbolism of dying/rising, putting off the old/putting on the new, and being baptised into Christ, inculcates a strong sense of breaking with previous social ties and crossing the threshold from one world to another. What Meeks points to (following V. Turner, [88f]) is that the experience of the Pauline community is here untypical of many such rites of passage. In the normal pattern, separation from one's existing social ties is followed by a period of liminality in which the initiates enjoy *communitas* and a close, undifferentiated mode of social relationship, followed by reintegration into the structures of the given society. However, if the initiatory rituals are exercised not for the dominant society, but within a sect or marginal group that distinguishes itself sharply from the society, that group may continue for some time to exhibit features of *communitas* (90f). It is this pattern of intimate and spontaneous association which is, in Meeks's view, reinforced by the language of brother and sister, the emphasis on mutual love, the talk about the Spirit and its gifts. The development of tighter structures emerges out of this initial period. In the earlier period existing social structures must have had some effect on the house-churches of the Pauline communities.

The same process of interaction is to be posited, though with much greater tentativeness, when Meeks comes to give a more systematic account of the patterns of belief and life in the Pauline churches. In the section on evil and its reversal (183-9) Meeks traces out the web of metaphors by which Paul develops a vision of evil and in so doing focuses, interprets and answers the group's 'disgruntlement' with the way things are (184). These powerful images of bondage and liberation, of guilt and justification, of estrangement and reconciliation, deformity and transformation were operational within a particular social context. What Meeks points to is the striking lack, in relation to the negative images Paul uses, of direct reference to social or political factors. On the one hand, the letters are concerned with personal problems, immorality, weakness, fear, suffering; on the other the scale embraces the whole world and Satan. The whole framework is theological, bounded by the final judgment of God.

> That is, this symbolism derives not from social relations like master and slave, father and son, judge and accused, friend and enemy, but from organic images of growth and decay, life and death, division and union, and from physical or magical notions of changing shapes or of visual transformation by mirrors. This imagery appears sporadically and fragmentarily in the Pauline letters, and its interpretation has been especially troublesome (187).

In his final four pages Meeks cautiously points to correlation between the social realities of the Pauline churches and the patterns of belief which he has sketched. Belief in the unity of God and the attribution, indeed, of some of the divine functions to Jesus may correlate with the remarkable commitment to unity of the scattered groups of Christians around the Mediterranean. Belief in the activity of the divine Spirit in the community relates to the degree of commitment and the intimacy of social intercourse within the local communities. Belief in the coming end of the present age correlates with the break that Christians have made with the existing order. Belief in the crucified and risen Messiah links with expectation about the opposition and suffering that Christians will encounter and with a joy in the liberation they already experience in the community itself. Such beliefs have the power to shape people's perceptions of their world and to structure the life of their communities, but the process whereby such notions are fully embodied in communities is long and diverse and cannot be simply read off the symbols themselves. It requires close scrutiny of the history of the many diverse communities which took their inspiration from these texts.

Meeks's book is full of rich and suggestive studies and shows how ideas, images, metaphors and rituals have their setting and life in communities, how they affect these communities and in turn are affected by them. It helps us to understand the nature of such ideas as it points to their power to shape whole communities and churches.

In a sense this is, of course, not an answer to Sanders's search for a category by which to interpret Paul's 'participationist eschatology'. What Sanders asked for was a concept which would adequately represent the *res* to which Paul referred when he spoke of Christians' unity in Christ. Albert Schweitzer had attempted to offer this in speaking of various types of mysticism and locating Paul's beliefs within them. Meeks, at least in some passages, suggests that Sanders's quest needs to be redefined. Religious doctrines and ideas are to be seen not so much as referring to certain theological truths and realities as providing societies with cultural-linguistic tools for making sense of and for constructing their worlds. Of course, Meeks properly recognizes that language can fulfil such a function only insofar as it actually says something. But we understand it only when we abandon the search for some transcendent reality to which it refers and see it as creative of new worlds. We shall consider such views further in chapter 10.

Note

1. Quoted in D. Way, The Lordship of Christ, 123

List of works cited

D. Bonhoeffer, *Letters and Papers from Prison*, Munich, 1951 (German); London, 1953 (English)

E. Käsemann, *Perspectives on Paul*, Tübingen, 1969 (German); London, 1971 (English)

E. Käsemann, *Commentary on Romans*, Tübingen, 1973 (German); London, 1980 (English)

E. Käsemann, 'Justification and Saving History', in *Perspectives on Paul*, 60-78

W.A. Meeks *The First Urban Christians. The Social World of the Apostle Paul*, London and New Haven, 1983

E.P. Sanders, *Paul and Palestinian Judaism*, London, 1977

K. Stendahl, 'The Apostle Paul and the Introspective Conscience of the West', in *Paul Among Jews and Gentiles*, Philadelphia, 1976, 78-96

G. Theissen, *Psychological Aspects of Pauline Christianity*, Göttingen, 1983, (German); Edinburgh, 1987 (English)

G. Theissen, *On Having a Critical Faith*, Munich, 1978 (German); London, 1979 (English)

G. Theissen, *The Social Setting of Pauline Christianity*, Edinburgh, 1982

D.V. Way, *The Lordship of Christ: Ernst Käsemann's Interpretation of Paul's Theology*, Oxford, 1991

8

The Development of Markan Study since Bultmann

Markan scholarship in Germany up to the early 1950 had been greatly indebted to the view of the form-critics that the evangelists were principally collectors of the tradition, rather than original authors in their own right. In this, scholars were not simply acting out of lack of interest in the theological contribution of the New Testament authors as such — Bultmann had, after all, devoted his major energies to discerning and expounding the theologies of John and Paul. They were acknowledging the justice of a literary historical judgement about the nature of the Gospel genre or *Gattung*.

The last fifty years have certainly seen remarkable shifts of opinion away from the apparent consensus of Markan studies in Germany in the 1940s. They have not, however, seen the emergence of anything like a consensus within the discipline. There has been a diversity of reasons for the growth of interest in the authorial role of the Evangelists: different views of the literary nature of the Gospels; different views of the Evangelists' independence over against their sources; and different assessments of the reliability of scholarly judgements about the history of the Synoptic tradition. There has too been a diversity of reasons why some have wished to express caution about what might have been an emerging redactional critical consensus: a more positive assessment of the form-critics' understanding of the genre; an increasing scepticism about the results of tradition-historical studies; a critical response to the variety of theologies which has been attributed to the Evangelists; and a more radical questioning of the value of any kind of search for authorial meaning. We might say that there is a radical divide between those who see the task of Gospel studies as being to discern, as far as is possible, the original meaning of the author and those who believe that such a task is, for whatever reason, misconceived.

Moreover within each of these two camps there are further sharp divisions. Those who seek the theology of Mark may differ radically about the extent and nature of his sources, his manner of dealing with them, his situation within the early church and, of course, about the nature of his theology. Those who are cautious about giving so much attention to the author's intention may do so because they believe that he was heavily constrained by his tradition; or they may do so because they believe that the search for authorial intention simply mistakes its importance and in consequence distracts from a proper reading of the text itself.

Markan studies, we have suggested, are divided. One reviewer, considering three of the major German New Testament commentaries produced in recent years, declared that the 'state of confusion is total'.[1] A brief review of the history of Markan studies may help to elucidate this. Thereafter we shall consider some of the representative works in the field and offer some analysis.

At the turn of the century enquiries into the sources of the synoptic Gospels had arrived at a broad consensus, the 'two document hypothesis', which declared Mark and Q to be the two major sources of Matthew and Luke. This directed attention towards Mark as the earliest Gospel and therefore the primary source for the life and work of Jesus. The hypothesis was also taken as the basis for the vast majority of subsequent work on the Gospels, tradition-historical, form-critical and redaction-critical. This means, *inter alia*, that the investment of the discipline as a whole in the hypothesis is enormous: any attempts to replace it with an alternative view meet with sustained opposition and, to date, little success.

The most obvious effect of the two-document hypothesis on Markan studies was to establish it as a primary source for historical studies of Jesus; perhaps more interestingly and subtly, it provided a basis for a sketch of early Christian history, seeing the Gospels as evidence for different stages of the earliest Christian communities' beliefs. Here, as we have already seen (chapter 2), the work of Wrede in *The Messianic Secret* is of prime significance. He drew attention to a range of theological motifs in the Gospel which were not easily explained as straight historical observations: the command to silence to demons and to the disciples; similar commands to those healed; secret, private teaching to the disciples; a parable theory; and the disciples' lack of understanding. He himself believed that these motifs were the product of the early Christian community, and that Mark had focussed them around the idea that the secret of Jesus' Messiahship would not be revealed until the resurrection (Mk 9:9).

The debt of Markan studies to Wrede is enormous, and we shall have occasion to discuss it further when we consider Räisänen's work in the next section. It is often hailed as the forerunner of redaction-ritical studies of the Gospels. Yet, while its importance for these can hardly be overstated, it is not the case that Wrede attributed the secret as such to Mark.[2]

This emphasis on the primacy of the community was, moreover, as we saw in chapter 4, strongly endorsed by the work of the form-critics published after the First World War, and this in two ways. In the first place their whole focus was on the traditions which lay behind the Gospels. They sought to isolate the original units of the oral tradition and to make conjectures about their particular histories. They also analysed the form of the Gospels themselves and concluded that they were principally collections of tales. Unlike contemporary Graeco-Roman lives and biographies they were very loose collections of stories from the oral tradition, not dissimilar to medieval collections of legends of the saints or of Faust. They were works of popular literature, rather than of developed *Hochliteratur*. At most, the Evangelists were responsible for providing the setting for the individual tales and a broad narrative framework by means of which to string them together. They were not in any obvious sense creative literary figures.

Reaction against these views came in the early 1950s and swelled into a great tide of PhD theses on sections of the Gospels as redaction-criticism moved into its heyday. We can consider here only the story of Markan studies but similar trends could be traced in studies of Matthew and Luke. In Markan studies the important early works were by E. Lohmeyer (1890-1946), R.H. Lightfoot (1883-1953), W. Marxsen (b.1919) and J.M. Robinson (b.1924). They attempted to discern ways in which the Evangelist had expressed his own views of the story which came to him through an albeit fragmented tradition: in his handling of topology (Galilee v. Jerusalem), and through his exploitation of certain theological motifs (parousia and resurrection, cosmic struggles with Satan, the Messianic Secret). Studies of various aspects of the Gospel followed: Mark's treatment of the miracle stories, of the passion narrative, of discipleship; and eventually there emerged a number of major commentaries which reflected these more specialized treatments: E. Schweizer (1967), H. Anderson (1976), W. Pesch (1976-77), J. Gnilka (1978-79), W. Schmithals (1979), D. Lührmann (1987), which occasioned U. Luz's (b.1938) remark quoted above, that the state of confusion was total.

The reason for this was, principally, the quite different views which the three commentators took of the Evangelist's relation to his tradition. At one level what this reflects is quite simply the imperfections of the tradition-historical method of enquiry. We simply do not have the means for making accurate judgements about the history of the development of the pre-Markan tradition up to and including its redaction by Mark. Formal criteria may, it is true, suggest interesting ways of reading the documents. We can perhaps see in our present text an amalgam of originally separate units and thus begin to hazard a guess as to the process whereby these texts came together. But even that, speculative though it is, rests on the assumption that the process of tradition is one of gradual accretion, rather than one of a series of performances, each of which realises variously some of the potentiality of the tradition itself (see G. Theissen, *Miracles*). While this in itself is enough to explain the confusion, there is another dilemma at the heart of redaction-critical studies. Little attention has been paid (though see Güttgemanns (b.1935) and Kelber (b.1935)) to the question of orality and literacy. Literary histories, we should at least assume, are different from oral traditions. The continuities and discontinuities between oral performances of unwritten traditions (stories, disputes, etc.) and literary recastings of written texts, we must surely assume, are of a different nature. Consider the difference between an accurate scribe and a skilled editor, between someone who retells 'accurately' but 'murders' someone else's story and the variations that may occur in the retelling of the same story by the same person on different occasions. Reconstructions of the history of traditional material have tended to be created by analogy from observations of the editorial changes which Matthew and Luke have made to Mark. Just as we can (more or less) get back to Mark by paring away the Matthaean and Lukan additions, so too, it is thought, we may be able to get back to the — many — layers of the tradition by similar 'paring'. But, even so, Matthew and Luke do not only add: they omit, they modify. If we were to pursue the analogy strictly, then we would also have to reconstruct earlier phrases which have been lost by deletion or modification and this clearly becomes impossibly speculative.

Furthermore, the disjunction between orality and literacy points to a further confusion in the discipline, not sufficiently noticed. It is this: there is a relatively smooth fit between source and redaction-critical studies; there is something approaching rivalry between form-criticism and tradition-historical criticism on the one hand and redaction-criticism on the other. The way this is manifested can be seen most clearly in Mark and goes back to the puzzle which Wrede posed: are the various motifs which compose the Messianic Secret the product of the community or of the Evangelist? How much of Mark's Gospel do we attribute to him, how much to his tradition? The more we see his Gospel as a deposit of the Early Christian community's traditions, the less we shall be disposed to see Mark as a creative author. One of the most illuminating if daunting facts to emerge from the comparison of the commentaries of Pesch, Gnilka and Schmithals is the fact that they disagree so radically about the distribution of material between tradition and evangelists.

Yet of course such rivalry is in a sense quite unnecessary: the tradition may have comprised all of and more than the Gospel; the Evangelist certainly wrote down all of the Gospel. It is also certain that some of the Gospel is unique to the Evangelist: equally true that some of it is the product of the community. But these two quests, for the Gospel's meaning and the community's tradition, may be pursued amicably only when an adequate understanding of the different 'laws' of orality and literacy has been achieved.

All that is to overlook the particular achievements of Markan study, and to concentrate on certain admittedly fundamental problems in its methodology. A closer look at some of the more significant works in the field may help to point the way forward out of some of the dilemmas.

One of the major contributors to Markan studies in the 1950s and 1960s was the Swiss scholar Eduard Schweizer (b.1913). He is someone whose theological commitment is clearly expressed through his exegetical work. Like Bultmann's, however, Schweizer's work is disciplined by a careful attention to literary-critical and philological studies. His commentary on Mark remains one of the most balanced examples of redaction critical work, even if there is never any real doubt about his commitment to a broadly Barthian conception of the freedom and radical grace of God.

For Schweizer, the Gospel of Mark has its place at that juncture in church history when the Pauline gospel had triumphed. At that point there was a danger that the link between the Gospel and the risen Christ who called his disciples to preach his gospel to all the world, even at the cost of suffering and death, would be lost. Jesus would become a mere symbol of 'freedom from superstitious observance of the law and incomprehensible cultic practices, the overcoming of death or victory over the demons'. There was a danger of a kerygmatic theology developing which had 'lost all its roots in history' ('Mark's Theological Achievement', [43]).

Mark's Gospel is seen as an answer to that dilemma. Its very form is remarkable for Schweizer. For while there might be collections of sayings of itinerant Hellenistic philosophers, there was nothing comparable in contemporary literature to the Gospel with its concentration on the deeds of Jesus and, even more remarkably, on the Passion. The only model here is the Old Testament with its concentration on the history of Israel, of all that 'God caused to happen to Israel' (44). The question for Schweizer, as a follower of Barth, is then how far Mark is attempting to develop or return to a theology of history which sees history as such, or a particular saving history within it, as the 'direct revelation of God' (*ibid.*).

Clearly, purely formal considerations will not suffice to answer this question. For Schweizer the task is to 'distinguish between tradition and Mark's own theological interpretation' (*ibid.*) and he believes that this can be achieved by attending, in the first place, to certain terms which occur in those sections of the Gospel which are undoubtedly redactional, above all in the 'short links between individual pericopae or in the brief summaries' which Mark provides (*ibid.*). Significantly Mark starts by emphasizing the preaching of the gospel and the need for repentance. As such he shows the extent to which he stands in the tradition of the post-Pauline congregation: 'Eschatological salvation consists first of all in the gospel breaking through the boundaries of Palestine and Judaism in the Church's proclamation' (45). But significantly for Mark, Jesus is referred to as teacher and assumes as such a special place within the saving dispensation of the kerygma. Not that the substance of his teaching is much reported: what is important for Mark is that this teaching occurs with authority. 'Mark proclaims what can only be understood by faith: that in Jesus' teaching God himself has broken into this world' (45). Third Schweizer points to a group of terms — 'parable', 'privately', 'not understanding', 'hardened hearts', 'knowing', 'seeking' and 'commanding' — which all describe the 'fact of the world's not understanding, which Jesus confronts with his parabolic speech and his private instruction' (46). Jesus' speaking in images is crucial for Mark. Such discourse challenges the listener because it can be understood only by the person who opens himself to the speaker, as indeed is shown by the figurative language of love.

Schweizer's task is thus to explore the development of these themes in the Gospel as a whole and he does this through an analysis of the structure of the argument of the book. It falls for him into five parts. The prologue and the first part, (1:1 to 3:6), speaks of Jesus' authority over demons, sin and the Law and of the blindness of the Pharisees. The claim is made that with Jesus the time of salvation has begun. He subjects the dark powers to himself and frees people from the Law: but the Pharisees respond to this by plotting to kill him (3:6). While such claims are made for Jesus, they are not to be seen as giving theological importance to the historical Jesus. Quite the contrary, the commands to silence to the demons (1:44 etc.) are 'prohibitions against handing on the historical Jesus' (47). What is important is not stories about Jesus but the Evangelist's pure witness. Jesus' miracles are subordinated to his teaching with authority. Similarly the second block of material in this section, a collection of controversy stories taken over by Mark, serves to underscore Jesus' authority over the Law and also points forward to the cross and the world's blindness to the revelation.

The theme of the world's blindness is explored further in the next section (3:7 to 6:4) which contains Jesus' parabolic discourse. The section starts with a summary of Jesus' activity and success, followed by the call of the twelve. This, however, leads on directly to a section which, in Schweizer's view, shows clear signs of Markan redaction, and which emphasizes the double rejection of Jesus by 'his own' and by the scribes from Jerusalem. It is now that Jesus begins to speak in parables and such speaking characterizes his whole ministry (4:34). 'Everything that Jesus has to say is *mysterion* (a "mystery" or "secret", 4:11), as regards its significance, incomprehensible to mankind. Only God himself can disclose to mankind the meaning of the parables. . . . Without God's "giving" there is no *ginoskein* ("knowing") (49). This again means that no salvation can be found in the historical Jesus. The revelation reveals first the blindness of humanity and in consequence the fact that it is God's mercy alone which can rescue humanity from such judgement. The section finishes with Jesus' rejection (6:1-4).

In the third section (6:5 to 8:21) the theme of the world's blindness is further developed in relation to the disciples, but now it is interwoven with a new note of hope for the Gentiles. The story of the Syro-Phoenician woman points forward beyond the story of the increasing blindness of the world, and the disciples' misunderstanding of the feeding miracles which is underlined in the final exchange of the section, 8:14-21.

The Gospel now (8:27 to 10:52) moves towards its climax with Jesus speaking openly, no longer in code. This is preceded by Peter's confession of Jesus as the Christ to which Jesus responds by predicting his own suffering and death. The mystery of God's speaking directly to men and women occurs; and it occurs by describing suffering and death. 'The word must become flesh in the body of the Crucified One. In no other way can he reach the hearts of men and women' (52). But mere teaching does not succeed in communicating. The gap between the 'mind of God' and the 'mind of men and women' is total. Only in discipleship, in the concrete calling of individuals to follow him on the way that he is going, can that disjunction be overcome, can men and women receive the gift of the mystery of God, know themselves chosen. For the time, however, Jesus' predictions of his passion meet with misunderstanding by the disciples. Only the blind man, whose eyes are miraculously opened 'follows him on the way'. Such discipleship is itself the gift of God.

Thus the Gospel reaches its climax (11:1 to the end) in the Passion. Mark's account, according to Schweizer, lays particular stress on the way this points to the opening up of the gospel to the Gentiles, with its culmination in the confession of the centurion and the rending of the veil of the Temple. For the disciples, God's grace comes through the promise that Jesus will meet them in Galilee. Mark's Gospel is thus revealed as the 'Gospel of the amazing, incomprehensible condescension and love of God which in Jesus seeks the world'(57). Only in the hiddenness of his crucifixion can God's love be grasped and then only by those who go with him step by step on his way. It is this fundamental hiddenness of God which the Messianic Secret expresses. The centurion, the women and disciples point forward as signs to the miracle of the congregation which is to come, which the Risen One will call into life and which he will send out into the world.

Schweizer's account of Mark's theology, which finds its detailed elaboration in his commentary, has provided much of the subsequent agenda for Markan studies. Certainly, as we have already seen, his perception of the need to distinguish tradition and redaction has been widely shared. Even Luz, in his review, effectively reverts to Schweizer's solution to this question by suggesting that the only reliable way forward is through some form of word statistics. Again, much of the detail of his exegesis will continue to engage scholars. However it is his proposal for understanding discipleship in Mark and his interpretation of the Messianic Secret as giving expression to a theology of the cross that have provided the major areas of discussion. We shall follow this principally through the works of two scholars, E. Best (b.1917) and H. Räisänen (b.1941). At this stage we shall therefore make two rather broad comments only.

Schweizer's account of Mark's theology is much concerned, we have seen, with the question of the theological value of the historical Jesus. Moreover his own theological position disposed him strongly against according it any value at all, except insofar as it served to underscore the particular, 'concrete' encounter between the believer and God in the word of the church. This then leads Schweizer systematically to downplay the sheer force of Mark's narrative. This is in large measure made possible by his procedure, which looks for Mark's contributions in the margins of the texts, the link passages and summaries, and ignores the sheer power and dynamic of Mark's story. Theological *parti pris* leads him to ignore essential characteristics of the text, and consequently to undervalue the miracle stories and their significance for Mark. This matter will be taken up by Theissen and Belo (b.1933).

Second, Schweizer's account of the history of Christian theology remains a highly idiosyncratic one in which the theological issues which are held to give it its dynamic bear a remarkable resemblance to the theological agenda which Karl Barth had set at the end of the First World War. In this sense Schweizer's work on Mark bears interesting structural resemblances to Bultmann's work on John and Paul. However it can obviously be asked whether Schwer's sketch of the theological factors which brought Mark's Gospel into being will do. In raising such questions we will have to attend much more closely to the cultural, social and even political conditions out of which Mark's Gospel grew.

Not that that is an easy task. Nevertheless scholars like Kee (b.1920), Kelber and, in rather different ways, Theissen, Belo (b.1933) and Hengel have offered a rather different picture of Mark's place within early Christianity, and we shall at least look at representatives of their work.

For all that the continuing attraction of Schweizer's work is that it attempts to unpack Mark's theology, to see how he addresses fundamental questions about how to give expression to the mystery of God, what to make of the 'blindness of the world' to the truth. These themes have been explored imaginatively in a thesis by Joel Marcus (b.1951), *The Mystery of the Kingdom of God*, which looks specifically at the treatment of parables in Mark 4. Marcus reads the chapter in the light of Jewish apocalyptic, identifying the giving of the mystery referred to in the redactional passage 4:11-12 with the giving of the parable of the Sower. By contrast with the very similar parable in 4 Ezra 4:27-29, where the good soil will come into being only once the evil soil has passed away, in Mark the good soil exists alongside the bad. The Kingdom is present but not yet fully revealed. The mystery is still hidden, still in need of interpretation. To those who have eyes to see, however, 'the kingdom of God is making its dramatic but hidden advent without totally abolishing the kingdom of Satan' (49). This message is, moreover, addressed appropriately to Mark's divided and persecuted community where the 'clash between belief in God's kingdom and experience of evil' (50) is addressed by the parable with its emphasis on hiddenness. Such a view suggests that there is a greater ambiguity about the life of the disciple than Schweizer argued for and leads us, appropriately, into a discussion of the work of Ernest Best. Marcus' book opens up a number of fruitful areas of enquiry. What of Mark's debt to Jewish apocalyptic thought? Where is Mark's community to be situated? He locates Mark's community in Syria and sees it as caught up in the Jewish war. It is in this situation of war and persecution that Mark has produced a reworking of apocalyptic traditions which attempts to see the unveiling of God's purpose in the tribulations of history. It is a message of caution for those who take too triumphalist a view of the life of discipleship; more importantly, it is a message of hope for those who are tempted to despair. 'There is hope for the world', according to the parable of the Mustard Seed:

> but one can see it only by looking in the unlikeliest places, where God seems at first to be most notably absent, where God's people are subjected to the most terrible pressures, but where the mysterious power of his kingdom is secretly at work (218f).

Thus Mark is seen as a creative theologian, one who 'writes about Jesus' word in such a way as to *embody* it, and to produce — by God's graceful power — an instrument for the creation of a new world' (220).

Ernest Best's work on Mark has been appearing over some 25 years since his monograph *The Temptation and the Passion* (1965). It includes a full-length study on discipleship, *Following Jesus* (1981), his Lund Memorial Lectures: *Mark: The Gospel as Story* (1983), and many articles, some of which have been collected as *Disciples and Discipleship* (1986). This material represents some of the most balanced and judicious work in the field of redaction-criticism (Best himself would prefer, for Mark, 'composition-criticism') and presents interesting contrasts with the work of Schweizer.

His method is in many ways close to that of Schweizer. He, too, stresses the importance of examining the seams in the Gospel, specifically with regard to distinctive Markan vocabulary. He does, however, believe that it is possible to detect Mark's hand in his handling of the individual pericopae of the Gospel and in his more detailed studies he is firmly in the school of those who believe that they can distinguish Mark from his tradition. But the most important evidence for him is the order in which Mark places his material and the way he 'sandwiches' one event within another so that the two throw light on each other. A prime example of the ordering of material is Mark's creation of 'a journey for Jesus from Caesarea Philippi to Jerusalem in such a way that it is studded with predictions of his death and directed to instruction on discipleship' (*MGaS* 11).

Best does however stress Mark's closeness to, and respect for, his tradition. In an important article 'Mark's Preservation of the Tradition'(*D&D*, 31-48) he has argued that Mark did not feel free to alter his tradition at will; that even where it would have suited him, for example, to alter 'holy one of God' (1:24) to 'Son of God', he does not do so. Mark's readers, so Best asserts, would have known the stories he used. He could not therefore alter them radically and so preserved their detail, even though he might have sometimes preferred not to (*MGaS* 13).

Collectors of traditions, while they have responsibilities as guardians of the inherited tradition, are nevertheless creative. Mark's material, even where it had already been collected together into small complexes, did not supply the structural principle(s) for the Gospel as a whole. For that 'a fresh set of structural principles would be necessary' (17) which Mark would supply. It is here rather than in the production of new material that his creativity is to be seen. But why did Mark cross the line between orality and literacy, putting the stories into written form?

Best is certainly someone who attends to the differences between orality and literacy, while being aware that those differences may themselves differ significantly from one culture to another. 'Written literature' is not necessarily more stable than oral — it can be changed, as Matthew and Luke make clear (though the very remarkable history of the New Testament text also makes clear how, at a certain point, change becomes very restricted). Written material can, however, be planned, and use can be made of rhetorical devices apparent to the eye rather than to the ear. Even so, Mark's Gospel was almost certainly intended to be read aloud, and the character of the story telling would be closer to oral narration than to a purely literary one (19).

In answering the question: why did Mark write (chapter VI), Best distinguishes between the occasion and the purpose of Mark's writing. The occasion is not easy to determine: some believe that Mark wrote because the witnesses to the life of Jesus were dying out; others that he wrote to counter certain heresies. Best doubts, not least in the light of the considerable stability of oral tradition, whether the former would have been the principal reason for writing; he considers evidence for the existence of a specific heresy to be deficient. Mark wrote because he wished to strengthen his congregation in times of persecution and trouble. His purpose was above all pastoral. Thus the question arises: How was it realised? How did telling the stories in this particular way help him to strengthen and console, comfort his congregation?

Here we shall necessarily have to be selective and consider Best's treatment of miracles, of discipleship and of the passion-resurrection in Mark.

Best deals with the Markan miracles within a wider treatment of Jesus as 'the One who cares' (chapter X). Whatever the original intention of the stories and collections of stories, they are now contained within a larger whole, whose 'structural principles' are related to certain images and conceptions found throughout the Gospel. Best points to the image of Jesus as the shepherd leading his flock, to the family images and to the stress on Jesus' teaching which runs through the Gospel. In considering the miracle material, the notion of Jesus as the one who cares can provide a useful guide.

Here Best is arguing on at least two fronts: first against those who believe that the dominant theme in the miracle stories (and possibly in the Gospel as a whole) is the cosmic struggle between Jesus and Satan; second against those who see the Gospel as combatting a contemporary understanding of Jesus as a 'divine man' who triumphs painlessly over all suffering and disease (against which view Mark stresses Jesus' cross and passion).

Best's notion of Jesus' caring allows him to thread his way between these two views:

1. It is true that in his exorcisms Jesus is seen in combat with the Satanic powers, indeed as triumphing over them. Best believes this is possible because

in the Temptation Jesus has already overcome Satan. But this is not to say that this theme dominates the Gospel. Jesus' hearers would indeed have taken the reality of demonic forces seriously and needed to have been reassured that they were vanquished; but they are not the only forces which threaten Jesus' opponents: persecution, wealth, physical

illness, death itself are not seen as demonic in the Gospel, yet the community needs reassurance about these too (56-8).

2. Hence it is not, in Best's view, correct to suggest that Mark's attitude to Jesus' healing is a negative one. He clearly portrays Jesus as a charismatic healer, indeed as instructing the disciples in how to heal (9:28f which Best regards as Markan redaction, [59]). Mark emphasizes Jesus' healings in the summaries and includes a very substantial number of such stories. He need not have drawn such attention to them, had he not wished. He needs to reassure his community that Jesus has power to heal, but not only to heal. His bringing of forgiveness, of a 'salvation' which is greater than physical healing, his teaching, are ways of caring for his people which are of wider significance. His death will be a ransom for his people: his death and suffering, and their discipleship, will provide the true means of life: only because he rose from the dead is he now alive to care for the community:

He died and rose and therefore is alive; it is because he is alive that he can now care for the community; he could not do this if he were dead or isolated from the community. Thus that section of the Gospel which precedes 10.45 tells us of the care of Jesus for the community as it is exercised in the present, i.e., Mark's present, and the section which follows 10.45 tells of the death he died and its meaning for the community. It is as if Jesus were alive all through the first part of the Gospel; he comes to men in his words and in his deeds; he instructs them in the meaning of discipleship and of his own life and death and he ministers to their needs, defending them from evil and delivering them from their spiritual and physical illnesses. Whereas in Acts Luke sets out the Spirit as the guide and aid of men in the period after the ascension, Mark has little to say about the Spirit; it is Jesus himself who is alive and who is therefore the guide and aid of the community (65).

What then of Jesus' death and resurrection and the discipleship that is laid on those who would draw life from them?

Best gathers his clues to Mark's theology of the 'cross' where he can. Unlike Schweizer he does not seek so much a grand design running through the Gospel, rather a series of hints which indicate at least broadly where Mark stands.

That the death of Jesus is important for Mark is not in doubt. He has included four predictions of the Passion in the narrative of Jesus' journey to Jerusalem; indeed the 'death of Jesus broods over the entire Gospel' (66). Moreover the context of the predictions, linked as they are to Peter's rebuke to Jesus, to the disciples' fear and misunderstanding, suggests that Mark is aware that 'it is not easy for disciples...to grasp the need for Jesus' death....If Jesus is able to heal the sick and raise the dead why should he have to suffer?'(67). But while Mark is aware of the difficulties that Jesus's death creates in the minds of the disciples, he does not suggest that they simply fail to understand. Understanding comes only slowly, by stages, as the story of the healing of the blind man in two stages suggests. Only as the story develops beyond the resurrection does Peter see fully.

What account then does Mark offer of Jesus' death? Mark certainly stresses that it is part of God's plan, that the Son of Man 'must' suffer (8:31). He suggests that his dying is a ransom without which men and women could not be set free from their sins (10:45), that his death is of benefit for others. Further, according to Best, he sees it as a bearing of the judgment of God. This is suggested by the quotation from Zechariah in 14:27b (suggesting that it is God who smites the shepherd: a Markan insertion) and by the references to the cup (10.35ff; 14:36) which Best, following Jeremiah 25:15-7, sees as 'more than a cup of suffering...a cup of judgement' (70). Again the cry of dereliction on the cross is seen as evidence that Jesus 'stands outside the mercy of God because he bears the judgement of God' (*ibid.*).

This view of Jesus' death as a bearing of the judgement of God has implications. It means that Best cannot accept the views of those, like J.M. Robinson, who see Jesus' death as a victory over the demonic powers of evil. That victory had already been won in the Temptation. It means, further, the rejection of Israel. Those who reject Jesus are themselves judged. The story of the fig-tree, which frames the narrative of the cleansing of the temple, symbolises the barrenness of Israel. 'The temple has not turned out to be what it was intended to be, a house of prayer for all nations, i.e. the Gentiles' (71). Jesus' death, by contrast, as the rending of the veil of the temple and the confession of the — Gentile — centurion shows, is the means by which the gospel is extended from Israel to all men and women.

Of course, his death is not the end. In his resurrection Jesus becomes present to the disciples. The message of the resurrection is that Jesus will go before the disciples to Galilee and that they will thus continue their pilgrimage with him in the preaching of the gospel. Unlike those scholars (Marxsen, Perrin) who see the message to the women as a prediction of the parousia, Best thus sees the message as opening up a new stage in the life of the disciples where they are called to engage in the mission of spreading the gospel in the Gentile world, where Jesus is with them on their journey, strengthening and restoring them on their way. Thus the story of the disciples' journey with Jesus to Jerusalem and the cross casts light on their continuing journey with the risen Jesus. It is a journey which has its goal not simply in the cross. 'The journey on which the disciples go is open-ended, a journey in mission towards the world. It is a journey outwards and beyond, determined in its nature by the cross and the resurrection, but never a limited journey' (92). It does, however, look towards a final fulfilment when the mission has been fulfilled and Christ will return.

We may now consider briefly the relation of Best's account of Mark to that of Eduard Schweizer. As we have noted, they are largely agreed on matters of method, though in practice it seems to me that Schweizer is more inclined to look for some overall theological schema (such, indeed, as that which he himself had broadly inherited from Karl Barth) whereas Best sees Mark as someone more in the grip of his tradition who leaves his imprint on it where he can and who is more of a pastor and a preacher than a full-blown systematic theologian (perhaps not a wholly inaccurate characterization of Best himself).

Such differences are, however, argued out. Best has made a strong case for seeing Mark as both a preserver and a respecter of his tradition. He could not, even if he had wished, have made substantial changes to his tradition. Nevertheless it is, in Schweizer's view, not so much in the modifications of the tradition, as in the way in which he puts it together, that Mark's views are to be seen.

The debate between the two interpreters may be focused as follows. For Schweizer, the cross is above all the place of revelation:

[T]he word has to become flesh, God has to give himself over completely into solidarity with mankind, and that in the radical way that Mark depicts it in his report of Jesus' crucifixion. . . . Here is the hiddenness of God at its most radical ('Theological Achievement', [57]).

It is the revelation of God in his hiddenness, *sub contrario*. For Best, it is the place where Jesus bears God's judgement on the sin of the world, where the old order is set aside and the new world opened up into which the Risen Jesus will lead his followers. This difference in opinion corresponds to a difference in understanding of discipleship. For Schweizer, the salient feature of Mark's presentation of the disciples is the motif of lack of understanding which Wrede had earlier drawn attention to. For Best, the disciples stand not so much for the blindness of the world, of men and women before faith, as for the Christian believer himself as he struggles for understanding, not least of the cross and the need for suffering. Such understanding is partial; it may be accompanied by trials and tribulations, and by failure. The story of the disciples on their journey with Jesus to the cross and beyond reflects that complicated history which is that of all believers.

Such debates are of crucial importance both for the future of New Testament study and indeed for the future of theology. At stake for New Testament study is its ability to resolve central interpretative issues by recourse to its own canons of judgement. Both Schweizer and Best agree very largely on the methods to be applied, yet they disagree quite significantly about the meaning of discipleship and of the cross and resurrection in Mark's theology. Is the discipline as a whole able to resolve such debates within its present frame of reference? If not, it might well seem that it will have to change that frame.

At stake for theology is a fundamental set of questions about the transcendence, the 'wholly otherness' of God, about the infinite distance between the 'mind of men and women' and the 'mind of God', such that only a radical change to men's and women's understanding can bring them to faith, to true knowledge of God. Such questions are in one sense perennial questions with a long history in the grand tradition of Western philosophy and theology, not least in the Reformed tradition to which both Best and Schweizer belong. It is interesting to note the particular cultural and historical constellation in which the debate is played out between the two interpreters. Schweizer stands in the Barthian tradition of reaction to the breakdown in liberal culture and values after the First World War. For him there is no doubt about the radical blindness of the world, in which ultimately even the disciples share. Only in the radical gift of faith can that blindness be overcome. Bartimaeus is the symbol of the universal blindness of the world. Best's situation is arguably a very different one. He comes from Ulster where there is a great deal of religious belief and activity but where true faith and understanding are hardly and often painfully won. It is certainly a situation in which there is a great readiness to castigate the blindness of one's — religious — opponents. It is one where it is perhaps less easy ever to be confident that one can properly claim to have received the gift of true faith (though such claims are, of course, made all the time). The Barthian strain of theology, which may have offered strength and consolation to those facing the attacks of the Nazis on the Confessing Church, may prove a more questionable ally in the confessional conflicts of Northern Ireland. Can the reading of Mark help to resolve such questions? We shall return to them after a further review of the work of Rhoads (b.1941) and Michie (b.1934), Räisänen and Belo.

Rhoads and Michie's *Mark as Story* appeared in the United States in 1982 shortly before Best's very similarly titled book. For all the similarity in the titles, the aims and quality of the two works are very different. Best is an Ulsterman, coming from a culture with a lively tradition of oral story-telling; Rhoads and Michie's approach is fundamentally literary, seeing the Gospel as a coherent literary whole, designed to be read as such. Perhaps 'designed' is inappropriate in such a context. Rhoads and Michie do not ask so much about the author's intentions as about the nature of the text, its rhetoric, settings, plot and characters. Nevertheless they do assume that there is a consistent design throughout the Gospel, that the notorious vagaries of Jesus' movements in Galilee have a meaning within the overall structure of the story; that the various conflicts which are recorded throughout the Gospel, between Jesus and Satanic agencies, between Jesus and the authorities and his disciples, fit into and comprise a coherent plot; that the various sayings and deeds ascribed to Jesus 'create a rich characterization' (104).

A number of things are striking about the way this schema is worked out in detail. One is the relatively weak attempt to relate their own reading of the text to earlier discussions of the matter. It is, of course, quite proper that any attempt to bring new concepts and perspectives to bear on a subject should be free to pursue its own agenda. What would have been interesting would have been to see some attempt to consider alternative readings and to justify the choices that they make. Thus Rhoads and Michie propose the interesting thesis that the parables in Mark's Gospel are to be seen as riddles, 'allegories that Jesus tells which interpret Jesus, events, and people in the story world as part of the rule of God' (56). They link here the Sower, the saying about defilement in Mark 7:15, the fig-tree and the saying about the door-keeper, Mark 13:34. The problem with this rather brief discussion is partly that it is extremely selective in the passages it takes from Mark, partly that it simply does not meet the obvious objections to the extension of some form of 'parable theory' to cover the whole of the Gospel. It is hard not to form the impression that for the authors a narrative approach assumes as *a starting-point which need not be argued for* that there is a coherent story-world, and that therefore motifs in the Gospel will always be consistently carried through. The point they are making can indeed be developed in interesting ways, as J. Drury (b.1936) has shown in *The Parables in the Gospels*; but, if the discipline is not to fragment, it needs to be argued.

Another problem is the contradictoriness of some of the judgements that are made. We are told, not unreasonably, that Jesus' '[f]requent movement suggests a hurried journey underscoring the urgency of Jesus' message' (68), but we are also told that he often has to move on because of the difficulties he encounters. We are told that his movements enhance his authority 're-established in city after city', while we also learn that all this activity accentuates for the reader Jesus' 'frustrations at not being able to control these obstacles and conflicts at every turn' (69). It seems that it is as difficult to give a coherent account of the narrative purpose of Jesus' movements as it is to construct from Mark's account a coherent itinerary (which one American in Oxford once memorably described as 'the meanderings of an intoxicated fly').

A further rather disturbing feature of the work is the strong tendency it displays of psychologizing. In the account of Jesus' 'conflict' with his disciples explanations are offered for both the disciples' and Jesus' behaviour in terms of their feelings and reactions. Thus we are told that Jesus' 'expectations and demands are just too much for them', that he expects 'too much too fast' (89). He did not prepare them for their call, for '[t]hey did not know about his baptism, the voice from heaven, or about his confrontation with Satan in the desert' (89f). This may be a legitimate filling out of the story, but it is certainly not something that the story as such points out. Perhaps more striking — and, one might venture to say, banal — is the portrayal of Jesus' 'frustration'. He is 'shocked and surprised' when the disciples fail to understand 'the riddles about the kingdom of God'. 'In his impatience and frustration, Jesus hurls rhetorical questions at them so that they may see how blind and dense they are' (93). He 'becomes especially upset when he realises that his own disciples are blind like the authorities' (94). Jesus' last words to the disciples in the Garden 'express a frantic effort to arouse them' (95). Quite apart from the very one-sided portrayal of the disciples (cf. Best's discussion of the matter above), this appears to assume an interest on the part of the text in such matters which needs to be argued for. The problem here is to know what sort of literary strategy is being followed. Are we simply being invited to read this text in this way as modern readers with an interest in such matters? Or is it being suggested that this was the way in which first-century readers would have read it? Certainly the exploration of contemporary literary analogies to Mark's Gospel is not a theme in the book.

Rhoads and Michie's work has been influential among a growing circle of scholars working in the States who wish to see the abandonment in biblical study of historical in favour of literary modes of investigation. There are here, without question, issues of great importance which are far from having being resolved. There is no doubt that the Bible has spawned an enormous literature of its own, and that this literary history is an area which has been largely neglected by those who have concentrated on the recovery of the original intention of the author. But it is clear from the state of the debate in Gospel study that a simple substitution of literary for historical studies both underestimates the extent to which form- and redaction-criticism have been interested in literature (while distinguishing different kinds of literature), and loses too much by abstracting from the particular setting in which a text is communicated and read.

Räisänen's work is certainly not uninterested in questions of the meaning and coherence of Mark's Gospel, but the answers he gives are very different from those of Rhoads and Michie. His work has focused very strongly on those elements which Wrede isolated as distinctive of Mark or Mark's tradition. His two early studies from the 1970s on the Parable Theory and the Messianic Secret have now been revised and published in a single volume, *The 'Messianic Secret' in Mark*, which deals quite extensively with more recent literary-critical studies of Mark. Throughout he is concerned with the question: how far can Mark be seen as an author with his own voice? At the same time he is equally concerned to understand what is being said through the various motifs which we find in Mark's Gospel, to adjudicate between the various claims which are made about its meaning by historical argument.

In a sense Räisänen's approach to the question of Mark's theology differs from that of Schweizer and Best in that he sets himself the specific task of examining the motifs associated with the Messianic secret in an attempt, first to see how far they can be attributed to Mark, how far to his tradition, and second to discover to what extent they form part of an integrated understanding of Jesus and his ministry, how the various elements are unrelated or even contradictory. Interestingly, since the publication of the first two monographs which presented the various elements of the 'secret' as being only loosely connected, Räisänen has worked more closely on Paul, specifically on the question of the interrelation of Paul's various pronouncements on the Law. His conviction that there is a good deal of inconsistency, and indeed contradiction, in Paul's statements about the Law has led him somewhat to revise his views of the attribution of relatively diverse motifs in Mark's Gospel.

This is not to suggest that Räisänen has greatly modified his views since the writing of the first two monographs. Certainly he is not tempted to follow more recent developments which suggest that we should abandon attempts at distinguishing Mark's work from that of the tradition altogether and instead attempt to read the Gospel as an integral text in its own right. Against those who like N. Petersen (b.1933) and Rhoads and Michie have attempted to explore Mark's 'story-world', he argues that there is simply not the consistency within the text as a whole to make this possible. Those who argue, for instance, that it is the disciples who give coherence to a story which is certainly episodic, still have to face the question about the consistency of the disciples' behaviour, indeed of their treatment in the text itself. If at 4:11 Jesus tells the disciples that the secret of the Kingdom has been given to them, the reader is certainly not told where. Nor subsequently does the behaviour of the disciples greatly tally with that claim (4:13). Nevertheless Jesus does entrust them with the task of teaching (6:7-13, 29-30) in which they are successful. Despite this they 'fail to understand what they can expect from Jesus (6:34ff) or who he is' (18) (6:52: due to hardening), and even fail to understand his simple teaching on the Law (chapter 7). Similarly there are inconsistencies relating to the disciples' ability to exorcise. In 9:14ff they are unable to exorcise, whereas in chapter 6 they could. Räisänen concludes:

> I cannot deem the resulting picture coherent. There is some chaos, at least, in the story world . . .it is misleading to construct a story world which does not allow for the possibility that *the characters serve different functions and operate at different levels* at various points (19).

What then of the Messianic secret? At the end of a long and careful examination of the various elements which Wrede had identified Räisänen sums up his conclusions as follows. First he analyses the various elements in the secret:

a) The commands to silence to demons and to the disciples belong closely together and 'constitute the messianic secret *proper*.' They are concerned with Jesus' identity and are not broken.

b) The disciples' lack of understanding is only loosely connected with the commands to silence, is concerned not only with Jesus' identity but with his fate and his message, and could stand without the Messianic secret.

c) The motif of secret healings is distinct from the messianic secret proper; the associated commands to silence are often broken and serve to highlight Jesus' authority.

d) The parable theory (4:11f) is to be separated from the messianic secret. There is no such consistent theory in the Gospel. Räisänen sees it as one explanation of the Jews' rejection of the Gospel.

e) Once the Messianic secret is broken up into its constituent elements Räisänen believes that one can see that substantial parts of the Gospel are concerned with openness, for example in chapter 2; that Mark has diverse motifs which cut across each other. Even in Mark's own redactional contributions, there are contradictions: the opponents know the secret (242f).

Räisänen then poses the question of the origins of the secrecy theme. He believes that Wrede was right to stress the epoch-making nature of the resurrection. 'Both the Easter experience and the crucifixion had to be interpreted in the light of (i) the scriptures and (ii) the traditions concerning the Lord' (244). What had happened, it would have been argued, must have been anticipated and clues to this anticipation would have been sought in:

a) hidden meanings in sayings and parables, such as the sign of Jonah and the parable of the Wicked Tenants. This would be reflected in the view of the parables as riddles;

b) 'the elaboration of the idea of secret teaching given by Jesus to his disciples'. This would provide a guarantee of the continuity between this and the teaching of the church drawn from the encounter with the risen Lord;

c) the disciples' misunderstanding which would serve to explain discontinuities between the church's teaching and inherited understandings;

d) the passion predictions;

e) stories of glimpses of the divine glory in Jesus' life, notably the transfiguration;

f) the treatment of the miracle stories as epiphanies (244f).

Such concerns may have already been reflected in Mark's tradition by:

a) the idea of parables as riddles, 4:11f;

b) 'the notion of secret teaching given by Jesus to his disciples';

c) 'the motif of Jesus' silencing demons' as part of the exorcism itself;

d) the injunction to temporary silence to the leper;

e) 'some incidents of incomprehension on the part of the disciples who were seeking glory for themselves and trying to avoid suffering' (245f).

Mark himself then:

1) preserved a) but brought it to bear on the missionary work of his community, seeking in it a source of consolation for them in times of difficulty;

2) took up and developed b) 'stressing the role of the disciples as mediators between Jesus and the community';

3) took up and changed the point of c) taking it to relate not to Jesus' exorcistic technique but to the christological confession of the demons;

4) developed d) drawing out the impact made by Jesus on the witnesses to the healings;

5) 'greatly elaborated' e) suggesting that the disciples did not understand 'the necessity of suffering and resurrection', nor parts of the teaching of Jesus (that is, in relation to the Law). This rather runs counter to the notion of secret and effective teaching given to the disciples (246).

In all this, the Secret was only one concern of Mark's. It runs counter to the stress which he elsewhere lays on the public nature of Jesus' ministry which was one of the main reasons for his death.

Thus Räisänen has dissolved the Messianic Secret into a number of parts which he sees as relatively independent of each other. Mark emerges as a writer of some independence and creativity, not as a major literary figure with an overall conception worked out through the piece. We can certainly ask about Mark's story-world, but we shall have to concede that it is a somewhat disjointed one, something which may fit better — one might add — in terms of lectionary reading than in sustained public literary performance (though here Mark's sheer pace and skill as narrator may surprise us).

One of the advantages of Räisänen's analysis is that it enables him to pick up the relative merits of the theological accounts which have been offered of Mark. These fall, on Räisänen's classification, under four heads (56ff and 247ff).

1. The apologetic explanation, which sees Mark as having been written to explain why the Jews rejected the Gospel, because of the divine hardening. But on the above analysis the texts which might point to this as a central part of Mark's theology, above all 4:11f, are shown to be traditional and their ideas not to have been developed by Mark.

2. The epiphanic theory which sees Mark as bearing witness to the glory of God which is manifest in Jesus. While such a view can appeal interestingly to the way in which the commands to silence are indeed broken in the case of many of the healing narratives, and to the story of the Transfiguration, it does not overall do justice to Mark's views. Nevertheless the existence of such a strand of thought in the Gospel serves to point up the looseness of the overall configuration of Mark's theology.

3. Views which stress the theology of the cross in Mark can appeal properly to Mark's development of the motif of the disciples' lack of understanding. This clearly emphasizes the sense in which for the disciples the cross presents a dark mystery which has yet to be appropriated. Nevertheless such a motif stands in tension to other commands to silence, notably the command in 9:9 which emphasizes the resurrection as the point at which the secret will be revealed.

4. Others, notably Wrede, have argued that Mark attempted to offer an account of the history of revelation which embraces not only the life and death of Jesus but also his resurrection and which culminates in the latter, though the final parousia is still awaited. This too is close to the view taken by Best. Such a view, according to Räisänen, does justice to the Messianic Secret proper and reflects the divide between Jesus and the church. It does not, however, altogether explain the centrality of the cross in Mark,

nor indeed do justic to the centurion's confession in 15:39.

In all this, Räisänen is working still within the framework suggested at the very beginning of the debate by Wrede: namely that the development of the Messianic Secret occurs as a response to certain specific christological questions which were occasioned by belief in the resurrection of Jesus. His own refinement of this is to suggest that Mark is wishing to correct a low prophet-Christology, such as may have been found in Q, and also to counter those who may have based such a view on an appeal to the historical Jesus. By contrast Mark emphasizes that Jesus deliberately concealed his messianic nature. Whereas for Q the casting out of demons is a sign of the coming of the Kingdom of God, for Mark it reveals Jesus' divinity: 'the proclaimer has become the proclaimed, a development which goes directly against the Christology of Q' (252). Similarly, while Q in the temptation story emphasizes Jesus' refusal to perform miracles as a proof of his divinity, Mark exalts Jesus' miracle working as just such a proof. Q has no passion narrative; Mark by contrast has some notion of atonement and expiation (Mk 10:45). Thus Mark has a Hellenistic christology of a wonder-working son of God and a spiritualising view of the Law.

It will be clear that in all this Räisänen is in many ways adding powerful support to Best's arguments against interpretations of Mark in terms of a theology of the cross. Best argues that Mark's portrayal of discipleship as a journey which extends on into the mission of the church points beyond the cross to the life of the church in the presence of the Risen Lord. Similarly Räisänen stresses the revelation-historical character of the motif of the Messianic Secret: the Secret is temporarily limited, waiting to be revealed after the resurrection.

Again Best and Räisänen, despite their rather different points of departure, come to very similar views about the literary character of the Gospel and about Mark's relation to his tradition. They differ, it is true, about Mark's purpose and about the particular historical setting of its composition. Best stresses Mark's pastoral purpose in strengthening a congregation facing persecution; Räisänen sees it more as a theological document designed to correct or combat variant christological views.

Does this mean that one can speak of a consensus in the discipline about the theology of Mark? In practical terms, not at all. The works of Best and Räisänen both have their origins in the 1970s and predate the kind of crisis that Luz describes in his review. They also predate the later literary studies to which I have referred only briefly and which they have attacked sharply in their subsequent writing. Thus there is still considerable diversity which is unlikely to be resolved in the immediate future. Nevertheless I would suggest that their work is likely to prove increasingly persuasive to New Testament scholars as the nature of the present dilemma in Markan study becomes clear. In the first instance what the situation revealed by the later commentaries shows is that a comprehensive reconstruction of the history of the tradition behind Mark is impossible. To make such a reconstruction the basis of any account of Mark's theology is to condemn the discipline to confusion. At the same time, literary-critical attempts to show that Mark himself has a developed a rounded 'story-world', an integrated theological schema, have also, so far at least, proved unconvincing. Mark is certainly a story-teller; but he is weaving together material that is significantly disparate. He may give hints and pointers, his juxtaposition of material may tell us not a little about his own views and concerns, but we must not expect too developed or sophisticated a theology from someone working with such constraints. The dilemmas encountered by subsequent developments in Markan study will in time be seen to have vindicated the more judicious approaches of Best and Räisänen.

Of course, those who look for theological meaning and practical applications from their study of the Gospels may not be entirely satisfied to leave it there. One of the difficulties with both Räisänen's and Best's work is that the theological meaning of the texts is not really explored beyond a certain level. Thus, while Räisänen suggests that Mark has indeed developed the motif of the disciples' misunderstanding, and Best notes their continuing failure to understand all that Jesus teaches them — indeed their betrayal and abandonment of him — neither of them offers much by way of an account of the subsequent role of the cross and suffering in the life of faith, the extent to which it provides illumination and understanding, and reveals the nature of God.

To this of course the answer will be simply, 'Nor does Mark'. In two senses I would question whether that is adequate. In the first place I suspect that there is more written into the fabric of Mark's Passion narrative than either Best or Räisänen would allow. Certainly, if Best is right to suppose that the Gospel is written for those in Rome who have recently undergone the traumas of Nero's persecutions, then this is a story that cannot fail to have evoked powerful associations with their own experience. Jesus' cry in the Garden to his father will have echoed their own agony at the thought of the barbaric torments which their Father God had allowed their fellow Christians to undergo. How would those early hearers have heard these texts as they were read out in the shadow of such terrible events? Would not Mark himself have been aware of and taken into account such resonances as he told his story?

Allowing that Räisänen and Best are right about their general account of Mark's literary role, this does not of itself answer the question: how are we to read the text he produced? Is the historical critical task which they have undertaken simply a useful preliminary to answering that question? Is it, at least in Best and Schweizer's case, as we suggested above, itself an appropriation of the text and not just a distanced exploration of the history of the early Christian church? And if it is such an appropriation, how does it relate to other so-called 'literary' approaches? Certainly Best's view can rightly claim to take seriously the narrative and literary character of the

Gospel. He does not, as does Eduard Schweizer, simply limit himself to a consideration of the strictly speaking redactional elements in Mark: he looks at the way Mark has composed and juxtaposed his material. He recognises Mark's gifts as a story-teller, while also seeing clearly the constraints under which he operated. In this sense his reading of the text is one which seeks an appropriate understanding of this kind of literary product.

It is not, however, an approach which asks about the forces and factors which lay behind the text; nor does it concern itself directly with the relation between the present reader and reading communities and that text. The latter question is one which is only now beginning to be asked in New Testament study, though it is overdue, not least in the light of the running together of historical readings and literary approaches in Best and Schweizer. The former has received attention in a remarkable work by a Portuguese engineer.

Fernando Belo is a Marxist Catholic who writes with considerable passion about the Gospel of Mark, offering a 'materialist' analysis of it. By 'materialist' he means seeing the text, not as the deposit of some spiritual, ideal act, but as the product of the socio-economic realities of its time. One might say that what he does is to substitute for the search for authorial intention the search for the social and economic system which has produced the text, rather as industrial society produces various goods which are owned by some and are the product of others' work. Of course it is not in any way an easy task to offer such an interpretation. We would need to know a very great deal about the particular setting of the text before we could give a full account of this kind; but that in a sense is true of most undertakings in ancient historiography.

Belo combines his materialism with a structuralist analysis of literary texts much indebted to Roland Barthes (1915-1980). Texts are produced by the weaving together of codes, cultural 'signifiers' which together make up the textile, or texture of the work. The critic's job is to decode, to show how the meaning of the text is encoded. A further consideration is important to the understanding of Belo's work: it is that different social forces or constraints may bear upon the production of texts; where a text emerges from a community in change, one might say, then different social forces and interests will be at work in fashioning that text, forging the meanings which will give direction to the community's aims and hopes.

The question for Belo and for subsequent attempts to address such questions is how we can identify such interests/constraints from a literary investigation of the texts themselves. For Belo, it is not oversimplifying to say that he attempts to do this by linking the different interests to different modes of literary production, namely narrative and discourse. Narrative is said to be impersonal (using the 3rd person predominantly), with the aorist as its dominant tense, whereas discourse is personal (use of 1st and 2nd persons), focusing on the present tense with the avoidance of the aorist.

For Belo, Mark's Gospel is subtly strung between the narrative of Jesus'

Messianic praxis and the mythological discourses which introduce a more abstract theological (ideological) note into the Gospel.

The narrative reflects the goals of the poor and oppressed, and their sense of conflict as this is expressed in Jesus' struggle against demonic forces and sickness, his rejection of the dominant economic modes of commerce (exchange) in favour of an economy of giving and use. It is reflected above all in his rejection in the narrative of the whole Levitical system of purity which is centred in the Temple cult and which gives power to the dominant priestly class. This is expressed in Jesus' rejection of purity (Mk 7) and in the attacks on the Temple and the motif of the tearing of the veil of the Temple at the end of the Passion narrative.

Belo's reading of the text, for all its rather alienating technical apparatus (though can it be said that, for example, the technical apparatus of tradition-historical criticism is less alienating?) contains much that is remarkable. He traces for instance the motif of tearing: of the old wineskins when they are filled with new wine; of his garments at Jesus' confession; and of the veil of the Temple as making the radical break between Jesus and the old order. He draws attention to the body language — hands, feet, eyes and ears — which permeates the texts, and points to the theme of giving/healing, hope, faith which structure the text. The journey, as the disciples and Jesus set their feet towards Jerusalem, symbolizes the disciples' commitment to the new praxis of Jesus, their hopes for a new world in which they can fully share. More controversial is his reading of the feeding narratives in which he contrasts the money (exchange economy on the one hand 'send them away, to . . . buy themselves something to eat') with the economy of gift expressed in Jesus' rejoinder 'You give them something to eat' (Mk 6:36f).

The analysis here is not only somewhat strained, but it relates necessarily to Belo's reading of the socio-economic systems of the time. Here there are, I think, real problems. Belo distinguishes two competing systems in Israel, the Levitical and the Deuteronomic; the former was dominant in the Pentateuch and placed the priests in a position of supremacy. The Deuteronomic 'system' with its much greater emphasis on social justice is the one favoured by Jesus and drawn on in his praxis. It is not clear how this relates to the actual economic realities of the day where the Palestinian economy has become entangled in the Roman system of provincial administration. Jesus may be showing himself to stand outside the Roman system of taxation by not possessing Roman coinage, but that requires a more intricate account than can be given in terms of a simple contrast between money/gift. Such a contrast, which may well be reflected in the texts, may be more a product of a millenarian frame of mind which longs for a complete end to the present order of things and looks forward to a mythological 'time of gifts', than to a new economic order as such. It is, in other words, less than clear how this would relate to actual economic options, past (Deuteronomic) or future, though, of course, utopian visions will draw on traditional exemplars, however strikingly they may be reworked.

The narrative of Jesus' Messianic praxis, his struggles against the dark powers of oppression and economic dominance, contrasts in Belo's view with the mythological discourse which is also woven into the narrative, notably in the prologue, the Baptism narrative, the passion predictions and the Little Apocalypse of chapter 13 with its vision of the return of the Son of Man. This strand is christological (Jesus as the transcendent Son of God) and sees the Cross, resurrection and the final parousia as the way of salvation and release for an oppressed people (as opposed to the present messianic powers). It is, says Belo, the ideology of a people who discover the impossibility of realizing their own hopes and goals through revolutionary praxis because of the iron grip which the dominant class has on the political economy. Here is the beginning of a long process of disempowering the poor within Christianity, of neutralizing the Messianic Gospel.

Again, one must ask whether this separation of narrative and discourse is not too simple a division. In the first place it is often a less-than-sharp distinction: in what sense is the Prologue discourse, rather than narrative? Does the inclusion of first- or second-person direct speech in narrative destroy its narrative character? Second it is clear that some of the key passages for Belo's account of Jesus' messianic praxis are themselves principally discourse or controversy: such as the Beelzebul controversy. Third and perhaps most critically, his proposal for distinguishing later tendencies in the text from earlier simply ignores the careful work that has been done by New Testament scholars. This might be acceptable if what Belo was offering was simply a deconstructionist reading, arguing that all texts contain the means of their own dissolution. But he is not: he is arguing passionately for a reading of texts which sees them as reflecting — as the 'products' of — social realities which are themselves part of a continuing history of human struggle. There is no ideological dispute, in this respect at least, between Belo and conventional New Testament history of the tradition.

Belo's book remains as a challenge to the discipline to explore the links between the Gospels (and indeed other New Testament writings) and the social and economic realities of the time. It is rooted in a metaphysical dispute between idealism and materialism which is in need of deep scrutiny. His attempt to substitute a structuralist reading of the text for previous methods of Synoptic tradition-historical study fails to convince. Yet we are left with important questions about the relation of such texts to, on the one hand the early millennial visions of Jesus' followers, and on the other these followers' subsequent bitter experience of suffering and tragedy. Are we simply to see in Mark the imposition of an ideology on a utopian vision; are we to see in it simply the history of, albeit pastoral, qualifications to that vision; or is there, however elusive to the readers two thousand years later, some synthesis, some deepening of the initial vision born of such tragedy which may also speak to us in a troubled, if hopeful, world?

Notes

1. U. Luz, reviewing commentaries by W. Pesch, J. Gnilka and W. Schmithals in *ThLZ*.
2. Cf. H. Räisänen, p. 44, n.2. The Evangelist was responsible for the presence of the Messianic secret in the Gospel; the conception itself was that of the early church. Wrede opens up the question of the Evangelists' contribution to the tradition as they collect and present it. He himself, certainly as far as the messianic secret was concerned, stressed the primary creative role of the community.

List of works cited

H. Anderson, *The Gospel of Mark*, London, 1976

F. Belo, *A Materialist Reading of the Gospel of Mark*, Paris, 1975 (French); New York, 1981 (English)

E. Best, *The Temptation and the Passion*, Cambridge, 1965, 2nd edn 1990

E. Best, *Following Jesus*, Sheffield, 1981

E. Best, *Mark: the Gospel as Story*, Edinburgh, 1983

E. Best, *Disciples and Discipleship*, Edinburgh, 1986

J. Drury, *The Parables in the Gospels*, London, 1985

J. Gnilka, *Das Evangelium nach Markus*, Zurich, 1978-9

E. Güttgemanns, *Candid Questions concerning Gospel Form-Criticism*, Munich, 1970 (German); Pittsburgh, 1979 (English)

M. Hengel, *Studies in the Gospel of Mark*, London, 1985

H.C. Kee, *Community of the New Age*, London, 1977

W. Kelber, *The Oral and the Written Gospel*, Philadelphia, 1983

E. Lohmeyer, *Das Evangelium nach Markus*, Göttingen, 1937

D. Lührmann, *Das Markusevangelium*, Tübingen, 1987

U. Luz, 'Markusforschung in der Sackgasse', *ThLZ*, 105, 1980, 641-55 (review of Pesch et al)

R.H. Lightfoot, *The Gospel Message of St. Mark*, Oxford, 1950

J. Marcus, *The Mystery of the Kingdom of God*, Atlanta, 1986

W. Marxsen, *Mark the Evangelist*, Göttingen, 1956 (German); Nashville, 1969 (English)

N. Perrin, *The Resurrection Narratives: A New Approach*, London, 1977

N.R. Petersen, *Literary Criticism for New Testament Critics*, Philadelphia, 1978

W. Pesch, *Das Markusevangelium*, Freiburg, 1976-7

H. Räisänen, *The 'Messianic Secret' in Mark*, Edinburgh, 1990

D. Rhoads and D. Michie, *Mark as Story: An Introduction to the Narrative of a Gospel*, Philadelphia, 1982

J.M. Robinson, *The Problem of History in Mark*, London, 1957

W. Schmithals, *Das Evangelium nach Markus*, Gütersloh, 1979

E. Schweizer, *The Good News According to Mark*, Göttingen, 1967 (German); London, 1971 (English)

E. Schweizer, 'Mark's Theological Achievement', *Evangelische Theologie*, 24, 1964, 337-55; and (English) in W. Telford, ed, *The Interpretation of Mark*, London, 1985, 42-63

G. Theissen, *Miracle Stories of the Early Christian Tradition*, Gütersloh, 1974 (German); Edinburgh, 1983 (English)

W. Wrede, *The Messianic Secret*, Göttingen, 1901 (German); Cambridge, 1971 (English)

9

Recent Developments
in Johannine Study

Bultmann's major achievement, we have seen, was to weave together a thoroughly historical reading of the Fourth Gospel with a theological interpretation of rare originality. His work on John was inspired by two central questions that he posed with great intensity, even if it was the second which towards the end of his life intrigued him the more: How is the Gospel to be located in the history of early Christian theology? What contemporary account can be given of the central theological claims of the Fourth Gospel? Scholars since Bultmann have been more intrigued by the first of these two questions than the second; their criticism of Bultmann's literary and historical proposals has seriously undermined the synthesis that he forged. Few however have made substantial contributions to the task of contemporary theological interpretation of the Gospel.

Bultmann's commentary appeared some fifty years ago, and its continuing ability to command scholars' attention is in itself no mean achievement. Nevertheless those fifty years have been productive ones for Johannine scholarship: the great commentaries of Dodd (1953), Barrett (1955, 1975²), Brown (1966, 1970) and Schnackenburg (1965, 1971) have appeared, together with a host of others, less bulky for the most part, but by no means inconsiderable: Sanders (1968), Lightfoot (1972), Lindars (1972), Becker (1979, 1981), and Haenchen (1980). At the same time there has been a steady stream of influential monographs and essays which have made significant contributions to the literary, historical and theological questions that Bultmann raised. Surveys of this literature are readily available, most recently in the opening section of John Ashton's (b.1931) splendid *Understanding the Fourth Gospel*. For my purposes, it makes best sense to review some of the more significant monographs and articles that have affected the course of Johannine study over the period and that still set the agenda at the present.

Of course, Johannine study is not a discipline hermetically sealed from other aspects of New Testament study. In so far as scholars have attempted to place the Fourth Gospel within the religious world of its time and to plot its position in relation to the early developments of the Christian church, Johannine study is necessarily related to wider study of the first-century

Mediterranean world. Within that field of study, two discoveries of far-reaching significance have occurred since the writing of Bultmann's commentary: the discovery of the Dead Sea Scrolls and the discoveries at Nag Hammadi. Such discoveries threw open the question of the religious milieu of the Fourth Gospel. Bultmann had supposed that it was significantly influenced by some form of Gnostic myth, indeed that John had taken over and reworked specifically Gnostic discourses. Qumran would show that Jewish literature could also contain forms of dualism which were interestingly analogous to the Fourth Gospel. Nag Hammadi on the other hand would begin to convince scholars that the relations between Christianity and Gnosticism were complex: that earlier criticism of Bultmann's theory of a pre-Christian Gnostic myth might itself need substantial revision. This, together with the continuing debate about the history of the earliest Christian communities, has injected an element of provisionality into historical debates about the Fourth Gospel, not that it is always reflected in the tone of scholars writing in this field.

Such provisionality is, however, a hallmark of much of the work of Ernst Käsemann. In his 1966 Shaffer Lectures, *The Testament of Jesus*, he starts with the 'unusual confession' that he intends to address a subject that 'he profoundly fails to understand' (1). The history of earliest Christianity, of the development of the early communities, their beliefs and organization, is an area where little firm ground is to be found and where often the best a scholar can hope to achieve is to have sharpened up the questions. The problem that Käsemann addresses is clear enough: it is how to locate the Gospel of John historically. His chapters on christology, ecclesiology, diversity and unity within the first-century church are all directed towards the resolution of that problem. Thus there is a significant shift in perspective from Bultmann's commentary. For Bultmann such matters were treated as resolvable and their solutions were incorporated into a general historical hypothesis that was intended to elucidate the sense of the Gospel text. By contrast, Käsemann brings such historical questions into the foreground, emphasises their intractability, and appeals to his understanding of the Gospel's christology and ecclesiology as a means of tackling the 'Johannine problem' of the historical location of the Fourth Gospel. Paradoxically, it has often been Käsemann's remarks about Johannine theology which have engaged scholars' attention; Käsemann's inaugural lecture, 'Heretic and Witness', however, demonstrates the leading role that historical questions played in his own work.

What is clear is that in answering the question, 'What kind of community produced the Fourth Gospel?', Käsemann takes as his starting-point the Gospel's christology and that he reads this as, very broadly, a docetic type of christology. He had already laid the way for such a view in his article on 'The Structure and Purpose of the Prologue to John's Gospel' in 1957. That article was a detailed discussion of Bultmann's analysis of the Prologue according to which it was based on a Baptist hymn with additions by the

Evangelist. Käsemann argued, *per contra*, that the basis of the Prologue was an early Christian hymn that underlay only the first 13 verses of the text. Verses 14-18 were the Evangelist's own composition.

Bultmann's position, though theologically attractive, was problematic. He saw verse 14 as part of the original Gnostic hymn; at the same time he saw the opening clause of the verse, 'And the Word became flesh' as expressing the Evangelist's theology of a hidden revelation which was deeply opposed to the Gnosticism of his source. This clause expressed *in nuce* the paradoxicality of the revelation in Christ, his hiddenness in the world of the transitory and the futile flesh. For Käsemann, by contrast, this first clause of the verse did no more than summarise what had been said in the second half of the Christian hymn that John was quoting, verses 5-13. It was a transitional formula, picking up the claim already made that 'he was in the world' and paving the way for the Evangelist's emphasis on the Christian vision of the glory of the Revealer: 'and we beheld his glory'. The Gospel is nowhere, so Käsemann believes, concerned with the hiddenness of the Word; it proclaims the *praesentia dei* (presence of God) in Jesus which is the true purpose of the incarnation. It is this that is the real cause of offence to the Jews: Jesus's claim to be equal to the Father, to confront men and women with the call of the creator. The miracles, while they may be misunderstood, are truly a manifestation of that creative power, true 'epiphany'; but this is not to detract from the fact that in Jesus men and women are confronted by the living word of the creator. It is their faith and hearing of the word that brings life. The Gospel proclaims, not the historical past, that the Logos was once incarnate in Jesus, but the presence of God in its midst, the presence of Christ, whose earthly history lies now nineteen hundred years in the past, as 'the Creator of eschatological sonship to God and of the new world'(*NTQT*, 165).

It is, then, this christology that provides the starting-point for Käsemann's investigation in *The Testament of Jesus*. His way into the discussion is via chapter 17. This he takes as a convenient summary of the Evangelist's thought, which treats the subject of eschatology from the standpoints of christology, ecclesiology and soteriology. But the main theme of his book is not theology as such but the historical location, within the history of early Christianity, of the Fourth Gospel. The theology may provide the clue to this problem, but Käsemann warns his reader not to expect too much. The book, following chapter 17, is then subdivided under three themes: the glory of Christ; the community under the Word; and Christian unity.

The chapter on the glory of Christ picks up the discussion of christology which Käsemann had initiated in his debate with Bultmann about the Prologue. The incarnation does not mean the assumption of a human incognito by the Logos, but is merely the affirmation that the heavenly Logos 'descended into the world of man and there came into contact with earthly existence, so that an encounter with him became possible' (9). Even the occasional references in the text to Jesus's humiliation are no more than the bare minimum necessary to present this story of the Logos's brief stay with men and women, in which he seems 'to be one of them, yet without himself being subjected to earthly conditions' (10). There is no paradox or dialectic in the Evangelist's portrayal of Jesus. The Johannine Christ is 'the Son of God who strides through the world of men' (transl. modified, 9,13). Whereas elsewhere in the New Testament Jesus's obedience in his earthly life is the ground for his subsequent glorification, here his obedience is the manifestation of his glory: it is the 'result of Jesus' glory and the attestation of his glory in the situation of the earthly conflict' (19). There is then no development in Jesus' sstatus, from humiliation to exaltation; all that changes is his situation. This understanding of christology corresponds closely to the Evangelist's eschatology. As Bultmann had argued, what is striking about this is its concentration on present eschatology. The early Christian expectation of some imminent end, indeed all forms of future expectation, yield to the sense of the *'praesentia Christi'* which is 'the centre of his proclamation' (15).

The replacement of the earlier patterns of present and future eschatology by an exclusively present eschatology further suggests, for Käsemann, ways of making sense of John's treatment of the Passion. At one level the Johannine motif of the 'hour' seems to point forward to the glorification of Christ in the Passion as something quite distinct from the glory of his earthly life. We should, however, be careful not to read these in terms of earlier forms of eschatology. John transcends the apparent distinction between the two by linking them to the notion of pre-existence. He 'understands the incarnation as a projection of the glory of Jesus' pre-existence and the passion as a return to that glory "which was his before the world began"'(20).

Again, whereas Bultmann had seen a sharp contrast between the Evangelist's theology of the incognito Christ and the miracle source, Käsemann regards the miracles as, for John, expressive of the glory of God which is manifested in the life of the incarnate Son. They are, that is to say, an integral part of the Evangelist's presentation of Christ. So, too, the discourses are not simply to be read as expressive of the new self-understanding that the believers receive as they make their confession to him, but as explicitly dogmatic reflections. 'The internal divine relationship of the revealer as the Son is just as strongly emphasised as his relation to the world' (23).

The theological positions that have been set out so far lead quite consistently into John's ecclesiology and soteriology. In a sense there is no doctrine of the church in John, no more than there is a doctrine of history. Or better, John has no real interest in the church as an institution, no sense of its place in the development of the world's history as it moves towards some final climax at the eschaton. We hear little of the standard elements of congregational life: sacraments, offices, worship, gifts of the Spirit, etc. To some extent Peter stands as the representative of the circle of the disciples, but other figures dominate and John introduces the esoteric sounding term 'friends' to refer to Jesus's followers.

If all are disciples, brothers, and friends of Jesus, then differentiations among them can no longer be decisive. The relationship to the Lord determines the whole picture of the Johannine Church to such an extent that the differences betwen individuals recede, and even the apostles represent only the historical beginnings of the community (31).

For just as the world provided only the stage for the coming of the Logos to men and women, so too, here history and the world's institutions have no significance except in so far as they provide the setting for the encounter between the Revealer and the — individual — believer. This disregard of history is again linked to the clear, if 'naive docetism' in John's christology.

In the same way, the tradition of the church is only there to point to Jesus. As an Evangelist, John clearly needs the tradition, although the form he uses is a later, wilder form than that found in the Synoptics. Nor does he contrast Spirit and tradition, as may have been the case in some earlier forms of Christianity. The Spirit recalls Jesus's words and the Gospel itself is an actual example of just such activity of the Spirit. But the tradition is not preserved for its own sake; only in so far as it enables the words of Jesus to be heard is the tradition of importance. John's use of the tradition, that is to say, is a prophetic, free use, which stands in the service of the realisation of Christ's presence to his hearers. Again, John's present eschatology controls his understanding of the institution and the tradition of the church.

In the final chapter Käsemann turns to the question of the unity of the church, a subject to which the early church attached no small importance. Paul developed his ideas in relation to the idea of the body of Christ, while for the Deutero-Paulines the unity of the church has become an essential characteristic which is guaranteed in heaven; John's treatment is quite different. The unity of the church is rooted in the unity of the Father and the Son; in so far as believers are united to the Son, remain in him, they are united to the Father and have unity among themselves. It is in virtue of his unity with the Father that Jesus is the Revealer of the heavenly world and that he appears in this world to draw the believers to him. He does not, despite the traditional saying of 3:16, love the world. Everything is focused on the relationship between the Revealer and the believers, and in this sense the Gospel lays the foundation for later Gnostic ideas. 'For gnosticism regards the gathering of the souls scattered on earth as the goal of world history' (73).

What then does Käsemann have to say about the historical location of the Fourth Gospel? It must have come from a time when the process of consolidating the churches into a unity, 'early Catholicism', was already well under way. Its nearest parallels are the enthusiasts who Paul attacks in 1 Cor. 15 and who are again the subject of polemic in 2 Tim. 2:18. Käsemann sees it as an enthusiastic sect, Hellenistic and enthusiastic in character, a 'relic of a Christian community, existing on, or being pushed to, the Church's periphery' (39).

It is interesting to compare Käsemann's monograph with the very different work published two years later by J. Louis Martyn (b.1925) in the States. Both scholars are interested in the same historical question about the Gospel's place in the development of the early Christian community's beliefs and practices. Some of the differences are strikingly obvious. Whereas Käsemann starts by giving a bold and provocative sketch of the Fourth Gospel's theology, Martyn's approach to the question is more pragmatic. He works away quietly looking for tell-tale marks that might suggest something about the immediate circumstances of its writing. Whereas Käsemann exhorts us to look for what is 'particular and concrete', Martyn displays an extraordinary sensitivity to the stray phrase that may provide an unexpected window onto the pressing concerns of the community in which the Gospel was produced.

Of course, such clues have to be searched for, and the historian needs to have a sense of where to look. The writing of a Gospel is foremost an exercise in handing on the traditions of the community. Thus if we are to detect something of the circumstances under which such traditions were handed on we shall need to attend to those points where, at least, we may sense that the Evangelist has created space for himself to shape his material, where 'elements of [his] own interests and experiences are more or less clearly reflected' (xxi). Such a point may be found in those miracle stories where the Evangelist has taken a traditional story and developed it into a dramatic cycle, to create a *literary genre* quite without counterpart in the body of the gospels' (*ibid.*).

The nub of the book centres around two such cycles in the Fourth Gospel: chapters 9 and 10 and 5-7. But there are clues that point to the questions raised in the two cycles. In John 16:2 the Johannine Christ warns his followers: 'They will put you out of the synagogues (*aposynagogos*); indeed, the hour is coming when whoever kills you will think he is offering service to God'. The two notions of excommunication and killing form the themes of the two cycles.

What is common to each is that John has taken a traditional miracle story and expanded it by adding a series of scenes. The resultant 'drama' must now be read on two levels. On the one level (which Martyn refers to as '*einmalig*') it refers to an event in the life of Jesus; on the other it refers to events in the life of John's own community. Events and characters in the narratives thus have a dual reference. The blind man and Jesus refer clearly to characters at the time of Jesus; they also refer to contemporaries of John and his community: a Christian healer and one of his 'patients'.

Some of these dual references work well; others are puzzling on the *einmalig* level and may be better explained when taken as referring to the Evangelist's own situation. This is the case with the reference to becoming '*aposynagogos*' in 9:22, compare 9:34. The term is so far known only in the

Fourth Gospel, and there is certainly no mention of Jesus or his followers having been excluded formally from the synagogue during his lifetime. *Prima facie*, at least, it seems more likely that this should refer to circumstances in the life of the early Christian community. But what circumstances?

9:22 reads in part: 'for the Jews had already agreed that if anyone should confess him to be Messiah, he would become an excommunicate from the synagogue' (Martyn's transl. [18]). There are four elements which require explanation: 1) the Jews; 2) the reference to some prior agreement; 3) the messianic confession of Jesus; 4) the adjective '*aposynagogos*'.

The adjective itself must mean, in some sense, 'away from the synagogue' and in context what is being referred to is clearly exclusion from the synagogue. Those who confess Jesus as Messiah are to be removed; they are no longer disciples of Moses but of Jesus (9:28). Parallels for this kind of deliberate attempt to exclude members from the synagogue are not easy to find. The types of ban found in rabbinical literature refer either to measures against scholars for the protection of purity regulations; or to measures which are relatively late and which were intended as a means of inner-synagogue discipline and not as a means of exclusion. Similarly the measures that Acts attributes to Paul in his persecution of the Christians are designed to discourage people from leaving the synagogue.

Martyn's suggestion is that there may be a connection here with the reformulation of the 12th Benediction of the synagogue prayer that dates from the time of the Academy in Jamnia after the fall of Jerusalem. According to the Babylonian Talmud, Samuel the Small reformulated the 12th Benediction at this time to exclude the heretics. This was in response to a request by Rabban Gamaliel and it was known as the Birkath ha-Minim (bBer 28b). Of this benediction we are specifically told that it was instituted in Jamnia (Ber 28b) and this ties in well with John 9:22 and its reference to a formal agreement.

It is less easy to know what the precise form of Samuel the Small's reformulation was. An early form of the benediction contains the words: 'Let the Nazarenes [Christians] and the Minim [heretics] be destroyed in a moment. And let them be blotted out of the Book of Life and not be inscribed together with the righteous' (Martyn's transl. [36]). Martyn believes that Samuel the Small probably added these lines against the Christians and other heretics, though he acknowledges that the originality of 'Nazarenes' is disputed by some.

If he is right, then the phrase 'let them be blotted out' suggests strongly: rooting them out. But how would a prayer have functioned as a means of exclusion? Perhaps, suggests Martyn, (38f) suspect members were made to read out the benedictions in the assembly. Christian believers, namely those who recognised Jesus as the Messiah, would have been reluctant to call down such a curse on themselves. On the other hand, rulers of the synagogue may have been able to avoid being put to the test in this way (see 12:42), because they controlled who it was that was called on to recite the Benedictions. All this supposes, of course, that the decision taken by the Academy at Jamnia was communicated to the synagogues elsewhere in the Mediterranean world, as is suggested by the reference (bBer 28b) to its 'institution' by the Academy.

The effect of the communication of such a decision on the early Johannine community is, then, not too hard to imagine. A group of Jewish 'disciples of Jesus', that is those who confess him as the Messiah, is suddenly challenged by the new benediction, and its members then have to decide whether they will leave the synagogue or whether they will remain secret believers (like Nicodemus) *unless otherwise challenged*. Martyn concludes this section:

Thus the Fourth Gospel affords us a picture of a Jewish community which has been (recently?) shaken by the introduction of a newly formulated means for detecting those Jews who want to hold a dual allegiance to Moses and to Jesus as Messiah. Even against the will of some of the synagogue leaders, the Heretic Benediction is now employed in order formally and irretrievably to separate the church from the synagogue. In the two-level drama of John 9 the man born blind plays not only the part of a Jew in Jerusalem healed by Jesus of Nazareth, but also the part of Jews known to John who have become members of the separated church because of their messianic faith and because of the awesome Benediction (40f).

The introduction of the 12th benediction as a means of excluding Christians was not the only measure that Jews took against Christians. 16:2b and the cycle in chapters 5-7 suggest that in some cases sterner measures were envisaged. The development of the story of the healing of the crippled man focuses attention on the healer, (not, as in chapter 9, on the healed) and on the Jews' attempts to kill him. In chapter 7 we hear of attempts to bring Jesus to court on charges of leading the people astray and of further deep divisions within the Jewish community.

We cannot here attempt to summarise Martyn's careful discussion of these passages. He offers a by no means implausible picture of developments in the synagogue from which the Johannine church sprang. Those who have been excluded continue, at considerable risk, to preach to the Jews. The synagogue rulers respond by trying to apprehend the Christian preachers on charges of leading the people astray, and there is continued evidence of considerable division of opinion with the synagogue.

Nevertheless, there is a continuing dialogue or debate with the synagogue. In a final section Martyn shows how these developments are reflected in the Fourth Evangelist's theology, both in discussion of expectations of a prophet-messiah like Moses and in the reworking of the notion of the Son of Man to refer to the dwelling of the Logos among men and women. What is of particular interest here is the way in which he attempts to correlate the duality of level of the stories with the Evangelist's christology.

Before going on to discuss what Martyn has to say about the reflection of all this in the theological debates of the Fourth Gospel, we should cast our minds back to Käsemann's discussion of the Fourth Gospel's location in the history of the early church. We have already mentioned the basic difference in their approaches to the subject: Käsemann argues from a reconstruction of the Fourth Evangelist's theology to his various relationships with other groups in the early church; Martyn picks up hints in the Evangelist's editing of the tradition, which lead him to detect echoes of struggles within the synagogue from which the Johannine community has emerged. These two approaches are, however, by no means mutually exclusive. The Fourth Gospel, on any reckoning, is a closely woven text, whose various strands, drawn as they are from many different contexts, may provide clues to different stages of the community's development. Käsemann's account of the Gospel's theology in terms of debates internal to the church — doceticism and gnosticism — may quite possibly give an accurate picture of a *later* stage in the history of the community, when it had become detached from the synagogue altogether. Thus it is more fruitful to note certain convergences between the two accounts, which may then provide the basis of further debates about the history of the theology of the Johannine community, than to seek to polarise them too sharply. Such convergences come in the portrayal of the Evangelist's theology and understanding of Christian existence, which Martyn treats in his last section.

The Fourth Gospel's theology, so Martyn argues, develops out of the identification of Jesus with the prophet-messiah like Moses into a strikingly original Son of Man christology which can speak of the presence of the Son of Man both in the historical figure of Jesus (*einmalig*) and, through the working of the Spirit, in the Christian preachers of his own day (see chapter 7). Martyn's view has important points of contact with Käsemann's claim that in the Fourth Gospel we have evidence of an enthusiastic form of Christianity that is rooted not in a particular form of sacramentalism (being baptised into Jesus' death and resurrection) but in a particular form of *christology*. How far do such resemblances reach?

One of the puzzles of the Fourth Gospel is that it links the notion of the Messiah with the performance of miracles, 'signs'. This is strange if the Messiah is thought of as a Davidic figure, as there is no evidence for the expectation of such a Messiah having been connected with miracles. On the other hand, there is evidence for a prophet-messiah like Moses (Deut. 18:15) who would perform miracles such as striking water from the rock and giving manna from heaven, and these themes are reflected in the Gospel (chapter 6). Martyn provides detailed argument for the following situation in the synagogue out of which the Johannine church emerged.

There were some Jews who were persuaded that Jesus was the Messiah like Moses. Such a belief was encouraged by the Gospel of Signs that emphasised Jesus' miraculous deeds and the belief that they engendered

(101-3). Others, however, true to Jamnia, disputed this claim on scriptural grounds, claiming that a more expert (midrashic) understanding of scripture showed that Jesus could not possibly be the expected prophet-messiah (104f). Yet others, represented in the Gospel by the figure of Nicodemus, looked for a midrashic justification of their incipient belief in Jesus as the Messiah (105-7). This is the force of Nicodemus' question to Jesus in John 3; but the question is cut short by the counter-statement that life can only come as a gift from the Spirit; all attempts to provide a justification for belief in Jesus from the scriptures are hopelessly bound to this world of the flesh. That is to say, the Evangelist, rather than attempt to strengthen the argument of the Gospel of Signs by providing midrashic support for it, rejects midrash as a means of securing faith and points instead to the need for election by God (110ff). The crucial text for this debate is John 6, where John deliberately contrasts Moses with God: It was not Moses who gave you the bread from heaven but my Father who gives you the true bread from heaven (6:32). This is not to say that the Evangelist wholly rejects the identification between Jesus and the prophet-messiah: he looks to a faith that goes beyond it (112ff).

If this is so, and John deliberately distances himself from the expectations of the prophet-Messiah, how does he himself develop Christian faith, christology, and on what basis? In the crucial texts which deal with the prophet-messiah, John introduces, by way of contrast, the figure of the Son of Man (121ff). Thus two factors are of importance in the story, for example of the man born blind: a) John's creation of a two-level drama 'which shows Jesus to be present in the activity of the Christian witness'; b) John's insistence that 'Jesus makes his presence unmistakably clear not as the Mosaic Messiah, but as the Son of Man on earth' (126f). In both points John is indebted, so Martyn contends, to apocalyptic. The notion of a two-level drama is to be found there, though it is certainly very differently worked out; and so is the figure of the Son of Man, the heavenly figure who will come to judge the world. But what is striking in John is the reference of this title to the earthly figure of Jesus. This goes beyond the Synoptics' proleptic use of the title, and Martyn quotes with approval Käsemann's statement:

Jesus is the Son of Man because in him the Son of God comes to man. It is characteristic of John's radical re-interpretation that he uses this title that designated the apocalyptic World Judge to refer to the earthly existence of Jesus (*TJ* [13], quoted in Martyn [132])

The point for both is that the same claims that are made about the Jesus who once encountered the man born blind are also being made about the believers: they too share in the life of the Godhead — are sons of God.

Yet in what sense is Jesus identified with the believers? What is meant by saying that the Son of Man must ascend, must go away? How did the Evangelist address the problem of the separation between Jesus and his disciples that is caused by Jesus's departure? Two possibilities would have presented themselves to him: either to point to the heavenly home that awaited the disciples, or to offer the hope of some kind of mystic union with the exalted one. John does indeed use both these motifs, but in an interestingly modified form. While in 14:2 Jesus promises his disciples that he goes to prepare rooms for them in heaven, in 14:23 he also promises that he and his Father will come to dwell with believers. Again while he speaks, in the image of the vine, about the union between believers and himself, he does not do so in a way that promises to take the believers out of the world; rather the Risen Lord 'makes clear that the union about which he has spoken is played out in the earthy drama of everyday life' (139). All of this is possible because of the Spirit-paraclete who comes to them in the place of the Son and takes them into the work of the divine Son. '*It is, therefore, precisely the Paraclete who creates the two-level drama*' (140).

This in turn 'creates an epistemological crisis' (141). For those outside the Johannine circle, 'the world', it is seen only at one level — it is either a story about Jesus that may be debated in a midrashic manner, or it is about the contemporary Christian, but without reference to the Paraclete who makes Jesus present in the Christian's words and deeds. For John, it occurs on both levels; and the fact that it does so is 'to a large extent, the good news itself' (142).

It is now easier to see what Martyn had in mind when he wrote at the beginning of his book of his desire to find 'passages in which elements of John's own interests and experiences are more or less clearly reflected' (xxi). Easier, but not altogether easy. Obviously, Martyn wishes to relate the Gospel text to circumstances in the life of the Johannine community both within and without the synagogue. But in what sense does it reflect John's own 'interests and experiences'? The term 'interests' here is clearly used without sociological malice aforethought, and presumably refers to John's own theological or religious preferences/beliefs. In fact we are told very little about these, though we may properly infer from Martyn's account that he was at least well-versed in certain forms of Jewish theological debate, and also not unfamiliar with apocalyptic literature. Why he rejected midrash and scriptural interpretation as a Jew we are not told, though one inference from Martyn's account might be that it was because of his belief in Jesus's divinity. It was after all for this reason that the Jewish leaders sought to put Christian teachers to death. Is the reason for John's rejection of midrash and the search for scriptural justification of his Christian beliefs, the recognition that such proofs cannot easily or persuasively be found? The grounds then for such a belief in Jesus's divinity would lie in John's and his community's own experience, the experience, as Martyn suggests, of been taken by the Spirit into the work and mission of the Son. It is this that is most clearly expressed in the two-level dramatic cycles which the Evangelist has created.

Such an account may help us to clarify further the relation of Martyn's portrayal of John's theology to Käsemann's. Martyn agrees with Käsemann that John 1:14 forms John's initial comment on the Logos Hymn with which he introduces his Gospel; but he sees it, interestingly, as supporting his view that the Evangelist wishes to tell his story on two levels. Just as the Prologue proclaims that the 'Word did not remain in heaven, but rather came and dwelt among us, so the Risen Lord does not remain in heaven, but rather comes to dwell with his own' (142] referring to 14:23). There is, presumably, no doubting the 'humanity' of the believers, and no suggestion in Martyn's treatment that John's Jesus is less than an historical, earthly figure, on the *einmalig* level. The linking of John's christology with his doctrine of the Spirit suggests that his christology, for all that it makes high claims about Jesus as the Son of God, does nothing to detract from the actuality of his earthly life.

In what sense, in Martyn's view, was John an 'enthusiast', someone who acknowledged no variety of gifts within the church but saw all believers as equally filled 'without measure' by the Spirit of the Lord? Martyn gives no direct answer to this question. What he does say is that John recognised stages of belief and was concerned to help those who had an initial belief in Jesus as the Messiah to come to a fuller understanding of him as the Son of Man. In this respect it is important to note that Martyn does not believe that the Johannine epistles with their perfectionist elements stem from the Evangelist.

Thus while there are important convergences between Martyn and Käsemann there are divergences too. Their work opened up a rich field of enquiry, which was taken up not least by R. E. Brown (b.1928) in *The Community of the Beloved Disciple* (1979), into the development of the theology of the Johannine community, once it was cut free from the synagogue. What Martyn's work unquestionably showed was the extent to which that tradition had been moulded by debates with the synagogue. His own suggestion that this was reflected in the creation of a two-level drama was certainly fruitful in bringing out some of the possible associations that John's hearers would make when listening to such stories. However, the notion that such stories should be construed as having two parallel senses is itself rather artificial. This is clear when for instance we press on the question of the precise character of the second level equivalents of Jesus and the blind man: do they represent a Christian healer and the one whom he has healed, or a preacher and his convert? The point is simply that stories about Jesus's confrontation with the Jewish authorities of his day would inevitably be linked by the teller and his hearers with their own experiences of such encounters, in such a way that that experience influenced their telling and hearing of the story and that the story influenced the way they understood their own experience. One of the difficulties with Martyn's talk of a two-level drama is that it can too easily suggest that the Evangelist was simply setting out two different sets of events without doing justice to the interaction between story and experience, the way in which the story shapes the world of John and his hearers. The latter view is however supported by what Martyn says about the author's belief in the Paraclete, as making possible the two-level drama. It is indeed a very powerful expression of the belief that the life of the community will be shaped by the story of Jesus's life.

There is another way in which Martyn's notion of a two-level drama could be misleading. By suggesting that there are two distinct but, in principle at least, determinate senses that the stories have, Martyn's work leaves the impression that the composition of the Gospel itself must be located at a particular point in the history of the Johannine community, namely that referred to by his second level. If, however, we see the interaction between story and community-experience as an on-going process, then the question of the precise location of the Gospel in the community's history becomes a more open one. Earlier debates with the synagogue may have left their mark on the stories; but the Gospel as a whole may still date from a later stage where the trauma of separation from the synagogue has been overcome and other, internal, issues may also have left their mark on the stories.

Questions about the nature of the interaction between the Johannine literature and its community are central to a remarkable article by W. A. Meeks, 'The Man from Heaven in Johannine Sectarianism' (1972). He takes his lead from Bultmann's view that any study of the 'Johannine puzzle' must start with the Johannine picture of the descending and ascending redeemer, and that, moreover, in approaching this topic 'it is not simply a question of explaining the *concept* of 'pre-existence', but rather of perceiving the origin and function of a *myth*' (141). For Meeks, the exegetical task is not simply to relate the Johannine myth to contemporary philosophical ideas; it is also to understand the way the myth functions within its community. The myth, he suggests, served to make sense of the varied history of the community: its relations with followers of John the Baptist, with the Jewish community and subsequent struggles within the church itself. 'More precisely', Meeks suggests, 'there must have been a continuing dialectic between the group's historical experience and the symbolic world that served both to explain that experience and to motivate and form the reaction of group members to the experience' (145).

Meeks starts with an investigation of the linguistic phenomena of the Fourth Gospel. 'The uniqueness of the Fourth Gospel in early Christian literature consists above all in the special patterns of language that it uses to describe Jesus Christ' (141). One of the features to which he draws attention is the occurrence of 'parallel, slightly varying formulations of similar thematic complexes' (144). Such repetition, he suggests, following Edmund Leach (b.1910), is sometimes part of a deliberate strategy of countering other complex signals in a particular society by repeating one's own signal as many times as possible, in different ways. 'From the repeated impact of varying signals, the basic structure that they have in common gets through' (*ibid*.). Thus the task for Meeks is to discern the underlying structure of the Evangelist's myth and to give some account of its social function, how it may have shaped the social world of the Fourth Gospel.

In his article, Meeks chooses to examine the Evangelist's handling of the motif of the descending and ascending Son of Man. Whereas such motifs occur elsewhere in connection with a narrative of the descent from heaven, which often identifies the figure as a hero or god, no such narrative is to be found in the Fourth Gospel. Indeed the '*motif belongs exclusively to discourse, not to narrative*'. It is used solely to identify Jesus, but not as a hero, rather as 'the Stranger *par excellence*' (146). It is, as we shall see, this notion of strangeness which, according to Meeks, the Evangelist uses to shape his community's awareness of themselves as sharply distinguished from all other religious and cultural groups.

Meeks's method of structural analysis is most clearly exemplified in his treatment of the theme of descent and ascent in John 3. The theme, or pattern, has previously been introduced into the Gospel in the promise made to Nathanael in 1:51. There it was associated with the title 'Son of Man' with which it is elsewhere closely linked in the Gospel. It is announced, moreover, to Nathanael who is characterised as the 'true Israelite' and to whom is promised a vision of 'greater things'. In this way Nathanael is contrasted with Nicodemus, who appears at the title's next occurrence as 'the teacher of Israel' who is told that he cannot or will not see certain superior things. Thus initially we learn something about the pattern: that the figure of the Son of Man is connected with a great promise; and that this promise is made, not to the Jews but to 'the true Israelites'.

The enigmatic and exclusive nature of the Son of Man's vision is brought out even more clearly in the dialogue with Nicodemus (3:1-21) and its sequel (3:31-6). True to his suggestion that the Evangelist works by weaving together traditional material of a closely similar, but not quite identical, nature, Meeks does not look for a tight line of argument in the chapter but rather the reinforcement of certain basic patterns of thought. At one level, the surface level, the initial dialogue affirms that 'Jesus alone has access to heavenly secrets' (147). In this, he connects the statement in verse 13, 'No one has ascended into heaven except the one who has descended, the Son of Man' (construed as a denial of claims so to have ascended made by apocalyptic seers) with the two Amen-sayings in vv. 3 and 5. There too the phrases 'see/ enter the kingdom of God' also refer to the notion of a heavenly journey, while 'v.13 shows that *anothen* has to mean "from above" and that "the one born from above/from the spirit" can only be the Son of Man, Jesus' (*ibid*.). That is to say, the passage asserts the uniqueness of Jesus's revelation by denying that any but he can have enjoyed the heavenly vision. For Bultmann, of course, verses 3 and 5 were key texts for his existential reading of the Gospel; on Meeks's reading they are, at a surface level at least, almost exclusively christological. Nevertheless at a deeper level, indicated by the form of the dialogue, there are social-anthropological claims being made. On the surface the motif of descent/ascent is being used as a warrant for the revelation that Jesus brings. The form of the dialogue however indicates, at a deeper level, Jesus's '*own* superiority to the questioner' (150). As in much Greco-Roman literature, the repeated pattern of misunderstanding provides an occasion for the reader to feel superior to those who have misunderstood *and* for the Sage to deliver a discourse. Yet there is more here than just bolstering the readers' sense of their superiority. Nicodemus, of course, stands for the Jews, specifically (and here Meeks agrees with Martyn in large measure) those who partly believe but are unable to risk expulsion and so fail to comprehend the identity of the Son of Man.

All this, the emphasis on the exclusivity of the revelation that Jesus brings and on the superiority of those who confess him over those who partially believe but cannot bring themselves to cut their ties with the synagogue, is reinforced by the passage, 3:31-6, with which this section concludes. Commentators, particularly since Bultmann, have recognised both the thematic links between this passage and the earlier dialogue with Nicodemus, and also felt the awkwardness of the transition which is provided by the bridging passage about the relationship between John and Jesus. This has led many to suggest some form of rearrangement, relocating verses 31-6 within the earlier dialogue. 'Such rearrangement hypotheses', so Meeks asserts, 'result from failure to perceive one of the most striking characteristics of the evangelist's literary procedure: the elucidation of themes by progressive repetition' (150).

Such a procedure was perhaps in part the product of necessity; the Evangelist inherited a good deal of material which was similar in content. This could either, as is the case in other examples of revelation discourses, be simply juxtaposed; alternatively, it could be linked to similar material by the interspersal of narrative episodes, as in the case here. This creates a certain distance from the earlier 'ambiguous and paradoxical statements, so that the internal tensions of the material begin to work in a progressive, didactic spiral' (*ibid.*). Specifically, certain points that had been hinted at in the previous section are here clarified. *Anothen* in verse 31 can only mean 'from above' and this, moreover, explicitly affirms Jesus's superiority over all other revealers. Indeed the section as a whole emphasises not so much the specific information which Jesus is to bring, as his status as the revealer; and this is then developed in a complex dialectic in the Gospel about true and false testimony (see esp. 5:31-41 and 8:12-20).

All this is highly illuminating. The question, however, remains how verses 31-6b relate to the intervening section about the Baptist. To put the question rather more sharply than does Meeks in his paper: How can the Evangelist, who has earlier asserted that it is through the witness of the Baptist that 'all would believe in him' (1:7), now apparently assert that the Baptist 'speaks of the earth'? Meeks answers this by pointing to the statement in Q: 'among those born of women none is greater than John; yet he who is least among the kingdom of heaven is greater than he' (Luke 7:28/Mt. 11:11). Thus the Evangelist is asserting firmly that 'John and his movement belong among those who are "of the earth"' (151), thereby, of course, further marking out the Johannine community from its rivals.

Of course, the passage contains more than just this. It introduces new themes that will be explored further in the Gospel and that will in turn help to develop the community's sectarian self-consciousness. What dominates the section, however, is precisely the theme of Jesus's strangeness. The dialogue is a parody of a revelation discourse. 'What is "revealed" is that Jesus is *incomprehensible*, even to "the teacher of Israel" . . . and even to the Baptist who has been his primary human witness (5:32-5)' (*ibid.*). At the same time the sense of the Gospel is one that is accessible only to those within the community for whom the complex allusions and repetitions make sense precisely because they are already familiar with them. It is a book for insiders, designed to assure them of their superiority over those outside.

Meeks's article is a fascinating attempt to make sense of the peculiarities of Johannine language, particularly its repetitiveness, and at the same time to show how it serves to inculcate a myth that exerts powerful social controls on his community. That is to say, he is concerned both with the expression and the function of the Johannine myth: how it is built up and communicated, and what effects it has on those who absorb it and make it their own.

Two points only can engage us here. The first concerns the relation between the numerous similar sentences and phrases that occur throughout the Gospel. To many commentators these have been best explained as the products of a community (or school) which has explored the same theme over a period and has preserved various utterances as part of its tradition; John has preserved these traditions and woven them together as best he can. This accounts for the stylistic unity of the material on the one hand and the strange breaks in sense and continuity on the other. Meeks largely accepts this account, but further suggests that in combining such varied yet similar material John had a specific purpose in mind: namely, reinforcing the basic pattern of the myth by constant repetition. This is intriguing but does it quite work? In his exposition of John 3 Meeks suggests that the last section, 3:31-6, resolves some of the ambiguities of the earlier discussion in 3:1-21 and, further, that it explicitly states things which were merely implicit in the previous passage. Now it is, of course, possible that simply juxtaposing elements from the tradition could have this neat effect of clarifying and making explicit what was contained in other parts; but if this kind of account is repeated, it is soon seen to rely too heavily on happy circumstance. One might then be tempted to see whether, despite the apparent disjunctions in the thought of the Gospel, there is not a kind of logic running through it which is more the product of an individual mind that the work of a school or community. Not that there has to be too sharp a distinction between the two alternatives: even a creative and original writer may be moulded by a school of thought and owe much to its forms of thought and language. We shall return to this question in the discussion of our next contribution.

The second question concerns the relation of the sense and function of the myth of the descending and ascending Son of Man. Like Martyn, Meeks wants to discover how the surface level of the text relates to the life of the community to which it was addressed. Martyn offered an answer in terms of his 'two-level drama'; Meeks in terms of the social function of the structure of the myth.

The question about the function of stories or discourses is of course a perfectly legitimate one and one that needs to be asked a great deal more by New Testament scholars. On the other hand we also need to distinguish carefully between the sense and the function of texts, and not to assume that there is no direct correlation between the literal, theological sense of a text and its social implications. Leach, to whom Meeks refers, often seems to suggest that the social dimensions of the texts he studies are not understood by those to whom they are addressed and that it is the job of the social anthropologist to draw out such a dimension by seeing how in fact they function. But may it not be that, at least at certain stages of a community's history, the social import of a text is clearly understood by the community, precisely because it is a clear implication of the high-level theological statements that are being made? The myth of a heavenly Son of Man who comes to reveal the Father only to those who believe and to draw them into union with him would seem clearly to imply that only those who believe can enjoy such life. There is, that is to say, a clear logical connection between the claim to uniqueness of the Son of Man as revealer and the claim that believers enjoy a unique status as sons of God. This may certainly reinforce a sense of the group's exclusivity; but such exclusivity may again be tempered by what the Gospel has to say further about the election of believers, about the mystery of belief and unbelief. Thus, again, much will depend on whether we see the Gospel as an extended attempt to explore and clarify central theological claims, together with their social implications, or whether with Meeks we see it more as the attempt to reinforce the sectarian nature of the church by inculcating certain patterns of mythological thought. Meeks insists that he wishes to distinguish sharply between philosophy and myth. Yet even myth, so far as it engages in discourse, is, as Meeks acknowledges, concerned with the exploration of ideas, their clarification and explication, and this will, on occasion at least, include their social implications.

The last piece that I wish to look at in this very selective review of Johannine studies was published in the same year as Meeks' article, though it had in fact been delivered as a public lecture two years earlier in 1970. C.K. Barrett (b.1917) has, of course, written one of the major commentaries on the Fourth Gospel, and this article clearly presupposes the careful detailed exegetical work that distinguishes his commentary. In common with the other scholars whose work we have reviewed, Barrett is also in constant dialogue with Bultmann and this article, 'The Dialectical Theology of St John', addresses itself to one of the central issues raised by the latter's *Gospel of John*: What kind of account can we give of the Evangelist's theology and mode of theologizing in the light of the apparent breaks and jumps in the Gospel?

As we have already seen, one of the preferred solutions to this problem is to look for some explanation in terms of the Evangelist's use of disparate but stylistically similar material: the Evangelist has imposed such order as he could on his material, but an element of disjointedness remains. This is of course an alternative to Bultmann's attribution of the breaks in thought to a physical disruption of the text and the subsequent, less than successful, attempts of an editor to reconstruct the original order. But as we have just seen, even highly sophisticated attempts such as Meeks's may end up by discovering such a measure of rational purpose in the ordering of the material as it now stands as to cause one to wonder whether the disjointedness of the text is not more apparent than real.

Barrett's proposal then is that the Evangelist's thought is dialectical, that is, that he seeks clarity on any matter by considering different opinions on the subject, revising, rejecting and selecting as he may be guided by the continuing dialogue that he thus holds with himself. This is, of course, a very wide definition and a more detailed understanding of the Evangelist's thought must be derived from close attention to the text. Can such a way of conceiving his thought serve to explain the apparent breaks in the argument in, say, John 6, a chapter which some have seen as evidence of dislocation of the text, others as the product of a particular mode of meditation on the theme of the manna, whether sermonic or midrashic (cf P. Borgen (b.1928) [1965]).

That there are tensions in the thought of the chapter is not in dispute. At the most obvious, the chapter speaks on the one hand of salvation, life, as a present reality: He who believes has eternal life (6:47); and on the other of the future resurrection of the believer on the last day (6:39, 40, 44 and 54). Again, so Barrett argues, the chapter speaks about such life being a gift to those who believe, who hear his word and abide in him; but it also talks in 6:53-8 as if life were dependent on the reception of the Eucharist. 'Does John then teach that communion with the Son, and the gift of eternal life, are exclusively dependent on sacramental means (v.53)? or that such physical media (*sarx*) are worthless (v.63)?' (53). Or are such tensions better explained as part of a dialectical process, a dialogue which the Evangelist holds with himself by which he seeks to gain greater clarity about the central claims of the Christian faith?

Such a suggestion is by no means far-fetched. The Gospel certainly contains themes in regard to which it 'presents a double front' (54). It is both Jewish and anti-Jewish, and this stems from John's understanding of 'the theological — the theological rather than the sociological — setting of Christianity, and this may be traced back certainly to the earliest Christian tradition, and with a high measure of probability to Jesus himself' (55). Was not Jesus himself a Jew and yet one who was rejected by his fellow Jews? Such tensions within the thought of the Gospel, that is to say, are directly related to John's understanding of the Christian theological tradition and are — therefore? — not to be related to the specific situation from which John writes or in which the traditions he uses developed. The same is true of the gnostic and anti-gnostic elements in the Gospel: they relate to 'an antinomy that is written into the stuff of the Gospel' (55). Are there similar tensions within John 6 that also relate to the central themes of the Christian Gospel?

Barrett identifies a number of themes that have a dialectical twist: signs, which are 'seen' and yet 'not seen' (58ff); faith which is both 'work' and 'not work' (60f); which may be read by the Jews as endorsing Moses, but which for John points not to Moses but to the God who works through him and who is now working through Jesus (61f); and the great themes of predestination and incarnational christology. (62-5)

To take an example in more detail: John 6 speaks frequently of 'coming to Jesus'. People come to Jesus, and although he refuses to accede to their desire to make him king, he does meet their needs, feeds them physically and satisfies their spiritual hunger and thirst. 'None is refused; whoever comes is received' (63). But there is another side to the matter. Those who come to the Son are drawn by the Father, with its negative implication that 'no one can come to me unless the Father who sent me draws him' (6:44).

> The fact is that this chapter . . . contains material that suggests that it lies within the competence of man freely to make up his mind to come to Jesus and thus to receive at his hand the gift of life that he offers without distinction or reservation, and that equally it contains material that suggests that this coming lies wholly within the freedom of God, who alone determines who shall come to Jesus (64).

This dialectical approach to predestination is the only tolerable way of dealing with the theme which has continued to exercise theologians throughout Christian history. For:

> [p]redestination is in fact a dialogue between God and man, though it is one in which God, because he is God, will always have the last word. Seeing is not necessarily believing, coming is not necessarily believing, for the faith that unites with Christ and receives the gift of life is not a human property. Effective coming means being drawn by God (44); effective seeing means being taught by God (45). Yet, when this is said, the seeing is real seeing, the coming real coming, and the believing real believing, man's seeing, man's coming, man's believing

(64).

Such a view of the workings of the Evangelist's mind may then provide a way of understanding the tensions in the chapter that were noted at the outset. The tension between present and future eschatology is 'a feature of New Testament thought in general, and constitutes one of its unavoidable problems' (66). John, by setting it within the framework of his dialectical understanding of faith, affirms both that the believer does indeed enjoy life, but also that he himself is not the source of that life. 'There is "an infinite qualitative distinction between time and eternity"' (*ibid.*) and for John both the heights of religious experience and the life of Jesus itself 'stand under the dialectic of "I will raise him up at the last day"' (66). The Cross is not simply a moment in the past, but something that must be seen — dialectically — 'as a moment of disclosure but equally as a moment of concealment (12.36-40)'. Similarly, too, the believer's participation in the Eucharist stands under the same eschatological dialectic. 'He who eats the flesh and drinks the blood of the Son of Man has life, but he does not have it as a personal possession that he holds in his own right; he will never cease to need what is expressed in the words: "I will raise him up at the last day"' (67).

This, in turn, provides a key to the problem of John's relation to the tradition. His eschatology is a deepening of the traditional Christian eschatology with its tensions between present and future realization. His eucharistic theology makes:

> explicit, and at great depth, what was already present in the traditional material . . . (1 Cor 11.26). The Supper, as Christians observe it, takes place between the historical event of the Lord's death, to which it looks back, and the meta-historical event of the Lord's coming, to which it looks forward (68).

> It may link with the reference to thirst in verse 35; but the essential motivation for its inclusion 'was John's insight into the older tradition' (*ibid.*).

Thus John is the theologian who, above all, perceives the 'turbulent dialectic of the primitive Christian tradition, and of the life of Jesus himself'. Resisting the tendency either to historicise it or to turn it into a form of gnosis, he offers instead

> a creative and perceptive handling of the earlier tradition, free in that it addresses to the basic Christian conviction whatever new questions a new age might suggest, obedient in that it is bound to the original apostolic witness to Jesus. The 'dialectical theology of John' is not a novel invention, but an authentic insight into the meaning of Christian origins (68).

It is clear that Barrett is here wrestling with the same problems as the other commentators we have been considering, namely, the particular nature of John's thought, of his relation to the tradition and of his place within the development of Christian theology. Like them he too is deeply influenced by the work of Bultmann, indeed in many ways more so, for he, like Bultmann, sees John, with Paul, as the great theologian of the New Testament. Where he differs from Bultmann is in his understanding of John's method and his relation to the traditions with which he works. For Bultmann, John is a more straightforward thinker: it is the accident of the Gospel's disruption which has created the disjointedness of his thought as it stands. Again, for Bultmann, John's relation to his tradition is more adversarial: he sets out to correct the naive faith of the signs source and to de-mythologise the Gnostic *Offenbarungsreden*. For Barrett, both John and the early Christian tradition with which he works (and here Barrett is referring less to sources that the Evangelist has used slavishly than to a broad range of Christian tradition including that represented in the Pauline literature) were dialectical. The tension between present and future eschatology ru. s through from the earlier tradition to John. John's merits are to have cultivated such traditions more faithfully than those who historicised them or turned them in a Gnostic direction.

It should be clear that in all this Barrett is not following Käsemann and Martyn in a search primarily for the location of the Fourth Gospel, be it in the development of the church or in the church's emergence from the synagogue. Certainly, he sees the relationship of Christianity to Judaism as a major theme for the Fourth Evangelist, not simply because it was a matter of pressing concern for his community, but because the issue was one that was of central and enduring import for the church. As he writes elsewhere (*The Gospel of John and Judaism* [76]), 'The merit of John does not consist in his having satisfied a passing, practical need by means of a fly-sheet, but in his having known abiding elements of theological truth. These evolved out of the tension between Judaism and Christianity, but they led out beyond this original frame of reference'.

There is, thus, again a sharp divide in Barrett's work between the theological and the sociological. This is reflected in his view of John's relation to his tradition: John is not principally working with traditional material (which he juxtaposes, redacts) which bears the marks of particular stages of the community's history; he is drawing on a rich and varied tradition and working freely and creatively within it to develop and clarify its theological sense.

It is also reflected in a relative lack of interest in the social implications of what John is saying, in the ways in which his work may have been influenced by immediate concerns of his community. In attempting to locate the Evangelist's thought in the development of early Christianity he is less interested in the ways in which it may have influenced the development of particular forms of community than in its permanent value to theology.

This is not to suggest that there is anything wrong in being interested in the permanent theological significance of New Testament texts. Quite the contrary: the question is a real one; but there is a question whether what may be construed as a quite sharp reaction against more recent interest in the social-historical aspects of the Fourth Gospel has not, perhaps, gone too far. What, I have been attempting to suggest, is wrong with some recent analyses is the separation of the sociological and the theological senses of texts, however that is done. It would be unfortunate, in reacting against treatments that seem to play down the theological importance of John, to accept that same separation. We learn much about the theological meaning of texts by understanding their social implications; just as we can fully understand the social import of a religious text only by understanding its theology.

The question can be raised nicely in conjunction with Bultmann's fundamental question about the nature of myth. Bultmann's view of myth was in an important sense ambiguous. In one view he saw it as a form of pre-scientific cosmology, a set of beliefs about the world that could simply no longer be held without loss of intellectual integrity. In another view myths were, as a matter of fact, the means by which people in the ancient world were able to give expression to their sense of human finitude, of the need for salvation, of the different modes of human existence. Certainly, Bultmann saw the Fourth Evangelist's articulation of such mythology as being first and foremost an exercise in the expression of his new self-understanding, and as such already a withdrawal — implicitly, at least — from its cosmological sense. What he did not do was to consider the role of such myth-making or breaking in the new development of John's community and indeed of the early church.

The studies we have reviewed pick up such questions in interesting ways. J. L. Martyn's work, like Käsemann's, is, first, a work of historical reconstruction. The outcome of his essay is to locate the Fourth Evangelist at the point at which his community severs its connections with the synagogue. It is at this point, when it can no longer rely on the myth and methods of mythological interpretation of the Jewish community (midrash) — at least in Martyn's view — that it begins to develop its own mythology. Here, too, E. Käsemann and Martyn agree, although they would take differing views of what that mythology is. That is to say, there is a significant consensus between Martyn, Käsemann and indeed Meeks — against Bultmann — that what John is doing is not myth-breaking but myth-making. Meeks's essay is concerned partly with the ways in which the myth of the man from heaven is inculcated, partly with the function of the myth in reinforcing sectarian attitudes within the community. This latter move is analogous to Bultmann's existential interpretation in so far as it abstracts from the 'objectivity' or cosmological content of myth and focusses on its import for the ways in which men and women make sense of their experience. The difference, of course, is that Bultmann considered such questions in terms of the individual's self-understanding, whereas Meeks is interested in the way the myth moulds the 'self-understanding', the attitudes and behaviour of the community as a whole. By contrast, Barrett is at pains to trace out the form of theological discourse in the Fourth Evangelist to see in it a rehearsing and elucidation of perennial themes of Christian theology: free-will and predestination; present and future eschatology; and word and sacrament.

Interestingly, it seems to me that Barrett is right to see such themes being articulated in John 6 and right to read the Fourth Gospel as above all a work of dialectical theology. No more than I can agree with Bultmann that John is essentially contributing to the discarding of myth in early Christianity, can I agree with Meeks that John's undoubtedly repetitious language is simply a device for reinforcing the contours of his myth. But to say that John is a theologian does not, of course, mean that his theology was not mythological; nor does it mean to say that it had no function in respect of John's community or of individuals within it. What is required is a theological interpretation of John's Gospel that exposes the social and ethical implications of his high theological claims.

List of works cited

J. Ashton, *Understanding the Fourth Gospel*, Oxford, 1991

J. Ashton, ed, *The Interpretation of John*, London, 1986

C.K. Barrett, *The Gospel According to St John*, London, 1955, 2nd rev. edn, London, 1978

C.K. Barrett, 'The Dialectical Theology of St John', in *New Testament Essays*, London, 1972, 49-69

C.K. Barrett, *The Gospel of John and Judaism*, London, 1975

J. Becker, *Das Evangelium des Johannes*, Gütersloh, 1979, 1981

P. Borgen, *Bread from Heaven*, Leiden, 1965

R.E. Brown, *The Gospel According to John*, New York, 1966, 1970

R.E. Brown, *The Community of the Beloved Disciple*, London, 1979

C.H. Dodd, *The Interpretation of the Fourth Gospel*, Cambridge, 1953

E. Haenchen, *A Commentary on the Gospel of John*, Tübingen, 1980 (German); Philadelphia, 1984 (English)

E. Käsemann, 'Ketzer und Zeuge' ['Heretic and Witness'], *ZThK*, 48, 1951, 292-311

E. Käsemann, 'The Structure and Purpose of the Prologue to John's Gospel', Munich, 1957 (German); in *New Testament Questions of Today*, London, 1969, 138-167 (English)

E. Käsemann, *The Testament of Jesus: A Study of the Gospel in the Light of Chapter 17*, Tübingen, 1966 (German); London, 1968 (English)

R.H. Lightfoot, *St. John's Gospel*, London, 1972

B. Lindars, *The Gospel of John*, London, 1972

J.L. Martyn, *History and Theology in the Fourth Gospel*, New York, 1968

W.A. Meeks, 'The Man from Heaven in Johannine Sectarianism', *JBL* 91, 1972, 44-72, in J. Ashton, ed, *The Interpretation of John*, 141-73

J.N. Sanders, *A Commentary on the Gospel According to St John*, London, 1968

R. Schnackenburg, *The Gospel According to St John*, Freiburg, 1965, 1971, 1976 (German); London, 1968, 1979, 1982 (English)

10
Towards a Theology of the New Testament

We ended the first half of this book with an account of the major achievement of New Testament interpretation this century: Bultmann's *Theology of the New Testament*. That was a work which attempted two tasks: on the one hand to give an account of the different stages of development of New Testament Christianity, with its roots in Jesus's preaching and the emerging forms of Hellenistic Christianity, culminating in the Pauline corpus and the Johannine writings, flattening out, as it were, in the Deutero-Paulines and the Pastorals; on the other to lay open the New Testament corpus to the modern reader in such a way that he/she can transcend the enormous cultural differences which set him/her apart from the text and read/hear them as texts that address the same fundamental questions of existence that move us today as they moved men and women then.

Thus Bultmann's *Theology of the New Testament* is an attempt to hold together two, in a sense quite separate, tasks that have each their own goals or norms. The historical-critical task, as pursued most rigorously by the History of Religions School, seeks to give an — objective — account of developments in religious faith and practice, as early Christianity emerges from its matrix in Second Temple Judaism and takes its place among the new Mediterranean religions of the Roman Principate. Such an account should seek to provide an historical narrative that is guided and tested by analogy with human experience and must be prepared to argue its case in the humanistic circles of modern academia. The theological interpretative task is of a very different kind: it seeks to read the texts in such a way that they may address the reader's deepest concerns, that in reading he may hear the Word of God speaking through them, may know himself judged and graciously upheld by the Word that speaks through the many different witnesses of the New Testament. In this process the interpreter has a maieutic (midwife) function only. Her task is to show how the New Testament texts are themselves the product of such a dialogue between the believer and her God; but it is only as the particular reader allows her own existence to be questioned by such texts that the concrete encounter of Word and faith may occur.

There is no doubt that there are real tensions between these two tasks that made Bultmann's synthesis of the two precarious. The requirements of historical detachment on the one hand and existential involvement on the other seem hard to reconcile. Bultmann's attempted resolution of the dilemma is twofold. First it is to attack the notion of historical detachment: an historian needs to enter the world of his subject imaginatively (Collingwood (1889-1943)) and will only succeed in understanding ancient texts when she has seen them as expressions (*Lebensäusserungen*) of the great forms of singular human existence (*der grossen Formen singulären menschlichen Daseins*, W. Dilthey (1833-1911), quoted *Glauben und Verstehen*, [II, 211]), not simply as the product of external causes. Her task, that is, is to recreate the world of the text imaginatively, to see how indeed it created or expressed a world of meaning for its readers/hearers. This, moreover, is something that is equally applicable to the study of non-religious texts, not an activity restricted to theologians. Second, the task of the New Testament theologian is to be distinguished from that of the preacher of the Word: it is not to give utterance to the Word; it is, rather, by showing how such texts once spoke, to point to the possibility of such 'speaking' as others enter into dialogue with them.

It is important to see how in the subsequent development of New Testament study this synthesis has been put under strain and why it eventually, in 1968, snapped. In the first place, Bultmann's way of reading a text as an expression of the particular self-understanding of its author has been felt not to do justice to the sense in which texts are the expression and product of particular communities. This can be seen most clearly in Johannine studies, where American commentators like J.L. Martyn and R.E. Brown have emphasised the way in which the Johannine literature reflects a number of different stages of the community's development. Second there has been concern, expressed most classically by K. Stendahl, that even the maieutic role claimed by Bultmann may lead the New Testament theologian to underplay the sheer otherness of the texts he is discussing, to overlook the distinctiveness of the past meanings of such texts in the search for their present meaning for us. Thus there has developed again a (purportedly) more rigorously historical treatment of the beliefs and practices of the New Testament communities that has by and large eschewed the task of relating such beliefs and practices to the faith of today's readers. The synthesis has broken, to be replaced — in America and Europe at least — by a resurgence of the work of the History of Religions School for one part; and a rich variety of attempted theologies on the other: biblical theologies in Germany (Stuhlmacher (b.1932), Hübner (b.1930)); the work of Liberation theologians in Latin America, Asia and Africa (Boff (b.1938), Sobrino, Pixley (b.1937) and many others); with literary critical and feminist approaches in North America and elsewhere (J.D. Crossan (b.1934), L. Russell (b.1929), E. Schüssler Fiorenza (b.1938)). It would require a separate book to discuss these in the detail they deserve. In an important sense it is too early to discuss them, for their contours are not yet set. Our task must be the more cautious one of tracing out developments in the tradition that stems from Bultmann. Certainly, there is no consensus among more recent attempts as to what is the most appropriate way forward for New Testament theology, whether indeed such a term is appropriate at all (see H. Räisänen). Nor, *a fortiori*, is there any agreement about how such a theology might relate to the work of historical critics.

It would, of course, be a mistake to suppose that Bultmann's New Testament theology went without serious challenge at the time of its publication; or that it was accepted without qualification by his followers. Some of these early debates must, at least, be mentioned in order to set the context for later developments.

Oscar Cullmann's studies of New Testament theology, *Christ and Time* (1946) and *Salvation as History* (1965), mounted a direct challenge to Bultmann's programme of existential interpretation. Whereas Bultmann had rejected the subject-object distinction as something that skews our understanding of faith (which is personal knowledge and therefore cannot properly be 'objectified'), Cullmann claimed that it was proper to speak of an object of faith that resists all attempts at appropriation. It was this object that holds together the biblical witness, namely 'saving-history'. Specifically, it was the belief that God acted in Christ that provided the unity of the New Testament, which in turn also represented the culmination of the Old Testament with its own witness to the saving acts of God in history.

There are many problems with Cullmann's work. While views similar to those that he wants to attribute to the New Testament as a whole are, indeed, to be found in Luke, it is much less easy to argue for their presence in Paul and John. Whereas Bultmann's theology focusses centrally on the latter two, Cullmann's work may be seen as an attempt to urge the claims of a rather different kind of faith which, also, is found in the New Testament, though by no means universally. Cullmann's attempts to read salvation-history into other parts of the New Testament provided relatively easy targets for his critics. Again, he largely ignored the hermeneutical questions that had been so central to Bultmann's enterprise. How can the beliefs of the New Testament writers be appropriated by readers in the twentieth century? The ways in which God's action in Christ is referred to in the New Testament are problematic for a modern reader, and Cullmann, like much biblical theology of the time, does little more than paraphrase them.

Nevertheless, it would be a mistake to dismiss Cullmann's work altogether. In his criticism of Bultmann's personalization of the knowledge of faith, he has drawn attention to matters which require further, and rather more careful, discussion. Is it right to see the 'object' of faith as simply subsumed in the 'self-understanding' of the believer? Bultmann himself would have denied that this was what his own programme of theological understanding intended. To claim that there is no knowledge of faith outside the act of self-understanding itself is not to claim that the object of faith is simply reduced to that act. On the contrary, what the faithful act of self-understanding tells the believer is that he only ever truly understands himself as he is addressed by the Word of the living God and that he only truly knows the living God as he is addressed by his Word. The words of the New Testament may mediate such an encounter between the believer and the Word; but it is only within such an encounter that the Word may be grasped.

Such questions take us back to the debates in the early 1920s between Bultmann and Barth. Subsequently they have rarely been pursued with the same rigour. Perhaps only in the work of von Balthasar (1905-87) is fundamental theological reflection on the nature of faith and exegetical work similarly combined — though even so his exegesis will appear strange and wilful to many. I will return to these issues when I come to give a fuller appreciation of his work.

Cullmann was not alone in criticizing the anthropological concentration of Bultmann's theology. Within his own camp Ernst Käsemann argued, as we have seen, that Paul's theology had a cosmological reference: that Paul's proclamation of the righteousness of God announced the extension of God's rule over the world, not just the possibility of a new self-understanding for individuals. Käsemann's reaction to Bultmann can been seen at one level as a reassertion of the historical programme of New Testament studies. He is seeking to place Paul historically both in relation to contemporary Jewish apocalyptic ('the mother of Christian theology') and to his Christian fellows and opponents. Thus it is important for him to see how Paul picks up Jewish apocalyptic beliefs about the End and the setting to rights of God's world, to see as clearly as possible the relation between Paul's doctrine of the *justificatio impii* and similar views in Qumran, and also to set Paul's beliefs in proper relation to the enthusiasm of his opponents in Corinth and to the various Judaising forces ranged against him. Much of the fascination of Käsemann's work lies in the historical rigour with which he pursued such questions.

At the same time his work was not without its theological pathos. It is, however, interesting to see whence this came. In part, as his preface to his commentary on Romans makes clear, it derives from his commitment to the Reformers' search for the heart of Paul's theology, his struggle to find a coherent centre to his work, and his belief that it lay in his preaching of the cross. In this struggle the historical search for Paul's intended sense and the theological attempt to establish the meaning of the texts went hand in hand. But the pathos of Käsemann's work also lay in the way that he chose to expound that preaching of the cross and justification, namely as the proclamation of God's assertion of his will over history! Käsemann wrote consciously as a church theologian, and for all the controversy he provoked within church circles his historical work was intended as church theology. When Käsemann affirmed that Paul's doctrine had a cosmological reference he was, in part at least, engaging in ecclesiastical debate, attempting to set the agenda for the church's action·as well as to discover the original sense of the New Testament writings. The irony is that he could do this only by recovering those mythological elements of the New Testament that Bultmann had 'interpreted existentially', that is to say, to which he had given an exclusively anthropological (and therefore, he believed, intelligible) sense. Thus in one sense Käsemann merely returns us to those problems which were Bultmann's starting-point, namely the problems of interpreting 'mythological eschatology'. His work is none the less instructive, not merely for the host of individual insights into the text that it brings, but also because it again brings out the precariousness of Bultmann's synthesis, of his marriage of history and theology.

It is interesting to reflect how these two theological tendencies in Käsemann's work both in their different ways militate against the task of providing a theology of the New Testament.

In the first instance the search for the intention of the authors of the New Testament must in the end create problems for any attempt to offer a comprehensive account of New Testament theology. Without question such a search was an important part of the Reformers' programme. Nevertheless precisely the focus on what Paul, John and other New Testament writers meant at a particular time must inevitably throw up the significant differences in understanding that exist between them. How such differences are to be reconciled is certainly not a problem solved by Luther or Bultmann.

There is another point here that is perhaps not always so clearly seen. Why should our historical interests stop at Paul's intention? Why should we limit our interest in these extraordinarily rich ancient documents simply to what it was that Paul was wanting to tell his readers/hearers? A genuinely historical interest in such documents would embrace not only what they were saying but also what they might indirectly tell us about Paul's opponents, about the way of life of the churches to which they were written, about their setting within the culture and society of the time.

What is happening when such questions begin to be raised? In one sense a very profound shift in the way that the texts are being read. It is clear that the Reformers' view of the texts was that they were in some sense vehicles of God's revelation, that properly read and understood they brought us face to face with the Word of God. To see them on the other hand as windows on to the world of early Christianity, as providing evidence for economic and social conditions in the first-century Mediterranean world is, on the face of it at least, to take a different view of such texts: they are documents of a former age, sources that, together with other contemporary documents, archaeological material and so on, can help us to reconstruct a picture of the 'social realia' of early Christianity.

Such views were presented to the Society for New Testament Studies Conference in Paris in 1978 by W. Meeks and R. Scroggs ('The Sociological

Interpretation of the New Testament: The Present State of Research') and perhaps an anecdote from that meeting may be permitted. It so happened that I was sitting immediately in front of Käsemann and some of his German colleagues as Meeks and Scroggs were making their presentation. Clearly there was considerable agitation behind me as matters proceeded. This culminated in Käsemann exclaiming *sotto voce* to his colleagues: '*Da ist nichts von Anrede.*' (approx. 'There is no sense of "address" in this', i.e of being addressed by God through the text). The observation was just; the agitation understandable in one who saw 460 years of tradition being discarded by the guild of New Testament scholars. Whether or not such moves mean the rejection of any form of New Testament theology is one of the questions to which we shall turn later in the chapter.

Käsemann's emphasis on the cosmological reference of Paul's doctrine of justification stood, we have said, in the service of his attempts to urge on the church a more active engagement in political and social issues. God wished to set his whole world to rights, not simply to reign in individual souls. Within the broad framework of a belief in the Bible as the vehicle of God's revelation such appeals to the cosmological references in ancient texts may be effective enough. Nevertheless they lack hermeneutical sophistication, and others would not be slow to suggest other ways forward that would both do justice to the historical meaning of ancient texts and to their original social significance. To achieve this it would be necessary to turn to the social sciences for an account of the function of religious belief both in effecting social change and in managing established or relatively stable societies.

We should not move on from these discussions without mentioning one very significant, if characteristically independent-minded view of these matters, offered by Krister Stendahl in his article in the *Interpreter's Dictionary of the Bible*, 'Biblical Theology, Contemporary'[1] Here Stendahl pleads for allowing historical study of the Bible its head, before proceeding to the task of attempting to discern the present meaning of the texts. Moreover, any such attempt should be preceded by careful hermeneutical reflection on the nature of such a translation of old meanings into new. Thus Stendahl identifies three stages of work, all of which are necessary for the successful writing of a biblical theology. First a descriptive, historical task, spelling out what the words meant when originally uttered or written, without regard for their later exploitation in the Christian tradition. Such a task can be undertaken by believer and agnostic alike. Second there is the task of devising an interpretative strategy by which to translate such historical findings into something of meaning and relevance to modern society. Last there is the task of translation itself.

Stendahl's insistence on the distinction between 'what it meant' and 'what it means' (14) has been widely welcomed. It cleared the way for a whole-heartedly historical approach to the New Testament, open to scholars of all persuasions, and this has subsequently been enthusiastically embraced by

American scholars working in Liberal Arts programmes. At the same time it appeared to allow a place for a theologically committed approach to biblical theology, one which might involve biblical scholars in co-operation with their colleagues in theology and philosophy. It appealed, that is, to a pluralist society that wished to permit both universally accessible modes of study and understanding of the Bible as well as confessionally orientated ones. The latter might, however, best find its place in the professional training schools and seminaries, rather than in the Liberal Arts Colleges and Universities.

It is not hard, I think, to find reasons why Stendahl's 'program', as he renamed it in his volume of essays *Meanings*, has had no takers. Most obviously, it is a programme that cannot easily, if at all, move beyond its first stage. The work of the descriptive historian is never done, and the biblical theologian who embarks on the task of translating such original meanings into some meaning for today is chronically in danger of being false-footed by subsequent developments in New Testament historiography. 'Actualizing interpretations' as Räisänen has subsequently dubbed them, are, on such a view, parasitic upon historical descriptions that are themselves constantly in flux. Stendahl's programme only confronts the would-be biblical theologian with the dilemma of Lessing's ugly ditch in a variant form. 'Accidental truths of history can never become the proof of necessary truths of reason'. It does nothing to resolve that dilemma. In fact, one might say, its appeal has in a measure lain in the sense in which it has concealed its full force. For the historical task is by no means exhausted, as we have just seen, by the description of the original sense of the words when uttered or written by the prophets and apostles. Such a formulation not only excludes all the other senses that we might derive indirectly from the New Testament texts; it also begs a host of questions about the ways in which, even in the original context of utterance, words may be understood and received. It also raises questions about why the task of historical description should be tied to the New Testament texts, excluding, that is, other Christian writings from the same period. The more one presses on such questions, as we shall see when we come to consider Räisänen's own contribution to the debate, the more the gap widens between an historical description of the life and beliefs of the early Christian communities and the task of seeing their texts as yielding normative senses for Christian communities in the twentieth (or twenty-first) century.

Certainly the effect of Stendahl's article was to drive a firm wedge between the two halves of Bultmann's synthesis. How far the subsequent dearth of serious New Testament theologies may be attributed to the unworkability of his own proposals is another question less easy to resolve. There was nothing in principle to stop scholars developing alternative programmes. Whatever the reasons, there has been no notable successor to Bultmann's *Theology of the New Testament*. This means that for the purposes of this chapter we shall drop the format of the last four chapters, where we were able to review some of the most interesting contributions in each of the areas of study. Here instead we shall deal thematically with the issues raised in a number of recent preliminary studies of the topic. Before turning to such a final survey, however, I want to introduce into the discussion a figure who presently stands on the margins of a number of areas in theology, but who has made his own distinctive contribution to the subject: Hans Urs von Balthasar.

Von Balthasar's major work is a large three-part theology that runs to 15 volumes. The first part is subtitled *A Theological Aesthetics* and its last two volumes offer a biblical theology of the Old and New Testaments. It is important to understand the location of these two volumes within the design of the first part that is devoted principally to the recovery of the aesthetic dimension of theology. The way in which something appears and the way in which it is apprehended are not minor matters. They should not be dismissed as distractions from the central matters of importance, namely questions about its truth and goodness. Against such all too prevalent views von Balthasar wants to argue that the beauty of a thing or person and our apprehension of it are central to our appreciation of its truth and goodness. The more we learn to appreciate such beauty, to know and understand its form, its proportions, its measure, the more readily we shall see it as it is, the less we shall be inclined to explain it away, to reduce it to the status of a mere product of other factors and forces.

Such views have a direct bearing on modes of interpretation that have been current in biblical study. At heart von Balthasar is opposed to all reductive modes of interpretation. Thus he is opposed to attempts to understand biblical ideas simply as the *product* of ideas that were current in other religious groupings at the time. But he is equally opposed to Bultmann's existential interpretation, in so far as this reduces the Word made flesh to the believer's experience of a changed self-understanding based on his encounter with the Word.

As I have already hinted, the debate at this point is by no means simple. Bultmann can reply that he is in no way attempting to equate the Word with the states of the pious self-consciousness but rather to insist that it is only in so far as we encounter the revealer as the one who transforms our self-understanding that he is the revealer at all (see *The Gospel of John*, 68f). Indeed at this point von Balthasar and he are in one sense agreed: namely that the 'true' meaning of the texts is disclosed only to those who believe. The issue turns on the nature of such belief. Does it allow for the element of disinterested contemplation of and wonder at the object of faith, a growth indeed in our 'knowledge' of that object? Or is our only 'knowledge' of the Word knowledge of the Word as the transformer of our self-understanding? Von Balthasar, following Augustine and P. Rousselot (1846-1924) speaks of the 'eyes of faith' and stresses thereby the aesthetic dimension of such belief.

To believe is to have one's eyes opened to the glory of God revealed in the *Gestalt* (figure, form) of the Christ-figure.

The language of *Gestalt* is appropriate here because the Christ draws together into himself the whole history of God's dealings with his people, and in his death and descent into hell opens up a new life that flows from the resurrection. What is revealed in such a form surpasses all attempts at comprehension; it is a glory so transcendent that even the theologies of the New Testament cannot comprehend it and so require each other, in their very considerable diversity, to complement one another. Yet the glory of the revelation *Gestalt* is mediated through the writings of the Bible, and their meaning is to be grasped not in terms solely of the new life that they bring to the believer but in terms of what they continue to show of the inexhaustible glory of that which is revealed. Hence von Balthasar's sustained polemic against Bultmann's reduction of the texts' sense to the effect that they have on their hearers.

We may place this in relation to our discussion of Stendahl's proposals. Stendahl, it will be recalled, argued that the task of historical studies was to discover what the words of the Bible meant when uttered in their original context. That may be seen as evincing a comparable concern against blurring the lines between our own appropriation of texts and their own — historical — meaning. But the question here is: what is being safeguarded? Is it the author's intention, what Paul had in mind when he wrote to his addressees, which we need to preserve in order that, suitably interpreted, he may still address us? So, I think, Stendahl. Or is it the glory of the Word made flesh, to which the texts bear witness, texts that indeed von Balthasar would claim are themselves the witness of the Word to itself?

> The word of scripture is the word in the mode of contemplating his own action, recording and elucidating it, something that can only be performed properly and perfectly by the word himself, since God alone compasses the entire range of his revelation; and only he can assign a valid human expression for it (*Word and Revelation*, [10]).

If the latter, then belief itself becomes part of the process whereby that glory is 'sighted', is given expression in each generation. Biblical theology is not just a matter of accurately and faithfully reproducing the various theologies of the New Testament and then rephrasing them in modern language, it is part of the continuing reflection and witness of the church to its central mystery, a reflection albeit that has its source and supreme exemplar in the New Testament writings themselves.

What is in question is the relationship between Paul's actual utterances and that to which he refers. Both Stendahl and von Balthasar differ from Bultmann in wanting to assert that what is referred to is not to be equated with the believer's self-understanding (even allowing that such self-understanding properly entails a sense of obedience to the Word of God). They want to assert *per contra* that the New Testament texts witness in some sense objectively to the transcendent reality of God's actions in Christ. Where they differ is in their understanding of how such transcendent reality is to be appropriated by the church to which it is given. Stendahl's insistence on the 'originality' of the New Testament writings (40f) suggests that, for him, there is a sense in which the understanding of the object of faith is only ever fully achieved by Paul, such that subsequent attempts at understanding always fall short and stand in constant need of revision in the light of the biblical text. For von Balthasar, the scriptural texts are, like indeed the church and its sacraments, forms that mediate the glory of the Word made Flesh, which continually generates itself new forms of faith and life, as new generations perceive fresh aspects of its infinite richness. Thus the biblical canon has a central and generative function in the faith and life of the church; and this does not therefore relegate all subsequent forms of church life to the status of translations of an original. The canonical writings mediate to each generation the living mystery of the Word made Flesh and it is this which is fruitful in the life of believers.

What all this means in practice is not easy to convey in a short space. Von Balthasar does not offer a biblical theology as such; rather a study of glory in the Bible. But whereas one might expect a treatment of the subject book by book through the Old and New Testament, the pattern offered for the New Testament is significantly different. For von Balthasar the Old Testament vision of glory has its high-point in the Mosaic covenant and in the prophets. From then on the vision becomes fragmented, leading to the apocalyptic seers' dreams of future glory. The glory of which the New Testament speaks is not simply the culmination of what had already been seen in the Old. That vision, partial as it is, is gathered up and renewed in a wholly unexpected way in the Word made flesh.

For at the heart of this new glory is the wordless figure of the crucified Christ. This caesura in sacred history: the coming of the Word made flesh, the claim he makes, his poverty and self-abandonment, his kenosis, death and descent into hell — all this needs to be marked out as the centre around which all the writings of the New Testament cluster, to which they all bear witness.

Yet the writings of the New Testament are not simply distinct from the Word; rather it is part of what it is for the Word to come in the flesh that he should give 'his own' to be taken by the Spirit, to be formed as he wills. In this sense the diverse texts of the Bible can be spoken of as the Word 'witnessing to itself'. Indeed, the very multiplicity of the New Testament texts points to the richness of what they express; and such multiplicity is to be seen not as an embarrassment but as the proper expression of the glory in Christ (see *The Glory of the Lord*, 7 [103-114]).

Von Balthasar's reading of the texts is in many ways bewildering. While he draws freely on the work of historical scholarship, it is clear that the framework within which he operates is quite different from that of the usual historical critical enquiry. This is partly because, as he says, the Word made flesh simply hands over 'his own' to be formed by the Spirit in the church. The New Testament is then the new form in and through which the Word is mediated to the church. It does not point beyond itself, either to a transcendent free Word that may speak through it as it pleases, or to the historical life of Jesus or the apostle Paul. Rather, in itself it mediates[2] the resurrected Word, as it is read within the life of the church. But, precisely because the Spirit 'takes of mine', we should expect consonance between the form of the Word which is presented in the Gospels and Epistles and what historical scholarship may show us of Jesus.

Where his work is, perhaps, most surprising is in his reading of the Gospels. Here an example may be helpful, and it will be practical to consider a passage that bears on the earlier discussion of the biblical understanding of time. What kind of understanding of time is presupposed by the Gospel accounts of the Word-flesh, of his claim (*Anspruch*), poverty and self-abandonment? (*ibid.* 162-201). Von Balthasar is aware at this point of the wide diversity of views among scholars about the timing of the Kingdom. What can be said about the time of Jesus? Von Balthasar is first keen to avoid drawing too sharp a distinction between Greek and Hebrew notions of time. He does, however, insist that for the Bible time is marked out in terms of God's *kairoi*, the moments in which God intervenes on behalf of his people. It is these moments that frame biblical history, not some chronological schema. This scheme of 'saving-history' marks out God's time from the time of humanity — which for the Old Testament is essentially the time of the individual who goes to meet his death — in such a way that the time of God and of humanity stand in tension with one another. God's time, that is to say, is 'filled time' — but there are distinctions to be made within it. Von Balthasar speaks of an analogy of time and distinguishes the time of the Old Testament, the time of Jesus and the time of the church. In such a scheme the time of Jesus is unique; it is the divine-human time.

Nevertheless Jesus's time is the time of an individual mortal man. God alone knows the hour of his death. His time is embedded in the time of others and limited by others who come before and will come afterwards (cf Mk. 2:19f; Mt. 26:11; Jn. 12:35). His time is limited and so therefore is his work (Mt. 15:24). Yet this limited sphere is to be the place where God's final drama with the world is to be played out, here in this unique 'existence unto death'. It is as he goes on his way to death and judgement, that the Kingdom comes. He must drink the cup that the Father gives him (Mt. 20:22) and undergo the 'baptism' with which he must be baptised (Lk. 12:50). Whether or not Jesus thought of himself precisely as the suffering servant of Isaiah 53 is ultimately of no great importance. If, however, Jesus had no consciousness of his representative role in God's judgement *at all*, then the foundations of the church's proclamation would be swept away.

If this thesis is accepted then the questions so hotly debated by Schweitzer,

Dodd and others can be resolved. On such a view the Kingdom is neither purely future, nor is the eternal simply present in the fleeting moment. The eternal is present in a wholly unprecedented way, not as that which is timelessly valid but as that which is occurring here and now, 'in the going and passing away in time of this one life' (168). This gives an urgency to his life: like the seed growing *automate*, Jesus has already embarked on his course and there is no turning back (Mk. 4:27; cf Jn. 12:35). That such language has apocalyptic overtones is not to be doubted, but it finds its particular sense as it is predicated of the one whose mortal life is caught up representatively in the divine judgement.

This, however, still does not answer the question how Jesus's time is to be understood theologically, that is to say, in relation to God's dealings with his world. How is one to understand the apparent discord between claims that the end is about to come within the lifetime of Jesus's hearers and those which speak of an interval between cross and resurrection on the one hand and the parousia on the other in which the world continues to exist? Questions like these are important both for Stendahl and von Balthasar. What is at issue is the question of how the theologian is to move from simply giving a description of the acts of God in the past to developing an understanding of God's continuing action in the world today. Von Balthasar suggests that for Jesus there has to be a 'double temporal horizon'. For himself, he reaches the end of time in the fullest sense with his death and resurrection: in death he passes into timelessness from where at his resurrection he breaks out into the eternal. But in so far as he is there for others and his time embraces their time, then there is still a time of the church and a time of discipleship. Such a double temporal horizon must be attributed to Jesus:

> because, in accordance with his mission, he must in the time of his own finite existence complete what has to be done with the 'world' as a whole (and that includes its temporal future), so that he attains the end of time in the fullest truth with his death and his Resurrection; and because . . . he can foresee a continuing period of chronological time for the others, for the disciples and for their commission, and with this chronological time also a continuation of the time of salvation that has been transformed in the coming of the Spirit (171).

All this was taken up again in the profound meditations on God's actions in Christ in *Theodramatik*, notably in volume 3, *Die Handlung*, which centre around the theme of *Stellvertretung*, or representation.

It is clear that we are in a very different world from that of much recent New Testament study with its concern to identify and characterise individual strata of the early Christian tradition. Von Balthasar moves with remarkable ease from statements about the historical Jesus to theological claims by the Evangelists or by Paul. His justification for this is two-fold: on the one hand it is the church which has created the texts of the New Testament and given the earlier traditions an overall sense ('The point that gives perspective, gathering the traditions together and finally interpreting them, lies in the Church: for she makes explicit the meaning that has lain in the earlier strata, mostly discoverable only in the traces they have left behind' *GL* 7, 162). On the other hand he moves all the time from a position of faith, from a theological *a priori* which predisposes him to see the continuities between the historical life of Jesus and the claims of the church. This enables him to retain a refreshing openness to historical questions, such as whether Jesus thought of himself as the suffering servant of Isaiah, while still finding it unthinkable that Jesus should not have thought of himself in some way as the representative of sinful humanity, because this would mean abandoning the perspective of the church that has gathered and preserved the traditions.

Thus there is a reversal here of the role of historical research. It is no longer being used as a critical tool; nor is it being used apologetically to produce, as it were independently, a view of Jesus and his mission that could at least be seen as in broad continuity with the church's tradition (as scholars as diverse in their theologies as Harnack, Dodd and Jeremias all variously did). Here historical research is drawn on, where appropriate — but only where appropriate — to flesh out the statements of the church. One might recall the position of Charles Gore in *Lux Mundi*.

Thus what von Balthasar offers us is a reading of the texts as they stand, which is literary and theological, rather than purely historical — where, that is to say, the role of historical enquiry has been significantly recast. He resists all attempts to probe behind them into the tradition-history, and while he is in no sense indifferent to the individual voices of the writers is also working on the assumption of their — at least eventual — complementarity. The Bible for him is a unity, though by no means a monochrome unity; its diversity, however, serves to illumine the central mystery that is always greater than that which we can conceive. Yet his reading of these texts is not purely descriptive. What the passage on Jesus's time shows is his own willingness to continue the reflective process which has itself led to the production and collection of the biblical texts. His proposals about Jesus's 'double temporal horizon' are certainly not read off the New Testament texts directly: they do, however, represent one way of taking and developing their meaning which von Balthasar will deploy with great virtuosity, not least in the volumes of *Theodramatik*.

In a strange way, what von Balthasar offers in his New Testament volume anticipates a number of things which have recently been advocated as desirables in New Testament theology, *stricte dictu*, and which stand in contrast to Stendahl's programme. It is a reading that takes the texts as they are and allows them to present the image, the *Gestalt*, which they intend. At the same time such a reading is not unrelated to a whole literary history of readings of the Bible. Von Balthasar would not agree with Stendahl that we should simply attempt to say what the biblical writers meant — 'regardless of their meaning in later stages of religious history — our own included'. For him such a disjunction would be too sharp. The texts themselves are part of such a reflective history, and the interpreter himself cannot stand entirely outside that tradition. His reading of the texts must be as close and attentive a reading as it may be; but at the same time it will continue the unending process of reflection on the reality to which the texts bear witness. In this respect von Balthasar's sense of the importance of the tradition of biblical theology, in the Fathers, the Middle Ages and the Reformers, and some modern literary theorists' emphasis on the role of literary history in shaping the reader's 'horizons of expectation',[3] are interestingly analogous. Such a view of course puts serious question marks against Stendahl's emphasis on a return to the original. Such a purely descriptive reading of the texts of the Bible must seem more and more impossible as we become aware of the way in which all our readings are conjunctions of the text itself and our own horizons of expectations. This is not to deny that the text has any particular meaning 'of its own'; nor, indeed, to dismiss as irrelevant the author's intentions in creating the text. It is to draw attention both to the way the text transcends any reading that we may give of it, and also to the way in which *any* reading of a text will indeed have its place within a literary history of interpretation.

Von Balthasar's work appeared in 1969 and thus essentially predates many of the recent developments that have led to the present resurgence of interest in New Testament theology. It is hard to characterise the massive shift in the intellectual, social and political climate that has occurred since 1968. On the political plane the pace of change has been remarkable. The era that started with Dubcek's Prague Spring and the student revolution of 1968 led on into the 'velvet revolution' of 1989 and brought with it immense and disturbing changes in the balance of power in the world. Outside Europe, the United States' hegemony was seriously challenged in Asia and Central America but equally vigorously and ruthlessly defended. Indeed, with the dissolution of the Soviet Union in the wake of the revolutions of 1989 the United States now appears as the dominant power.

Exactly how such changes in the political sphere correlate with changes in the intellectual climate is more difficult to say. If various forms of Marxist theory commanded great attention at the beginning of the 1970s, it is now deconstructionism and various kinds of literary theory which exert a powerful and arguably fateful attraction on many, not only in the United States, but also in Central Europe. But the picture is in no sense uniform. Indeed, the sheer plurality of intellectual theories on offer is itself perhaps the most significant development of all. The almost iron grip that a certain form of empiricism had gained in the English-speaking world by the 1960s has been shattered and there is now apparently no limit to the kinds of theory which can claim some kind of intellectual standing.

Such developments have not passed by theology, or even New Testament studies. Over the last twenty years the influence of the social sciences in all branches of theology has grown significantly. In New Testament study the work of Gerd Theissen, Wayne Meeks and others in advancing social historical modes of enquiry has increasingly come to be regarded as central to the discipline, though this is still not a view wholeheartedly supported in Germany. Latin American materialist readings of the New Testament and feminist readings of the Bible in the United States also pay their tribute to the social sciences. All of this can be seen as in some ways continuous with the socialist and revolutionary movements of the 1960s, although it is also a reflection of the way in which historical critical modes of enquiry with a long tradition have joined forces with the social sciences, preferring functional rather than metaphysical modes of explanation. At the same time there has been a growing interest in literary-critical modes of interpretation which are often strongly ahistorical in their assumptions and methods. Again, there is a diversity — and, indeed, contradictoriness — in such developments, which must at some point raise doubts as to whether New Testament study can be regarded any more as a single discipline, albeit with its various parts, but parts which contribute by agreement to a total enterprise.

These questions are focused with considerable sharpness in an article by Wayne Meeks in a volume of the *Harvard Theological Review* offered to Krister Stendahl (*HTR* 79:1-3, 1986, [176-86]). The distinction, made famous by Stendahl, between 'what the text meant' and 'what it means', Meeks suggests, has to be rethought in the light of radically new accounts of religious meaning. For these he turns to George Lindbeck's (b.1923) *The Nature of Doctrine* (1984) which has distinguished three broad theories of religious meaning: (1) the 'cognitivist' model, where religious statements, specifically church doctrines, are understood as 'functioning as informative propositions or truth claims about objective realities' (16); (2) the 'symbolic-expressivist' model which 'interprets doctrines as non-informative and non-discursive symbols of inner feelings, attitudes, or existential orientations' (16); and (3) the 'cultural-linguistic' model which sees religious doctrines as defining the grammatical rules of a language which believers learn and then use to make sense of the world of their experience. On such a view, religious statements do not properly refer to some world of transcendent being or reality (as the 'cognitivist' view suggests), but they do have 'cognitive dimensions' in so far as it is an 'idiom that makes possible the description of realities, the formulation of beliefs' (33). Again, it is not denied that religious doctrines are related to believers' experience. But whereas on an 'expressivist-symbolic' view they are merely the manifestation of an individual's subjectivity, on the cultural-linguistic view religion is a 'communal phenomenon that shapes the subjectivities of individuals' (*ibid.*). Religions, that is to say, are 'comprehensive interpretive schemes, usually embodied in myths or narratives and heavily ritualised, which structure human experience and understanding of self and world' (32).

Clearly such a view is distinct from those of von Balthasar and Cullmann, and, indeed, Stendahl, all of whom hold views which seem closer to Lindbeck's 'cognitivist' position; it is also distinct from Bultmann's position which seems closer to Lindbeck's 'symbolic-expressivist' view. (In fact, as I would want to suggest, Lindbeck's classification does justice neither to von Balthasar, nor to Bultmann, something which may in itself prove fruitful for further reflection.) What is novel about such a view? And how does it redefine 'meaning', when we ask 'what it meant' and 'what it means'?

In the first place, Lindbeck's view is opposed to a 'hermeneutics of referentiality'. That is to say, interpreters of texts should not have as their principal aim to discover what the texts refer to, 'what really happened', the 'objective reality' which they supposedly, but perhaps one-sidedly or misleadingly, describe. By contrast such a hermeneutics sees the task of the interpreter as being to discover and to chart the world of signs, 'the semiotic universe', which informs particular texts, or which enables certain groups to shape their lives and make sense of their experience.

Second, meaning here is being defined as 'intratextual', located within the texts themselves, as opposed to being determined by reference to things or objects outside the texts. In the text a system of signs is encoded which, third, enables a particular group to shape or to make sense of its experience, which, indeed, enables the group to come to terms with its history; it is not the history that shapes the language of the group. On this view, the semiotic system of the group has an autonomy that gives it a privileged position in relation to experience and historical accident. That is not to say that it is unrelated to such experience and accident, only that it has a certain priority over against it. (Lindbeck even compares it to Kant's notion of *a priori* categories, though it would have to be said that the force of Kant's categories is to constrain the freedom of the human imagination to make of sense perceptions what it will; the categories are universal and necessary, [33]).

Meeks accepts such an account of religious meaning without further critical discussion. He accepts it, moreover, as providing the basis for an important restatement of the task of biblical theology, to which the rest of the essay is devoted. It is to be noted in this that he still accepts Stendahl's overall distinction between 'what it meant' and 'what it means'. Thus the historical descriptive task, that Stendahl argued was the basis for subsequent attempts at translation, now turns out to be very much like the kind of social history that Meeks has been practising himself in *The First Urban Christians*. There he has offered a '"thick description" of the ways in which the early Christian groups worked as religious communities, within the cultural and subcultural contexts peculiar to themselves. . . . In order to determine what a given text *meant*, therefore, we must uncover the web of meaningful signs, actions, and relationships within which that text did its work' (*HTR*, 179). The social historian is 'not only or even primarily trying to reconstruct "what really happened" as "objective" reality. She or he is more interested in trying to understand the meaning of what the actors and writers did and said within their culture and their particular subculture' (181). Moreover, we should recall that Meeks's handling of this kind of social history is functionalist, which is to say that it focuses attention on the way the symbolic universe encoded in the texts *works*, which is, of course, not to deny that he is interested in decoding the texts to reveal the symbolic systems.

The question then is: How does this kind of historical descriptive work relate to the theologian's quest for the present meaning of the texts? Here Lindbeck's account of religious meaning seems to produce a mis-match between the kind of social historical work that Meeks has done so well in studies of first-century Christianity, and the kind of work on the present meaning of the Bible that he (Lindbeck) proposes. Lindbeck in talking about intratextuality (that is, the sense in which the meaning of a text is immanent to it, not defined by reference to that which is external to it); takes 'text' not simply in a metaphorical sense, to refer to the 'entire cultural system of the religious community', but in a literal sense to refer to the 'semiotic universe encoded paradigmatically in holy writ' (116). The task of the theologian would be to 'redescribe reality within the scriptural framework rather than translating Scripture in to extrascriptural categories' (*ibid.* [118]).

This, in turn, might well suggest that the natural ally in such a task would not be the social historian at all, but rather the literary critic for whom historical readings of the text are at best of secondary importance. The literary critic could offer a decoding of the 'semiotic universe paradigmatically encoded in holy writ' (Lindbeck, 116) which would provide a 'test of faithfulness' of the readings offered by the theologian.

Meeks wants to suggest ways in which his kind of reading of the New Testament and other texts can in fact interact with a biblical theology such as is proposed by Lindbeck. Lindbeck and Frei (1921-199) have criticised historical critical readings of texts for their concern with 'what actually happened', that is to say with 'referentiality', rather then with the systems of meaning which the texts encode, in the case of the Bible, paradigmatically for the Christian community.

Much post-Enlightenment Biblical criticism was concerned precisely with such a quest for the reality behind the texts, and this was responsible for the 'eclipse of Biblical narrative' (Hans Frei). Meeks suggests that this is a charge that can be less easily directed against the social cultural historian, for '[s]he or he is more interested in trying to understand the meaning of what the actors and writers did and said within their culture and their peculiar subculture' (181).

This, however, does nothing to diminish the dilemma to which Stendahl had pointed, namely the gap between historical study of 'what it meant' and modern interpretations of 'what it means'. The social historian's task is no less difficult than any other historical task; his results just as provisional. This is by no means the only point at issue. What divides the social historian and the modern interpreter is, not least, the canon. The early Christians simply did not have a 'New Testament'. 'Foremost among the factors that separate the use, and thus the meaning, of the New Testament texts in the first century from those texts' use and meaning in the church today is this: then there was no New Testament, now there is' (181).

Striking as this fact is, there has been little attempt 'to describe or define the significance of the crucial transition between precanonical and canonical situations' (182). How did the all-encompassing biblical narrative that Frei and Lindbeck see as so significant for the reading of the Bible develop? Was it accidental that the texts in the Bible lent themselves to being read in this way? 'Or had the idea of that story, the plot itself, already taken shape in the rituals, preaching, moral exhortation, story-telling, prophesying, and midrash practised by the early Christians? . . . Did the canon make the story or the story the canon?' (183).

Again, such a question is not a purely literary one. 'Canon' is not a neutral descriptive term; it is a sociological concept by means of which the community invests these texts with a particular kind of function and authority. By the same token, understanding the canonical texts entails knowing how to use them within a particular community (whether we choose to do so or no). Precisely because canon is a sociological concept, the act of its understanding has a social, as opposed to a purely individual, existential dimension.

This means not only that the interpreter needs to know how to use the text within a particular Christian community, but even, so Meeks argues, that he or she may 'be obliged to find or to try to help to create a community competent to understand, and', he adds significantly,

that means a community whose ethos, world-view, and sacred symbols . . . can be tuned to the way in which that text worked in time past. . . . The goal of a theological hermeneutics on the cultural-linguistic model is not belief in objectively true propositions taught by the text nor the adoption by individuals of an authentic self-understanding evoked by the text's symbols, but the formation of a community whose forms of life correspond to the symbolic universe rendered or signalled by the text (184f).

The task of the modern interpreter of the New Testament is clearly seen now to have a social dimension, closely related to that of the social historian of the early Christian movement. The social historian needs to discover how the texts he studies interacted with 'the whole range of passive as well as active learning that members of a given culture and of particular subcultures within it have absorbed' (184). The modern interpreter needs to assist people to attain the competence to embody such texts in living communities. Moreover, the two exercises may, now that we have understood their common base, mutually help one another. 'The story of the origins of the community, of the dialectic that produced both church and canon, ought to be suggestive for the present task'. We need to see the church 'struggling to discover, adapt, and invent appropriate forms of living in the world' (185) if we are to understand better what it is to embody such texts in our present communities.

Meeks's essay repays close reading. Its implications are wider than could have been teased out in the course of a short article for a journal. Let me simply spell out the following. In the first place it proposes a quite different paradigm for biblical theology than that of Bultmann. Theology is no longer seen as reflection on the believing self-understanding but as a process of redescribing reality by means of the Christian symbolic universe. In this process, as indeed with Bultmann, the theologian has an enabling role: he assists the community (no longer, as with Bultmann, just the individual) to find itself, to be attuned to its inherited world of signs. Whereas for Bultmann the believer achieved authenticity by discarding inherited values and attitudes, here it is almost the reverse. The believer is most truly a believer when he or she has mastered the language of the group, has become competent to 'redescribe reality' in its terms — even though she may still decide to refuse to use such language. If, for Bultmann, the believing self-understanding was the result of the obedient response of the believer to the Word, for Meeks it is the result of schooling in a particular tradition of religious language and symbols that produces an ethos and world-view all its own. This quite properly takes seriously an aspect of our humanity that is in danger of being undervalued, indeed seen as inimical to human authenticity in Bultmann's account. On the other hand, it runs the danger of seeing humanity as being simply determined by inherited beliefs and attitudes. What such a view may miss is the sense in which individuals may rise over their inherited beliefs and attitudes, which are mediated by the world of signs that they inhabit. On the other hand such a view of the text as encoding a particular cultural language also allows for a more creative use of texts. Now the texts become the means by which we may redescribe our world, responding freely and creatively within the constraints of *this* set of cultural signs.

Second, we should note that there is a linkage between the careful study of the history of the social embodiment of Christian belief systems that Meeks proposes and the social or ideological critique that some, like Belo and a number of Latin American scholars, have been asking for. It is not just that, as Meeks rightly points out, the churches had to adopt more worldly ways in order to survive. We need also to investigate the way in which particular interests controlled and shaped the tradition, suppressing elements that were threatening to them. Such questions were of course raised by W. Bauer (1877-1960) in his remarkable *Orthodoxy and Heresy in earliest Christianity* (1934).

They need to be extended into a full treatment of the development of the canon, which represents one of the most significant attempts in Christian history to control the tradition. We need, suggests Meeks, a different way of construing terms like 'story', 'kerygma' and 'salvation-history', which the older biblical theology had taken as referring to particular 'objective' theological truths (attempts which as we noted never seemed to get beyond rather flat paraphrase). We must learn to see them as notions that come alive only when we understand how they helped the 'early communities struggling to discover, adapt, and invent appropriate forms of living in the world' (185). We also, one might suggest, need to see them as notions that can be pressed to one's advantage, or which alternatively need to be suppressed or neutralised lest they disturb the fragile balance of power that has been achieved within a particular community.

Thinking about how the interests and experience of different Christian groups may have shaped and influenced the development of the canon (and indeed of the individual texts themselves) may raise some sharp theoretical questions for the cultural-linguistic understanding of religion. On the latter view it is the semiotic universe that defines reality and experience. Here, however, we are being invited to consider how social, political and economic interests may shape the texts. A dialectic between experience and belief is being proposed which seems better able to deal with historical accounts of religious movements. Meeks's alliance of social *historical* studies of early Christianity with 'intratextual' biblical theology is threatened.

Such considerations also pose questions for theologians like von Balthasar. In the first place, is a reconciliation possible between a view of the biblical writings as the Word witnessing to itself, and one that sees the canon as emerging out of a long history in which different embodiments of the early Christian symbolic world have been competing with each other? Such a reconciliation is not, indeed, impossible, and will depend ultimately on one's understanding of the nature of the tradition. Certainly, a theologian like von Balthasar has no difficulty in principle in recognizing that the process of the formation of the canon is a prolonged one. What social historical studies of the process emphasise is the turbulent nature of that process, the way in which it is marked by the clash of powerful interests in the church. Clearly this has implications for the way one understands the workings of the Spirit in the tradition of the church. It must inevitably raise questions as to how far one can recognise the canon as paradigmatic for the church, as indeed mediating the revelation-*Gestalt* to the church.

This is still not the main point that needs to be raised. Von Balthasar's central claim is that the Bible mediates the transcendent God to its readers. It refers, albeit not by pointing beyond itself but by analogy with a work of art, by embodying in its texts the glory of the Lord. The question that has to be asked of Lindbeck's cultural-linguistic model (which Meeks embraces wholeheartedly) is whether its sharp disjunction between the propositional and the cultural-linguistic model of religion does not too quickly dismiss the possibility of religious texts mediating the transcendent to their readers.

What the cultural-linguist properly observes is that religious language may be extremely effective in shaping the way that a whole people looks at life and makes sense of its changes and chances. The interest of such language, that is to say, *is not exhausted when we have considered its theological referents*, that is, the divine being/s to which it may refer. For whether or not the beliefs that religious sentences about gods and goddesses express are true, there can be no denying their power to shape the lives of whole peoples. Hence the analogy with a language. Acquiring religious beliefs is, in important senses at least, like learning a language: it enables one to make sense of the world in ways that would be impossible to those without language. But this is only an analogy. In another sense, acquiring religious beliefs is not like learning a language at all. I do not have to ask myself whether Italian is true before I decide to speak it, only whether it is appropriate in the circumstances. By contrast, I would be wise to ask such questions before I adopted, for example, Satanist beliefs. Of course I could simply learn what Satanists believe without assenting in any way to such beliefs, and in certain cases it may be important that I understand what Satanists do in fact believe. But the point I am making here is simply that when I learn Italian I do not also require to make up my mind whether I assent to it, before I use it. I merely need to know when it is appropriate to use it. My grounds for drawing on particular religious beliefs to make sense of my world will, that is to say, be of a different kind to the grounds that I may have for speaking in Italian to a garage mechanic who knows nothing but that language, even though I may be for other good reasons hesitant to do so. The reason for this is that the religious sentences which we learn make claims about, attempt to express something about the way things are; and that you cannot adopt such sentences without in some sense assenting to them.

This is a point of vital importance. Cultural-linguistic models are attractive because they are able, in a way that propositional models of understanding have often failed to do, to explain the power of religious beliefs to shape the lives of communities. But, as von Balthasar has urged,[4] this may be because such propositional models have been too narrowly conceived, and have denied the aesthetic dimension in religion, which is able to do justice, both to the transcendental referentiality of religious language and to its fecundity in spawning a rich diversity of forms of life.

What such a discussion suggests is that while there is much to be learnt from cultural linguistic accounts of religions we should not simply abandon the notion that religious beliefs refer to transcendent being/s — attempt to express the inexpressible. Language, that is to say, is not just a convenient tool for constructing social reality, but it may, as indeed it clearly does when it speaks about God, purport to refer to that which transcends the social cultural world of a particular community. We do not need to decide the difficult question as to whether religious language refers *successfully* in order to see how the claims adherents make about divine beings have implications of a wide variety for their beliefs, attitudes and behaviour in their everyday life as they engage with their fellow men and women in society. The danger with the cultural-linguistic understanding of religion is that it may encourage scholars to ignore the explicitly theological aspect of religious language and behaviour, whereas, in fact, one of the great fascinations of studying religious belief systems is to see the great diversity of social worlds which they spawn.

A further point needs to be made here that bears on the discussion above about the ways in which different groups have struggled to gain control of the tradition. It is clear that not all religious codes shape society in the same way. Different groups may be at loggerheads with each other in an attempt to control the content of the tradition. It matters to them which traditions are preserved and which have precedence in the tradition, the canon. Traditions, which encode different sign systems, are not indifferent as to the kinds of worlds and experience which they may generate; so it matters which ones gain credence and acceptance within the community. The reason for this is, I think, because there is a rather different link between language and experience than that proposed by Lindbeck. As I suggested in the discussion of my book in chapter 6, linguistic conventions work by prescribing certain regularities of linguistic use that are known and acknowledged within a particular community. These regularities concern not only the way in which sentences are linked to one another, but also the way in which sentences are linked to certain kinds of experience. Thus there is a more than accidental link between the language-games we play and the kind of world we inhabit; though the precise nature of that link may be difficult to describe. The fact that certain accounts of that relationship may have been shown to be problematical (empiricist theories of description) does not mean that there is no relationship at all.[5]

An awareness of how texts can shape and mould society is of course something that feminist biblical critics have in full. Such an awareness is kindled as soon as one raises the question: what place do these texts allow for women in the communities from which they came and which they will subsequently generate? One of the most remarkable works in this field is Elisabeth Schüssler Fiorenza's *In Memory of Her* (1983). In the introductory chapter she states her position with all necessary clarity:

> A feminist hermeneutical understanding that is oriented not simply toward an actualizing continuation of biblical Tradition or of a particular biblical tradition but toward a critical evaluation of it must uncover and reject those elements within *all* biblical traditions and texts that perpetuate, in the name of God, violence, alienation, and patriarchal subordination, and eradicate women from historical-

theological consciousness. At the same time, such a feminist critical hermeneutics must recover *all* those elements within biblical texts and traditions that articulate the liberating experiences and visions of the people of God (32f).

Precisely because the Bible is revealed to be a thoroughly patriarchal, 'androcentric' text, it seems clear that the basis for such a critique cannot be derived from the Bible itself. What gives the critic authority to take on the text, 'the revelatory canon for theological evaluation of biblical androcentric traditions and their subsequent interpretations' (32), is the experience that women have of suffering and oppression. Like liberation theologians, she insists 'that revelation and biblical authority are found in the lives of the poor and the oppressed whose cause God, as their advocate and liberator, has adopted'. Feminist critical hermeneutics, that is, claims a particular revelatory authority for women's experience, which, however 'elaborates not only women's oppression but also women's power as the locus of revelation' (34f).

There is, in practice, a dialectical relationship here. Women's power to criticise the Bible is derived from their experience of the 'struggle for liberation from all patriarchal oppression'. This is in turn a power to evaluate the authority claims of the Bible and to discover those texts that keep alive the *memoria passionis* of women's suffering and that can offer a prototype that will enable the transformation of Christian communities. That is to say, such a critique not only stands over against the biblical tradition but opens up a way of reading the Bible that is creative and powerful.

Clearly such a reading is primarily historical. It is so, however, not in a detached, neutral way, but by adopting 'an advocacy stance'. It starts from an awareness of the way in which powerful forces have oppressed women in society and moves on to a greater understanding of the way in which the biblical texts have themselves been commandeered by androcentric forces in society. Its aim is to restore the balance, to recover the actual historical experience of women in the early church and to reinstate those traditions in Jesus and Paul that empower women. It is therefore very far from seeing the text as that which alone provides us with the means of making sense of the world, which determines our experience, though it recognises the power that such texts can possess. But it resists that power in the name of a greater power that is derived from the experience of the struggle. It is a reading of recovery that attempts to reassert traditions and values that have been suppressed.

Precisely as an historical task, it is far from simple. The task of recovering what has been effectively suppressed cannot be easy, even if those who do the suppressing are rarely as thorough as they would like. This is not the place for a full discussion of her historical thesis; nor is it in any sense intended as a criticism of that work, which is full of illuminating insights and possibilities of reading the texts. She argues, rather as did Christopher Rowland (b.1947) in his later *Radical Christianity* (1988), that there is a radical strand of support for and empowerment of the poor in the New Testament. This, she asserts, also gives prominence and status to women in the church, as is evidenced by the story of the woman who anointed Jesus or by the activities of women in the Pauline mission and indeed by some, but not all, of Paul's theology (notably Gal. 3:28). Of course, such a summary merely flattens and distorts. Nevertheless, such a thesis, if it can be sustained, clearly poses a major challenge to the dominant patriarchy of the New Testament texts. This in turn forces home the point that a purely literary interpretation of the text runs terrible dangers, namely of canonizing that which is oppressive. It is therefore not enough, as Phyllis Trible (b.1932) would wish, to differentiate within the text that which is essential and that which is accidental. The basis of feminist hermeneutics must lie outside the text in the experience of the struggle. Only from there can it confer authority, and derive strength and support from those texts that enshrine the experience of women's oppression and liberation.

Such an approach to the reading of the New Testament is obviously very different from that of Meeks, though both of them are committed to an historical enquiry, and both seek guidance for their communities. There are important points of overlap. The kind of work that Meeks has done on the communal life of the early Christian communities is grist to Fiorenza's mill when she sets about arguing for the prominent position of women in Paul's communities (108). It is, indeed, not easy to characterise exactly where the difference lies between Fiorenza's *In Memory of Her* and Meeks's *The First Urban Christians*. Appearing in the same year, they contain no direct discussion of each other; but clearly their aims are very different. Meeks is principally concerned to give as careful and 'thick' a description of the Pauline communities as he can. He does, indeed, provide a detailed and careful discussion of the position of women in the Pauline churches, and notes that they enjoyed a position more nearly akin to that of men in the synagogue (*First Urban Christians*, 80). He suggests that the baptismal formula in Galatians 3:28 may, indeed, be more than a symbolization of a transitional state for the initiate, but then suggests that it was of most practical significance in respect of the relations of Jews and Gentiles. But the discussion of women takes up a relatively small amount of space; the question of women is clearly not on his agenda in the same way that it is on Fiorenza's. We are led to ask: Is the relative brevity of the treatment that Meeks gives to the position of women in Paul's communities a function of his relative lack of interest in the subject, of the general enterprise in which he is engaged, or of the subsequent suppression of the evidence in the tradition? The answer would seem to lie somewhere between the two last possibilities. He is certainly attempting to do more than focus on the position of women, as is quite proper; but equally, there is a sense in which he submits to the evidence of his letters and, precisely as a historian, does not attempt to offer more than the evidence will allow. Fiorenza, by contrast, has a very different agenda that means that, again quite properly, she is interested in the position of women and the subsequent suppression of traditions about them. Thus she comes to the study of the text, less as a polite enquirer, carefully listening to the nuances of the conversation to build up a picture of the network of relationships that hold this strange group together, than as an inquisitor, deeply suspicious of what she will hear.

Both Meeks and Fiorenza are, as we have seen, committed to historical modes of enquiry. Robert Morgan and John Barton's *Biblical Interpretation*, by contrast, takes more seriously the new forms of a-historical literary criticism that have been vigorously developed in the United States by scholars like D.O. Via (b.1928), R. Tannehill (b.1934) and J.D. Crossan, and proposes a synthesis between these and historical approaches to the Bible in the search for theological understanding of the texts.

Morgan's argument is subtle, and any summary is likely to distort. A brief account may be offered as follows. Biblical interpretation is concerned with explaining the meaning of — biblical — *texts*. Such explanation needs to be, as far as possible, accessible to all, and should therefore avail itself of generally agreed, rational methods of enquiry — historical, social scientific or literary. None of these is to be ruled out in principle. Nevertheless, it is the aims of the interpreter that will determine which methods are most suitable for her/his purposes. There is nothing in the nature of any text that demands that it be read in a particular way. 'Texts, like dead men and women, have no rights, no aims, no interests'(7). In the present academic climate, the aim of the biblical theologian should be two-fold. It is firstly to give an account of the theological sense of the biblical texts which can inform, correct and revivify the church's thinking, its systematic theology. Second it is to give an account of that *theological* sense which is intelligible to colleagues in other fields and disciplines and which can therefore provide the basis for a fruitful interdisciplinary debate.

In order to give a *theological* interpretation of the texts of the Bible we need some theory of religfion and reality in terms of which that account can be offered. In the past such an account has often been drawn from the church's own theological tradition, and such is still the practice within Roman Catholic and conservative evangelical theology. The liberal tradition, by contrast, tried to develop an independent understanding of religion and reality (whether explicitly stated or no) and to link this closely with its *historical* reading of the biblical texts.

Both of these modes of operation have their advantages and disadvantages. The confessional approach clearly offers a theological reading of the texts, and in so far as it engages in historical readings of the texts may both stimulate theological thinking within its own tradition and keep open the lines of communication to the scholarly community outside. On the other hand, the religious community may well wish to set limits on historical questioning of its received teaching, and in practice this kind of approach has tended to be wary of historical hypotheses that would embarrass Christian theology. We may think again of Gore, and also of von Balthasar. The liberal approach has run into two main difficulties: the practical one that the close 'fit' between historical accounts of Christianity and the theory of religion that they espouse is harder and harder to find (consider the embarrassment caused to liberal Protestant theology by the works of W. Heitmüller and A. Schweitzer); and the theoretical one that within a 'pluralist culture no theory of religion and reality can command wide assent' (196). On the other hand its great achievement was to keep open the dialogue with other disciplines and to allow the texts to have their own voice over against the theological tradition. In these respects it has been the great enlivener of theology, and its loss must be made good.

Morgan's own proposal is that historical (including of course social historical) modes of study of the Bible need to be supplemented by literary ones. More radically, not only should they be supplemented by them but the respective roles of literary and historical studies in relation to theology should be redefined. Historical studies should have a predominantly negative, as opposed to a prescriptive role. Whereas for Harnack it was historical study that would provide the answer to the question 'What is Christianity?', now history's role is to be reduced to that of eliminating certain — false — understandings of Christianity. Where there is a clear conflict between a theological interpretation of the texts and an historical one, then we should decide in favour of the historical one. On the other hand, theology should not consider itself bound to historical hypotheses of doubtful probability, nor, indeed, be dependent on such hypotheses for its own development. That is to say, while Morgan wishes to maintain the critical function of historical study of the Bible, he looks to literary studies to provide the creative stimulus for theology proper. Literary study can provide a rich variety of possible readings of the biblical texts with which theology can interact, thus releasing theology from the endless search to find a single normative (historical) sense of the texts as a necessary condition of making any theological judgements at all. Equally, because the subject of literature and art is in many ways very close to that of religion, it can often provide readings of the texts that are theologically more fruitful than historical ones that may be controlled by an overtly anti-religious animus.

This is an attractive proposal as well as an original one. We need, however, to see more closely what is actually being said. What is it to call for a literary reading of the texts? In one sense Morgan is clearly asking for readings that abandon questions of authorial intentionality in favour of exploring the way in which readers — or, better, communities of readers — receive and understand a text. Certain texts, at least, like works of art, cease to be the property of the author once they have been published. It is for the public to make of them what they will. This may entail looking closely at what the author herself intended, but that is a decision for the interpreter, not something the author can simply require. What this marks is a turning away from the search for a single meaning for the text that could be established by careful historical research, to the cultivation of a plurality of meanings that is the outcome of the interrelation of the various readers and the text itself.

Clearly, the question that concerns Morgan at this point is whether such an approach will not ultimately lead to a radical indeterminacy of meaning where there is no control of any sort on the kinds of interpretation which may be offered. But how is such control to be achieved without invoking again the notion of authorial intention? What else indeed could be implied by his appeal to historical study of the Bible as an — albeit negative — norm? I am not convinced that Morgan's answers here are entirely consistent. Sometimes he talks about the text itself exercising some sort of control: 'The balance between determinate meaning and the necessary element of indeterminacy can be achieved by respecting the two poles in interpretation. The written text is fixed, and sets limits to how it can rationally be read. It cannot mean anything the interpreter likes' (257). On other occasions he appeals to a commonsense belief that in interpreting a text we are looking for the message which the author intended to communicate.

For all the emphasis that literary criticism now places on the reader, common sense continues to look for the grammatical meaning of the text, on the assumption that this usually corresponds to the intention of the writer. Even after two generations of emphasizing the text at the expense of the author, the natural instinct is to ask what the speaker or writer intended (269f).

Morgan expresses this understanding of texts in a metaphor. A text is like an electric wire. It '"lives" only as an electric wire is alive. Its power originates elsewhere: in a human author'. Equally, the text only comes alive when it makes contact with some form of receiver, that is, with a human reader. 'Only then can the human power, imagination, and intellect carried by the marks on the page strike a light, communicate warmth, or give a nasty shock' (269). This image is striking for its functionalism and the lack of attention it pays to the wire itself, which is simply conceived as a medium for the creative power of the author. But artistic creations outlive their authors and have an existence independent of them with a literary history of their own which needs to be recognised. Flaubert (1821-1880) in his final illness lamented: 'I am dying like a dog and that whore Emma [Bovary] lives'. There is a vital question here whether we regard texts as essentially a medium, however sophisticated and difficult to decode, which conducts us back to its source, the author's creative impulse, with which we as readers can then interact; or whether the creation of texts is more like the creation of great works of art that are essentially independent of their creators and that remain as cultural monuments which in the end defy analysis. It is this latter view which von Balthasar holds when he talks about texts as *mediators* of the divine glory.

But what is it that texts say? Specifically, what do religious texts like the Bible say to us about the nature of the living God? Of course such a question is not by any means the only question which we can put to such texts; they may quite properly be used as windows on to the world in which they originated. The theological question is nevertheless a legitimate question which subserves the aim of those who wish to offer a theological interpretation of the Bible. As Morgan is at some pains to stress, it is for the interpreter to chose what aims he may have in approaching a text.

Morgan's central thesis here is again not without ambiguity. He rejects, as we have seen, one of the classical ways in which New Testament scholars have 'translat[ed] Scripture into extrascriptural categories' (Lindbeck, 118), namely liberal modes of interpretation. This, not least, because there is no longer any consensus about such a philosophy of history. On the other hand, he does say quite clearly and indeed repeatedly that what is required is a theory of religion such that it could communicate both to those with a religious faith and those within the academic community who do not share such a faith but who are interested in understanding what Christians have believed. For some it would be the basis for providing an account of Christianity that would enable them through it to encounter the living God; for others it would be the principle around which a coherent and systematic account of early Christian faith and practice could be constructed.

If liberal views of history will no longer serve, because of their controversiality, will the literary theories that Morgan seems to prefer serve any better? It is difficult not to think that his preference for literary theories is less a function of their non-controversiality, than a product of Morgan's cautiousness about historical readings of the Bible in general, which is linked to his belief in their conservatism, their inability to spawn new meanings. On the other hand the authority with which he ultimately invests historical readings of the texts suggests that some account of that authority, that is to say some view of history, even if not a liberal, evolutionary one, is still required.

Clearly, what is attractive to Morgan about literary theory is its links with literary *readings* of the Bible. The advantage of such readings is two-fold. First they provide an agreed method, or series of approaches to texts, which is allowed to generate a diversity of views: rationality in search of agreeable diversity, surely a foundational principle of modern pluralist society. Second, literary readings appear to take us into areas of experience and reality that are closely associated with those that traditionally have been the territory of theology. Morgan does not offer any very full discussion of which particular versions of such theory he would prefer, though he does quite properly allow that there are theories that would be wholly antipathetic to a religious stance.

Morgan's discussion remains at a distance from the actual interpretation of texts. It is, he says, a recipe for interpretation rather than a piece of interpretation itself. It will undoubtedly contribute significantly to the process of re-evaluation of the place of historical studies within biblical interpretation. In such a process it is of course important that the two methods or sets of methods should be clearly differentiated; but, equally, it would be mistaken to draw the lines of contrast too sharply. Morgan properly insists that the historical quest for the original meaning of the text can provide a certain benchmark against which to test subsequent interpretations. However, his stress on the singularity of historical interpretation is, I think, misleading. An historical understanding of the diversity of readings of a particular text actually underscores the point that texts do not have single meanings but rather a quite possibly rich literary *history*. The point about this is that it underscores the sense in which that diversity is neither entirely arbitrary nor wholly unrelated to the — literary — readings of texts. Each generation reads a text differently; not a small part of the reasons for such different readings lies in the change in the readers' 'horizons of expectation' which has been effected by the text itself. Thus historical readings of texts, if they do not confine themselves simply to the search for authorial intentions but look also for the range of understandings which is generated by a text, may, indeed, help to inform and enable our present readings of texts, making us more sharply aware of the literary context in which we stand, at the same time as illuminating the dialectic in this literary history between text and experience. This, in turn, may prompt theologians to search for an understanding of history that can underpin such a practice.

The 'dialectic between tradition, experience and interpretation' is at the heart of another refreshingly crisp presentation of the problems of work in this field, *Beyond New Testament Theology*, by Heikki Räisänen. Räisänen recognises the need for a 'synthesis of the religious contents of the New Testament' (93) that would be of interest, not only to the churches, who already have more material than they can digest, but also to other scholars and indeed a wider public. Such a work should be 'orientated on the concerns of society rather than on those of the church' (95) and such concerns are not merely local but global, embracing questions about the co-existence within the world of a number of different religious communities. A synthesis that met such concerns would provide critical information to Westerners about the 'roots of our religion . . . how it all began' and would eschew propaganda. 'A globally meaningful aim is to make a tradition (be it one's own, be it an alien one) comprehensible and to relate it to other traditions'(99). Clearly, such a study would not limit itself to the books of the New Testament canon, but would examine all relevant sources for early Christian belief and practice and would be interested in the subsequent history of influence and interpretation of the biblical texts. It would need to strike a balance between the scholar's own concern that his work should be relevant to modern societal and global issues and historical objectivity. In practice this means that 'actualizing interpretations' should be kept distinct from historical work, but that the structure of any synthesis would reflect such contemporary concerns. Thus one might well, in the light of modern questions about tolerance, consider how the New Testament texts and the actors in them deal with those of other religious and philosophical persuasions. In this context it would be appropriate to consider too the effect of the texts on subsequent Christian generations, the extent to which they have encouraged fanaticism, for example. Such an approach can facilitate the use of the historian's material by others mostly concerned with the modern situation, but 'such shaping is only possible as regards the questions asked and the manner and order of presentation' (109). In all this, the historian would not require to adopt a particular faith commitment, as had been urged by Barth and Bultmann; she would, however, need to empathise with the subject of research, not only with those figures and groups who had subsequently received the seal of canonical approval but with others as well.

Räisänen makes further specific proposals about the shape which such a synthesis might take. He, himself, intends to offer a synthesis of early Christian religious thought which would be systematically or topically arranged. However, we will pass these proposals over in order to concentrate on the model of historical interpretation which will underlie his work. It is here that he offers a discussion of the dialectic between tradition, experience and interpretation. True to his interest in providing an account of the origins of Christian thought that will be useful to those grappling with modern societal and global issues, Räisänen centres his chapter on interpretation on the question of how religion is to be understood. Here, too, of course, he comes close to Morgan's proposal that any attempt to offer an account of the New Testament that would be of use to the wider academic world must develop some acceptable account of the nature of religion.

Räisänen starts by noting the attempts of scholars like Rudolf Otto, G. van der Leeuw (1890-1950) and Mircea Eliade (b.1907) to explore the core religious experiences of humanity, but himself prefers to work with 'the whole spectrum of experiences, including quite mundane ones, as reflected in the material' (129). He questions, indeed, whether there are specifically religious experiences at all. May it not simply be that 'a certain type of religious experience is *interpreted* by some persons or groups in religious terms, and by others in different terms'? (*ibid.*). From this, it follows that Räisänen is interested in the way that the 'symbolic universe' (P. Berger (b.1929) and T. Luckman (b.1927)) of a particular group makes sense of — and is itself modified by — the historical experience of that group. Symbolic universes provide the conceptual framework that enables a group to make sense of its experience and that in consequence weld it together. The experience of the individual is integrated into this framework. As he learns the language of the group so he is prepared 'to perceive the world in a particular way' (130).

All this is reminiscent of Lindbeck's views. The terms that different groups use constrain the way in which they experience their world. Where he differs is in the account he offers of religious change. 'All socially constructed worlds are inherently precarious' (Berger, *The Social Reality of Religion* , 38). Where members of a group become aware of a lack of fit between their tradition and their experience, they will mostly be able to reinterpret such experiences in the light of the tradition. Where this is not possible or acceptable to all, there:

> is the possibility that reflection on a particular experience leads to a *change* within the symbolic universe. If the change is accepted by [leading members of] the community (which often involves acts of *legitimation* that actually camouflage the change and suggest that none has occurred or at least stress the continuity with the past), the symbolic universe will be modified. If a new turn is not thus accepted, this may lead to a break with the community on the part of some of its members who are then forced to construct a new symbolic universe. In this process they will legitimate their stance by drawing heavily on elements of the old one and often stressing their continuity with the past. Often they will be anxious to maintain that it is *their* interpretation, rather than that of the early community, which upholds true continuity with the great values of the past.[6] (130f).

It is not hard to see how such an understanding of religious change and development can serve the wider task which Räisänen sets himself, of explaining the nature of early Christianity to those outside the church. It draws on categories which are widely accepted in the social sciences, and offers an account of religious development which is at least in some respects neutral on the question of whether the impulse for the growth of religions is transcendent or not. Räisänen goes on to sketch out some possible ways in which New Testament scholars might contribute to 'actualizing interpretations' of the New Testament, but is careful to insist that the task of constructing or modifying 'a present-day viable theology' goes beyond the competence of the biblical exegete as such. She may, however, act as critic, and historical work such as Räisänen proposes will clearly assist the task of 'check[ing] religious truth claims in terms of their consistency and their effects on the life of believers, and . . . against present experience' (138). Reflection on its past significance ('what it meant') will begin to shade over into reflection on its present meaning ('what it means'), but the distinction between the two must be jealously preserved.

Before drawing together these discussions, let me highlight one central point. In his discussion of the dialectic between tradition, experience and interpretation, Räisänen effectively identifies 'experience' as the initiator of religious change and development. By 'experience' he has in mind, at least principally, '"profane", everyday reality, bound in time and history' (125). What this effectively does is to cast religion into the role of the conservative force in society, which attempts to rewrite aberrant experience in its own terms and whose principal function is the integration of individuals into the group. Certainly, on Räisänen's understanding it would be possible (though he shows little enthusiasm for this) to allow that there were certain kinds of religious experience: Otto's encounters with the numinous, that might be genuinely innovative and critical of society. What it does not at all allow for is the generative and *innovative* power of religious texts and indeed rituals and symbols in which the symbolic universe is encoded. Precisely because there is a link between language and experience, religious beliefs have the power to redescribe, to throw new light onto the nature of the experience which we make and thereby to allow us to see it anew. Räisänen's apparent reluctance to recognise this fact is strange when one considers the history of the Bible's influence. It has of course unquestionably exerted great conservative force. Räisänen quotes Ranke's view that Rom. 13:1-7 is the most important text that Paul ever wrote. But it is equally true that Luther's reading of Romans and Galatians contributed effectively to one of the major revolutions in European society. Whatever Lutherans may subsequently have made of Paul, one should not allow one's vision to be clouded when viewing Paul and Luther himself.

We have reviewed a perhaps bewildering set of proposals for the future of New Testament theology. One thing, at least, is clear. None suggests that it might be possible to revive Bultmann's synthesis between historical study of the New Testament and an existentialist understanding of Christian faith. All indeed, with the exception of von Balthasar in the 1960s, have abandoned Barth's attempt to break down the barriers between the interpreter and her text and to produce a biblical theology which is at the same time historical and 'actualizing'. All but von Balthasar wish to free the student of the New Testament from any particular faith requirement, so that he may address himself freely to his colleagues in other disciplines and even faiths.

What has brought about this change? In the first place social historical studies of the New Testament have established themselves firmly in the discipline (for how long?) and this means that there is a wide acceptance of the view that religion is a social phenomenon which shapes the individual and makes him what he is. Bultmann's existentialism, which was born out of the great crisis in European culture in the wake of the First World War, has yielded to the views of social and cultural anthropologists. Such views can provide an account of the diversity of modern cultures which is neither dismissive of cultural values and inheritance (as was existentialism) nor judgemental about cultures other than one's own (as was the liberalism of the colonial period). Such a shift in perception has been internalised in the historical work of at least an influential school of New Testament scholars, and this makes a return to Bultmann's position unlikely for the present. Studies like Martyn's on John and Theissen and Meeks on Paul have established a different view of the nature of the individual's place and role in the early Christian communities which contrasts rather sharply with the view of faith as obedience to the word of the gospel which Bultmann argued so persuasively in his day.

This in turn throws open the question of religious truth. We have seen how there is substantial disagreement between Räisänen and Lindbeck/Meeks over the question of the role of experience in shaping the individual's response to and acceptance of his inherited tradition. Does experience cause people to rethink their religious traditions? Or do religious traditions shape the individual's consciousness and integrate her into the group? And what does this tell us about the truth or adequacy of a particular religious tradition? Again, Räisänen and Morgan lay different emphases on the way in which any account of the religious thought of the New Testament should in principle be able to be construed as an account of the encounter with the living God. Most importantly, there is a significant divide between those like Morgan and von Balthasar who see the texts of the New Testament as creative and generative of new ways of theologizing and living out the gospel, and those who see the tradition as a conservative force which has to be read critically in the light of experience. The latter view would be shared, if for different reasons, by Räisänen and Marxist critics alike.

This deep divide also leads to a disagreement about the relation of historical, literary and contemporary theological studies. Those who believe that reflection on historical events and experiences can significantly shape religious traditions will of course see historical study of the tradition as a vital tool for its understanding. Some, like Räisänen, may be correspondingly modest about their competence to engage in present reflection on present experience, while hoping that their historical work may provide guidance for those who do so. Others, like the Marxists, may have clearly developed views about the nature of reality which enable them to translate their reading of the New Testament into more concrete proposals for present praxis. Those who see the symbolic universe of a given religious tradition as that which breathes life into the community will be much less interested in the historical study of Christian origins. They will want to find acceptable methods by which to draw on the texts' creativity, and may well find literary methods to be most satisfactory. The appeal to historical study, as with Morgan, may now be no more than a last court of appeal to adjudicate in cases of intolerable disagreement. The literary critic in this sense may see himself as contributing fully to the renewal of the church as a biblical theologian, at least according to von Balthasar. These are mostly quite high-level theoretical questions, which are unlikely to be quickly resolved.

It seems, then, that we can continue to expect a steady flow of detailed treatments of isolated aspects of New Testament historiography, and that where we do get more general accounts of the religion and religious thought of the New Testament we can expect a considerable diversity of approach. Räisänen at the end of his book suggests that biblical scholars are facing a major choice: either they can continue as the guardians of confessional traditions providing normative advice squeezed out from the sacred texts, or they can choose fearlessly to reflect on the biblical material 'from a truly ecumenical, global point of view' (141). Rather less excitingly, one might say that the lines are nowhere nearly so clearly drawn. Those who wish to reflect on the history of the Christian tradition from a global point of view may still do so from the standpoint of a faith that is schooled in a particular confessional tradition; even those whose primary interest is to serve a particular confession may see the future of that confession as lying in a greater openness to other traditions and religions. While one may resist the way in which Räisänen puts the options, one can at least wholeheartedly support his belief that a viable biblical theology of the future, whatever route it takes, must reflect in its questioning and searching the very different world that we now find ourselves in.

It may be an open question as to which of the various theologies of the New Testament that will be produced over the next decade will contribute most to the development of a new global consciousness. One may, at least, hope that it is those which do so contribute which will most be heard.

Notes

1. Reprinted in *Meanings*, 1984 as 'Biblical Theology: A Program', to which reference is here made.
2. The notion of mediation is crucial to von Balthasar's understanding of biblical aesthetics. Just as a painting does not *point* to the artist's vision or merely represent a scene, but itself encapsulates or embodies that vision, so too the biblical texts *mediate* the*Gestalt* of the divine glory in Christ.
3. Cf. among others, H.R.Jauss, *Literaturgeschichte als Provokation an die Literaturtheorie*, Frankfurt, 1970
4. Cf. *The Glory of the Lord*, volume 1, *Seeing the Form*, 70-117
5. See especially J.M. Soskice's illuminating study, *Metaphor and Religious Language*, Oxford, 1985
6. See his discussion of Lindbeck's views, 33, 197ff

List of works cited

H.V. von Balthasar, *Word and Revelation*, Einsiedeln, 1960 (German); New York, 1964 (English)

H.U. von Balthasar, *Theology of the New Covenant*, volume 7 of *The Glory of the Lord: A Theological Aesthetics*, Einsiedeln, 1969 (German); Edinburgh, 1989 (English)

H.U. von Balthasar, *Theodramatik*, III: *Die Handlung*, Einsiedeln, 1980

W. Bauer, *Orthodoxy and Heresy in Earliest Christianity*, Tübingen, 1934 (German); Philadelphia, 1971 (English)

R. Bultmann, *The Gospel of John*, Göttingen, 1941 (German): Oxford, 1971 (English)

R. Bultmann, *Theology of the New Testament*, Tübingen, 1948ff; London, 1952-5 (English)

R. Bultmann, *Glauben und Verstehen*, Tübingen, 1958

O. Cullmann, *Christ and Time*, Zürich, 1946 (German); London, 1949 (English)

O. Cullmann, *Salvation as History*, Tübingen, 1965 (German); London, 1967 (English)

H. Frei, *The Eclipse of Biblical Narrative*, London and New Haven, 1974

G. Lindbeck, *The Nature of Doctrine: Religion and Theology in a Postliberal Age*, London, 1984

W. Meeks, 'A Hermeneutics of Social Embodiment', *Harvard Theological Review*, 79:1-3, 1986, 176-86

R. Morgan with J. Barton, *Biblical Interpretation*, Oxford, 1988

H. Räisänen, *Beyond New Testament Theology*, London, 1990

C. Rowland, *Radical Christianity*, Oxford, 1988

R. Scroggs, 'The Sociological Interpretation of the New Testament: The Present State of Research', *NTS*, 26, 1980, 164-179

E. Schüssler Fiorenza, *In Memory of Her*, New York, 1983

K. Stendahl, *Meanings*, Philadelphia, 1984

Some Concluding Reflections

The abiding temptation of the historian is to pretend to know more than he knows. Such temptation may present itself differently: at times it may be the temptation of supplementing one's sources with the theories and ideas that one holds dear; at others that of allowing comment and analysis to run over into prediction and knowledge of the future; or, indeed, of offering comment and analysis before things have fallen into place, found their course and taken their place in history.

How far I have avoided such pitfalls in this book must be left for others to judge. The most I can hope for is that, in judging, they would not wish me to have committed indiscretions worse than those I already have.

What, then, can one say of the last hundred years of New Testament study? At the least, that it has shown vigour and creativity, that it has adapted to changing moods in the humanities, that it has engaged seriously with new methods of study. More, much more indeed, could have been done to show how the discipline as a whole has met the challenges of new discoveries (Qumran, Nag Hammadi) as well as the introduction of new methods. But others have followed that path, and I have instead tried to show how developments in the discipline have also corresponded to wider cultural shifts, which have their complex roots in major political and economic changes in our societies.

The old liberal school with its historical apologetic and its, more or less, evolutionary view of religious and cultural history gave expression to a mood of cultural optimism, at times, one would have to say, of cultural imperialism. True, such a mood is manifested more in works of popular apologetic, like Harnack's *What is Christianity?* and Bousset's *Das Wesen der Religion*, than in detailed historical studies.

There is, indeed, as R. Morgan has rightly pointed out, a considerable discord between some of the historical work of the History of Religions School and the dominant liberal Protestant understanding of religion which most of its proponents shared. Heitmüller's work showed a Paul who was much closer to popular religiosity (*Volksreligion*) than to liberal Protestant views of inwardness and ethical probity. Bousset, in *Kyrios Christos*, tried to correct this view by suggesting that Paul at least shook himself free from the sacramental and cultic piety of the earliest Hellenistic Christian communities. Again, Weiss pointed to apocalyptic tones in Jesus's preaching which suggested that he saw all human endeavour in this world as being under the judgement of God and of no significance for the coming Kingdom. Albert Schweitzer took up such suggestions and worked them into an account of the origins of early Christianity that showed it as arising out of the world-denying apocalyptic visions of Jesus into the fully developed Christ mysticism of John. Such views were countered by Harnack, who disputed the significance which Weiss had attributed to the apocalyptic tones in Jesus' preaching, and portrayed the prior Hyalinisation of the church in piety and dogma as a corruption of the original Gospel, from which it had been freed only by the Reformation and the Enlightenment.

Liberal theology, that is to say, carried the seeds of its own destruction within it. Yet it was the major loss of cultural confidence occasioned by the fratricide of the First World War that actually brought about its demise in Germany. By contrast, in a Britain enjoying the Indian summer of its imperial dreams, liberalism was alive and well. It is, of course, important to distinguish between a general cultural mood and its various expressions. Headlam and Dodd are very different figures, however much they were both influenced by the age in which they lived. Indeed, Dodd's espousal of an evolutionary view of history is qualified by his understanding of eschatology, which sees the Gospel of the Kingdom as judging human efforts as well as empowering them. In the darker times of the 1930s he wrestled with the political questions facing the church, and perhaps some of his finest theological writing comes from this period. Nevertheless in his historical scholarship he remained firmly opposed to the work of Schweitzer and Heitmüller. His doctrine of 'realised eschatology' is, I wanted to suggest, as much an attempt to retain some form of evolutionary doctrine of history as it is a serious piece of historical exegesis.

Meanwhile in Germany major changes were afoot. Barth's attack on liberal theology ended its dominance of the universities. The emergence of form-criticism after the First World War, together with Bultmann's critique of Baur's understanding of the Spirit in Paul, hastened the end of standard interpretations of Jesus and Paul. At the same time Barth was uttering dark warnings against the work of the History of Religions School. The connections here should not be oversimplified. A complex realignment of theological and historical views occurred, which produced some strange pairings. Weiss's view of Jesus's eschatology was adopted by many in the Barthian camp, not least because of its strong prohibition against all attempts to plan or to devise programmes for the hastening of the Kingdom. The radical historical criticism of the form-critics that made it increasingly difficult to assign sayings to Jesus with any confidence, was harnessed to a theological programme that declared the impropriety of all attempts to base faith on historical knowledge of Jesus. At the same time, Bultmann boldly linked his existential interpretations of Paul and John with historical accounts of the development of earliest Christianity taken over from the History of Religions School, and then further developed. In each case, the result of such couplings was to lend historical support to theological views that had at least so much in common that they were opposed to any alliance between religious belief and doctrines of history. Eschatology, as Hoskyns put it, was brought in to protect the doctrine of God from evolutionary doctrines of history.

Foremost among those who embarked on such a course of action was Rudolf Bultmann. His work marks the achievement of a new synthesis between historical study and a particular view of the nature of religious belief which would, for some twenty years at least, dominate the field. Paul and John were to be shown to be the apostles of a Christian inwardness that was effected by the preaching of the Word. Their writings were the theological explication of such a renewed self-understanding; in turn they would form the basis for the re-enactment of that founding moment of proclamation that lay at the heart of their authors' own faith. The work of the exegete was not only to lay bare the sense of these ancient theological formulations, but also to do so in such a way that those who read would themselves be enabled to be proclaimers of the Word.

Bultmann's theology is, in more ways than one — but not by any means in every way — Lutheran. The word has latterly become something of a term of abuse in New Testament circles (not least among those whose knowledge of Luther and Lutheranism is at best sketchy). Certainly, Bultmann agrees with Luther in seeing Paul as one among the principal figures in the history of the West who has explored the human self-understanding and thus significantly advanced the understanding of what it is to be human. Like Luther, too, he saw in Paul's term 'the righteousness of faith' (as opposed to 'works-righteousness', 'own righteousness') the key to his understanding of the Gospel. It is for both these reasons that he and Luther have recently been attacked by Stendahl and Sanders and Räisänen. There is, however, another, equally important, sense in which Bultmann is to be compared with Luther, which distinguishes him from certain forms of Lutheran orthodoxy that he would have opposed with vigour. The Gospel for him is not to be confused with a set of 'objectifiable' doctrines; it is not something which can ever be translated into a certain kind of social and cultural life to be passed on from one generation to another (*Kulturprotestantismus*); it is Gospel only in so far as it cuts across all cultural traditions and social and political codes, judging and liberating men and women so that they may be free to oppose those who seek to oppress and enslave. The Gospel is the power of salvation precisely in so far as it liberates men from their inherited patterns of behaviour, belief and association that hold them in bondage ('the Babylonian captivity of the church') and enables them to enjoy the 'freedom of the Christian man/woman'. In a word, it was in the Gospel that men and women might seek renewal, new life, after the collapse of Western culture that was brought about by the massive political upheavals of the early twentieth century. The Gospel did not of itself offer a particular form of culture, 'Christianity'; rather it cut across all cultures, judging them and freeing those who would hear to enable them to find their own true existence.

The difficulty with such a view of the Gospel and faith is, classically, that it so focuses on the prophetic, critical function of the transcendent Word of God, 'the *viva vox evangelii*', that it is unable to give an adequate account of the way in which the Gospel generates communities and living traditions of its own. Hence the danger that, after the first critical shock, Christian faith is restricted to the private sphere of inwardness, while the 'secular' world is left to the powers that be. Such dangers are, in Bultmannn's theology, particularly signalled by his assimilation of Paul to John, where the Pauline/evangelical theme of Word and faith is, so to say, played out in the orchestral colours of John's dualism and other-worldliness.

It was, then, no accident that one who had been as active in the Church Struggle in Germany as Ernst Käsemann should wish to find ways of exploring the social and political dimensions of the Gospel, at the same time as attacking Bultmann's close association of Paul and John. Thus he emphasised the cosmological sense of Paul's notion of God's justification — his establishment of his just rule over his world — and distanced John from Paul by attacking his christology and portraying his community in terms reminiscent of Paul's opponents in 1 Corinthians. The problem with Käsemann's strategy is that he wanted to have his cake and eat it. He claimed for his own political stance the authority of the living transcendent Word of the Gospel which cut across all this-worldly myths and dreams, precisely by appealing to the mythological elements in the Pauline epistles. At the same time he attempted to diminish the authority of the Fourth Gospel by emphasising the mythological character of its christology. He remains a fascinating figure because he straddles the era of Barth and Bultmann and the political reaction of the late 1960s. He remains a transitional figure; he is, however, at least that. Others in Germany have been content not to make the transition at all.

It is important to note what the nature of the transition is. In a word, it is a detaching oneself from the — broadly — evolutionary models of history, culture, religion and society which had captivated European biblical scholarship from the time of Lessing and Baur, in order to find alternative ways of expounding the relationship between religious belief and human society. It is perhaps significant that much of the creative work in this field has come from North American scholars like Martyn, Sanders and Meeks. In a country like the United States that is constitutionally, if not always actually, pluralistic and multicultural, it is perhaps easier to understand the need for and indeed to be able to deliver studies of early Christianity that are not judgemental or evaluative but which do nevertheless take a keen interest in early Christianity's relations with its contemporary culture and society.

Some of the most vigorous work in this field has been negative and critical. E.P. Sanders has attacked those who have, in his view, at least, engaged in apologetic or polemical readings of Judaism in order to exalt Christianity as a great evolutionary step forward. With some justification, he has hit on

Lutheran scholarship as incorporating all that is most noxious in Christian misrepresentation of Judaism — and indeed of Paul. By contrast, in his own portrayal of Paul and Judaism he is content to set the two systems of belief alongside each other, to show how they structure and pattern the lives of individuals, to compare but not to evaluate, not even, as we have seen, to explain. Interestingly, in Sanders work there is little attempt to take into account the closer social and political circumstances of the various communities who shared the beliefs that he so defines. Indeed, it is part of the limitations of his early work that he concentrates on the core beliefs of Judaism only, while neglecting the more detailed regulations. Others, notably W. Meeks, have been keener to offer the kind of 'thick' description of early Christian communities that explores the interrelations between belief and social custom and mores, and attempts to see how such beliefs enabled believers to make sense of and structure their world.

It is interesting to compare such work with the work of the History of Religions School that is often invoked. Whereas the History of Religions School attempted to trace the interconnections of different religious movements in the first century and so to offer some kind of historical account or explanation of their genesis, Sanders simply refuses to give such a causal explanation. The point about Judaism for Paul was that it was not Christianity. Paul did not become a Christian because he was inherently dissatisfied with Judaism, nor even because he was convinced of the superiority of Christianity; he was simply attracted by the otherness of Christianity. Sanders has all the energy of the History of Religions School to explore the religious world of the first century. He has neither their interest in historical explanation nor, indeed, in the social and communal aspects of a group's beliefs. Meeks, by contrast, shares much of the History of Religions School's fascination with ritual, imagery and symbolism, but is much less willing to explore the higher levels of religious belief or, indeed, to consider their place within some overall scheme of religious development. Here, cultural ethnography takes over from the charting of historical developments. It is social history, but history by vignettes, rather than on the grand canvas.

So what sort of transition is this, and where is it taking us? Has the shock of the crisis in Western European culture and society that was administered by the double blow of the First World War and the 1917 Revolution simply been absorbed by time, so that we can regain the cultural confidence that assured us of the essential continuity between Western European (and North American) civilisation and the great civilisations of the past? This at least was still the view of Dodd in 1970. Like Harnack, he sought to trace, historically, the golden thread that connected European civilisation to the *Founder of Christianity*. Certainly for Barth and Bultmann such a continuity was not only beyond our powers of reconstruction: it was an idol, a product of religious pride and self-aggrandisement, part of the false consciousness of sinful men and women who defer the confrontation with the living word of the text by historical analysis and reconstruction. Bultmann's dilemma becomes clear here, and it is only his internalising of the historical endeavour — Dilthey, Collingwood — that enables him to rescue historical research in theology. By contrast, Meeks' reconstructions, so painstaking, so minutious, of the social worlds of early Christian urban communities, present us with a series of miniatures where what we may learn is not something of the theological *contents* of their beliefs but something about how they functioned for them then, so that we might also learn something about how our beliefs should function for us now. Sanders's denial of the possibility of interpreting Paul's central concepts simply closes the door on Stendahl's programme of biblical theology, the road from 'what it meant' to 'what it means'.

There is even more at stake here than our confidence in our ability to reconstruct the past, and so to retain our sense of identity with the grand tradition of human cultural evolution. There is a deeper loss of confidence in the ability of our words, our inherited cultural traditions, any longer to signify. Barth gave voice to this in his early lectures where he spoke of the emptiness of so much preaching and its inability to answer the questions and expectations with which — still — people approached the sermon. He found his own answer in his denial of the *analogia entis*, of the power of natural language to speak of being and of God, and in his affirmation of the *analogia fidei*, the power of the Word of God received in faith to fill our broken words with meaning. Here, notoriously, the ways part: both between Barth and von Balthasar and between Barth and Bultmann.

Bultmann, as we have seen, denied that it was possible properly to speak of God at all, except in so far as we speak of the new self-understanding which springs from obedience to the transcendent word. We know Christ in so far as we know his benefits — but in knowing his benefits we know him truly as the one who reveals to us a new and authentic mode of existence. We need to see beyond the mythological language of the New Testament to the self-understanding that finds expression in such — speculative, objectifying, and therefore inauthentic — language. Barth, by contrast, could not accept that the language of the Bible was mythological or inauthentic: it was precisely the language that gave meaning to all other language.

Von Balthasar insisted, against Barth, that the language of myth, poetry and philosophy could indeed speak, at least analogously, of being and of God. To deny that there is any continuity between the vision of being, of truth, goodness and beauty in Homer, in Plato, in Virgil and the vision of God's glory in the Bible would ultimately be to evacuate the claim that the Bible speaks of God's glory of any meaning at all. It would be to cut the Bible off from the world of human discourse and to condemn it to unintelligibility, a monologue with itself. But what if the world itself becomes forgetful of being? If even the poets themselves lose confidence in the power of their words to 'recognise life, to catch the sudden moment of meaning'? What if such words do not shine in the darkness, but, like shooting stars, fade, leaving behind 'darkness again, monstrous, in the empty space around the world and me' (Gottfried Benn, 'Ein Wort'). Perhaps it is the task of Christianity to rekindle the vision of being as it is faithful to its own vision of truth, beauty and goodness. Thus von Balthasar's volumes on the Old and New Testament vision of God's glory come only after a prolonged examination of glory in the realm of metaphysics, just as it is important for him to chart the work of Christian poets and philosophers who since the fading of aesthetics from the theology of the schools have kept alive the vision of glory in the church. And this conviction that the biblical revelation of God is essentially aesthetic, that it is given in a form which has its own rightness and necessity, its proportion and measure, leads him, further, to assert that all Christian theology is, properly, biblical theology, marked by the form which is given in the Bible.

These debates about the nature of theological language, and, indeed, about the object of theology itself, are of lasting significance and will continue to inform the agenda of biblical theologians. Within the mainstream of biblical study it is, of course, Barth and Bultmann who have been most influential. Their views of the nature of mythological and philosophical language can hardly have failed to influence the new modes of working in the field of the history of religions that we noted above. Comparisons with, or, indeed, attempts to elucidate, the meaning of New Testament texts by reference to contemporary Greek philosophy have been rare over the last few decades. Sanders's refusal to offer any attempt to elucidate the meaning of Paul's 'participationist eschatology' is again like but unlike Bultmann's own declaration that the mythological language of the New Testament must be interpreted in an existential sense. Sanders simply denies that Bultmann's existential sense is an adequate rendering of the meaning of Paul's concept, which, he affirms, is unintelligible to us. More subtly perhaps, the work of Lindbeck and Frei on which Meeks draws in his programmatic essay owes a considerable debt to Karl Barth. Barth, we have just said, denied that natural human language was able to speak properly of God. Only the revealed language of faith could do so, and it was this language which could inform and give sense to our broken human language. The Bible, that is to say, schools us in the language of faith (paradigmatically encodes the semiotic universe) by which we make sense of our world, by which our natural language is transformed to give new meaning to our existence. It is only a short route from here to Lindbeck's cultural-linguistic model of religion, where religious language and beliefs provide the conceptual tools by which we construct our worlds. But if this is coupled with a denial that texts refer at all, there is no longer any means of discriminating between the worlds that are constructed on the basis of the Bible or the Koran or the works of Karl Marx. We would then be set on a course to a pluralist society where there would no longer be any common discourse by which to distinguish the absurd and the cruel from the balanced and the compassionate. The possibility of historical or metaphysical interpretations of texts is then denied; all that is permitted is increasingly virtuoso rhetorical performances of texts.

Not, of course, that either Barth or von Balthasar denied that texts refer: they asserted powerfully that the biblical texts speak of the glory of God. The danger with Barth was rather that, by denying the ability of natural human language to speak of God and being, he isolated the theological enterprise from the general human search for meaning. This is certainly not part of von Balthasar's purpose, and his most important contribution may still be his attempt to restore the connections between the world of Greek myth, metaphysics and poetry and the biblical vision of glory. In a world where there is serious possibility of major confrontation between peoples identified with different world religions, it is important, as Räisänen has suggested, to give an account of Christianity's debts to other religious movements at the time of its beginnings, just as it is important to give an account of its relationship with the traditions which are incorporated in the Old Testament — provided always that such an account can break free of the old polemical models. It is hard to see how such accounts can make a serious contribution to a multicultural world if they deny out of hand the claims of such traditions to speak of God and being.

The temptation, I have said, is to claim to know more about the provisional that one does, and to be drawn into predictions of the future which outstrip one's competence. Certainly, there is no shortage of vigorous new growth in New Testament study. It is no reflection on the vigour — and indeed in the case of literary and feminist studies, the considerable output — of much of these new movements, that they have not featured more fully in this book. My aim in what is only a selective journey through the landscape of New Testament study has been to give an account of developments in the major paradigm of biblical interpretation during the last century, namely the historical paradigm. I do not think that the time has yet come to pronounce it dead, or indeed to declare that its hegemony over the discipline is broken. What I have tried to show is both the interesting shifts that have occurred in the way that it has been operated and, at least tentatively, some of the difficulties that it has encountered as it has, largely, abandoned evolutionary models of historical explanation and the apologetic which was never far below the surface of such accounts. Historical and metaphysical readings of texts may presently be under serious attack from deconstructionists and post-structuralists. Those who wish to continue to work in this tradition certainly need to review radically their epistemological basis and their cultural stance. They will find themselves working in a more diverse discipline, borrowing, as indeed has always been the case, from literary and sociological modes of enquiry. But unless they wish to contribute to the fragmentation of the world with its diverse cultures and religions, they will, I suggest, be ill-advised to abandon the historical and metaphysical task altogether.

Author Index

Subject Index